Essentials of Real Estate Investment

Twelfth Edition

David Sirota, PhD, Denise Evans, JD (contributing editor)

ESSENTIALS OF REAL ESTATE INVESTMENT TWELFTH EDITION

Published by DF Institute, LLC, d/b/a Dearborn Kaplan Real Estate Education and
Kaplan Real Estate Education
1515 West Cypress Creek Road
Fort Lauderdale, Florida 33309

10 9 8 7 6

ISBN: 978-1-4754-8540-0

10 9 8 7 6 5 4 3

ISBN: 978-1-4754-8657-5 (custom)

CONTENTS

UNIT 9

Applications to Property Tax 119

UNIT 10

Financing for Real Estate Investments 127

UNIT 11

Residential, Land, and Commercial Investments 155

INTRODUCTION

The introduction to the 9th edition of this text expressed optimism about an economic recovery from the Great Recession. The introduction to the 10th edition of this text declared it an excellent time to invest in real estate because prices and interest rates were low, even if banks were being very selective screening potential borrowers.

That optimism proved to be warranted and the investment advice well-founded. In August 2015, the unemployment rate was down to 5.1% nationally, and by October 2018. it was down to 3.7%. Other economic indicators are strong, and economists predict continued job creation, which will fuel consumer spending, and in turn, entice businesses to hire and invest more.

All of this translates into optimistic news for the U.S. housing market. As of mid-2015, existing home sales (which make a comparatively large proportion of all home sales) had surged to their highest level since November 2009. According to the National Association of REALTORS®, existing sales climbed 5.1% month over month to an annual rate of 5.35 million sales. In May 2018, the U.S. had the fastest pace of homes sold relative to the inventory when months' supply was 4.1 months. In 2008, the U.S. had the slowest relative pace when it would have taken 10.8 months to sell the supply of homes on the market at the prevailing sales pace. Then in September 2018, existing-home sales declined after a month of stagnation in August. REALTORS® report "low inventory" and "interest rate" as the major issues affecting transactions in September 2018.

Democracy as a political system, when coupled with capitalism as an economic system, is based on the private ownership of real and personal property. Therefore, in the United States, individuals and corporations may own real property under the laws of this country. Such private ownership, called the *allodial system*, allows for fee simple ownership, which expands the simple rights of property use and control during an owner's life to include the powerful right to designate to whom a property passes upon the owner's death. As a result, owners may effectively translate their work efforts into tangible real and personal property assets, and thus, accumulate an estate to enjoy and control into the future.

The desire to accumulate a measurably valuable estate and generate a revenue stream is no doubt one major reason for the tremendous interest in the ownership of real property in this country. It appears that almost everyone gives high priority to the ownership of real estate—from the smallest condominium to the largest shopping center.

This 12th edition of *Essentials of Real Estate Investment* examines the current real estate market and describes the various opportunities for real estate investors. Real estate may provide a profitable alternative for an investor's portfolio, with much of the income sheltered by deductions for operational costs, interest expenses, and depreciation.

This text presents the units as follows.

- Unit 1 introduces the nature of the real estate market.
- Unit 2 explores purposes for investing in real estate as an alternative to other forms of investment. It also describes the advantages and disadvantages of real estate investments.
- Unit 3 discusses the importance of leverage.

- Unit 4 provides an inventory of the various forms of real estate ownership, including individuals, groups, partnerships, trusts, and leaseholds.
- Unit 5 describes the market and property analyses necessary to determine the feasibility of a real estate investment.
- Unit 6 reviews the current income tax laws governing real estate investments. Included are a number of tax-sheltering alternatives.
- Unit 7 discusses the time value of money.
- Unit 8 examines the financial requirements necessary to measure the economic feasibility of a real estate investment.
- Unit 9 explores applications to property tax.
- Unit 10 investigates the financing alternatives for leveraging real estate investments. Included are discussions of the government's role in finance, sources of funds, types and forms of real estate loans, special loan provisions for investment financing, and default and foreclosure consequences.
- Unit 11 is an examination of the various types of real estate available for investments: land, residential, office buildings, commercial properties, industrial properties, and special investment opportunities.
- Unit 12 explores managing the investment property, including differences in management needs, based on the type of property being managed.
- Unit 13 summarizes the transaction from contract to closing.

ACKNOWLEDGMENTS

David Sirota received his Ph.D. in Real Estate from the University of Arizona in 1971. He taught real estate subjects at many universities, including the University of Arizona in Tucson, Eastern Michigan University in Ypsilanti, National University in San Diego, and California State University in Fullerton, and at one time, headed the Department of Real Estate at the University of Nebraska in Omaha. Dr. Sirota has also written state licensing exam questions for the Arizona Department of Real Estate and ETS. He was involved as a consultant in the development of a congregate care center in Green Valley, Arizona, and acts in a consultant capacity for individuals and developers. He was a founding member of the Real Estate Educators Association (REEA), securing one of its first DREI designations.

Denise Evans is a semi-retired Texas attorney who specialized in banking and real estate litigation, and since that time, she has been a developer and real estate investor. She is the author of several nationally published real estate books, as well as locally published books of regional significance. She is a former adjunct professor in the College of Business at the University of Alabama, teaching Principles of Real Estate.

Thanks also go out to those who have contributed to this and previous editions of this textbook: Karen B. Abbott, Thurza B. Andrew, Donald G. Arsenault, Jack R. Bennett, Paul S. Black, Richard Blyther, Robert Bond, William J. Cahaney, Gene Campbell, Ken Combs, Bo Cooper, Gerald R. Cortesi, Larry B. Cowart, Valleri J. Crabtree, Samuel P. DeRobertis, Jack Flynn, Peter C. Glover, Ronald Guiberson, Lloyd L. Hampton, Byron

B. Hinton, James E. Howze, Carla J. Keegan, Sam Kiamanesh, Rick Knowles, Craig Larabee, Calvin Montgomery Sr., William E. Nix, William M. North Jr., Michael R. Phillips, Donald L. Pietz, Richard P. Riendeau, Jerry Rutledge, Jeff Siebold, Teresa Sirico, Walstein Smith Jr., James Sweetin, Steve Williamson, and Roger W. Zimmerman.

UNIT 1

Real Estate Investment Characteristics

LEARNING OBJECTIVES

When you have completed this unit, you will be able to accomplish the following.

- Describe the nature of the real estate market.

KEY TERMS

bundle of rights	highest and best use	real estate
buyer's market	integration	real property
cycle	longevity	relative scarcity
demand	market segmentation	risk
disintegration	market value	seller's market
easy money	permanence	supply
equilibrium	personal property	tight money
fixity	property	value in use

INTRODUCTION

Property is anything that can be owned. **Real property**—also called **real estate**—is defined as land and all natural and human-made improvements permanently attached thereto, and the rights appurtenant, including air and mineral. All other property is **personal property**. To own real estate is not only to possess the physical property but also to acquire certain legal rights to its continual peaceful use and redistribution. When we acquire real estate, we also acquire an accompanying **bundle of rights** in the property. These are the rights of use, possession, control, enjoyment, exclusion, and disposition, including the right to pass on the property by means of a will.

THE NATURE OF THE REAL ESTATE MARKET

Characteristics of real property investments

Each parcel of real estate is unique, and thus, requires an individual investment analysis relevant to its specific locational attributes. However, all real property has certain common characteristics that affect its value. These characteristics include fixity, longevity, permanence, risk, and market segmentation.

Fixity

Real estate is fixed in location, which greatly restricts the scope of its marketability. As a result of this **fixity**, real estate values are affected by any political and economic activities occurring in the immediate vicinity.

Longevity

Real estate is generally considered to be a long-term investment because of the durability of the improvements and the permanence of the land. This quality of **longevity** enables investors to estimate, with some degree of reliability, the present value of a future stream of income from their properties.

Permanence

It is the attribute of **permanence** that forms the basis for our system of long-term mortgage-debt amortization. Investment in real estate usually involves relatively large dollar amounts that require complex financial arrangements. These complexities, in turn, require the expertise of lawyers, accountants, brokers, property managers, real estate consultants, and other specialists.

Risk

Real estate investment is a relatively high-**risk** venture that reflects the uncertainties of a somewhat unpredictable market. In fact, there is no readily identifiable, organized national market for real estate as there is for stocks and bonds. The realty market is a combination of local markets that react speedily to changes in local economic and political activities and somewhat more slowly to regional, national, and international events.

Market segmentation

The real estate industry also suffers from **market segmentation**. The fractured aspect of this unorganized and largely unregulated market is further complicated by the lack of standardization of the product and the fact that many of the market's participants react intuitively, giving little attention to formal feasibility or marketing studies. The real estate investment market is divided into submarkets such as retail, warehouse, residential, and others, compounding the complexity of investing. However, the investor who seeks qualified help and takes advantage of available protective measures can often mitigate—or, minimize—some of the risks.

Besides these inherent characteristics of real property, many government activities also directly or indirectly influence property values. At the federal level, income tax laws can provide incentives or disincentives for particular types of investments. Some of those laws can change rapidly, while others remain stable for years and even decades. The government's regulation and control of money effectively dictates the extent of real estate activity through manipulation of the supply, as well as the cost of mortgage money.

Our various levels of government also function in other ways to affect real estate property values. Environmental controls and impact studies add time and costs to the development of land—costs that are inevitably paid by consumers. Local political attitudes regarding zoning and growth restrictions act to raise the prices of properties already developed, effectively creating a monopolistic position for their owners.

Fueling these political attitudes is the antigrowth philosophy of citizens in some areas where property taxes and other public costs are rising at an alarming rate to serve an ever-increasing population. "Not in my backyard," usually shortened to "NIMBY," has become the slogan in these cities.

Changing nature of the realty market

In the early 2000s, the subprime mortgage market more than doubled its offerings of hybrid adjustable-rate mortgages (ARMs) with artificially low initial payment schedules and other very liberal qualifying standards. Such loans were called *subprime* because the borrowers did not qualify for the prime lending rates available to those who are more credit-worthy. Fannie Mae and Freddie Mac loans also became available in various forms using very liberal qualifying standards, thereby creating many risky loan products. Exotic mortgage insurance and mortgage bundling and resale products further obscured and shifted default risks onto unsuspecting secondary market purchasers. Without personal risks, mortgage originators became ever more aggressive, loaning more than 100% of property values to anyone capable of signing their names to the documents. Easy access to money drove real estate prices higher and higher. The overall housing market boom began to decline in 2006. The subprime market was the first to crash, but by 2007, Fannie Mae and Freddie Mac were also in trouble. Borrowers found themselves unable to pay their sharply increased mortgage payments as adjustable-rate loans began to be reset at higher rates. Refinancing was no longer an option because realty values were declining, and a slow market made it very difficult to sell. In September 2008, Fannie Mae and Freddie Mac were placed into conservatorship under the newly formed Federal Housing Finance Agency.

Over the next several years, a variety of federal programs and tax incentives made it easier for borrowers to modify their home mortgage loans, obtain debt forgiveness without tax liability, and remain in rental housing despite foreclosure of the underlying mortgage. Most of the programs have now expired, but elements of each have been incorporated into other programs as a type of safeguard against another potential crash.

Programs such as those allowed many borrowers to keep their homes in spite of the financial conditions of the Great Recession. The resulting confidence—security in having home ownership—helped consumers increase retail spending after even modest improvements in the economy. Increased retail spending spurred investment real estate construction and redevelopment. The improving economy meant increasing demand for recession-era foreclosure housing available at steep discounts. That supply dwindled, housing demand increased, new construction started again, jobs in the construction industry and its suppliers saw dramatic growth, more people were employed and could afford housing and retail goods, and so on. The real estate cycle had turned. President Donald Trump's election in 2016 created wild exuberance in some circles and spurred the release of long-hoarded investment dollars. Barring an unforeseen catastrophic event, the realty markets seem firmly in recovery mode.

Supply of and demand for real estate

In the very broadest sense, the **supply** of land is unlimited. Although it is true that the earth represents a fixed supply, it is also true that this supply can be extended indefinitely by building under and over the landmasses and open seas, and by fractionalizing ownership interests into time-shares. Still, there are huge expanses of land that remain unusable in their present state or are currently uninhabitable because of geophysical circumstances.

It is the **relative scarcity** of usable land, however, that is important to real estate as an investment vehicle. Relative scarcity is what establishes the basic value for real estate. The economic worth of property fluctuates with the effective **demand** for strategically located and, thus, by definition, relatively scarce parcels of land. Even more important than the supply of and the demand for unimproved land are the interactions of these economic factors as they affect the existing stock of improved real estate.

One of the principal components of demand is population, not only in terms of the number of people, but also of subgroupings according to age and income.

The current U.S. population topped 326 million in 2018 and is expected to grow to more than 398 million by the year 2060 (see Figure 1.1).

Migrational trends and locational economic-base analyses can be developed to estimate variations in the demand for real estate within a given area. Changes in location, as well as changes in living patterns, determine where there will be growth in demand for real property and what this demand will require in terms of housing and related real estate developments.

Figure 1.1: Projections of the Population by Selected Age Groups and Sex for the United States: 2016 to 2060

Projected Age Groups and Sex Composition of the Population

Projections for the United States: 2020-2060

Main series. Table 2

(2016 base population. Resident population as of July 1. Numbers in thousands)

	2016	2020	2025	2030	2035	2040	2045	2050	2055	2060
Total	**323,128**	**332,639**	**344,234**	**355,101**	**364,862**	**373,528**	**381,390**	**388,922**	**396,557**	**404,483**
Under 18 years	73,642	73,967	74,654	75,652	76,664	77,131	77,561	78,225	79,148	80,137
Under 5 years	19,927	20,439	20,868	20,976	20,993	21,106	21,319	21,610	21,914	22,144
5 to 13 years	36,954	36,780	37,074	38,051	38,453	38,568	38,715	39,049	39,532	40,090
14 to 17 years	16,761	16,748	16,712	16,625	17,217	17,457	17,527	17,566	17,701	17,903
18 to 64 years	200,241	202,621	204,354	206,311	210,201	215,571	220,995	225,023	227,794	229,670
18 to 24 years	30,844	30,380	30,554	30,612	30,519	31,369	31,943	32,126	32,229	32,467
25 to 44 years	85,147	88,843	92,328	94,370	95,368	95,067	96,054	97,459	98,727	100,230
45 to 64 years	84,250	83,398	81,472	81,329	84,314	89,135	92,998	95,437	96,838	96,973
65 years and over	49,244	56,052	65,226	73,138	77,997	80,827	82,835	85,675	89,615	94,676
85 years and over	6,380	6,701	7,450	9,074	11,793	14,430	16,953	18,561	18,913	19,019
100 years and over	82	92	120	140	156	196	270	386	486	589
16 years and over	257,955	267,049	278,019	287,784	296,814	305,159	312,637	319,519	326,291	333,323
18 years and over	249,485	258,672	269,580	279,449	288,199	296,397	303,829	310,697	317,410	324,346
15 to 44 years	128,658	131,781	135,459	137,476	138,804	139,551	141,173	142,786	144,252	146,140
Male	**159,079**	**163,904**	**169,738**	**175,174**	**180,070**	**184,481**	**188,575**	**192,577**	**196,661**	**200,871**
Under 18 years	37,609	37,779	38,144	38,656	39,163	39,397	39,613	39,948	40,416	40,917
Under 5 years	10,187	10,446	10,662	10,717	10,725	10,782	10,890	11,039	11,194	11,310
5 to 13 years	18,861	18,789	18,947	19,438	19,641	19,698	19,771	19,939	20,184	20,467
14 to 17 years	8,561	8,545	8,535	8,501	8,797	8,918	8,952	8,971	9,038	9,140
18 to 64 years	99,677	101,111	102,293	103,596	105,811	108,760	111,697	113,897	115,366	116,291
18 to 24 years	15,819	15,526	15,591	15,637	15,605	16,029	16,316	16,405	16,452	16,569
25 to 44 years	42,753	44,837	46,795	47,970	48,528	48,348	48,846	49,576	50,217	50,952
45 to 64 years	41,105	40,748	39,906	39,990	41,678	44,382	46,534	47,916	48,697	48,770
65 years and over	21,793	25,014	29,301	32,921	35,096	36,324	37,265	38,731	40,879	43,663
85 years and over	2,225	2,418	2,780	3,463	4,564	5,590	6,599	7,246	7,408	7,477
100 years and over	16	21	30	38	43	55	77	110	137	168
16 years and over	125,801	130,396	135,900	140,781	145,309	149,560	153,461	157,134	160,780	164,537
18 years and over	121,470	126,125	131,593	136,518	140,907	145,083	148,962	152,629	156,245	159,954
15 to 44 years	65,045	66,768	68,806	69,995	70,733	71,078	71,893	72,722	73,458	74,384
Female	**164,049**	**168,735**	**174,497**	**179,927**	**184,792**	**189,047**	**192,815**	**196,345**	**199,896**	**203,612**
Under 18 years	36,033	36,187	36,510	36,996	37,500	37,733	37,948	38,277	38,732	39,220
Under 5 years	9,740	9,993	10,205	10,259	10,268	10,324	10,429	10,572	10,721	10,834
5 to 13 years	18,093	17,992	18,128	18,613	18,812	18,870	18,945	19,110	19,348	19,623
14 to 17 years	8,200	8,203	8,177	8,124	8,421	8,539	8,575	8,595	8,663	8,763
18 to 64 years	100,564	101,510	102,061	102,715	104,390	106,811	109,298	111,125	112,428	113,379
18 to 24 years	15,025	14,854	14,962	14,975	14,914	15,340	15,627	15,721	15,776	15,898
25 to 44 years	42,395	44,006	45,533	46,400	46,840	46,718	47,207	47,883	48,511	49,278
45 to 64 years	43,145	42,650	41,565	41,340	42,636	44,753	46,463	47,521	48,141	48,203
65 years and over	27,451	31,037	35,926	40,216	42,901	44,503	45,569	46,943	48,736	51,013
85 years and over	4,155	4,283	4,670	5,611	7,229	8,840	10,354	11,315	11,506	11,543
100 years and over	66	71	89	102	113	141	193	276	348	422
16 years and over	132,154	136,653	142,118	147,003	151,505	155,599	159,176	162,385	165,511	168,786
18 years and over	128,015	132,547	137,987	142,931	147,292	151,314	154,867	158,069	161,164	164,392
15 to 44 years	63,613	65,013	66,653	67,481	68,071	68,473	69,280	70,064	70,794	71,756

Note: 2016 is the base population estimate for the projections.

Projected Age Groups and Sex Composition of the Population: Main Projections Series for the United States, 2017-2060. U.S. Census Bureau, Population Division: Washington, DC.

Source: U.S. Census Bureau, Population Division
Original Release Date: March 2018
Revised Release Date: September 2018

Source: U.S. Census Bureau

A **tight money** market occurs when interest rates are high and loans are difficult to find. An **easy money** market reflects low interest rates and lots of money available for real estate loans.

Supply can sometimes be viewed as a function of demand when the bidding on scarce properties forces prices upward. Serving effective demand and anticipating its impact is a real estate supplier's most important skill, one that industry professionals and investors are vigorously pursuing with increasing degrees of sophistication to perfect investment strategies. Because most real estate developments involve a time lag, which exists because of the time it takes to prepare raw land and construct new buildings, shrewd investors constantly study the market to anticipate demand.

Often, supply itself may be viewed as an accelerator of demand. The imposition of growth controls, building moratoriums, and stringent environmental controls seriously inhibits the increase of new housing stock and puts the full pressures of demand on existing property owners. These owners then enjoy a virtual monopoly that affects rental rates and property prices. Thus, the available stock of improved real estate itself establishes the design, quality, price, and terms for the consumer.

Real estate cycles

Keeping in mind the cause-and-effect relationship between supply and demand, we can now examine the cyclical nature of the real estate market. A real estate cycle (see Figure 1.2) is frequently described as either a **buyer's market** or a **seller's market**. A buyer's market indicates a surplus of supply and a downward price trend, favoring the purchaser. In a seller's market, supply is short and demand is high; thus,prices are forced upward by the competitive market situation.

Figure 1.2: Real Estate Cycles

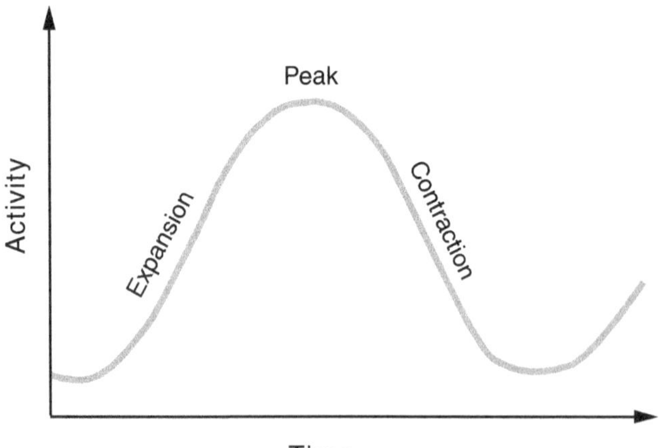

Because the term *cycle* implies repetitive, ongoing fluctuations in price, the buyer's and seller's markets are equal and opposite partners in the cycle. Thus, we can begin at any stage of a real estate cycle to examine the total cycle's fluctuation. If we enter a cycle somewhere near its peak, we can observe a shortage of supply, high prices as a result of competitive bidding, and, logically, high concurrent profits for sellers. Such high profits act to attract new investors who wish to capitalize on the opportunities, and it is reasonable to assume that new construction will take place, regardless of costs. With new buildings available as additional inventory to satisfy demand, the market cycle will level temporarily and then start to fall until supply exceeds demand. At this point, the cycle has reached its valley, and conditions are those of a buyer's market.

Other catalysts can affect a **cycle**, acting to speed it up or slow it down and to raise or lower its peaks and valleys. Included among these catalysts are tax reforms, interest rate fluctuations, a depression or recession, or even a national crisis such as 9/11, to name a few.

The inherent imperfections of the real estate market contribute to the perpetuation of the cyclical trend. Lack of communication among real estate building contractors, coupled with the time lag between the start-up and the completion of buildings, is a major factor in this problem. Another problem arises when contractors base a decision to build on gut feelings instead of market research. Real estate tends to have a longer contraction phase than other types of industry. A manufacturer of appliances may lay off workers and cut back production to ride out a contraction in the market. The owner of an office building still has the same amount of space to lease, and therefore, may stay in contraction longer.

Entering the market at the peak of a cycle involves planning, possible rezoning, and financing, as well as labor and material acquisitions in anticipation of construction. When building continues at a feverish pace to capture the profits of backlogged demand, little thought is given to overbuilding until the inevitable occurs and supply exceeds demand.

Now the situation is reversed, with few buyers and many alternative properties from which to choose. An associated lowering of prices results until little, if any, profits are left. Building ceases and market conditions continue at a low point until the excess supply is absorbed, at which time, the market begins to move toward the peak again.

Bubbles are a frequent phenomenon in the real estate cycle. A bubble is a sharp rise in real estate prices, fueled by speculation among those who operate under the greater fool theory of real estate investing. The *greater fool theory* supposes that whatever price is paid in a rapidly rising market, some fool will pay more to purchase it from the current investor. Fortunes are made during such times, until the fools are sated, prices decline, values crash, money becomes tight again, and there are long lines at bankruptcy courts and foreclosure auctions. The Federal Housing Finance Agency maintains statistics of home prices in markets around the country. There are various rules of thumb for signs of a bubble, but most can be summed up by answering this question: "Are local price increases significantly greater than national averages, and is there any identifiable economic factor, other than speculation, that would explain the increase?"

Despite the cyclical short-run fluctuations in any real estate market, property values, in general, rise over the long term. However, this trend is based on a summarization of activities involving many properties. Any individual property may react cyclically or counter-cyclically to the general activities of the marketplace, much as individual stocks gain or lose value within the stock exchange. Real estate investors are cautioned to consider each purchase carefully from both its micro and macro positions in the realty market. Investors must be aware of the long-term aspect of real estate investments.

Value theory of real estate

Although all the forgoing economic principles are important for potential real estate investors to keep in mind, in the final analysis, investors will be primarily concerned with the value of one particular property. Real estate has value only as one in a series of alternative investment opportunities. Value is, in reality, in the eye of the beholder, the occupier, or the user.

A seller's value is, more often than not, a reflection of personal and slightly sentimental feelings. Undoubtedly, the buyer or agent will have an entirely different opinion of the value of that particular property. Likewise, an insurable value, a condemnation value, and a taxable value, among others, may all indicate a different dollar amount for the same property.

In theory, the value of a parcel of real estate is interpreted to be market value or its value as established in an exchange. As such, **market value** is defined as that price which a knowledgeable buyer will pay and a knowledgeable seller will accept for a property that has been exposed for sale to the market for a reasonable length of time and with neither buyer nor seller acting under duress or enjoying any advantage, financial or otherwise. Most real estate transactions will require an estimate of the market value of the property involved.

However, market value, as estimated by the seller, appraiser, or perhaps a real estate broker, may differ substantially from market price, which clearly is established by what the buyer will actually pay for the property. To illustrate the difference, the market value of a three-bedroom, two-bath brick home in a good school zone might be $X. The product is fairly fungible and similar to many other nearby homes with recent sales records. If that same home has a famous former owner, or trendy new finishes, or supernatural phenomena, then emotional decision-making can drive the price up or down, varying from the value. *Price* is more in the realm of behavioral economics, while *value* is more in the realm of traditional economics.

When determining the value of a particular property at a specific point in time, an evaluator has several basic principles of value to use as guides. The *principle of substitution* contends that no rational, economical person would pay more for one property than for another of like design, quality, and utility. This principle is the basis for the comparable sales approach to estimating the market value of real property.

The *principle of balance* identifies the problems that result from an oversupply or undersupply of a particular type of real estate. For example, too many condominiums of the same size, design, and price in one area would act to depress the values of all of these properties within the market.

The *principle of contribution* states that the value of an addition to a property is a function of its contribution to the overall profitability of the property, not just its construction cost.

The *principle of conformity* states that homogeneity in design and quality creates the most reasonable value for a property, while a property that is dramatically different from or nonconforming to its surroundings is invariably lowered in value.

The *principle of anticipation* stipulates that most investors make their investment decisions based on the measurement of the present value of an anticipated net income stream. This principle is the basis of the income capitalization approach to realty evaluation.

The *principle of highest and best use* is fundamental to estimating the value in use of a real estate investment. This principle is defined as the legal and possible use that is most likely to produce the greatest net return from a property over a given period.

In addition to its market value, real estate also has a **value in use**. This is the value on which a number of real estate investors rely and a value that could differ from the property's market value. For example, compare the market value of a property currently used as a parking lot with its potential value as the site for a high-rise office building. Thus, *value in use* is that use of the property that may or may not be its **highest and best use**.

As discussed earlier, value is primarily a function of the interactions of supply and demand. A relatively scarce but desirable item's value may increase specifically because of its scarcity and desirability. It must also be remembered that change is ever-present, thus affecting attitudes concerning desirability and value.

Real estate is considered to be a relatively scarce and desirable item. Its value is in a constant state of change because of a myriad of continuously operating social and economic forces.

Estimators of real estate value must be acutely alert to three stages of change in property values:

1. **Integration**—a condition of developing value when building new
2. **Equilibrium**—a condition of stable value during the holding period
3. **Disintegration**—a condition of declining value during the aging process

A property's value is affected by the prevailing stage of change in its city or neighborhood. Because property cannot be moved, it may go through this evolutionary cycle many times during its economic life.

SUMMARY

In economic terms, land is considered a relatively scarce commodity, although from a practical point of view, land is infinite in supply because it can be developed into the air and underground and split into temporal units, such as time-sharing. Still, most of the earth's population gathers tightly in the great cities of the world, congregating where there are jobs. Thus, there is an ever-increasing demand for a limited supply of desirable real estate. This pressure of demand acts to force the prices of available real estate to new heights.

Real estate market activities fluctuate as a function of supply and effective demand. When the top of the cycle has been reached, with high prices reflecting high profits, the entry of new builders acts to add to the supply and reduce the prices and profits accordingly, resulting in a reversal of the cycle. The microcycle is local in character, while the long-term cycle shows an ever-increasing value for real estate over time.

In addition to the demands of a growing population, artificial limitations on the supply of real property add to the increasing costs of real estate. Concerns with pollution have led to environmental controls that limit new construction. Political attitudes regarding controlled growth have also inhibited construction in many areas of the country. Natural gas and water shortages, sewer inadequacies, central city decline, and resultant suburban expansions have all placed substantial burdens on current property owners to support their local governments on an ever-shrinking tax base.

Despite all these obstacles, real estate investors continue to seek profitable projects. Attempting to anticipate demand and, in some areas of this country, creating demand by the very design of their projects, real estate developers are adjusting the sizes of homes, rethinking the frills in office buildings, providing the magnetism necessary to attract customers to shopping centers, and creating new concepts in planned unit developments, manufactured-home parks, office parks, and industrial parks. All of this is in an effort to bring a usable product to a receptive market.

The measurement of a property's value is a function of its utility, its ability to generate income in the future, and its position in a spectrum of alternative investment opportunities.

Price often is based on subjective intuitive interpretations, although a body of principles has been developed to describe property value in terms that are more objective. These principles include those of substitution, highest and best use, balance, contribution, conformity, and anticipation, and they describe the function of value in conjunction with the activities of a rational, economic investor.

DISCUSSION TOPICS

1. Investigate the economic conditions of your community and identify the point in the real estate cycle at which you believe it to be.
2. Identify a specific neighborhood in your community and estimate where it is on the development spectrum: integration, equilibrium, or disintegration.

UNIT 1 EXAM

1. Real estate investments should be considered first and foremost from the viewpoint of
   A. the economic soundness of the project.
   B. the unique financing techniques available.
   C. the tax shelter opportunities.
   D. the unlimited growth potential.

2. Which of the following is *TRUE* regarding the characteristics of real estate?
   A. It has a central and controlled market.
   B. It is a short-term asset.
   C. Each parcel is similar to other parcels.
   D. Its market condition is seldom in balance with supply and demand.

3. Supply and demand theory indicates that if they both increase at the same rate, prices will
   A. go up.
   B. go down.
   C. first go up and then go down.
   D. remain constant.

4. A buyer's market indicates all of the following *EXCEPT*
   A. excess supply.
   B. lower prices.
   C. high demand.
   D. flexible terms.

5. Which of the following approaches to value reflects the actual price that a knowledgeable buyer will pay?
   A. Value in use
   B. Highest and best value
   C. Appraised value
   D. Market value

6. When properties in blighted areas begin attracting investors, they are entering a period of
   A. integration.
   B. equilibrium.
   C. disintegration.
   D. urban renewal.

UNIT 2

Purpose and Function of Real Estate Investment

LEARNING OBJECTIVES

When you have completed this unit, you will be able to accomplish the following.

- Explain the purpose and function of real estate investment, including the advantages and disadvantages.

KEY TERMS

betterments	mailbox money	sweat equity
liquidity	sheltering	

INTRODUCTION

The ownership and control of real estate is a fundamental part of our lives. We depend on real property to provide us with shelter and to satisfy other basic needs. In our country, these essential needs are met in various ways. Because technological achievements have advanced our living standards, we are no longer individually dependent on the ownership of land for the fulfillment of our basic needs. We rent or own an apartment or a house that is serviced by utility companies and financed by lending institutions. We work in office buildings, manufacturing plants, and shops, and we purchase our goods in stores, play in parks, and consume the products from far-off farms and ranches.

Many people now have the financial capability to step beyond using real property to supply only the necessities. These individuals also acquire real estate as an investment—a creator and a storehouse of value that represents the conversion of their work efforts into a tangible, valuable asset.

A real estate investment sometimes requires something as important as money—it often involves the application of personal time and effort. This hands-on approach to an investment is called **sweat equity**.

A real estate investment can be described as *the commitment of funds and time by an individual with a view to preserving and increasing capital and earning a profit to create a better life for the individual and others*. One must carefully evaluate investment opportunities in light of present and future needs for capital and time, and whether anticipated returns will be worth the cost. Mastery of the principles in this material will significantly increase the likelihood of making wise decisions.

PURPOSES OF INVESTING IN REAL ESTATE

To preserve capital

A primary reason for investing in real estate is the preservation and possible enhancement of the capital invested. Generally, owners have enjoyed rising property values over the years. Consequently, the capital value of the investment is preserved or increased by appreciation. It is precisely for this reason that real estate investments are described as hedges against inflation. Theoretically, the values of real estate fluctuate with local market cycles, but real estate values tend to rise over the long term.

A real estate investment may build up additional equity for its owner through reduction of the mortgage debt. The periodic repayments of the principal amounts owed on existing financing increase equity in property. This increasing equity can be secured for reinvestment either by refinancing the mortgage or selling the property, depending on the market. In fact, one of the more important benefits of investing in real estate is this ability to reuse the capital through periodic, tax-free refinancing, while at the same time preserving the value of the investment. In addition, the owner's equity in an investment may be raised by increasing the amount of the net operating income (NOI), which invariably raises the total value of the investment. Simply put, properties with better cash flows are worth more to potential buyers or lenders.

Although the problems associated with tenants are legendary, business tenants often improve the properties they occupy. These **betterments** tend to increase a property's value and are often left behind when the tenant moves. This not only preserves an owner's capital investment, but it enhances it, sometimes substantially.

To earn a profit

Fundamentally, all investors in real estate seek a profit on the money they invest. By definition, an investment of any kind is a commitment of funds with the intention of preserving capital and earning a profit. For real estate investors, these profits assume two forms. The income stream from the tenants' rents should generate one kind of profit. The gross amount of rent should be adequate to pay for all of the fixed and variable operating expenses of the property, with enough remaining to show a return on the investment. Thus, an investor anticipates that the income will provide a steady cash profit while the invested capital remains protected over time. When the property is sold, this investment will be recovered intact, or better still, a gain will be made. This gain reflects the increase in the property's value during the time it was held and is the second form of profit that can be earned by a real estate investor.

Before committing any funds, an investor should analyze carefully the returns available from opportunities other than the purchase of real estate. For example, a viable alternative to investing in a real estate venture is to deposit money into a government security that pays interest each year. The annual interest or profit (before taxes) that is earned on this investment becomes a benchmark against which the anticipated profitability of an alternative investment can be measured. The principal can be withdrawn from this security at a specific time so it meets the requirements of an investment: preservation of capital and generation of a profit. If we analyze a real estate investment that shows an annual return (before taxes), with the possibility of recovering the full investment within some identifiable future time period, we see a situation parallel to the government security. However, unlike this security, there is a greater degree of risk associated with real estate investments. This risk includes the likelihood of being able to collect the rents in the amounts and at the times anticipated and the chances of fully recovering the investment in the future. In addition, unforeseeable problems might occur over time.

Thus, the profit from a real estate investment should not be considered equal to this same profit from a government security. Something extra must be earned to offset the greater risks that are so much a part of real property ownership. In addition, to compensate for lack of liquidity, real estate investments must develop even larger returns. Unlike other investments, real estate is often difficult to sell at a specific point in time. Therefore, to be viable, a real estate investment should be designed to develop a relatively higher rate of return (profit) than is available from other safer, more liquid investment opportunities.

To enjoy tax relief

Under the current income tax code, and unlike many other investments, the income derived from rental real estate can be sheltered substantially to diminish the income tax liability, and thus, enhance the bottom-line return.

After all income from a rental property is accumulated for the year, the expenses incurred to develop this income may be deducted—effectively **sheltering** this amount from income taxes. *Sheltering income* simply means having the income deemed as either nontaxable, as in the deduction of expenses, or as tax-deferred, as in cost recovery (depreciation) deductions. Depreciation deductions reduce current taxable income but are recaptured and taxed when the property is sold, thereby deferring taxes rather than truly saving them. These expenses include all operating costs such as management fees, property taxes, utility expenses, repairs, maintenance, advertising, bookkeeping, and others as required. In addition, the interest paid on existing real estate loans is deductible. Thus, the gross income derived from rentals is effectively reduced to a net amount that is then subject to the imposition of income taxes at the taxpayer's bracket. Tax credits may further reduce tax liability, such as those available for energy efficiency features or low-income housing tax credits.

In addition, real estate investments are normally made for extended periods of time and, as such, currently enjoy the tax advantages available under long-term capital gains (other than depreciation recapture) when the investment is sold for a profit.

The full ramifications of the current tax laws, as they apply to investment decision-making, will be examined in later units. No investment decision can be intelligently made without one eye toward the tax consequences of various alternatives.

ADVANTAGES OF INVESTING IN REAL ESTATE

Any list of available avenues of investment will include stocks, bonds, savings certificates, life insurance policies, commodities, consumer merchandise, and real estate. The investment opportunities in real estate include open land, vacant lots, farm acreage, industrial properties, houses, apartment buildings, stores, shopping centers, office buildings, clinics, recreational projects, mineral deposits, securities, manufactured-home parks, condominiums, and airspace.

Competition for the dollars available for investment is high, and each opportunity has its own advantages and disadvantages. The general advantages of investing in real estate, however, include its relatively high-yield possibilities, tax flexibilities, and the retention of a large degree of personal control over the capital invested. The next lesson discusses more about leveraging these opportunities.

Relatively high yields

Bottom-line yields in excess of 20% are not unusual for many real estate investments. Yields can even exceed this amount, reaching infinity in those cases where 100% or more leverage—using borrowed funds to purchase property—has been achieved. More common, though, are real property investments that regularly develop 10%–15% annual returns over the life of the investment. These profits reflect the opportunities that exist in real estate and, when compared to average yields on other types of investments, explain its popularity.

The return on a savings investment is the rate of interest paid by the bank or savings association. These rates currently run slightly over 3%, depending on the type and duration of deposit. These are before-tax yields, which are eroded by the taxes paid, in accordance with the investor's particular tax bracket. Stocks often pay dividends that average about 2% of the value of the investment, but unlike savings, for which the amount of deposit remains constant over time, the value of the stocks fluctuates in the market. As a result, an element of risk is introduced for a stock investor who analyzes yield in terms of dividends received plus growth in value. If this growth is 5% per year and the shareholder receives 2% in dividends, the yield is 7% before taxes.

Bond yields fluctuate, sometimes dramatically, as a function of the money market. A bond owner may earn about 3% interest but may have to take a discount when selling in a market at more than 3%. Some bonds, such as municipals, are tax-exempt, and their yields are commensurately lower, depending on the bond's rating.

It is accepted in real estate investment that high profits are positively correlated with high risk. Although yields on real estate investments do fluctuate from time to time and from property to property, there are guidelines on which objective decisions may be based. For example, despite the fractured quality of the general real estate market, there are fairly definable submarkets. One such submarket is apartment projects. Depending on location, number of apartments in the complex, and their size and decor, an investor can usually find comparable projects, research competitive rents, and estimate the income possible from an anticipated investment. This analysis and others will provide data on which an objective decision concerning the profitability of the investment can be based. There are similar submarkets for houses, stores, office buildings, shopping centers, and other forms of real property.

Income tax flexibility

Real estate allows its owner a high degree of tax flexibility, due in part to the application of depreciation allowances and the ability to deduct the premises' operating costs from the gross income collected. Taxes due on the gain from sales can be deferred until later years because of advantages under Section 1031 of the Internal Revenue Code. Tax-free gifts of fractional shares of a limited liability company that owns real estate can result in lower tax rates for some of the income and avoidance of estate tax liability. Placing real estate in a self-directed IRA can defer taxes; placing it in a self-directed Roth IRA can eliminate taxes.

High degree of personal control

Real estate investments provide the opportunity for a high degree of personal control. Purchase terms can be designed to reflect specific financial circumstances. Often, rents can be arranged to anticipate changes in future realty cycles. Various bookkeeping techniques can be adopted to reflect individual needs as they change over time. Property can be periodically refinanced to capitalize on the equity accumulated. The investor usually retains the power to decide on when, how, and to whom the investment will be sold, under terms that satisfy personal economic requirements.

DISADVANTAGES OF INVESTING IN REAL ESTATE

There are no perfect investments. An investor who prefers the guaranteed safety offered by U.S. government securities must forgo high yields to achieve this safety. An investor who is interested in the relatively high yields offered by real estate will have to sacrifice a certain amount of safety and **liquidity** and be willing to take a more active personal role in managing such an investment.

The disadvantages associated with real estate investments include relatively poor liquidity, large capital requirements, constant management, being a landlord, and a relatively high degree of risk.

Relatively poor liquidity

Although real estate is usually easy to purchase, it is sometimes difficult to sell, with little certainty about the final sales price. Unlike the stock and bond markets, where there are almost always buyers to be found if the price is low enough, sometimes real estate cannot be given away, let alone sold at a reasonable price. For example, in good times, owners are reluctant to sell, while in bad times, everyone wants to sell at the same time, significantly reducing the property's marketability. If a property's current value is significantly less than the mortgage balance, then owners will be forced to choose among selling and bringing cash to closing, retaining and continuing to service the debt until better times, or allowing a foreclosure or short sale.

Large capital requirements

Contributing to the poor liquidity of real estate income property are the relatively large sums of money needed for property acquisition, maintenance, and reserves. Despite the high leveraging opportunities that exist in this field, a sound investment must be backed by adequate operating capital to protect it in the event of unforeseen major crises. An unexpected reversal in the economic cycle of a community could result in a high number of vacancies and, at the same time, eliminate any possible market for disposing of the suddenly declining investment property.

Necessity of constant management

Everything about real estate, as in most other areas of present-day living, is expensive. At current rates for repairs, everyday maintenance is costly, to say nothing of required replacement of worn-out items. Major maintenance expenditures such as a new roof, plumbing, or electrical systems can easily amount to thousands of dollars.

Constant property maintenance is an absolute necessity for improved real estate investments. Buildings need careful attention, including perpetual nailing, patching, painting, and replacement of worn parts to satisfy tenants and ensure continuing rental cash flows. In addition, the hallways, elevators, and grounds also require routine upkeep.

In other words, a real estate investment requires more active participation on the part of the individual investor than do most other investment opportunities. This management activity may be passed along to a professional management agent or service, but then the income from the property must be sufficient to justify the cash paid for these services.

Being a landlord

Most real estate investments require that the property owner enter into some form of personal involvement with the professional manager, the tenants, or both. These interpersonal relationships are often warm and rewarding, but they can also become distressing, especially when a manager must be dismissed or a tenant evicted. People are often deterred from investing in real estate because, as landlords, they are exposed to tenants' complaints and the problems of managing property, and this factor should be included in the acquisition decision. Investors seeking **mailbox money**—passive revenue—either choose other investments or rely heavily on third-party management companies.

Risk

Finally, it must be clearly understood that there are substantial risks involved when investing in real estate. It is true that there are risks in every field of endeavor—even in our daily activities. Still, it is important to reiterate that investing involves decision-making—a choice of what you should buy, when and where you should buy, and, most significantly, whether you should invest at all.

What makes real estate investment so hazardous is the number of agencies and events beyond the investor's control that influence its success. For example, the unpredictability of the income tax code may be enough of a detractor to discourage some investors. We also cannot ignore the fluctuations of the financial markets as interest rates shift in response to the natural laws of supply and demand, as well as the imposition of monetary controls by the Federal Reserve System (the Fed).

Add the other disadvantages, detailed previously, and you can draw a clear warning that, although real estate investment carries with it the potential for large rewards, there are indeed substantial risks involved. Yet even in real estate, there are varying degrees of risk. Investing in an office building with a successful and profitable track record that has a number of tenants on long-term leases presents less risk than investing in a proposed building with no history to consider.

SUSTAINABILITY

In today's world, sustainability is also a factor when developing real estate. According to the U.S. Environmental Protection Agency (EPA), sustainability is based on a simple principle: everything that we need for our survival and well-being depends, either directly or indirectly, on our natural environment. The EPA is the government's environmental watchdog. To that end, many government contracts include sustainability clauses. The Internal Revenue Code also includes incentives for energy efficiency. For more information, go to www.fedcenter.gov/programs/sustainability/.

SUMMARY

People invest in real estate with a view toward preserving capital and earning a profit. Real estate investments offer relatively higher yields, greater leveraging opportunity, greater income tax sheltering strategies, and a higher degree of personal control than most other types of investments.

On the other hand, real estate is definitely illiquid when compared to stocks and bonds. It also requires a commitment to personal involvement in management, either with a professional manager or with the tenants themselves. The role of landlord has probably turned many away from the profit opportunities available in real estate investments.

UNIT 2 EXAM

1. An investor in real estate must consider all of the following analysis aspects *EXCEPT*
   A. yield.
   B. risks.
   C. pride.
   D. value.

2. Real estate investments have all of the following advantages *EXCEPT*
   A. high yields.
   B. leverage.
   C. liquidity.
   D. personal control.

3. To increase the use of leverage when buying a real estate investment is to
   A. decrease its yield.
   B. increase its risk.
   C. decrease its operating expenses.
   D. increase its beginning book basis.

UNIT 3 Leverage

LEARNING OBJECTIVES

When you have completed this unit, you will be able to accomplish the following.

› Summarize the concept of leverage and how it is used in investment real estate.

KEY TERMS

leverage

INTRODUCTION

Leverage is the use of borrowed funds to purchase a property. Leverage is an important advantage of investing in real estate because the investor uses other people's money.

LEVERAGE OPPORTUNITIES

Leverage is an investment term that describes a popular concept called *OPM*, or using *Other People's Money* to make investments. If an investor has $100,000 in cash to invest in a rental property, he could purchase a modest single-family residence that might generate gross revenues of $10,000 per year. By borrowing money and using borrowed funds to leverage its available cash into a larger property, that same investor might be able to buy a 20-unit apartment building for $1 million. The revenues would be much larger than the single-family residence, even after debt service on the loan. This is the power of leverage in real estate. The power has a downside, however. Increasing leverage increases expenses from debt service and increases the risk of loss by foreclosure if gross revenues and reserves can no longer cover mortgage payments.

Although most lenders allow a purchaser to borrow up to 50% of the value of securities such as stocks and bonds, real estate offers an investor the highest leveraging opportunities of any investment alternative. Most realty transactions require 20%–25% of a property's value as a cash down payment, while others have 10%, 5%, or even no down payment requirements. Depending on the economic climate, it is not uncommon for investors to enjoy the benefits of arranging their real estate investment portfolios with greater than 100% leverage and ending up with cash in their pockets.

High-leverage situations include transactions involving carryback mortgages, land leases, subordination, joint ventures, syndication, sale-leasebacks, wraparound mortgages, participation mortgages, and other creative real estate ownership and financing arrangements. These concepts and their applications, among others, will also be examined in upcoming units. Some categories of investment historically generate opportunities for greater than 100% financing. These include rehab projects and real property development. Lenders will often approve loans for up to 80% of the anticipated value of the project after completion of all work.

SUMMARY

Leverage is an investment term that describes a popular concept called *OPM*, or using *Other People's Money* to make investments.

UNIT 3 EXAM

1. Because of the fractured quality of the market, a real estate investment is frequently considered highly
   A. profitable.
   B. illiquid.
   C. transferable.
   D. valuable.

UNIT 4

Ownership Interests in Real Property

LEARNING OBJECTIVES

When you have completed this unit, you will be able to accomplish the following.

- List and describe different types of individual ownership.
- List and describe different types of group ownership.
- Describe trust ownership and the role played by foreign investors.

KEY TERMS

ancillary probate
blue-sky laws
collapsible corporation
community property
conduit
curtesy rights
discretionary trust
dower rights
fee simple ownership
Foreign Investment in Real Property Tax Act (FIRPTA)
general partnership
inheritability
investment trust
irrevocable trust
joint tenancy
joint venture
limited liability company (LLC)
limited partnership
living trust
minority ownership discount
partnership
pierce the corporate veil
real estate investment trust (REIT)
real estate mortgage trust (REMT)
regular corporation
right of first refusal
S corporation
severalty
self-directed IRA
sole and separate ownership
syndicate
tenancy by the entirety
tenancy in common
testamentary trust

INTRODUCTION

How an investor holds title to real estate has a significant impact on the degree of personal involvement in management and the amount of profit earned, taxes paid, and asset protection—meaning loss of other assets because of personal liability for debts and damages related to a particular real estate investment. This unit includes a review of the major forms of interests in real property, including ownership by individuals and ownership by groups such as corporations, collapsible corporations, partnerships, and trusts.

INDIVIDUAL OWNERSHIP

Individuals may acquire legal interests in real property, called **fee simple ownership**. An estate in fee simple implies that the owner has the greatest bundle of rights to the use of the property, including the right to pass it to others through inheritance. Included in this bundle is the right to use, possess, finance, lease, devise (pass to another by a last will and testament), and sell, among others. Without partners to please or shareholders to impress, individuals may design their investment holdings to meet their own immediate and long-term goals.

On the other hand, individual owners assume a high degree of personal involvement, responsibility, and liability for their investments and all the problems inherent in such tight control. For example, legal suits for fraud or negligence, and demands for actual and punitive damages, can easily bankrupt an underinsured property owner. The eviction of nonpaying tenants may well be disliked by another. Individual ownership of real estate demands that the investor take an active role in investment management.

The various forms of individual ownership include tenancy by the entirety, tenancy in common, community property, joint tenancy with the rights of survivorship, sole and separate ownership, ownership in severalty, and dower and curtesy rights. Use of the word *tenancy* when describing ownership rights in real estate derives from William the Conqueror's invasion and subjugation of England in 1066, after which he declared himself the owner of all the land in the realm and granted tenancies to his lords. They, in turn, granted tenancies to those under them and so on down the chain. The tenancies carried with them broad rights, including that of inheritability, unless revoked for some transgression against the Crown. This practice, called subinfeudation, was discontinued in the 14th century, but the terms survive to this day.

Before examining each of these forms, an important distinction must be made concerning an individual owner's rights of property control. An owner can hold a fee simple title or an undivided interest in a fee, subject to the right of either inheritability or survivorship.

Inheritability implies that the control individuals have over their estates includes the right to designate who will inherit their property. These designations are described in the owner's will, which requires a legal probate procedure before the estate can be distributed to the heirs. Inheritability also implies the right to change one's mind—right up until execution of a new will moments before death. The opposite of inheritability is *survivorship,* which is choosing an ownership form that automatically determines who will receive the property upon one's death. Survivorship cannot be changed unless all owners execute a new deed and choose a new form of ownership.

The purpose of the probate process is to provide creditors of the deceased with a reasonable amount of notice and time in which to perfect their claims against the estate. To this end, a primary probate is initiated in the deceased's state of residency, and **ancillary probates** are initiated in each state in which portions of the estate's assets are situated. Thus, for a deceased Michigan resident who owned property in Arizona, the primary probate proceedings would take place in Michigan, and an attorney in Arizona would supervise the ancillary proceedings in that state.

On the other hand, **joint tenancy**—also called *survivorship*—eliminates this personal control over the distribution of an estate after death. When two or more persons enter into a survivorship form of ownership, they give up their inheritable rights and designate that on one owner's death; the other(s) in the agreement will be the recipient(s) of the deceased's portion of the property. The interests of the deceased pass automatically and immediately to the survivors in this form of survivorship ownership.

Holding title subject to the right of survivorship eliminates the necessity of probate proceedings, with accompanying savings in time and costs. See Figure 4.1 for inheritability and survivorship interests.

Figure 4.1: Real Property Ownership

Type	Relationship	Consequences on Death
Tenancy by the entirety	Married couples only	Automatic survivorship
Tenancy in common	Anybody	Inheritable
Community property	Married couples only	Inheritable
Joint tenancy	Anybody, although usually family members	Automatic survivorship
Sole and separate	A married person in her own right, but implying a living spouse	Inheritable
Severalty	Unmarried or divorced persons, widows, and widowers	Inheritable
Dower/curtesy	Surviving spouses	Inheritable
Life estate	Anybody	Ceases upon death
Remainders	Anybody	Inheritable

Tenancy by the entirety

Tenancy by the entirety is an arrangement limited to married couples that includes the automatic right of survivorship and is not available in community property states and some common law states. The owners are construed to be one entity, and when one spouse dies, the other becomes the immediate sole owner. Neither spouse may unilaterally dispose of the interest. Property is generally safe from creditors of only one spouse, making this form of ownership an asset protection tool.

Tenancy in common

Recognized in all states, **tenancy in common** is an arrangement in which each of several participants controls and has an interest in an undivided portion of the entire property. This relationship can be established between two or more people. The basic components of tenancy in common are the concepts of *inheritability* and *undivided interests.* Inheritability provides an individual owner with the right to designate to whom his proportionate share of the property will pass upon his death. Undivided interests implies that no single participant can identify a specific portion of the subject property, but rather, has rights to the entire property and its benefits as per the participant's proportionate share. Each tenant in common has an equal voice in the property's management, unless otherwise specified, and each assumes a proportionate share of the responsibilities, obligations, and profits of the tenancy.

Actions by any cotenant are assumed to be on behalf of all cotenants. For that reason, a cotenant cannot buy her property at a foreclosure or tax sale auction and gain 100% ownership rights in the property. The purchase will reestablish the tenancy in common, but with the obligation of contribution by other cotenants. They will each owe their pro rata share of the purchase price to the one who paid that price.

Some states recognize a tenancy in common with survivorship. This is legally complicated and beyond the scope of this book. Such an ownership mechanism is very similar to a tenancy by the entireties but is not limited to spouses. It is often used as an asset protection tool. Investors should seek legal counsel to see if it is available and research the local benefits and drawbacks.

Spouses would normally own an undivided half interest in a property. Four partners might agree on an equal ownership arrangement of one-quarter interest each. However, any proportion is allowable. For example, one partner may have an undivided 12/20 interest, another could have a 5/20 undivided interest, and a third partner might have a 3/20 undivided interest. In a $20,000 cash transaction, this would require the partners to contribute $12,000, $5,000, and $3,000, respectively. Unequal ownership shares typically arise because of death and intestate succession—meaning property distribution by statute because of the absence of a will. Children of the decedent might each inherit a 25% interest, but then a deceased child's children—the grandchildren—might own a proportionate share of their parent's 25% ownership. Child 1, 2, and 3 might own 25% each, while grandchild 1 and grandchild 2 own 12.5% each.

Anyone may own property as a tenant in common. It is a form of ownership whereby each participant may dispose of one's own interest at will unless there is a formal partnership agreement to the contrary. Each participant's undivided interest is inheritable and is distributed by will to the deceased partner's heirs. Thus, in a state that recognizes tenancy by the entirety, if spouses wish to exercise control over their estate by will and designate some other party their heir, they should hold title to property as tenants in common so that each will have an undivided half interest.

Should an owner die without a will (intestate), the owner's interest would pass to the deceased's heirs, as designated by state law. Of course, if the owner dies with a will (testate), the deceased's property passes to the devisees named in the will. Remember that these issues are legally complex and will differ from state to state, which necessitates the input of a competent attorney.

Joint tenancy with rights of survivorship

All but four states recognize joint tenancy, whereby participants—not necessarily spouses—own equal undivided interests in property, subject to the rights of survivorship. Any joint tenant may sell an interest or lose it through foreclosure or other involuntary transfer, but the joint tenancy arrangement will be destroyed as a result, and the new owner will assume a role as a tenant in common with the remaining owners.

Although anyone may hold title in joint tenancy, it is unusual for persons other than family members to enter into such an arrangement. Remember, survivorship effectively eliminates an owner's right to designate by will to whom property interests vest. They will automatically vest in the surviving owners.

Thus, a father's death in a joint tenancy arrangement with his wife and son results in the father's one-third undivided interest automatically vesting in the surviving wife and son, consequently raising each of their proportionate interests to an undivided half. When the wife dies, the son automatically acquires the full interest in the property, and probate proceedings are avoided each time. Again, legal counsel is needed for such matters.

Community property

Under **community property**, which applies only to married couples, money earned during marriage and property purchased with these communal funds belong equally to each spouse, who, simultaneously, maintains inheritable rights. Therefore, the community property spousal relationship is the opposite of the survivorship rights of spouses who are tenants by the entirety.

Most agree, however, that the participants may maintain separate personal controls under certain circumstances. For example, property inherited by one spouse can be maintained as separate property. In addition, any funds flowing from this separate property may be kept separate, as long as they are not commingled with communal funds in the family checking or savings accounts. If this income is deposited into a family account, the funds become community property, but the inherited real estate can still be maintained as separate property. On the other hand, if the income from separate property is kept apart from communal funds, any additional property purchased with this money will also be considered separate property, even if the acquisition occurs during marriage. Texas, however, considers any money earned during marriage to be community property, even those funds earned from separate property, unless the couple has signed a contract stating otherwise.

As shown in Figure 4.2, only nine states recognize community property, each with differing interpretations of the various intricacies inherent in this form of ownership.

Figure 4.2: Forms of Ownership in Each State

	Forms of Ownership				
	Sole	Concurrent			
	Individual	Tenancy in Common	Joint Tenancy	Tenancy by the Entirety	Community Property
Alabama ‡	•	•	•		
Alaska*	•	•		•	
Arizona	•	•	•		•
Arkansas	•	•	•	•	
California	•	•	•		•
Colorado	•	•	•		
Connecticut	•	•	•		
Delaware	•	•	•	•	
District of Columbia	•	•	•	•	
Florida	•	•	•	•	
Georgia	•	•	•		
Hawaii	•	•	•	•	
Idaho	•	•	•	•	•
Illinois	•	•	•		
Indiana	•	•	•	•	
Iowa	•	•	•		
Kansas	•	•			
Kentucky	•	•	•	•	
Louisiana**					•
Maine	•	•	•	•	
Maryland	•	•	•	•	
Massachusetts	•	•	•	•	
Michigan	•	•	•	•	
Minnesota	•	•	•	•	
Mississippi	•	•	•	•	
Missouri	•	•	•	•	
Montana	•	•	•	•	
Nebraska	•	•	•	•	
Nevada	•	•	•		•
New Hampshire	•	•	•	•	
New Jersey	•	•	•	•	
New Mexico	•	•	•		•
New York	•	•	•	•	
North Carolina	•	•	•	•	
North Dakota	•	•	•		
Oregon	•	•		•	

Figure 4.2: Forms of Ownership in Each State (continued)

	Forms of Ownership				
	Sole	Concurrent			
	Individual	Tenancy in Common	Joint Tenancy	Tenancy by the Entirety	Community Property
Pennsylvania	•	•	•	•	
Rhode Island	•	•	•	•	
South Carolina	•	•	•		
South Dakota	•	•	•		
Tennessee	•	•	•	•	
Texas	•	•	•		•
Utah	•	•	•		
Vermont	•	•	•	•	
Virginia	•	•	•	•	
Washington	•	•	•		•
West Virginia	•	•	•	•	
Wisconsin††	•	•	•		
Wyoming	•	•	•	•	

‡ Alabama allows ownership as tenants in common with survivorship. It is similar to a tenancy by the entireties but is not limited to married persons. It is primarily employed for asset protection purposes.

* Alaska does allow couples to opt into a community property arrangement; property is separate unless both parties agree to make it community property.

** In Louisiana, real estate can be owned by one person and by two or more persons, but these ownership interests are created by Louisiana statute. There is no estate comparable to those of joint tenancy, tenancy by the entirety, or community property, nor is there any statutory estate giving surviving co-owners the right of survivorship. Two or more people may be co-owners under indivision, or joint, ownership.

† Ohio does not recognize joint tenancy but does permit a special form of survivorship by deed through an instrument commonly called a "joint and survivorship deed."

†† Wisconsin recognizes "marital property," which is similar to community property.

Community property with right of survivorship

Community property with right of survivorship allows for the tax advantage of community property (step up in 100% of the basis of property upon the death of a spouse) with the outright ownership by the surviving spouse of the decedent's half interest. Probate is also avoided. Married owners of real estate must proactively title property in this manner.

Sole and separate ownership

All states recognize **sole and separate ownership** of property, which is an inheritable estate. This form of ownership vests title to property in the name of one spouse while implying that the other is still alive but has signed over the interest. Sole and separate ownership can be used to take advantage of special property tax exemptions, simplify property management, or avoid inheritance taxes.

For example, in Arizona and several other states, qualified veterans are eligible for special tax exemptions on their portion of a property. If a nonveteran spouse quitclaims interest to the veteran spouse, the veteran spouse can then claim the tax exemption for the entire property, not just the veteran's half. Although Arizona is a community property state, the veteran would own this particular property as separate property because, as described previously, property inherited or received as a gift by one spouse in a community property state may be held as sole and separate property.

Often, one spouse will quitclaim the interest in a property to the other for ease of management. This same purpose can be achieved if one spouse executes a power of attorney, legally granting the other full authority over the property.

In addition, sole and separate ownership is often used to transfer one spouse's share of a property to the other spouse as a gift to avoid probate costs and inheritance taxes. However, a transfer of this nature may be subject to gift taxes. The impacts of inheritance and gift taxes will be examined in a different unit.

Severalty ownership

All states acknowledge that single people, whether unmarried or divorced, as well as widows and widowers, own their real property in **severalty**—also called *sole ownership*. Severalty is confusing to students, who think it means "several" owners. The legal word *severalty* has its origins in an old French term meaning "severing" or "separating" ownership from the group into sole ownership. Severalty is an inheritable estate. Thus, owners in severalty should designate by will to whom they wish property to be distributed upon their death. Corporate ownership is in the form of severalty. The corporation might have more than one owner, but the corporation itself is a single legal "person."

Dower and curtesy rights

Finally, a few states recognize the legal rights of a surviving spouse concerning the real estate of the deceased spouse. The rights of a widow in the property of her deceased husband are called **dower rights**, while the rights of a widower in the property of his deceased wife are called **curtesy rights**. The rights are intended to provide some support for the surviving spouse, who might have received nothing under the will. The degree to which these rights are respected varies from state to state. In some states, dower and curtesy rights were abolished and replaced by *elective shares*, which do not distinguish whether the surviving spouse is a widow or a widower. An elective share allows a disinherited spouse to elect inheritance under a statute rather than under the will. It means that in those states that allow an elective share, a decedent cannot legally leave her spouse penniless.

Note that title companies are requiring the spouse who is not on the deed to sign the contract and the deed to reduce any liability arising from dower or curtesy rights or elective shares in the future. Such spouses are not selling current rights but merely releasing future rights. A promissory note might be in only one spouse's name, but both could be required to sign the mortgage because of these rights.

It is important that investors be familiar with the laws of the states in which they anticipate purchasing real estate because these specific laws will prevail for all transactions concerning property regardless of an investor's principal state of residence. Any income derived from property is subject to the laws of the state in which it is situated, as well as federal income taxes. In addition, although a deceased's main probate will be originated in the state of primary residency, ancillary probate proceedings will be required in each state where owned property is located. It is advisable to consult a real estate attorney in every case.

GROUP OWNERSHIP

In addition to individuals who own real estate investments singly, with their spouses, or with others as tenants in common, there are more formal arrangements for group ownership of realty. Five important property ownership types are the *corporation*, the *S corporation*, the *collapsible corporation*, *formal partnerships*, and *LLCs*. It is important to carefully analyze from a tax and legal liability standpoint each of the various titling and ownership structures.

Corporations

A **regular corporation**, also called a C corporation, is a separate legal entity created under the authority of the laws of the specific state of its incorporation. It is composed of any number of individuals who join together for mutual purposes and is considered to have an existence distinct from that of its members. Shareholders can be natural people, as well as other corporations and legal entities. Corporations are endowed with the capacity for continuous existence despite changes in ownership, and they act as individuals in matters relating to the common purposes of the association. These actions must remain within the bounds of the corporation's powers, as outlined in the corporate charter, and within the laws of the various states in which it is licensed to operate. As a legal entity, a corporation can hold title to real property in its own right.

Participation in a corporation is evidenced by stock certificates that are traded by various means, mostly in organized stock exchanges. Certain classes of stock owners have the right to vote but usually take a passive role in the activities of their corporations. The actual operation of a corporation is often left to professional managers who serve together with the company's president and board of directors for the shareholders' benefit.

Corporations formed for the purpose of investing in real estate are designed primarily as capital-accumulating vehicles. Using a public stock offering, the organization of a corporation may attract funds slated for an investment, giving smaller investors an opportunity to expand their participation far beyond their individual financial capabilities.

Corporations have four general characteristics: continual life, centralized management, limited personal liability, and easy transferability of interests.

Continual life

Corporations "die" only when they are disbanded intentionally, are absorbed into another company by merger or court order, or fail to file an annual report with the secretary of state. (Note that due to the continuity of life, death or bankruptcy will not terminate a corporation as long as someone continues to file the annual report.) Otherwise, they function perpetually, with new managers replacing those who retire.

Centralized management

Large corporations can afford to attract talented professional people. A corporation's functional design lends itself to centralized management in which trained and experienced teams are directed by and held accountable to a board of directors.

Limited personal liability

One of the most important characteristics of a corporation formed for real estate investments is its ability to shield a shareholder's personal assets from the debts of the corporation. Unlike a general partnership in which participants are personally responsible for their proportionate shares of a venture's liabilities, corporate shareholders' risks are limited to the extent of their investment in the company. In the event of a bankruptcy, other personal assets of the stock owners are not subject to attachment for any of the corporation's debts. Officers of the corporation are also protected by the corporate form of ownership. There are exceptions to this protection for criminal acts and trust fund liabilities such as employee FICA/Medicare and sales taxes. Also, it is possible for a court to **pierce the corporate veil** in cases where the corporation is managed as if it were a sole proprietorship or small partnership. In other words, the shareholders comingle personal and corporate funds and assets, fail to have regular meetings and votes, and otherwise ignore the existence of the corporate entity. If the shareholders ignore the rules of corporate management, the law will allow creditors to also ignore the corporate veil, thereby piercing it. This immunity is also eliminated on those corporate loans where officers are required to be held personally liable for the debt. Lenders may ask officers for a personal guarantee of repayment of the debt when a corporation is newly formed or has weak credit.

Easily transferable interests

Because of the efficiency of the organized public exchanges, corporate stock ownership is relatively easy to transfer. This characteristic is particularly desirable for real estate investors who normally face a difficult situation when they need to sell their holdings. There is an exception for small corporations, called *closely held corporations*, which typically have buy/sell restrictions written into the bylaws and printed on the stock certificates. Such restrictions routinely require transfer of stock to the corporation or other shareholders before being offered to outsiders. Stock may not find a ready market to outsiders, who might find themselves with only a minority interest in a corporation largely controlled by a few other shareholders.

S corporations

There is no such thing as an **S corporation** as a different legal entity. It merely indicates a corporation that has elected to receive income tax advantages in exchange for meeting IRS requirements under Subchapter S of Chapter 1 of the Internal Revenue Code.

Clouding the efficiency of corporate ownership for real estate investments is the problem of double taxation. The corporation is subject to income taxes on the profits it generates, and the shareholders must pay taxes again when these profits are distributed to them as dividends. This double tax has made corporations less desirable for real estate investors and has led to the popularity of the S corporation, the limited partnership, **limited liability companies (LLCs)**, and the **real estate investment trust (REIT)** as alternative ownership forms. These forms of ownership act as investment conduits, bypassing double taxation. A conduit is something through which other things travel, such as water or electricity. In tax law, a conduit is a mechanism that allows profits to travel through the vehicle that created the profits, without tax liability. Instead, profits are taxed to the person or entity that ultimately receives them. This is called **conduit** *tax treatment.*

The special form of corporation called an *S corporation*—also called an *S corp or Subchapter S corporation*—is available for small businesses. It offsets the onerous double tax while still preserving the advantage of limited personal liability intrinsic in the corporate design. The major disadvantage of an S corporation is its limited ability to pass-through losses to individual investors. However, this disadvantage is significant only for an organization that emphasizes tax shelter over current cash flows. The S corporation is a popular vehicle for real estate investment.

S corporations are a creation of the tax laws. To qualify, a company must file an election form with the IRS and meet the following criteria:

- It must be a domestic corporation.
- It must have only allowable shareholders, such as individuals, certain trusts, and estates. Partnerships, corporations, or nonresident aliens may not be shareholders.
- It must not have more than 100 shareholders. Married couples are treated as one shareholder.
- Nonresident aliens are not eligible to participate, although foreign corporations or partnerships are allowed.
- It must have only one class of stock, although designations for voting or nonvoting stock may apply, making the S corporation as flexible as a limited partnership.

The major advantages of an S corporation include limited personal liability, ease of transferability of ownership shares, centralized management, and comparative ease of formation. Its basic disadvantage is that aggregate losses may be passed through to the individual shareholders in an amount equal only to cash paid for the stock, plus any loans made to the company. This limits the S corporation's ability to shelter other income earned by its shareholders. Thus, the S corporation's most efficient application for real estate investment is for projects designed for purposes other than tax shelters. In addition, having an S corporation with few members is an IRS audit flag that perhaps one or more members is providing significant services to the corporation. If there are no reported wages and salaries and no withholding taxes paid, and the audit reveals substantial services, then the IRS will impute a salary. The corporation will owe employment taxes, and the IRS will also impute income to the working members, even if there are no actual distributions or wage payments. Shareholders who wish to avoid an audit and the resulting additional taxes, penalties, and interest, would do well to pay a reasonable wage or salary to any member providing significant services to the corporation.

Collapsible corporations

A corporation formed for a single purpose and then disbanded when the goal is achieved is called a **collapsible corporation**. It is similar to a joint venture except with the added advantage of the corporate shield from liability. For example, a corporation may be formed for the specific purpose of owning a property from its unimproved state through the completion of building construction on the site. The project is not an investment in the eyes of the IRS because it is not held for growth, income, or business use. This means that during the course of construction, certain operating expenses, such as management salaries, mortgage interest, placement fees, and title insurance premiums, are treated as ordinary costs rather than a capital expenditure. Unlike the case with investment properties, these losses can be used to offset other ordinary income. This usually results in a substantial tax shelter for the corporation's owners. However, when the building is finally completed and the property is sold, profits from the sale of the improved property are considered ordinary income. Ordinary income is taxed at regular tax rates, gives rise to self-employment tax liability, and does not enjoy long-term capital gains tax rates.

Partnerships

Most states have passed local versions of a recommended set of laws called the Uniform Partnership Act. Uniform laws are written by national scholars and practitioners, called Commissioners, who attempt to design statutes that meet fairly universal problems and goals in various areas of the law. Once those Commissioners are finished, their creations can then be adopted and tweaked by state legislators to meet local concerns. Uniform laws also exist in the areas of landlord/tenant law, commercial transactions, and many others. Under the Uniform Partnership Act, real estate may be owned by individuals or corporations in **partnership**, with every partner considered a tenant in common with each of the other partners. The various forms of this type of ownership include full partnerships, syndicates, limited partnerships, LLCs, and joint ventures. Because of the legal complexities involved in forming a partnership, and state variations in the Uniform Act, it is suggested that an attorney's services be employed to prepare a partnership agreement.

General partnerships

Many **general partnerships**, also called *full partnerships*, are relatively informal arrangements wherein some friends or family members join to purchase an investment property as tenants in common. The only evidence of the partnership is their names on a deed specifying their proportionate ownership interests in the property. Other general partnerships can be designed with a formal contractual agreement specifying in detail the various rights, duties, and obligations of each member and whether their ownership interests are freely transferable. Some agreements require that a participant's interest first be offered to the remaining partners before being sold outside the partnership. This condition is called a **right of first refusal**.

Under the general partnership form of ownership, each partner assumes an active management role. Any partner has the ability to bind the entire partnership to agreements the others might find objectionable, unless those commitments are outside the ordinary course of business or expressly require unanimous vote under the act or the partnership agreement itself. As a result, a general partnership requires a high degree of trust among the partners.

General partnerships are usually designed to unite compatible persons who have similar goals for real estate investments, thereby enlarging their individual capabilities to acquire property. Although the management votes are usually equal, the distribution of earnings and the mortgage and property tax obligations are based on each participant's proportionate percentage of ownership. Partners are then personally responsible for their own income tax liability. A partnership receives conduit tax treatment.

In a general real estate partnership, members are personally liable for all debts and obligations of the partnership, regardless of their proportionate share. In the event of bankruptcy, other personal assets of the partners may be attached to satisfy creditors. However, the partnership itself is not responsible for the private debts of any one partner. In the event of a personal bankruptcy, only the proportionate interest of the troubled partner may be attached by creditors.

A condition common to many formal general partnership agreements specifies what the surviving partners' relationship will be with the heirs of a deceased partner. Recognizing the need for continuing compatibility in a general partnership in which each participant has an equal voice in management, most formal realty agreements will grant the remaining partners an option to purchase the ownership interest of a deceased partner.

A buy-out formula is devised at the inception of the partnership, usually based on the fair market value of the share at the time of death. The funds for the purchase option may be secured from the proceeds of a partnership life insurance program or from contributions made by each surviving partner. In the absence of a buy-out agreement, or if the remaining partners do not exercise the option that does exist, the heirs assume the deceased's partnership position, and the realty investment continues to function.

Syndicates

A **syndicate** consists of two or more investors joining together for the purpose of purchasing and operating a real estate investment for a limited time. It is similar to the concept of the collapsible corporation. A syndicate may take the form of a corporation, full partnership, LLC, or limited partnership. It is merely a description of multiple ownership in real estate, not a form of legal ownership. Most syndicates are in the limited partnership format, with the syndicator taking the role of the general partner and the investors being limited partners. Real estate syndications were once very popular because of extremely favorable tax treatment that resulted in deals driven by tax advantages rather than true economic value. That popularity waned when the tax laws changed in 1986, but they are still good investment vehicles when the underlying investment is sound.

Limited partnerships

Unlike the general partnership in which each participant takes an active management role and is also subject to the personal liabilities involved, **limited partnerships** and syndicates attract realty investors who prefer to take a passive role in management and who wish to limit their personal liability to the extent of their specific cash investments.

A limited partnership or syndicate is formed when a real estate promoter, assuming the liability and responsibility of a general partner or syndicator, purchases or takes an option to purchase an investment property. The public is then invited to participate as limited partners by buying ownership shares in various denominations. It is a type of crowd funding. The result is a relatively large group of investors who rely on the management expertise of the general partner for promised profits. The limited partners take a passive role in management and enjoy the security of protecting their other personal assets from liabilities incurred by the partnership. Any losses by the limited partners are limited to the loss of the individual's investment in the group. General partners retain full liability for all the debts of the partnership.

Limited partnerships are investment conduits that pass the profits directly through to the investors in proportion to their ownership shares. Any annual income tax liabilities are thus imposed at the investor's level. When the property is sold, the proceeds are also distributed proportionately to each investor. Because excess losses cannot be passed through to the passive investors in a syndicate or limited partnership, the popularity of these ownership entities has diminished in favor of REITs.

Unit 4

Each share in the limited partnership is the individual property of the investor and is inheritable. The shares are evaluated according to current market prices at the time of the owner's death and then distributed to the heirs after payment of any required inheritance and estate taxes.

Many smaller realty investors are attracted to this form of ownership. They can not only limit their personal liability and avoid the burdens of active property management, but also expand their individual investment capabilities by becoming part of a group that invests in larger, more efficient—and hence, potentially more profitable—realty ownership ventures

Limited partnerships are relatively popular vehicles for real estate ownership because they offer a wide latitude of investment opportunities, the ability to attract large sums of venture capital, and great flexibility in organizational design. Their organizational flexibility stems from their ability to design investments that can fulfill individual investors' requirements. To illustrate, one investment may be organized to attract those interested in receiving income in the form of regular cash flow from one single specific property, such as an office building. Other limited partnerships can be designed to attract investors who prefer to purchase shares in a diversified investment portfolio consisting of a variety of properties, much like a mutual fund in the stock market.

As an investment conduit, and to preserve its single-tax profile, a limited partnership must actively avoid displaying, at any one time, the basic four characteristics of a corporation: continuity, central management, limited liability, and easy transfer of interests. In fact, the IRS looks with disfavor on any limited partnership in which more than two of these characteristics exist at any one time.

As a result, because centralized management and limited liability are absolutely basic to limited partnerships, they are often designed to terminate at a specified time, and certain restrictions are placed on the transferability of ownership shares. In the first instance, the termination date is often established in advance; in the second instance, the organizational agreements usually include the general partner's right of first refusal to purchase any shares before they are offered to the public. This is just one of many examples of how income tax laws influence real estate investing.

Because syndicates are concerned with selling units of ownership in an enterprise that relies on the management and control of other persons, they come under the definition of a *security*, the same as stock in General Motors. To protect small and vulnerable investors, states pass **blue-sky laws**. The term comes from an early court decision in which a judge said he wanted to protect people from speculative investments that had about as much value as a patch of blue sky. These blue-sky laws require every syndicator or general partner to prepare a comprehensive prospectus to distribute to potential investors. In addition to describing the physical property and the terms and conditions of the investment, full disclosure of the names and experience histories of each syndicator must be made, as well as a clear indication of all the risks inherent in the proposition.

When investors consider forming or joining a syndicate, it is imperative that they know precisely what is required in the way of organization, costs, and potential benefits. Syndicates are a popular mechanism recommended by many real estate investing experts for use by cash-poor promoters. As a result, the strategy attracts a large number of relatively unsophisticated users, thereby increasing the need for good legal and accounting assistance. A comprehensive outline for a syndicate offering is shown in Figure 4.3.

Figure 4.3: Syndicate Offering (Limited Partnership)

Article I. General Provisions

Formation
Name
Purposes
Place of business
Term

General partner
Certificate of limited partnership
Agent for service of process
Exhibit of limited partners

Article II. Definitions

Acquisition expenses
Acquisition fees
Adjusted invested capital
Affiliate
Assignee
Cash available for distribution from operations
Cash from sales or refinancing
Closing date
Distribution
Finders' fees
General partner(s)
Gross offering proceeds
Gross property revenue
Limited partners
Managing general partner
Majority vote

Net proceeds
Offering and organization expenses
Offering memorandum
Operation expenses
Original invested capital
Partners
Partnership
Partnership properties
Property management fee
Sales commission
Subscription agreement
Subordinated real estate commission
Total outstanding units
Unit
Unit holders
Working capital reserve

Article III. Capital Contribution and Related Matters

Capital contributed by general partner(s)
Capital contributed by limited partners
Payment for units
Subsequent offerings of additional units
No action or consent necessary by limited partners for admission of other limited partners
Return of capital
No interest on capital

No priority
Remedies for default in capital contributions
Subscriptions and admissions
General partner(s) may purchase units
No assessments or additional contributions
No withdrawal of capital contributions
Securities laws
Temporary investment of partnership capital

Article IV. Allocation of Distributions, Income, Losses, and Other Items Among the Partners

Distribution to the partners
Capital accounts
Obligation of general partner(s) to make up negative capital accounts
Limitations on distributions
Allocation for tax purposes
The limited partners' share of allocations and distributions among themselves

The general partner or partners' share of allocations and distributions among themselves
Allocation between assignor and assignee
Timing of distribution
Express consent of allocations
Special allocation for tax-exempt and foreign investors
Tax withholding

Figure 4.3: Syndicate Offering (Limited Partnership) (continued)

Article V. Management of Partnership

The management powers of the general partner(s)
Restrictions on powers of the general partner(s)
Decisions
Actions requiring consent of all general partners
Limited partners have no management powers
Duty of the general partner(s) to devote time
General partner(s) may engage in other activities
Dealing with the partnership
Liability of the general partner(s) and their affiliates
Consent of the limited partners not required
Liability of general partner(s) for capital contributions
Reserves

Article VI. Compensation to the General Partner(s) or Affiliates

Property management fee
Real estate brokerage commission on acquisition
Partnership management fee
Real estate brokerage commission on resale of property
Standby loan commitment fee
Loan guaranty fee
Fee for initial property management and marketing advice and rental marketing structure
Development supervision fee
Limitation on compensation to general partner(s)
Initial partnership, tax advice, and administration fee
Farm property management fee
Investment advisory fee
Mortgage brokerage commission
Subordinated interest
Sales commission
Incentive management fee
Rental consulting fee
Fees payable on removal

Article VII. Books, Records, Accounts, and Reports

Books and records
Limited partners' rights regarding books, records, and tax information
Accounting basis and fiscal year
Reports tax matters partner
Bank accounts
Designated person

Article VIII. Assignment of Interests in the Partnership

Assignment of interest in the partnership of the general partner(s)
Assignment units
No assignment allowed under certain circumstances
Substituted limited partner
Death, insanity, incompetency, or bankruptcy of a limited partner

Article IX. Dissolution and Termination of the Partnership

Dissolution
Continuation of the business of the partnership
Authority to wind up
Winding up and liquidation
No recourse against general partner(s)
Claim of limited partners or assignees

Article X. Termination of a General Partner

General partner(s) ceasing to be a general partner(s)
Termination of executory contracts with general partner(s) or affiliates
Removal of a general partner(s)
Continuing interest of terminated general partner(s) Reports after removal
General partner(s) ceasing to be a general partner(s)
Termination of executory contracts with general partner(s) or affiliates
Removal of a general partner(s)
Continuing interest of terminated general partner(s) Reports after removal

Figure 4.3: Syndicate Offering (Limited Partnership) (continued)

Article XI. Meetings and Voting Rights	
Notice of meetings	Voting rights of the limited partners
One vote per unit	Consents
Article XII. Partnership Expenses	
Reimbursement to general partner(s)	Direct payment of partnership expenses
Expenses of general partner(s)—nonreimbursable	Payment of expenses of the partnership
Article XIII. Amendments of Partnership Documents	
Amendments in general	Amendments by the general partner(s)
Amendments requiring greater than a majority rule	
Article XIV. Borrowings	
Loans by the general partner(s) to the partnership	Commercial loans
Loans by the partnership to the general partner(s) or others	
Article XV. Representations and Warranties of the Partners	
General partner(s)	Indemnification by limited partners
Limited partners	
Article XVI. Miscellaneous Provisions	
Notices	Waiver of action for partition
Article section headings	Attorneys' fees
Construction	Creditors
Severability	Remedies
Choice of venue and law	Authority
Counterparts	Tax elections
Entire agreement	Legends
Amended certificates of limited partnership	Signatures
Power of attorney to the general partner(s)	Election to be governed by successor or different limited partnership law
Further assurances	Arbitration
Successors and assigns	
Exhibits	
Description of property to be acquired	Name, address, number of limited partnership units, and capital contributions of each limited partner

The dissolution of a syndicate occurs on the expiration of its term or on the first occurrence of one of the following:

- Election by the general partner(s) to dissolve or discontinue the partnership, which is approved by a majority vote
- Bankruptcy of the partnership
- The sale or disposition of all or substantially all partnership assets, including the cessation of active business, the distribution of all cash, and the termination of reserves for liabilities

Unit 4

The benefits from the limited partnership form of ownership can extend beyond even the more usual income, depreciation, and growth in value potentials of most real estate investments. Because termination dates must be established in advance, promoters may design a number of separate limited partnerships, each controlling an individual property. These partnership units can then be traded regularly.

Limited liability company

A limited liability company (LLC) is an alternative to the limited partnership. An LLC has a corporate form and asset protection, but also the conduit tax treatment advantages of a partnership without the restrictions of an S corp.

Resembling a corporation by limiting the personal liability of its shareholders (called members in an LLC) and an S corporation by having the tax impact at only the member level, the LLC includes these additional benefits for its owners:

- Both gains and losses are passed through to individual members.
- It may be designed to dissolve on the death or bankruptcy of one or more of its members.
- It may include in its ownership nonresident aliens or foreign investors.
- Its basis may be expanded to add the LLC's debt to its investors' capital, unlike the S corporation, which limits the basis to the cash investment of its shareholders. *Basis* is a tax term that determines the amount of depreciation deductions, limitations on loss deductions, and amount of taxable gain upon a resale. For example, an LLC is formed with $1 million contributed by its shareholders; $500,000 is used to make a down payment on a $3 million office building. The LLC's basis is increased to $3.5 million to include the $2.5 million debt.

Many real estate investors choose the LLC form of ownership as an estate-planning tool. Under current IRS regulations, a minority interest in an LLC may be valued significantly less than that member's pro rata share of the underlying assets. In addition, most state laws allow a minority member to retain control of the LLC, as long as that is specifically stated in the organization's operating agreement. For example, the LLC might own real estate with an equity value of $100,000, and ownership by one individual, who has three children. Current tax laws allow annual gifts, tax free, of $15,000. If the owner were to sell a 15% interest in the LLC to an outsider, that buyer would pay significantly less than $15,000 because it would be acquiring only a minority interest. The buyer would have no meaningful input and no control over the LLC. As a result, there would be a **minority ownership discount** for the value, which might depress the value down to $7,500. Because of the 50% valuation discount, the owner of the LLC could give each child a 30% interest, which would be valued at $15,000 each, not $30,000. There is no gift tax, the membership shares have been effectively removed from the investor's estate, and the investor retains control of the LLC and the property.

LLCs can be organized only in states with authorizing legislation. Ownership interests are not freely transferable. Many states (such as California and Texas) charge an extra tax for the privilege of operating an LLC.

Some states now allow Series LLCs. A Series LLC allows single filing of creation documents but separate tax treatment for separate ventures in the series. There are savings in legal and accounting expenses. Series LLCs, when allowed, are uniquely attractive to real estate investors with multiple properties. Rather than holding title in separate LLCs to separately protect assets or attract investors, each property is held in one of the series under the master umbrella.

Joint venture

A special form of a general partnership, the **joint venture** brings together the skills and assets of a group of heterogeneous investors for a specific realty project. For example, a joint venture might be formed by a landowner, a developer, and a financier, each of whom contributes unique skills and assets to the overall project and receives, in exchange, a proportionate share of ownership.

The scope of a joint venture can be broadened to include, as partners, not only those individuals just mentioned, but also carpenters, electricians, plumbers, and other artisans who contribute labor and materials as their share and who receive in return a proportionate ownership.

Joint ventures must have a definite agreement setting forth the intentions of the parties, including provisions for treatment of the cash flows. This form of ownership can be entered into by individuals, corporations, and partnerships that become tenants in common with each other and are subject to the conditions, privileges, obligations, and liabilities of the full partnership discussed earlier. They typically have a limited lifespan.

TRUST OWNERSHIP

A trust is an arrangement whereby a person or legal entity holds title to a property and manages it for the benefit of another. The creator of a trust is the trustor, the holder of legal title is the trustee, and the receiver of the benefits of the trust is the beneficiary, who may also be the trustor under some agreements.

Trusts may be described as **discretionary trusts** or **irrevocable trusts**. The former can be altered or discontinued at the discretion of the participants. The latter are established for a specific purpose and cannot be changed until this purpose is achieved.

Trust agreements pertinent to real estate investments include the **testamentary trust**, the **living trust**, and the **investment trust** *(REIT.)* These real estate trusts are created for many reasons, including to

- provide continuity in ownership over several generations,
- enlist the expertise of professional management,
- protect assets and income from dissipation by imprudent beneficiaries,
- eliminate repetitive probate costs, or
- hide the identity of beneficiaries.

Testamentary trust

A trust may be established by the provision of a decedent owner's will specifying that certain portions, or all of the property in the estate, be placed into a trust for the benefit of designated heirs. This form of ownership is a testamentary trust and vests control and management of a deceased's property in the name of a trustee. In this manner, an estate may be kept intact through one or more generations of heirs and may enjoy the benefits of professional management during the intervening years until its final distribution per the terms of the deceased's will.

Living trusts

In the living trust (also called the *inter vivos trust*) form of real estate ownership, a trustor executes an agreement with a trustee to hold property in trust for the trustor's benefit and under the trustor's direct control for a certain time until specific goals have been attained. The living trust is terminated when these goals are achieved. Such a trust is originated by naming the trustors as primary beneficiaries during their lifetimes. Upon their death, the living trust changes to a testamentary trust, and the decedents' heirs move from a secondary beneficiary position into the primary position.

A living trust is often employed by land developers when acreage is purchased under the terms of an installment contract. The seller of the land must place the receivable contract in trust with a bank or title company together with instructions to release certain portions of the collateral land as stipulated payments are made to the trustee by the purchaser-developer. The trust ends when the contract is paid in full. Thus, the land seller, as well as the trustor, becomes the beneficiary of this living trust. The trustee is empowered to accept payments and issue releases, and sends the proceeds from the payments to the beneficiary.

This trust arrangement guarantees the developer periodic releases of parcels from the contract. These timely releases are vital to the success of the project because they maintain a constant flow of land for development. In the absence of such a living trust agreement, the developer would need to find the seller each time a payment was made to secure a release of the needed property from the lien of the contract. Because the trustee, which is usually a corporation, is the legal owner of the contract, the developer can quickly and efficiently secure the periodic releases when needed.

In the event that the seller dies during the term of the contract, the trust will continue uninterrupted, with the benefits passing through to the heirs under the testamentary provisions. Thus, the trust continues to function until the contract is satisfied, the property is fully distributed, and the goals are achieved.

Investors sometimes make use of the anonymous ownership advantage of a living trust to hide their names as beneficiaries. This technique is especially effective if the revelation of a property owner's name might have an adverse effect on the negotiations for the purchase, sale, or refinancing of a specific property.

Living trusts that are established to become testamentary trusts and control property over several generations eliminate the costs of repetitive probate proceedings because the secondary beneficiaries automatically advance each time the primary beneficiary dies. Generation-skipping trusts have been eliminated under the tax laws, and currently, the value of a trust's assets is included in the total value of an individual's estate for inheritance tax purposes. However, an irrevocable trust can still be established to avoid inheritance taxes. To create such a trust, a property owner must make an irrevocable gift of property to a trustee, with the property held on behalf of the named beneficiaries until the donor's demise. Thus, the donor may enjoy the income from the property and, at death, have the income accrue to the benefit of the heirs.

Investment trusts

In addition to the individual trust forms for property ownership already described, trusts can also be designed to act as investment conduits for small investors, enabling them to pool resources to participate in the field of real estate. By subscribing to and meeting specific IRS requirements, an investment trust avoids the double tax burden imposed on corporate earnings. The IRS requirements include the following:

- Transferable beneficial shares must be issued to at least 100 people by the end of the first year.
- More than five people must own more than 50% of the beneficial shares of the trust.
- At least 75% of the trust's assets must be in real estate.
- At least 75% of the gross income must be derived from rents from real property, interest on obligations secured by mortgages on real property, gain from disposition of real property that is not dealer property, and certain types of interest on dividends.
- At least 90% of the trust's earnings must be distributed to shareholders each year.
- The trust itself must be a passive investor, hiring others to manage and operate its investments.

The common types of investment trusts are the equity trusts called *real estate investment trusts (REIT),* **real estate mortgage trusts (REMT)**, and a hybrid form of these two.

In addition to these basic real estate trust forms, special investment trusts can be designed for the development and ownership of medical buildings, manufactured-home parks, recreational condominiums, mini warehouses, and other unique real estate developments. A synopsis of a trust offering is shown in Figure 4.4.

Figure 4.4: Synopsis of a Trust Offering

Synopsis of a trust offering
(Subject to state securities division approval)

REGENCY APARTMENTS
100 real estate investment trust units

Minimum investment: $30,000

This offer may be considered speculative, and there is no assurance that the property will increase in value or that the trust will realize a profit from the operation or upon the sale thereof. There is no public market for the trust interests, and none can be expected to develop.

The Regency Corporation shall be the manager of the trust. No dealer, salesperson, or any other person has been authorized to make any representations other than those contained herein. This publication does not constitute an offer to sell or the solicitation of an offer to buy any of the securities offered hereby to any person to whom it is unlawful to make such an offer. The trust intends to sell only those number of interests described herein.

The Regency Investment Trust is acquiring the Regency Apartments under an agreement executed with Allied Investment Corporation (the sellers). The purchase price is $3 million, to be paid in cash upon closing. It is the intention of this trust to generate positive cash-flow income to its investors for five years, then capital gains profits when the project is converted to condominiums and sold.

The Property. The Regency Apartments consists of 100 one-bedroom, 1½-bathroom, unfurnished rental units. It is located at the intersection of Bell and Center streets, close to Monterey Plaza Shopping Center. The complex is composed of 10 individual two-story red brick buildings on a three-acre lot. There are two heated swimming pools, saunas, whirlpool baths, dressing rooms, and improved patios. Each apartment has its own carport and storage area, as well as small private patio or balcony. The apartments are all 900 square feet and include built-in kitchens, paneling, wallpaper, separate air-conditioning, drapes, and carpets.

Figure 4.4: Synopsis of a Trust Offering (continued)

Pro Forma Statement		
Gross Potential Income:		
100 apartments @ $500 per month	$600,000	
Contingencies:		
Vacancies 5%		
Reserves 10%		
Operating Expenses:		
Management 5%		
Taxes 7%		
Insurance 3%		
Maintenance 20%		
Total (50%)	-300,000	
Net Operating Income (NOI)	$300,000	
		(10% on $3 million invested)

(Note that projected growth in value is up to $5 million in five years [$50,000 per apartment as a condominium]. This reflects a 15% additional annual return for a total overall projected annual yield of 25% before income taxes.)

All books and records shall be housed at the office of the Regency Corporation and shall be open to inspection by all members of the trust during regular business hours. Monetary distributions shall be made monthly, and all profits shall be distributed equally to each unit of the trust (1/100). No unit owner shall bear any financial loss in excess of the original contribution.

Real estate investment trust (REIT)

A REIT (pronounced "reet") uses the accumulated funds of its investors to earn real estate income via diverse properties as well as create long-term investments. A REIT is primarily an income generator for a group of small investors and is similar to the stock market's mutual funds. It may be publicly traded, publicly nontraded, or privately invested in.

REITs give the small investor the opportunity for broad-based participation in real estate equity investments, offering both regular income from rentals and long-term gains in property value as incentives. Unlike other forms of real estate ownership, REITs may not pass losses through to their beneficiaries. Therefore, their use as tax shelters is limited. Their greatest appeal is to those investors who can absorb additional active income but do not have either the financial capability or the inclination to invest directly in real estate.

REITs may be equity, mortgage, or hybrid in nature; that is, they may hold real estate, real estate mortgages, or both. Legislation authorizing REITs was signed into law by President Dwight Eisenhower in 1960, and REITs have enjoyed cyclical success over time. Although much commercial real estate is owned via partnerships, REITs have become a popular investment vehicle, as they are more liquid and less capital intensive. According to NAREIT, the national trade association, REITs have a combined equity market capitalization of $1 trillion. This is expected to grow. Because there are tax advantages for foreign investors in real estate via REITs, there has been an increase in their popularity abroad. Starting in 2018, the Tax Cuts and Jobs Act allowed ordinary REIT dividends to qualify for the new 20% pass-through deduction for income tax purposes, regardless of the wage and qualified basis limitation rules. The new tax advantages make REITs even more popular.

Traditionally, REITs had to conform to rules that required that they receive income primarily from rentals and could provide only limited services. However, the Real Estate Modernization Act, effective January 1, 2000, allowed REITs to create and own profitable subsidiary companies that provide noncustomary services to REIT tenants without penalty. These services include, among others, management of the buildings, land development activities, bulk-purchasing discounts for tenants, and partnerships with other entities to provide other services such as rental insurance. The income from these activities is taxable at the corporate level.

Real estate mortgage trusts

Real estate mortgage trusts (REMTs) are a form of investment that attracts participants who prefer the benefits offered by real property financing activities—a somewhat more stabilized form of cash flow—rather than the often-volatile activities of the real estate equities market.

The REMT uses monies secured from the sale of beneficial interests to establish a substantial line of credit with its bank or a similar financial institution. Then the REMT uses this credit to participate in the real estate financing market as a lender of junior mortgages, wraparound loans, gap loans, participation loans, and other sophisticated and often esoteric financing forms.

Hybrid trusts

Often REITs and REMTs are established as interlocking trusts, with the REIT dealing in property equities and the REMT financing these investments. In effect, this combination creates a hybrid trust arrangement and offers beneficiaries a greater opportunity for investment diversification.

Self-directed IRA

An IRA is a mechanism for retirement investing. Large institutions that invest in stocks, bonds, and other liquid assets manage most IRAs. Because of tax code incentives, a regular IRA can accept tax-deductible annual contributions from a person, and income earned within the IRA is not taxed currently. Later, when the retiree takes distributions, they are all taxed at ordinary income rates. A Roth IRA does not enjoy tax-deductible contributions. Earnings are not taxed in the years earned—the same as a regular IRA. However, all distributions, upon reaching the retirement age, are tax free.

Many real estate investors, firm believers in the benefits of IRA options, desire real estate holdings in their retirement accounts. To do this, they must choose REITs as part of their professionally managed portfolio or set up a **self-directed IRA**. There are national companies that act as custodians for the self-directed IRAs and make sure all IRS paperwork is filed timely and accurately, in exchange for a small fee based on the size of the equity in the properties. The investor is free to choose when and what to buy, as well as when and what to sell. The investment must be passive, however, meaning the investor cannot guarantee any mortgage debt and must hire a management company for tenant-occupied property.

Some states do not have enabling legislation that allows a self-directed IRA to hold real estate. Care should be taken to consult with local real estate lawyers on this subject, as well as with a national custodian company for IRS restrictions on particular transactions.

FOREIGN INVESTORS

According to the National Association of REALTORS® 2018 Profile of International Activity in U.S. Residential Markets for the 12 months ending March 2018, foreign investors purchased $150.3 billion worth of U.S. residences—approximately 8% of the total existing home sales dollar volume. Foreign clients are an upscale group of buyers, paying on average nearly $454,000 for a house compared to the overall U.S. average house price of approximately $290,600.

Any banks dealing with foreign investors must report cash payments of $10,000 or more to the IRS. The **Foreign Investment in Real Property Tax Act (FIRPTA)** requires that the broker handling a sale for a foreign national withhold 10% of the gross proceeds to ensure the proper taxes are paid to the IRS.

Generally, foreign investors purchase American property because of

- perceived security of investments in the United States, based primarily on the stability of the government;
- the appreciation in the values of their own currency when compared to the dollar;
- highly inflated values of real estate in their own countries; and
- easing of restrictions by their own governments on foreign investments.

China was the top source of foreign buyers for the NAR® survey year ($30.4B), followed by Canada ($10.5B), United Kingdom ($7.3B), India ($7.2B), and Mexico ($4.2B). According to NAR, most buyers from China, India, and Mexico were residents of the United States, while most buyers from Canada and the United Kingdom were nonresident buyers.

SUMMARY

This unit presented an overview of the various types of ownership interests in real property. Ranging from individual ownership to corporate forms, partnerships, and trusts, real estate investors have many formats to choose from to satisfy their specific preferences.

Individually, real estate can be owned with either survivorship or inheritability as a goal. Although ownership forms can be changed during a lifetime with the agreement of all parties, it is the distribution of property after death that dictates its lifetime ownership design. Thus, in most states, married couples may own property as tenants by the entirety, with the result that the deceased's portion will automatically vest in the surviving spouse. This eliminates the time and cost of probate, but it also eliminates the rights of the deceased to designate an heir other than the spouse.

To preserve the prerogative of designating, by will, to whom an estate will pass, an inheritable estate must be established. To this end, the community property form of ownership is recognized in only eight states, while the tenancy in common format is available in every state to provide spouses with an alternative to tenancy by the entirety.

For those who want to avoid probate costs in the community property states, and in those states that do not recognize tenancy by the entirety, the available form of ownership is joint tenancy with the rights of survivorship. This estate can be used by any two or more individuals, but because it effectively eliminates inheritability, it is usually limited to use by family members.

For the married individual who wishes to maintain control over property, sole and separate ownership is available. Finally, for the single person, ownership in severalty is the format under which to own real estate. Each of these forms—sole and separate and severalty—is inheritable because only one person is involved.

An alternative to the individual ownership of property is the establishment of a corporation. Here, personal liability is limited to loss of one's investment and expectation of future profit. In addition, the corporate form provides a basis for attracting a pool of investment funds from many smaller investors through the sale of stock. Its design guarantees continuity and affords the means for hiring professional management. Corporate earnings are subject to double taxation and, as such, are limited in use as real estate investment ownership formats. However, S corps can be used as investment conduits to avoid double taxation.

Partnerships are used to join investors together to share in a potentially profitable venture. A general partnership gives each participant an equal voice in the management, despite the proportionate share of ownership. In addition, each partner is personally responsible for the liabilities of the partnership.

On the other hand, limited partnerships and syndicates act to shelter passive investors' individual liabilities. In this form of ownership, the general partner, or syndicator, assumes full responsibility for management, in addition to full liability for the success of the investment.

Property ownership in the form of a trust is established to create continuity in the management of an estate and avoid repetitious probate costs. Living, or inter vivos, trusts, which after death become testamentary trusts for the benefit of the heirs, can be established to control property during the life of a beneficiary. This form of ownership directs a trustee to hold the legal title to property in trust for specified beneficiaries and follow the directions established in the trust agreement for the management of the properties involved.

Investment trusts such as REITs and REMTs are established on this living trust basis, as are family and special trusts. However, REITs and REMTs act as investment conduits for many smaller investors and qualify under specific IRS regulations to act as trustees in purchasing, managing, and financing real properties. Because of these special requirements, profits from these activities are taxed only once at the beneficiary level, not twice as in the corporate ownership form.

DISCUSSION TOPICS

1. Investigate your state laws regarding the distribution of the assets of an estate left by a person who dies intestate and without any discoverable heirs.
2. Secure a copy of a REIT prospectus. Would you recommend an investment in the enterprise?

UNIT 4 EXAM

1. Automatic survivorship is intrinsic in which of the following forms of realty ownership?
   A. Sole and separate
   B. Tenancy in common
   C. Tenancy by the entirety
   D. Community property

2. An S corporation
   A. requires 100 or more shareholders.
   B. is subject to double taxation.
   C. is available to foreign investors.
   D. limits the personal liability of its shareholders.

3. Tenancy in common includes which of the following?
   A. Automatic survivorship
   B. Married persons only
   C. Inheritability by will
   D. Equal ownership shares only

4. Participants in a general partnership usually take title as which of the following?
   A. Joint tenants
   B. Tenants in common
   C. Tenants by the entirety
   D. Tenants in severalty

5. Corporations are formed to own real estate for all of the following reasons *EXCEPT*
   A. to avoid double tax on profits.
   B. for broad-based capital accumulation.
   C. to limit shareholder personal liability.
   D. to develop continuity of ownership.

6. Which of the following is *NOT* an attribute of a limited partnership?
   A. The personal liability of the limited partners is limited to their investment.
   B. Taxes on profits are imposed at the investor's level.
   C. Each partner takes an active role in management.
   D. Operating losses are passed through to the partners.

7. Foreign investment in the United States represents
   A. less than 1% of home sales.
   B. more than 50% of commercial real estate.
   C. around 8% of home sales.
   D. an expensive investment because of the Foreign Investment in Real Property Tax Act, which imposes a 25% surcharge on property taxes for foreign owners.

8. Sole ownership of real estate is described as ownership in
   A. vivos.
   B. singularity.
   C. sole seisin.
   D. severalty.

9. A living trust usually evolves into
   A. an inter vivos trust.
   B. a testamentary trust.
   C. a collapsible trust.
   D. a limited partnership.

10. Blue-sky laws cover all of the following disclosures *EXCEPT*
    A. the experience of the syndicators.
    B. an indication of the potential risk of the investment.
    C. a guaranteed return on the investment.
    D. a description of the property, terms, and conditions of the investment.

UNIT 5

Techniques of Investment Analysis

LEARNING OBJECTIVES

When you have completed this unit, you will be able to accomplish the following.

- Describe how a market analysis leads to important data.
- List the attributes of a property analysis and how this information affects the real estate investor.

KEY TERMS

- come out of the ground
- deed restrictions
- deferred maintenance
- destination store
- due diligence
- Environmental Protection Agency (EPA)
- feasibility analysis
- innocent landowner defense
- market study
- minimum housing standards
- overlay
- Phase I, II, III, and IV
- plat
- pro forma profit and loss
- remediation
- rooftops
- setback requirement
- site selection
- stabilized occupancy
- subdivision restrictions
- traffic counts
- variance

INTRODUCTION

Many real estate investments are made in a relatively informal manner. A real estate broker offers a particular property to a client, who inspects it and briefly analyzes its income potentials using certain mathematical techniques to measure profitability. Usually, the services of an appraiser are sought to verify the market value of the property. If the investment meets the buyer's criteria, and the terms of the purchase can be arranged to satisfy the parties, the transaction is completed.

Under the responsibility of **due diligence**, a broker often recommends a more intensive analysis of the possible financial success of an investment to satisfy the requirements not only of the investor, but also of the financier and potential tenants. These formal feasibility studies are generally undertaken when large projects are contemplated, such as subdivisions, office buildings, shopping centers, industrial parks, and manufactured-home parks. They are also recommended for new investors with any size project until the investor develops better instincts and rules of thumb. Feasibility studies consist of three broad analyses: market analysis, property analysis, and financial analysis. This unit examines the first two.

MARKET ANALYSIS

The market analysis gathers data about the marketplace. It seeks to answer the questions, "What is the profile of the marketplace of potential customers, what properties are available for purchase, what competition is already in the market place, and what competition is likely to develop in the very near future?" The market analysis does not investigate economic viability of a purchase or development. That is the province of the financial analysis. The market analysis may reveal that spending time and money on a feasibility study will be fruitless. For example, a market analysis may show significant vacancy rates in luxury apartment units. One does not need a detailed financial analysis to conclude that a new luxury apartment project would be ill advised.

Market analyses include demographic data gathered from census studies and local chambers of commerce. It shows number of **rooftops**—households—plus employment rates, ethnic and age profiles, and median disposable income. The location of major traffic arteries and feeder roads will be identified, with traffic count data and travel patterns obtained from local departments of transportation. Average home sales and rental rates are usually obtainable from local REALTOR® associations. Chamber of commerce information, plus physical reviews of the area, will reveal location and sizes of competing properties or projects. Investigation of recent building permits or zoning **variance** requests will help identify competing projects about to **come out of the ground** in the near future. Many ill-prepared real estate developers have been surprised to discover four or five similar projects starting construction at approximately the same time, in a market that will support only one or two. All of this information will be necessary to evaluate market demand and possible near-future market competition.

Also important in the market analysis is the identification of interest groups that can affect an investment. These include location of a property within a local government's jurisdiction, which will determine what ordinances and zoning restrictions will apply. If specifically requested, the market analysis can also provide the identities and profiles of major competitors, lenders, and potential opposition groups.

An analysis generally begins with an on-site tour of the area. The investor obtains all available maps of the locale, zoning ordinances pertaining to the area, applicable building codes, and statistical data concerning the population. The investor then examines at least six major factors in the neighborhood: land usage, economic climate, occupancy rates, transportation and utility services, facilities, and community acceptance.

Neighborhood boundaries and land use

A neighborhood can be defined as an area within which common characteristics of population and land use prevail. There is no predetermined size for a neighborhood. In rural areas, it may consist of three square miles, while a city neighborhood may be five square blocks.

The investor must determine the boundaries of the area before a market analysis can be made. Rivers, lakes, mountains, parks, railroad tracks, or major highways help delineate the confines of a neighborhood. Particular note should be made of natural and artificial boundaries that may curtail the future growth of a neighborhood. Various types of land uses have differing neighborhoods. A major sporting goods retailer might be a **destination store** that draws consumers from a 75-mile radius. An all-you-can-eat buffet-style steak house would usually define its neighborhood as an area with a radius of five miles. Artificial boundaries, such as highways, might cut off part of the circle created by that radius.

In the absence of any obvious physical boundaries, an investor must determine the extent of land that is under common usage and that shares a similar population. Any variances or restrictions in zoning should also be noted. Depending on the type of property involved, these zoning regulations may have a positive or negative effect. Commercial and industrial enterprises are adversely affected by a zoning restriction that limits the area to residential or multifamily use. On the other hand, the desirability of a residential neighborhood could decline severely if a zoning ordinance favorable to industrial development were granted for the area. A prudent investor will also review any studies performed for the local planning commission or zoning board that might recommend future zoning changes.

Neighborhood economy

Various sources of statistical information are available to an investor for assessing the economic climate of a neighborhood. The local chamber of commerce accumulates data regarding the number and types of businesses in the area, the volume of their activity, and general trends in their growth or decline. A neighborhood with a well-diversified business sector is usually more economically stable than an area that depends on a single major industry for its support.

Information secured from local financial institutions also provides a reliable indication of the area's economy. The volume of mortgage loans outstanding and being issued reflects the overall confidence in the real estate market. Competitive rental prices currently charged for residential, commercial, and industrial space in the neighborhood also offer an accurate measurement of the area's economy. Low rents generally indicate an oversupply of rentals relative to a limited demand, whereas high rents generally indicate a shortage of rental space.

Occupancy rates

The occupancy rates for a particular type of property also reflect the relationship between supply and demand in the neighborhood. Occupancies constantly change, and vacancy rates fluctuate accordingly; this affects rents and values.

A high occupancy rate indicates a shortage of space and the possibility for rent increases. A low rate, as reflected by many *For Lease* signs posted in a neighborhood, results in tenant demands for lower rents and other concessions on the part of the landlord. The oversupply of space that results in low occupancy rates can be either technical or economic in origin. Technical oversupply occurs when there are more available units than potential tenants. Economic oversupply reflects asking prices beyond the purchasing power of potential tenants. Statistics on vacancy rates can be obtained from current housing reports, which are published by state departments of commerce and list vacancies by region. Local utility companies often provide information regarding vacancies, with the number of nonoperating meters corresponding roughly to the number of vacant apartments, stores, or offices, as the case may be.

The investor-developer must also be able to predict whether future occupancy levels will rise or fall and how quickly these transitions will take place. To answer these questions, existing competitive space must be inventoried according to building type, age, size of units, and rental schedules. In addition, careful attention should be devoted to securing an inventory of all new construction, both under way and contemplated.

To a great extent, accurate prediction of occupancy rates depends on matching the composition of the local populace to the available space. The investor-developer should know the number of potential buyers or tenants and their ability and willingness to purchase or rent the properties being developed. The stability and trends of their incomes must also be determined.

Statistics issued by state departments of labor list the total number of employed persons by region and also provide the investor with information regarding unemployment ratios. Information obtained from the chamber of commerce can furnish investors with a clear picture of local employment opportunities and the median income of the community's population. In addition, local financial institutions can provide information about the population's savings habits as an indication of economic stability. This employment and income data should develop some reliable benchmarks for establishing appropriate rental schedules.

To plan efficiently for the number and type of housing units needed, investors in residential rental properties must determine the most common individual family size and composition, in addition to the total number of people within the area. For example, the prospects for financial success of a high-rise apartment complex composed of studio and one-bedroom units in an area composed mainly of families with two children are quite different from those prospects for a similar property in a neighborhood of young singles or childless couples. Local marriage, birth, and divorce records will provide investors with information regarding the structure of family units within the area.

In addition to the family structure, investors in residential real estate must be aware of current shifts in population. When changes in the composition of a neighborhood are detected, these alterations must be carefully analyzed in terms of land use and income level. An increase in population due to an influx of middle-income families into an expanding community has a considerably different meaning from an increase in population due to overcrowding in lower-rental areas. The implications for the future use of the neighborhood are quite different in each case.

Transportation and utilities

Regardless of the type of development contemplated, transportation facilities are of prime importance to future tenants and must be included in the market analysis of the property. In large cities, close proximity to public transportation is vital to apartment dwellers who may not own cars. Employees in many office buildings often rely on public transportation to get to work. Traffic patterns, street networks, and **traffic counts** in a neighborhood are significant to such commercial ventures as strip stores or shopping centers.

Traffic counts are critically important to many property uses and will also reflect changes in neighborhoods. State and local departments of transportation maintain counts of the average number of vehicles that travel on major roads and their important feeder roads. Sometimes the counts are separated by time of day and direction of travel. Various retailers have **site selection** requirements such as *55,000 vehicles per day* and similar benchmarks. If, for example, morning rush-hour traffic shows the bulk of the vehicles traveling in one direction, then one does not want to place a coffee shop on the opposite side of the road. A review of historic traffic count data will show if the area is stable, growing, or in decline.

Industrial developments require convenient access to railroads, expressways, or airports for receiving and distributing goods. Most communities have industrial development boards that can provide maps that include this information.

In addition to public transportation facilities, access and linkage to various parts of the community are essential components of the market analysis process. Here, not only must the distance to work be examined, but also the roads and freeway networks to determine the amount of time it takes to reach various destinations. Site reports can be ordered from online services that show important demographic information within a certain number of miles of a prospective site or within a certain number of minutes of travel time. Minutes of travel time often shows a more accurate picture of the relevant neighborhood.

For example, a housing project constructed some distance from the center of a community on less-expensive land might be successful if a connecting freeway allows potential homebuyers to get to work faster than if the project were built in town with only surface transportation available. Thus, a time-distance study should be included in feasibility reports.

Residential, commercial, and industrial property users are also deeply concerned with the availability of adequate parking facilities. Off-street tenant parking can relieve the aggravation of overcrowded curb space in urban areas. Commercial enterprises need adequate parking facilities for their customers, and industrial concerns require dockside space for loading and areas for employee parking. Some communities have minimum parking standards that require a certain number of parking spaces per bedrooms in an apartment community or per square foot of retail space in commercial areas. Others, seeking to make parking difficult and encourage reliance on mass transportation and ride sharing, specify a maximum number of parking spaces.

The costs and availability of utility services are becoming increasingly important in their effect on profits from investment properties. Commercial and industrial users are particularly concerned with heavy-duty power lines, separate sewerage systems, and other unique services required by the nature of their businesses.

Neighborhood facilities

Although the existence of neighborhood amenities is of great significance to residential investors, any improvements that help attract potential residents will indirectly benefit commercial and industrial developers by providing a local pool of potential consumers and employees. When inspecting a neighborhood, an investor should note the location and number of parks, playgrounds, theaters, restaurants, schools, colleges, houses of worship, and other social or cultural organizations and facilities that will be attractive to future inhabitants.

Community acceptance

Community involvement with any new real estate development, especially if it involves zoning issues, has become extremely important and should be included in a feasibility study.

In one geographic area, it took Walmart many months and a good deal of money to finally find acceptance within the community for one of its supercenters. It was built on the third location recommended because citizens owning properties around the other two locations expressed too much opposition. The third location was approved only after making many concessions to the local neighborhoods, which raised the building costs considerably.

In another area, a drugstore chain battled with the local historic preservation committee to build in a neighborhood where some houses were to be removed to make room for the drugstore's parking area.

Environmental impact studies are required in many areas of the country. These studies describe the effects of the project not only on the immediate surrounding properties, but also on the community and region as a whole. In addition, project plans must be approved by various government agencies, including street and road, water, sewer, fire, building inspection, and other departments charged with protecting the health, safety, and welfare of citizens. Each of these stakeholders should be identified in the market analysis.

Any time lags necessary to satisfy these requirements must be included in the study in order for the investor to develop the strategy necessary to complete the project and enter the market in a timely manner.

Property analysis

There is often some overlap between the market analysis and the property analysis. If the investor is looking for a site for development or a property to purchase, it may consider several offerings in the marketplace. In that case, the market analysis will provide broad-brush stroke information about things like community acceptance, zoning, environmental requirements, and similar items. If the investor is interested in one particular opportunity, then detailed information about those matters just listed will be included in the property analysis, because the investigation is capable of specificity.

Environmental protection agencies

Meeting the requirements of environmental protection agencies is a constant concern of all property investment. A property might have toxic waste that must be remediated—cleaned up. It might be in an area that indicates the mere possibility of toxic waste, thereby requiring further investigation and expense to satisfy lender concerns. Environmental protection requirements will affect expenses for groundwater control, wastewater management, minimization of heat islands created by high concentrations of concrete and buildings, and creation of natural habitat zones, to name a few.

Increased pollution of the natural environment led to the passage of the National Environmental Policy Act of 1969. A federal administrative division, the **Environmental Protection Agency (EPA)** was established by this act. Among its other duties, the EPA determines environmental control guidelines for the development of real estate projects. In practice, the EPA encourages the individual states to adopt and enforce local controls of their own and steps in only when the states do not act to implement the minimum federal guidelines.

Consequently, real estate investors will probably come into contact with their state's environmental protection agency, not the national EPA. In addition, most municipalities have officials in charge of water control. Rainwater runoff from a site under development causes significant soil erosion; silts up the streets, stormwater systems, and waterways; and carries pollutants into other areas. Even after development and landscaping, a significant portion of the land that once held vegetation is now covered by concrete and asphalt; rainwater runs off instead of being absorbed into the water table. For that reason, many projects must now build retention ponds for the collection of rainwater. This is an expensive addition to a project that might not have been anticipated by the developer. Existing properties that do not have such stormwater control might be grandfathered and allowed to remain out of compliance while under the same ownership. Once ownership changes, however, the purchaser could be required to make expensive modifications to the property.

Real estate investors are most likely to encounter environmental reports that should be ordered by the investor, and that will most certainly be required by the investor's lender. As with so many things, lender requirements arise out of their own regulatory requirements and safe harbors. A lender evaluating a project must ask itself, "What happens if we foreclose?" Under federal law, any owner of real estate with toxic waste is liable for **remediation**, even if that owner was not responsible for the discharge. The safe harbor of nonliability, called the **innocent landowner defense**, is available only if the owner took all reasonable steps before its acquisition to make sure the property was free of toxic substances. For that reason, lenders require that their borrowers obtain environmental reports.

The first of these is the **Phase I** Environmental Site Assessment (ESA,) usually simplified to *Phase I.* It requires an exhaustive study of the past uses of the property and nearby properties to reveal any possible contamination. A former gas station slightly uphill from the subject property and already identified as suffering from leaking tanks is a clear indication that groundwater on the subject site is polluted, and possibly the soil, too. If there was a dry cleaning plant on the subject property 20 years earlier, there is a strong possibility of hazardous waste. In addition, the site itself is carefully examined for sources of contamination such as leaking tanks, dry wells, storage drums of hazardous waste, and so forth. Third-party materials might be added, such as USDA soil surveys and topographic maps, maps of known radon (naturally occurring radioactive gases released from the soil), and habitat areas for endangered species. All of the Phase I investigation is designed to answer the question, "Is there a significant possibility there might be environmental issues related to the subject property?" There is an abbreviated version of Phase I called a site screen, which limits itself to public records research but no site visit.

More research is required if any potential issues are revealed in Phase I. If it comes back clean, no additional reports will be needed. The additional report, though, is called a **Phase II**. It is an intrusive investigation that usually drills core samples from the property to identify the types and quantities of various pollutants and whether they are in the soil or the groundwater, and whether they are leaching into nearby properties. There could be a need to dig monitoring wells, which will then require the passage of time and frequent monitoring and testing, to complete the report. If indicated by prior usage of the property, exploratory efforts will have to find the location of underground tanks or other pollutants such as buried automobile batteries. Due to the possibly destructive nature of Phase II, many sales contracts require that the potential buyer return the property to its preinvestigation condition if the buyer declines to go through with the purchase for any reason at all.

Once all the contaminants have been identified and quantified, the investor must ask, "Will my planned used of this property require remediation?" An outdoor recreational facility will have different hazardous waste sensitivity than a commuter parking lot. The recreational park might mandate remediation. The parking facility might require a few extra inches of concrete.

If the property tests show contamination, then a **Phase III** must be ordered. It includes the report of the extent of the various problems, together with alternatives for remediation. Sometimes, a legitimate remediation plan will say something such as, "This problem will naturally dissipate over time through the action of bacteria already present in the soil." Other times, it might require introduction of large concentrations of certain bacteria, groundwater flushing, or even complete removal of all soil and replacement with new soil.

The **Phase IV** is the actual remediation plan selected by the investor and its engineers. It is the roadmap for remediation, just as engineering drawings are the roadmap for electrical and plumbing systems in a building. Phase V obtains environmental protection agency approval for the Phase IV plan, and Phase VI gathers all necessary data to obtain regulatory approval that the site now meets all environmental standards after it has been remediated. Most real estate investors will order a Phase I. Some will also need a Phase II. Except for the largest projects, most will never encounter anything beyond Phase II because the costs will far exceed the value of the investment. To protect themselves, most investors include a due diligence contingency in their purchase contracts, allowing cancellation if Phase I or Phase II reveals negative information.

Local government environmental protection agencies usually include departments responsible for wastewater and groundwater. **Wastewater management** means the ability to tap into existing sanitary sewer lines of sufficient size to accommodate the needs of a proposed project. If that route is not possible or is prohibitively expensive, a developer may need to investigate on-site sewage treatment using artificial or natural methods.

Groundwater control imposes demands during development when there is site disturbance, and after completion, when rainwater must be channeled into acceptance receptacles. In the early stages of development of an area, discharge into storm sewer drains might be sufficient. As the area matures, storm sewers will become overwhelmed, and the groundwater will become depleted because of the reduction of natural absorption. More concrete means less water returning to the earth via natural means. To address these problems, many local governments require water retention features to collect rainwater and allow its slow reabsorption in the soil. The beautiful lakes and ponds in modern office parks, with their dramatic fountains of water, are usually the result of bureaucratic requirements rather than aesthetic sensibilities of the developer.

Local government regulations

Just as the various agencies of the federal government and their local counterparts have an impact on real estate investment activities, so, too, do other local agencies affect the investment process. The following are some more specific ways in which the regulating bodies of local governments control the growth and development of communities. Their existence is usually noted in a **feasibility analysis**.

Subdivision regulations

Most major communities in this country have adopted laws to regulate the subdividing of land. In this context, it means any division of larger parcels into smaller parcels and is not intended to be restricted to only residential subdivision development. The purpose of these laws is to prevent the unplanned and haphazard division of large parcels of land into small building lots. City and county officials are charged with the duty of supervising the orderly growth of their communities. As a result, an investor who wishes to develop a parcel of land must present an application for plat approval and required zoning changes to the special local agency established for the purpose of subdivision control, such as a local planning and zoning department.

Plat approval

To control the design of a new subdivision, a developer must submit a plat for approval by all of the various departments involved in community services. A **plat** is a drawing of the subdivision by an engineer or architect that shows lot sizes, street widths, easements, and so on (see Figure 5.1). The proposed lot sizes must conform to acceptable standards. The street design must link up to existing roadways and incorporate special safety features such as proper widths, gradients for curves, access for firefighting equipment, and turnarounds in cul-de-sac streets. This plat is recorded so that the legal descriptions become effective. Property can now be described as "Lot 3, Block 4 in Enchanted Valley Estates, as recorded in the real estate records of Harris County, Texas," rather than a lengthy metes-and-bounds description.

Figure 5.1: Sample Plat

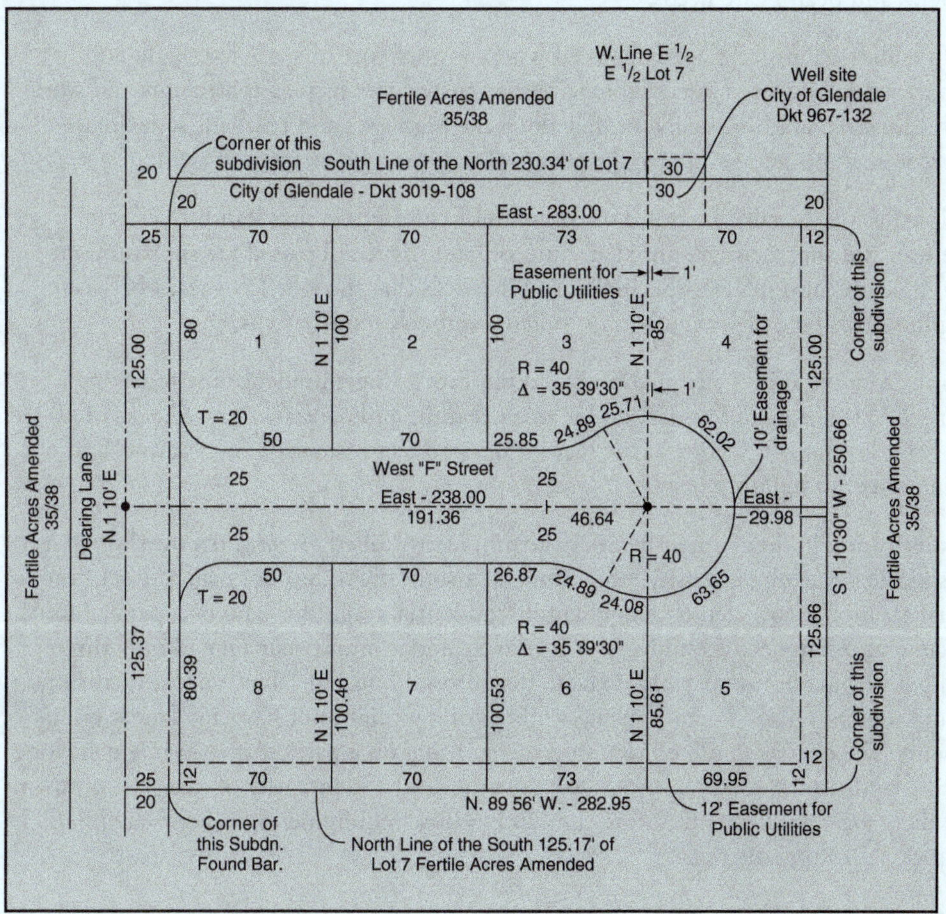

Adequate drainage must be provided to avoid potential flood damage. Utility installations must be situated in proper easements and be readily accessible for continuing maintenance. Adequate solid and liquid waste-disposal systems must be developed to prevent pollution of underground or surface water streams.

Before plat approval, any special circumstances surrounding each particular project must be solved to the satisfaction not only of the community agencies, but also of neighbors and other citizens whose rights are involved.

Zoning codes

In addition to subdivision regulations, most communities have local zoning ordinances that designate allowable land usage for particular purposes. Currently, Houston, Texas, is the only major U.S. city that has no zoning codes.

Historically, zones were separated according to types of use: single-family residential, multifamily residential, commercial, industrial, and special purpose (such as an airport or hospital). Each of these uses was felt to affect in different ways traffic size and patterns, water usage, school system growth, and police protection, to name a few areas. Zoning regulations help control development so it does not outstrip current or near-future government resources. In addition, zoning protects neighborhoods from undesirable uses that might affect property values, which then negatively affects the property tax revenues necessary for local government. That is why areas zoned for single-family residential use will prohibit industrial activities, for example. More progressive zoning schemes seek a multiplicity of allowed uses within designated areas to create mini-communities that can meet residents' housing, retail, employment, and health care needs.

Repeatedly, subdivisions have been designed with an inner core of space for single-family housing surrounded by areas intended for more intensive uses such as apartments and store buildings. Industrial land is usually located along the highways and railroads to facilitate shipping requirements and minimize the effects of pollution on residential areas.

Zoning designations usually are based on a system of code letters that stand for certain allowable uses and specify the required amount of land that can be used for construction. These zoning codes also include specifications for spaces that must be left vacant between adjoining lots. This type of specification is called a **setback requirement**.

For example, a county CR-1 designation could indicate a single residence use requiring a minimum of 36,000 square feet of total lot area per unit; and construction setbacks of 30 feet from the front lot line, 40 feet from the rear lot line, 10 feet from each side lot line, and not more than 34 feet in building height.

In addition to zoning, there might be micro-requirements called *overlays*. An **overlay** usually imposes specific aesthetic or density requirements in some areas, but not others. For example, all properties zoned as low-density single-family residential might have no occupancy limits. If a particular area has a college/university overlay, it might limit occupancy to only three unrelated persons per house to avoid de facto dormitories housing 10 or more students in a four-bedroom house. The standard business office zoning might not have any landscaping requirements. The overlay confined to properties fronting on a particular road might include very specific landscaping requirements to support the aesthetic integrity of that part of town. Overlays allow local government to fine-tune its land-use requirements without having to create additional zoning districts.

These requirements vary from jurisdiction to jurisdiction and depend to a great degree on the type of development anticipated for the specific location. It is important for a real estate investor to be thoroughly familiar with local zoning codes.

Rezoning a property from its present use to a more intensive use—such as changing a vacant lot zoned for a single house to a zoning that would permit four units—may result in substantial profits for an investor. The rezoning process involves the submission of an application to the appropriate government agency, a review of this application by the professional staff of this agency, and a public hearing in front of a commission, city council, or county board of supervisors who will rule on the acceptability of the professional staff's recommendations. Public hearings allow petitioners to state their cases and permit neighbors and other interested citizens to make their feelings known. Participants have recourse to the courts if they feel rezoning decisions are unfair.

Rezoning is often a difficult process because of local opposition to changing the use of an area indefinitely. In most jurisdictions, it is illegal to spot zone—rezoning one particular property and leaving all others the same. One alternative is a zoning variance, which leaves the zoning in place, but allows a particular nonconforming use on the property. Usually, these are granted only if the property is not capable of supporting its zoned used. For example, the corner house that was built on a quiet street might now be on a major traffic artery. Its use as a single-family residence is hampered by traffic noise, pollution, and dangers posed to children. Rather than allow the property to fall into disuse and eventual demolition, a local government might allow a variance for a small business, such as an attorney's office or a beauty salon. Another alternative is a conditional-use permit that is already preauthorized under the zoning plan, but which requires some additional conditions and approvals before final authorization for that use.

Because each jurisdiction follows its own specific techniques for conducting the rezoning process, investors interested in this form of activity are well-advised to know the requirements in their particular area and seek professional legal, engineering, or architectural help.

Deed and subdivision restrictions

Restrictions are covenants that run with the land, and once recorded, they remain in effect into the future or for a period specified within the restrictions. Each new owner of the property buys *subject to* the restrictions. Restrictions specify what the property can or cannot be used for or what can or cannot be built on the land. Restrictions supersede any zoning on the property, but only insofar as they are more restrictive than applicable zoning. The feasibility analysis should investigate relevant restrictions, which are usually obtained from a local title insurance company.

A landowner on property to be split off and sold separately from the main parcel usually imposes individual **deed restrictions**. By restricting the new parcels, the original owner can maintain the integrity of the main parcel.

Subdivision restrictions, on the other hand, are usually established by the developer on all of the lots in a new subdivision to maintain their homogeneity of use, as well as value. Subdivision restrictions generally run for 50 years or longer. Thus, buyers in the subdivision can rely on their investments maintaining their values for long periods.

For example, restrictions may include a minimum number of square feet per residence and prohibit any use other than residential in the subdivision.

Restrictions are only as strong as the individuals who will be responsible for their enforcement. In the case of deed restrictions, when the original owner dies or moves away, the split property owners may stop observing the requirements. If the new owner of the main property does not object within a reasonable period, the restrictions may be broken. Similarly, with subdivision restrictions, their enforcement relies on a strong neighborhood association that will not be afraid to sue those who do not observe the requirements. Some courts have ruled that an association's failure to enforce restrictions over time waives the association's right to enforcement.

Planned unit developments (PUDs)

Many communities use a form of subdivision called the *planned unit development (PUD)*. A PUD actively encourages mixed land uses. Thus, apartments and town houses can be joined together with common walls, while retail businesses and "clean" industrial plants can be incorporated into the subdivision.

FOR EXAMPLE

If a 100-acre tract can hold 300 individual single-family detached houses under a zoning designation of three house lots to the acre, a PUD can be designed to include three separate 100-unit complexes. Elimination of the side-yard setback requirement makes it possible to construct a 100-unit building that includes high-rise and low-rise apartments joined by common walls. Each 100-unit building is surrounded by open space that would contain lawn areas, playgrounds, swimming pools, bicycle and walking paths, tennis courts, golf courses, and similar recreational facilities.

Mixed land-use PUDs incorporate residents, retail businesses, office buildings, and even acceptable industrial plants into their designs. These PUDs become entirely self-contained small communities. For example, Reston, Virginia, has store buildings, apartments, a lake, and various employment centers built right into exclusive single-family home areas. Residents of this type of community, also called a traditional neighborhood development, can walk or ride a bicycle to work, school, stores, or recreational areas.

Minimum housing standards

Many communities have adopted uniform building and housing codes that designate **minimum housing standards** required for new construction, as well as for older homes. These requirements impact construction and rehab expenses and must be considered in the feasibility analysis if they are out of the ordinary. For example, low-rise, ADA (Americans with Disabilities Act)-compliant apartments in most of the country might cost $150 per square foot for construction. Minimum housing standards in a coastal community might require that all new structures withstand sustained winds of up to 150 miles per hour. That requirement alone could add another $75 per square foot to construction costs. This must be factored into the feasibility analysis to see if the project is economically possible at current rental rates.

Requirements for new housing include minimum specifications for foundations, underflooring, wood framing, roofing, and weatherproofing as well as general requirements involving light, ventilation, and sanitation. Apartments, townhomes, and self-storage often have requirements for firewalls between units—or a certain numbers of units—and for exterior walls if the building is within a certain number of feet of the property line. Knowing of the need for this additional expense in advance could result in making slight changes to building placement for a development. Some jurisdictions also require provisions for off-street parking facilities and fire warning systems.

For older structures, most cities maintain inspection staff charged with determining the safety of existing properties. Where a building or a portion of a building (usually more than 50%) is found to be unsanitary or unsafe, these inspectors have the power to issue appropriate citations to the owner, outlining failings that need to be corrected and penalties if they are not. At the same time, a sign is posted indicating that the building is unsafe and advising against entry. Ultimately, if the faults are not corrected, the structure may be condemned and destroyed as a public nuisance.

In great part, these minimum housing standards are a result of the activities of mortgage lenders. Historically, lenders have fought for better building codes for potential enhancement of the value of their collateral. The Federal Housing Administration (FHA) has been a pioneer in these efforts with its standardization of appraisal techniques, which led to the establishment of new housing codes in the mid-1930s.

Planned growth

Many communities throughout the country compete with each other to attract new industry by offering tax waivers and other incentives. In some instances, industrial development foundations are formed by local businesspeople and given large budgets with which to lure desirable industries away from other communities. New industry means new jobs, higher earnings, more taxes, and generally, growth, expansion, and prosperity.

In some areas, community growth has become uncontrolled because of a burgeoning population. City planners and citizens alike are displeased over these developments, and politicians move to a no-growth policy. However, some yield to pressure from the construction industry and modify their views to form a policy of planned growth. This vests more power in the bureaucratic agencies that control land use and development and inhibits new construction.

As a direct consequence of slowing new building, values of existing properties tend to rise. A case in point is the dramatic increase in values of coastal and lakeside properties in areas that have imposed building moratoriums and enforce severe controls on new developments.

Community profile

Most new real estate projects begin with an available piece of property, an investor looking for a property, and a broker acting as a catalyst to unite the two. Thus, a project starts with a predetermination of use—for example, a shopping center. The feasibility study must then include an analysis of the market this center is intended to serve.

Market analysis is predominantly concentrated at the local level. To determine the potential income that can be realized from an investment, a careful investigation must first be made into the economic climate of the community and, particularly, the neighborhood in which the project is located.

Evaluating the data

Once the **market study** and feasibility analyses are complete, the investor-analyst must combine the information to determine if the planned use is economically viable, if there will have to be changes to meet pecuniary or other challenges, or if the project should be abandoned or relocated.

The success of the analysis is only as reliable as the judgment of the person making the evaluation. In the absence of experience, an investor should seek the services of a professional property analyst who is fully knowledgeable about the nature of business and economic cycles and who can accurately assess their influences on the character and future trends of the subject market area.

PROPERTY ANALYSIS

An investor needs to carefully examine the physical characteristics of the parcel of land to be used in new construction or the nature and condition of the existing building considered for purchase. In the first instance, the land's geological and surface characteristics are investigated, as well as the costs of their probable modification and of the installation of utilities, roadways, and landscaping. In the second instance, the physical condition of the existing building, its functional capability, and costs of modernization must be analyzed for potential repair and maintenance expenses.

The site

Besides the locational characteristics described in the market study, a site's physical attributes must be examined to determine its capacity to support the structures the investor intends to build.

Surface attributes

The use of a parcel of real estate may be limited by its topography, vegetation, size, shape, or exposure. These surface attributes include hilly terrain, the presence or absence of fertile topsoil, woods, boulders, irregular shapes, narrow dimensions, obnoxious odors, and oppressive sounds. Topsoil is desirable for landscaping but is undesirable for construction. Many construction projects have gone far over budget when the ill-prepared developer discovered that 10 to 20 feet of topsoil had to be excavated and relocated, and the hole then filled with clay or piers sunk down to the bedrock. To cure any of these problems and to prepare a parcel of land for new construction involves expenditures that must be included in a feasibility study for a complete picture of total investment costs.

Subsurface soil characteristics can generally be learned from USDA soil surveys, coupled with spot drilling at the property site. The contours of a parcel of land can be seen from topographic maps publicly available or specially ordered. Figure 5.2 shows a sample topographic map, available from https://nationalmap.gov/ustopo/. The lines indicate changes in elevation according to the scale in use for the particular map. Each line might indicate a change in elevation of 20 feet, as illustrated in the following example. Circles in the middle of contours indicate the highest or lowest point. Closed circles indicate increasing elevations or hills. Closed circles with hashtags on them indicate depressions or holes.

In the following illustration, looking just north of the left-most body of water, we can see a measured elevation of 580 feet above sea level. North of that is a contour line with no elevation, and north of that is one with an elevation of 620 feet. Interpolating, the middle line must be at 600 feet. If we know the horizontal scale of the map, we will know that the terrain goes uphill at the rate of 20 feet per measured horizontal distance. Lines that are closer together indicate steep changes in elevation because one need cover a much smaller horizontal distance to climb another 20 feet of elevation.

Figure 5.2: Sample Topographical Map

While physical irregularities may be corrected with the services of landscaping engineers, it is often more difficult to acquire the amount of land necessary to ensure adequate areas for building and parking. Residential lots need ample frontage exposure to serve the tastes of modern high-income homebuyers who also are seeking the quiet and protection of a suburban or rural location. Commercial property must be easily accessible to people on foot or in cars. Industrial property must have access to railroads, highways, and adequate utility services, including solid and liquid waste-disposal facilities.

Subsurface attributes

The ability of a parcel of land to support new construction is of paramount importance to developers of high-rise apartment or office buildings. Soft or slippery subsoil conditions can result in high costs if a builder has to sink support piers to firm bedrock, often far below the surface. New construction techniques are opening up additional, formerly unusable, wet, marshy lands for development, but the costs are high.

Where the land is rocky and the subsoil hard and impenetrable, there will be additional costs for excavation. In areas where basements are desired, these costs may adversely affect the sale of houses. Where substantial foundations and a number of subsurface floors are included in the building's design, rocky subsoil creates physical barriers often difficult to offset.

High subsurface water tables and areas subject to flooding often create difficulties when providing for sanitary sewage disposal and adequate drainage runoff. Pollution of underground water streams is a serious problem in these areas.

The property

The purpose of a property analysis is to familiarize the investor with the nature and condition of the particular building under consideration and its position relative to similar properties in the neighborhood. On completion of the property analysis, the investor should know what expenditures would be needed to make the property competitive with the best units available in the area and what the average operating costs for the project will be.

Exterior attributes

The visual image, or initial impression, created by a building is of considerable importance to prospective tenants. Thus, an investor should note the age and style of the property, as well as the condition of the walkways, landscaping, and overall exterior appearance of the building itself. Any improvements required should be noted.

In addition, the investor should be alert to any major repairs deferred by the previous owner. The masonry, windows, eaves and trim, roof, porches, parking area, pool, other amenities, and building parts must be carefully examined for **deferred maintenance** that may require immediate attention and capital outlay.

Interior attributes

The investor should carefully examine the interior of the building, including the number of individual apartments or offices and their layouts; size; number of rooms, closets, and bathrooms; and views. In addition, property must be able to be renovated to accommodate the diverse uses of the tenants. Securing optimum rents is a function of desirability of design, location in the building, and physical quality.

When inspecting individual units, the investor should examine the condition of the hardware, plumbing, walls, and electrical fixtures. In apartment units, appliances, carpets, and drapes should be checked, and an estimate should be made of the expense of repairing or replacing worn or obsolete items.

The condition of entryways, halls, laundry rooms, storage rooms, and other common interior areas should be checked. Any redecorating and replacement that may be required to improve the general appearance of the building should be noted. This inspection should include the heating and cooling systems, plumbing fixtures, water heaters, elevators, swimming pools, and other tenant amenities, as well as the machinery required for snow removal and lawn and pool maintenance.

Asbestos

In addition to considering the condition of the site relative to the presence or absence of hazardous waste, it is important for purchasers of existing structures to address the possibility that construction materials containing asbestos may be present. The cost of its removal could affect the profitability of the venture.

Repairs for the removal of asbestos can be deductible expenses only if it can be shown that

- they are necessary to keep the property in an ordinarily efficient operating condition; and
- the costs will not materially add to the value of the property or appreciably prolong its life.

Otherwise,

- the costs must be capitalized as a permanent addition to the existing basis of the property, to be recovered at its sale;
- the costs must be depreciated independently; or
- the investor must identify which portion of the costs would increase the value of the building and capitalize that portion. The balance can then be deducted as a repair cost.

However, the hasty and careless removal of asbestos may cause more harm than leaving it in place. Researchers have determined that when existing asbestos materials have not been disturbed, the concentration of airborne asbestos is comparable to the level of concentration in outdoor air. The EPA agrees that when asbestos is not damaged or disturbed, it probably should not be removed. Often, the asbestos may be contained in place by encapsulating the asbestos with other material.

Toxic mold

The property must be inspected carefully for the existence of toxic mold, which must be removed to eliminate costly lawsuits. According to the American Bar Association, before 2000, mold insurance claims settled for $5,000 or less. Today, commercial developers and homeowner claims routinely exceed $100,000, and in 2011, the largest reported verdict for a mold-related claim was $7.7 million, awarded to the owners of 216 condominium units in South Carolina. Most states have adopted notice requirements to tenants or purchasers of real estate. In some states, tenants must report mold issues to landlords. Failure to disclose the existence of mold will likely result in lawsuits.

Chinese drywall

Between 2001 and 2009, an estimated 100,000 U.S. homes were built with Chinese drywall, a defective product that emitted sulfurous gases and volatile chemicals. There were also commercial uses of the product in office buildings and retail space. The emissions caused respiratory problems and corroded copper surfaces such as plumbing, electrical, and HVAC. As such, the drywall was a safety and a health hazard. Class action litigation identified many of the properties that contained Chinese drywall, with settlement funds available for remediation. Unfortunately, not all properties have been identified or remediated. Care should be taken when buying anything built or significantly remodeled in the relevant years, focusing on outside testing of drywall samples or close inspection of copper components.

Radon gas

This is a colorless, odorless gas emitted by radioactive materials contained in certain rock formations. In high enough concentrations, it can cause lung cancer. Typically, radon problems can be eliminated with proper ventilation of the structure.

Lead-based paint

Federal lead-based paint regulations must be followed if the property is a single-family or multifamily residential property built before 1978. There are six basic requirements under these regulations:

1. The buyer must be given the EPA booklet *Protect Your Family From Lead in Your Home.*
2. The seller/landlord must disclose any known lead-based paint hazards.
3. Sales contracts and leases must contain a lead warning statement.
4. The seller/landlord must provide the buyer/tenant copies of any lead-based paint reports concerning the property.
5. Buyers must be given a 10-day opportunity to conduct a lead-based paint inspection by a qualified lead inspector.
6. As of April 2010, federal law requires anyone who is paid for work that disturbs paint to be trained and certified by the EPA.

More information on lead-based paint may be found at www.hud.gov.

Other environmental issues

There are many other environmental issues that may affect the investment, such as carbon monoxide, urea formaldehyde foam insulation, polychlorinated biphenyls, groundwater contamination, electromagnetic fields, and underground storage tanks. A wealth of information on these issues is available at www.epa.gov.

Because of the many and varied problems that may exist within structures, investors are advised to enlist the services of a qualified private building inspector for a professional opinion of the structure's condition. Many inspectors specifically exclude structural and roof issues, which might require additional experts.

Together with the payments necessary for debt service, the investor is then ready to do a financial analysis to complete the feasibility study.

Financial analysis

Acquisition costs

The cost to buy a property, including expert reports, surveys, appraisals, real estate agent commissions, and lender fees must all be estimated.

Construction costs

Construction costs, or rehab expenses, will vary with the type of property and local construction requirements, including wind and snow load resistance, fire walls, rainwater control, and parking, to name a few. Experienced investors and lenders usually have rules of thumb for standard construction projects in their market and can be consulted for advice for purposes of the feasibility study. Of course, detailed architectural and engineering plans and finish schedules (exterior siding, flooring, fixtures, etc.) will be necessary to create a final construction budget, but that is not necessary at the feasibility study stage.

Holding costs

All projects have holding costs until they reach their planned maturity. Those consist of normal and customary operating expenses such as utilities and insurance, plus debt service. For a new apartment project, holding costs are estimated into the future until a time of projected **stabilized occupancy**. That is the point at which the owner is no longer rapidly leasing up first-use apartments and has reached a plateau with some continued growth, but also attrition as old tenants depart and their units are filled with second-generation tenants. For an office building that is largely preleased, holding costs might be projected just until the certificate of occupancy is issued and the property is ready for tenant move in. Holding costs must be estimated to see if the investor has the capital reserves to cover those costs until rents are sufficient or if money must be borrowed for future cash shortfalls.

Projected revenues

Investment properties can have several types of projected revenues. Periodic revenues include rental revenue, ancillary revenue, and miscellaneous revenue. *Ancillary revenue* increases or decreases depending on occupancy levels, such as laundry room revenue, pet fees, late fee charges, and forfeited security deposits. *Miscellaneous revenue* is independent of occupancies, such as billboard rental or roof rights. *Periodic revenues* for a subdivision development include lot sales. *Disposition revenue* is estimated for a property that is being acquired or developed for resale and estimates the net sale proceeds after deducting marketing and sales expenses. Disposition revenue should also have a time frame when that will happen so time value of money calculations can be made. If Project A can be sold for a $500,000 profit in one year, and Project B can be sold for a $550,000 profit but only after the passage of three years, Project A might be the more profitable one.

Operating expenses

The investor should verify the amount of property taxes with the local tax assessor and the amount of insurance premiums with an agent. Constant attention must be paid to adequate insurance coverage in the face of inflation and ever-increasing legal settlements. In addition, changes in zoning might mean that a grandfathered and nonconforming building will need to be rebuilt in a much more expensive manner if there is significant damage due to fire or natural disaster. Adequate insurance coverage for a particular building might be insufficient to build its replacement.

An investor must accurately estimate ongoing maintenance expenses, in addition to monies earmarked for future replacement of major items such as the roof, furniture, carpets, and elevators. Some lenders require each month that investors place agreed amounts of money into a restricted bank account to be used for only approved purposes. Other lenders merely require listing a reserve for repair and replacement as an expense item on the profit and loss statement.

Vacancy and credit losses are typically listed as an expense item. If the gross scheduled rents for a 100-unit apartment project are $1.2 million ($1,000 monthly rent per unit × 100 units × 12 months) then, depending on the marketplace, the investor might allocate 10% of that number to vacancy and credit losses as an expense. This would add another $120,000 of expenses. Even if an investor is wildly optimistic that she will never suffer any vacancies or credit losses, the lender will demand that such an expense be included in the **pro forma profit and loss** submitted with the loan request.

Management fees in the local market must be included as an expense, even if the investor will self-manage the property. The reason, again, goes back to lender fears that it might have to foreclose, in which case, it will always hire third-party management. The lender's decision about the size of its loan depends on its projection of what the property will be worth in its hands after a potential foreclosure. Management fees will increase its expenses and reduce its net recovery. Aside from lender concerns, any prudent investor will assume outside management. Whether buying, borrowing, or selling, management fees must be ascertained or imputed, then expensed.

For tenant-occupied properties, turnover expenses must be estimated and included in the operating expenses. Assume an apartment tenant departs, leaving his unit in near perfect, clean condition. No amounts can be deducted from the security deposit for damage or cleaning. Despite that, the landlord must usually steam clean the carpeting and make minor repairs due to normal wear and tear. The unit will require a least a perfunctory wipe-down cleaning. The locks will have to be rekeyed. If each tenant turnover costs the landlord $500, and if 10 units are expected to turn over each year, then $5,000 of turnover expenses must be accounted for.

As will be explored more thoroughly in later units, proper calculation of NOI, net operating income, is critically important to the evaluation of any income-producing property. *NOI* is the total of all revenues, minus all operating expenses. It forms the basis of virtually all appraisals, loan approvals, and buyer evaluations. Care must be taken during the feasibility analysis stage to estimate those numbers as accurately as possible, otherwise the buying or development decision will be based on nothing more than wishful thinking.

SUMMARY

Many real estate investments are made in a somewhat informal manner, with a buyer purchasing a property after a cursory examination of its physical condition and a rudimentary analysis of its profit potential. Other realty transactions require more definitive feasibility studies, including analyses of the environmental impact, local government regulations, and an analysis and market profile of the community where the property is located. Then a complete, in-depth examination of the property itself, both land and buildings, plus a financial analysis of the quantity and quality of the income stream need to be derived.

A market study includes a description of where the property is located. Often, there are no clear-cut physical boundaries, such as mountains, streams, or roadways, to delineate a market neighborhood. Rather, the area is described as that which is under common usage and shares a similar population. The economic climate of the neighborhood is then examined to discover types of business activity, volume of sales, and general trends in growth or decline. Included in the trend analyses is the availability of money for mortgage and business loans and competitive rental prices charged for properties similar to the projected investment.

Occupancy rates aid in measuring the economic quality of the market that a realty project will serve. High current occupancy rates (low vacancy rates) indicate a shortage of space and the possibility for rent increases. An oversupply of space, on the other hand, indicates a weak market and the possibility of developing less cash flow from the project than anticipated. Careful projections must be made of future trends in the development of comparable rental space from new construction, both under way and contemplated.

A complete profile of the neighborhood's population is included in the economic analysis. In addition to the number of persons located in the area, their family structure and financial positions can provide information that can be helpful in planning the number and types of housing units needed or the composition of a shopping center. Current population shifts must be diagnosed for an indication of potential changes that may affect the investment.

Once the economic profile of the market neighborhood is acquired, its locational qualities should be identified. These attributes include the type and availability of transportation facilities and utilities, as well as neighborhood amenities that would enhance a contemplated project.

A careful investigation must be undertaken regarding the community acceptance of a major new realty development. In addition to the immediate neighbors' attitudes, the requirements of all the various public agencies that will be involved in the project's supervision before and during construction must be analyzed. Any substantial negative points of view will have to be met forthrightly before the project is initiated.

An in-depth study of the physical qualities of the land on which a project will be constructed—or, in the case of a used property, of the building itself—must be coupled with the economic analysis of the market the project will serve. Both surface and underground attributes of the site must be analyzed in terms of its ability to support a new project. An already existing building must be inspected in terms of its appearance and functional efficiency so that the owner can learn of potential refurbishing costs and ongoing operating expenses.

DISCUSSION TOPICS

1. Select a property in your area that you think is not currently enjoying its highest and best use. Choose a potential use for the property. Create a checklist of all publicly available sources you would use to develop a market study and feasibility analysis.
2. An increasing awareness of the effects on the environment of uncontrolled growth suggests an emerging trend toward a no-growth attitude. Investigate the attitudes in your community from the points of view of both citizens and politicians.

UNIT 5 EXAM

1. The primary purpose of subdivision regulations in most states is to
   A. enable developers to profit from rezoning.
   B. divide large parcels of land into small lots.
   C. prevent unplanned and haphazard subdividing.
   D. inhibit growth in developed areas.

2. A mixed-use subdivision describes
   A. properties having no deed or subdivision restrictions.
   B. proportionate grouping by population age.
   C. a legally prohibited method of development.
   D. different but compatible developments in one designated area.

3. A permissible request to change the allowed use of one property to something different from current zoning laws is called
   A. rezoning.
   B. variance.
   C. site zoning.
   D. nothing. It is not allowed.

4. In a market analysis, the occupancy rates for a particular type of property should be compared with
   A. the community's overall occupancy factor.
   B. the nation's occupancy factor for that type of property.
   C. the community's occupancy factor for that type of property.
   D. the U.S. Department of Labor's employed persons list.

5. When analyzing the site of a new commercial investment project, all of the following factors must be considered *EXCEPT*
   A. the site's surface attributes.
   B. the site's subsurface attributes.
   C. the site's possible contamination.
   D. the site's fertility.

6. When examining a building included in a proposed commercial investment, all of the following factors regarding the property must be considered *EXCEPT*
   A. appearance.
   B. location.
   C. physical condition.
   D. the appeals period following a city's environmental review determination.

7. Two expenses that will be imputed to a project's operating expenses, whether actually incurred or not, include
   A. leasing commissions and debt service.
   B. management fees and repair expenses.
   C. corporate overhead and key man insurance.
   D. market studies and feasibility analyses.

8. Which of the following statements about residential subdivision restrictions is *FALSE*?
   A. They are enforceable only against the original homeowner.
   B. They are covenants that run with the land.
   C. They are effective as long as they are enforced.
   D. They are established to maintain the homogeneity of property use and value.

9. A feasibility analysis is primarily designed to provide an investor with information appropriate to
   A. avoid paying income taxes.
   B. guarantee a profit on the investment.
   C. make an economically rational investment decision.
   D. satisfy various government regulatory agencies.

10. The Environmental Protection Agency (EPA) establishes guidelines for the prevention of all of the following *EXCEPT*
    A. air pollution.
    B. soil contamination.
    C. water impurities.
    D. property accessibility.

UNIT 6

Tax Characteristics and Strategies

LEARNING OBJECTIVES

When you have completed this unit, you will be able to accomplish the following.

- Calculate income subject to tax and income tax rates.
- Describe tax shelter opportunities for real estate investors.

KEY TERMS

active income	dealers	real estate professional
active participation	deferred exchange	realized gain
adjusted basis	depreciation	recaptured depreciation
alternative minimum tax (AMT)	exchange	recognized gain
at risk rule	passive activity loss limitation	straight line
boot	passive income	tax credit
capital gains income	portfolio income	taxable income
cost recovery	pyramiding	tax shelter

INTRODUCTION

This unit examines the important income tax considerations for real estate investors, whose handling of various tax alternatives has a direct effect on the profitability of their investments. On one hand, the rents from investment property or the profits from the sale of real estate increase the owner's taxable income. On the other, operating expenses, depreciation, refinancing, installment sales, and exchanging can all provide the investor with a shelter for this income and profits. In addition, an appropriate management strategy can develop a tax shelter for some of an investor's income from other sources.

INCOME SUBJECT TO TAX

For federal income tax purposes, there are four categories of real property: residential, investment, trade or business, and dealer. Each class of property has its own unique set of tax rules.

Active income

All money earned in the normal course of working or conducting a trade or business is identified as **active income**. The bulk of active income is derived from wages, salaries, commissions, and annual operating profits from operating nonpassive businesses. Other earnings also included in this category are tips, prizes, awards, alimony, gambling winnings, jury duty fees, and so on. Active income is taxed at ordinary income tax bracket rates and is subject to Social Security and Medicare taxes.

Real estate used in a trade or business may generate active income depending on facts and circumstances. Investments in real estate may generate active income only if the investor meets the definition of a **real estate professional** (when more than 50% of the taxpayer's personal services during the year are performed in real estate businesses and when more than 750 hours of services in real property businesses are performed during the year). A taxpayer who materially participates in a trade or business on a regular, continuous, and substantial basis is defined as being *active*. This is important because a tax loss generated by an active trade or business may be used to offset active income such as salary.

All real estate rental activity is considered passive no matter how involved the owners are, except for corporation-owned rentals and the operation of a hotel, motel, or inn, which are considered active. Despite that, passive losses from rental property can be used to shelter active income, as described in the next section on passive activity loss limitation rules.

Portfolio income

Portfolio income includes interest, dividends, royalties, and annuity income, as well as gains or losses from the sale or exchange of portfolio and certain investment assets. Deductible expenses directly allocated to such income reduces portfolio income.

Portfolio activity of concern to real estate investors includes REIT dividends, income from a real estate mortgage investment conduit, and certain gains on investment real estate property, none of which can be sheltered by passive losses.

Passive income

Passive income is an important concept in real estate because passive activity losses can be used as a deduction to reduce tax liability for passive activity income, but not ordinary income. In prior years, high-income individuals such as doctors and lawyers could invest in real estate limited partnerships that generated massive paper losses and use those losses to reduce or eliminate taxable income from their primary—active—business. Tax law changes closed those loopholes. There are exceptions explained in the *passive activity loss* section, which follows.

All rental income is considered passive income unless it has a strong services component, such as hotels and office business centers, or it is a short-term vacation rental with very frequent marketing and turnover. Any activity in which the taxpayer does not materially participate is passive. As a result, limited partners are always passive because they are not legally allowed to be active. If a limited partner takes on an active role in an investment, it loses the protections of a limited partner and has the full liability of a general partner.

Capital gains income

Money earned as profit on investments made outside the ordinary course of work and business is identified as **capital gains income**. Such income includes profits made on the sale of real property, stocks, equipment, and other assets not held for regular business purposes. In other words, noninventory assets produce capital gains income when sold for a profit. This category also includes property held for the production of income, such as apartment buildings and machinery in a plant, but specifically excludes all property held as inventory stock for resale to customers. Capital gains profits are the difference between the realized selling price of the property and its adjusted basis.

The realized selling price is most often the contract sales price (the actual price paid on the sale of the property), less the allowed costs of sale such as the following:

- Real estate commissions
- Accountants' fees
- Settlement charges
- Appraisal fees
- Escrow fees
- Document preparation
- Surveys
- Attorneys' fees
- Points paid by the seller to buyer's lender
- Closing fees
- Advertising
- Title insurance
- Recording fees
- Pest inspection

The **adjusted basis** of the property begins with the basis, which depends on the method of acquisition. The three most common examples are as follows:

- If the property was purchased, the basis is the purchase price.
- If the property was inherited, the basis is the market value at the time of death.
- If the property was received as a gift, the basis is simply the same as the giftor's basis.

Once the basis is determined, certain adjustments (additions to and subtractions from) are made over time to arrive at the adjusted basis. The most common of these adjustments include the following:

- Add the costs of purchase, which are very similar to the above-listed costs of sale.
- Add interest expenses during development and before project completion.
- Add the cost of post-acquisition improvements to the property.
- Subtract depreciation on the improvements only (land cannot be depreciated).

- Subtract any casualty losses that are not reimbursed by insurance.
- Subtract any part of the property that has been sold.

Consequently, the capital gains calculation is as follows:

1. Contract sales price less allowed costs of sale equals the realized selling price
2. Realized selling price less the adjusted basis equals the gain/loss
3. Gain less **recaptured depreciation** (that portion of the gain that represents the total of all prior depreciation deductions taken over the years by the current owner) equals capital gain.

Assumption of debt

If the buyer assumes some or all of the seller's debt on property, that amount is included as part of the sales price for purposes of calculating taxable gain.

	Seller A	Seller B
Adjusted basis	$200,000	$200,000
Mortgage balance	$250,000	$250,000
Sale to buyer, cash paid at closing	$30,000	$280,000
Mortgage assumed	$250,000	$0 mortgage paid off at closing
Taxable gain	$80,000	$80,000
	($250,000 mortgage principal balance assumed by buyer + $30,000 boot − $200,000 adjusted basis)	($280,000 sales price − $200,000 adjusted basis)

A special word about dealers

Dealers in real property buy and sell real estate much the same as if it were a retail store's inventory. They are the opposite of investors, who buy and hold real estate for investment income through rental revenue or appreciation and sale or who use real estate as the premises for their trade or business. Flippers and subdivision developers are dealers. Landlords are usually investors. Dealers must report all profits as active income—taxed at ordinary income tax rates—the same as wages. They owe self-employment taxes on their income. Dealers do not enjoy Section 1031 tax-deferred gain benefits, they must report all gain in the year of sale even if they hold the financing and receive payments over many years, and they cannot take depreciation deductions. On the other hand, dealers can deduct many business expenses that must be capitalized by investors. Losses by a dealer can shelter other active income such as wages and salaries.

Investors can sell property at a profit and defer taxes until a much later date using the Section 1031 tax-deferred exchange. They can deduct depreciation each year as an expense, thereby sheltering income. Depending on the holding period, investor profits are taxed at the lower long-term capital gains rates. Investors do not pay self-employment taxes on their gains. Those who sell property and hold the financing may split annual payment receipts into four parts: nontaxable return of basis, recapture depreciation currently taxed at 25%, long-term capital gains with favorable tax rates, and interest taxed at ordinary income rates. Only the money received during the tax year is taken into consideration. Investors must add many expenses to the basis of their property and do not enjoy current-year tax deductions as a result. Losses by an investor are limited in their ability to shelter other income.

The tension between dealer and investor status is one of the great fears for aggressive real estate investors. They ask, "How many properties can I buy and sell each year before the IRS considers me a dealer?" Miscalculation and taking benefits intended only for investors can result in audits, loss of benefits, large additional taxes, penalties, and interest. Unfortunately, there is no safe harbor for determining when one is a dealer or an investor. The IRS looks at many factors on a case-by-case basis, including time spent in the activity, self-description as an investor or flipper, extent of improvements to the property, use of outside professionals for sales, and use of a dedicated sales office. For the real estate novice, it probably boils down to this: Are the profits from regular sales of real estate necessary to meet the ordinary living expenses of the taxpayer? If so, then it is probably a dealer and not an investor.

Taxation of gains

As explained earlier, the gains on the sale of dealer property are taxed at ordinary income rates with the additional liability for self-employment taxes. Currently, self-employment taxes are 15.3% up to $128,400 of ordinary income, and 2.9% on amounts over $124,800.

Investors must divide their realized gain into two parts. One part, called *recaptured depreciation*, is the sum of all the depreciation deductions taken over the years of that investor's ownership. Recaptured depreciation is taxed at 25% no matter what the taxpayer's ordinary tax bracket. The balance receives capital gains tax treatment. Capital gains are taxed at a different rate than ordinary income. For capital gains, the amount an investor is taxed depends upon both the investor's tax bracket and the amount of time the investment was held before being sold. If the asset is held for 12 months or less, the gains are taxed at the taxpayer's ordinary income tax rate. However, if the asset was held for more than 12 months, the tax rate is 0% for taxpayers in the 10%–15% brackets, 15% for the 25%–35% brackets, and 20% for the 39.6% bracket.

If the taxpayer has real estate gains over certain thresholds for the year, she will also owe Net Investment Income Tax of 3.8% on amounts above the threshold. The two most common thresholds are $200,000 of modified adjusted gross income for single people and $250,000 for married people who do not file separately. The tax is on sales of true investment property, plus sales of one's principal residence. The tax was part of health care reform and is called the *Unearned Income Medicare Contribution Tax*. In reality, however, the money collected goes into the nation's general fund, not into Medicare.

Seller financing, for income tax purposes, means any arrangement in which part of the purchase price is received in a tax year different from the year of sale. A property sold in December 2018 for $1,000 down, with the remaining $199,000 due by January 31, 2019, is considered seller financing if the seller is a calendar year taxpayer. Assuming a $60,000 adjusted basis, dealers will have to report $140,000 of taxable gain in 2018. This is true even if the remaining $199,000 is financed over 30 years. Investors, on the other hand, will split all payments for the tax year into portions representing return of basis, recaptured depreciation, capital gain, and interest, and only the capital gain and interest portion of the actual receipts is taxed in that year. Recaptured depreciation is fully taxed in the year of the sale.

Estate and gift taxes

For 2019, the annual gift tax exclusion is $15,000 per person, per donee. In other words, spouse A and spouse B can, together, donate up to $30,000 per year to each of their children. There is no restriction of who can receive the gift, however. The nontaxable estate and lifetime gift exclusion is $11.4 million per donor for 2019. If a widow has four children and gives each of them a 25% share in real estate worth a total of $1 million, then $60,000 of the gift is free from taxes under the annual exclusion (1 donor × 4 donees × $15,000) and the remaining $940,000 will be tax free under the lifetime exclusion, leaving $10,400,000 of exclusions to be used for future gifts or to shelter her estate from taxes. In 2019, the top bracket for estate taxes is 40%. The current exclusion amount will adjust each year for inflation and then expire in 2025, when it will return to $5 million unless the law is changed.

INCOME TAX RATES

Taxes are imposed only on **taxable income**, which is the net amount remaining after all allowable deductions and adjustments have been made from the gross amount of income earned in a specific year. The tax rates are incremental; that is, all earnings listed under a specified rate are taxed at that rate, whereas earnings over the stipulated amount are taxed at the next rate, and so on. In other words, receiving a raise that pushes the taxpayer into a higher tax bracket does not mean that all income will now be taxed at a higher rate, but only the amount that is over the threshold of the new tax bracket.

Remember that corporate income is subject to double taxation—once as corporate earnings and again as dividends distributed to shareholders. To avoid this double tax, realty investments may be held by individuals as an S corporation or in a trust.

Alternative minimum tax

The **alternative minimum tax (AMT)** is a special levy on investors and corporations that take so many deductions and credits that they would pay little or no tax. It was passed in 1969 after Treasury Secretary Joseph Barr announced that 155 high-income households had not paid a dime in federal income taxes because of various tax deductions to which they were entitled, and that 21 people among those households were millionaires. The public was outraged, causing Congress to pass the AMT. The theory behind the tax is that even though individuals might be entitled to the benefit of some tax preference items like depreciation deductions, they must pay some sort of minimum tax. While the tax was originally designed to limit benefits to high-income households, it has, over time, taken a heavy toll on many middle-class taxpayers. There has been widespread pressure for repeal because it is claimed to be unfair and far too complex to allow for planning except by wealthy individuals who can afford good lawyers and accountants—in other words, the people on whom the tax was originally imposed.

The Tax Cuts and Jobs Act of 2018 minimized the consequences for middle-class taxpayers by increasing the exemption amount and dramatically increasing the phase-out thresholds. For purposes of this course, calculation of the AMT is not important. It is important to know that one's estimate of tax liability for a particular year might be greatly understated because of AMT, which should spur the taxpayer to seek assistance or use one of the free online AMT calculators.

REAL ESTATE INVESTMENTS AS TAX SHELTERS FOR ACTIVE INCOME

Real estate investments are defined as **tax shelters** where the operating costs, mortgage interest, and allowable depreciation are deducted from gross income to derive the net income that is subject to tax.

Operating costs and interest expenses

Investors in income-producing real property are allowed to deduct all operating expenses, and interest paid on property loans, from the investment's gross income. Every real estate investment incurs operating expenses in one form or another and to varying degrees. Vacant, unimproved land is subject to property taxes; improved property develops a multitude of operating costs, including property and sales taxes, insurance premiums, maintenance charges, management fees, bookkeeping, advertising, pest control, and snow removal. Any investment purchased with a loan also incurs interest expenses.

These and other charges are all deductible from the gross annual income when determining the net income, which is subject to tax at the owner's rate. In addition to these operating and interest expenses, improved income property may enjoy another deduction: depreciation of the improvements.

Depreciation

Appraisers describe **depreciation** as a loss in value from any cause. This loss can result from a physical wearing out or from functional and economic obsolescence. The appraiser attempts to measure this loss in value for a particular property.

On the other hand, depreciation from an accounting viewpoint is a recovery of investment costs and makes no effort to reflect any real loss in the property value. It is a theoretical loss of value for tax purposes and is more technically called **cost recovery**. The more commonly used term, *depreciation,* is also acceptable, however. The following schedule provides the tax depreciation schedule that has been allowed by the IRS.

- Residential rental properties placed in service after January 1, 1987: 27.5 years straight-line (3.63% per year) for only the improvements portion of the real estate. Land is never depreciable. In other words, if a four-plex is purchased for $200,000, and if $40,000 of that represents land, then $160,000 is depreciable. There is no precise formula for allocating between land and improvements, but it is usually safe from IRS disallowance if the buyer uses the same ratio employed by the local tax assessor. Once a ratio is established, it remains unchanged over the lifetime of that person's ownership.

Calculation: $160,000 × 3.63% = $5,808 per year in depreciation deductions.

- Nonresidential real estate: 39 years straight-line (2.564% per year) for only the improvements portion of the real estate. *Straight-line depreciation* means the same amount each year for the full depreciable time period.
- Autos and light trucks: Five-year write-off, 200% declining balance allowed. Declining balance depreciation allows larger deductions in early years and then smaller ones over time. The total dollar amount of all the deductions will be the same as **straight line**.
- Personal property and manufacturing equipment: Seven-year write-off, 200% declining balance allowed.
- Land improvements (e.g., sidewalks): 15-year write-off, 150% declining balance allowed.
- Rehabilitation **tax credit** for nonhistoric structures placed in service before 1936: 10%. A tax credit reduces tax liability, dollar for dollar. A $1,000 tax credit will save $1,000 in taxes. A tax deduction reduces income. If someone is in the 25% bracket, a $1,000 tax deduction will save $250 in taxes.
- Rehabilitation tax credit for certified historic structures: 20%.

Bonus depreciation was sometimes offered to spur investment after a catastrophic event such as the 9/11 attacks and Hurricane Katrina. Historically, as much as 50% of the improvement's basis could be deducted in the first year, thereby sheltering large amounts of income. The 2018 Tax Cuts and Jobs Act allowed $150,000 of bonus depreciation to assist economic recovery.

Section 179 of the Internal Revenue Code allows 100% depreciation of certain personal property used in a trade or business, up to annual limits. In 2018, the limit is $1 million, except for most vehicles, which are capped at $25,000. Section 179 used to be called the "Hummer Loophole" because it allowed people to buy luxury vehicles, like Hummers, and fully deduct them in the year of acquisition. Full-sized pickup trucks and a few other vehicles do not have the $25,000 limitation.

FOR EXAMPLE

To illustrate how real estate investments act as tax shelters, consider the following analysis:

$50,000	Gross annual income
−17,000	Annual operating expenses
−3,000	Nonoperating expenses, such as advertising and leasing commissions, and perhaps a share of corporate overhead
30,000	Cash flow before debt service
−25,000	Interest paid on loan (limited to investment income)
5,000	Cash flow before depreciation
−10,000	Depreciation allowance
(5,000)	Net paper loss

The gross annual income reflects income from all the property's sources, such as rents, vending machines, and laundry. The operating costs include property taxes, insurance premiums, maintenance, utilities, and management. The $30,000 cash flow is the net taxable income and is considered profit.

Note: Gross annual income less operating expenses results in a number called ***Net Operating Income (NOI)***, which is the foundation of a very popular financial analysis model. Expenses that are not part of the routine operation of a property, such as leasing commissions, are not considered part of the NOI for purposes of the model, but are fully deductible as business expenses.

This profit is sheltered from income tax by allowable interest expenses and depreciation deductions. Thus, this investment generates a $5,000 passive loss. This loss can be used to offset the owner's other passive profits or, if the owner qualifies, it can reduce other active or portfolio income accordingly, thereby saving tax dollars.

Note that this example does not include an amount for reserves for replacements in the operating costs. Many prudent investors allocate a portion of the property's income into a reserve account each year toward future major repairs or replacements. These reserves are not deductible operating expenses until they are actually spent.

Cost segregation depreciation

Cost segregation depreciation is a method of depreciation in which some individual parts of a real estate asset are depreciated separately and not as a part of the whole unit. Real property improvements are called *Section 1250 property* because that is the IRS section that defines them. Personal property is called *Section 1245 property.* Property has different allowable depreciation schedules depending on whether it is Section 1245 property (shorter schedule) or Section 1250 property (longer schedule.) Longer schedules mean smaller deductions each year.

The taxpayer is allowed to determine whether an item, even if it otherwise appears to be a part of the real property, can be classified as personal property under Section 1245 of the IRC. The art of separating out these components is called *cost segregation*. The IRS *Cost Segregation Audit Techniques Guide* states: "In general, a turnkey construction project includes elements of tangible personal property (e.g., phone system, computer system, process piping, storage tanks, etc.). It is relatively easy to identify that these are Section 1245 property and allocate a portion of the total project costs to them. However, a cost segregation study may also report certain building occupancy items (e.g., carpeting, wall coverings, partitions, millwork, lighting fixtures) as Section 1245 property that would have likely been classified or grouped under Section 1250 property without the completion of the cost segregation study. These items may or may not constitute as qualifying Section 1245 property depending on the particular facts and circumstances for which the project was designed." Examples may include the following:

- Restaurants and hotels that include significant machinery, fixtures, and specialized food storage and handling facilities that might be considered separate from the building.
- Office buildings where improvements can be constructed to be removable.
- Computer rooms and trading floors that are fitted with specialized telecommunications equipment, electrical service, and enhanced heating, ventilation, and air-conditioning equipment.

For more information regarding tax treatment of residential rental property, see *IRS Publication 527.*

Passive activity loss limitations

There is a limit on the amount of real estate losses that can shelter other (active) income, such as that from wages, salary, or dealer real estate. The first rule is that all rental income is passive income. Passive losses can offset passive income, but not active income. This is the **passive activity loss limitation** rule.

However, taxpayers who actively participate in a rental activity can deduct up to $25,000 per year of passive losses against active income, but only if the taxpayer makes less than $100,000 in Modified Adjusted Gross Income (MAGI). Many tax benefits are tied to MAGI. It is calculated by taking the adjusted gross income on a tax return and then adding back certain deductions (such as IRA contributions) to arrive at MAGI. It does not change the taxes due; it merely determines if the taxpayer is entitled to certain benefits. **Active participation** means participation in management decisions using independent judgment and not just reliance on a third-party manager. By IRS definition, limited partners can never be active participants, nor can anyone who owns less than 10% of the investment. Trusts and corporations are never active participants.

However, taxpayers who meet the definition of a *real estate professional* are not capped at $25,000 per year but can fully deduct their passive losses against active income. A real estate professional must meet two requirements: an activity requirement and a time requirement. The only allowed activities are real estate

- development or redevelopment;
- construction or reconstruction;
- acquisition or conversion;
- rental;
- management or operation;
- leasing; or
- brokerage.

The time requirement includes the taxpayer spending at least 50% of his time in the previously stated activities (it can be a combination of them) *and* at least 750 hours per year. Investors seeking to maximize deductible losses in the early years of an investment should review the IRS' *Passive Activity Loss Audit Techniques Guide*, which is available on its website.

Another limitation on deductible losses is the **at-risk rule**. In its simplest form, it provides that an investor cannot deduct more than it has at risk in an investment. A limited partner who invests $5,000 and has no personal liability can deduct only $5,000 of losses, no matter what the underlying asset does. There are many variations on how to calculate how much is at risk. For additional guidance, *IRS Publication 925* provides explanations and examples.

REAL ESTATE INVESTMENTS AS TAX SHELTERS FOR CAPITAL GAINS

The tax laws allow other sheltering mechanisms, including tax-free refinancing, pyramiding through refinancing, special exemptions for profits made from the sale of principal residences, installment sale deferments, exchanges, and inheritance tax exemptions.

Tax-free refinancing

Refinancing involves the securing of a new loan to replace an old loan. Logically, the new loan should be sufficient not only to satisfy the balance of the existing loan, but also pay all of the placement costs involved and generate new cash the borrower can use for additional investments. Any money acquired by refinancing is not subject to tax, even if these funds exceed the original purchase price of the specific property. This money is considered borrowed money and, as such, is not taxable.

In this regard, a distinction should be drawn between two types of gains; **realized gain** is the actual profit derived from a transaction, such as the money received from refinancing, and **recognized gain** is that portion of the profit recognized by the IRS and subject to tax. In the case of refinancing, a taxable capital gains income from this transaction exists only when the realized gain becomes recognized gain upon the sale of the property. In the meantime, property can be financed and refinanced repeatedly over time to generate tax-free cash that can be invested and reinvested for additional profits.

Pyramiding through refinancing

One way to acquire a substantial amount of real estate is to periodically refinance those properties already owned and then use the proceeds to purchase new properties. This procedure is called **pyramiding** *through refinancing*.

Unlike *pyramiding through selling* (where an investor purchases a property, improves it for resale at a higher price, and then purchases additional properties with gains from the sale), pyramiding through refinancing is based on retaining all properties acquired. By not selling, the investor is constantly increasing the refinancing base while avoiding capital gains taxes.

Pyramiding through refinancing begins with the purchase of one property. If more than one property can be purchased to start the plan, then the refinancing base will be enhanced at the outset. The type of property to be purchased should be improved income property that has the ability to generate at least enough cash flow to cover all operating costs plus mortgage payments.

It is in the best interests of the investor to purchase better properties in stable or growing areas. An older property in a declining neighborhood would make a poor investment with which to pyramid through refinancing. Rents and values of such buildings might decrease, and thus destroy, the refinancing cycle.

With the appropriate application of deductible allowances, most, if not all, of the net income earned during the years of ownership could be sheltered, while capital gains taxes could be avoided through the refinancing process. The estate could then be left to the investor's heirs at the stepped-up values determined at the date of death, without the investor ever having to pay capital gains tax on any profits derived from ownership of this property.

Note: Under current tax law, if an investor dies owning real estate, the investor's adjusted basis becomes irrelevant, and the adjusted basis of the heirs will be the fair market value at the time of death. In other words, the investor can buy land worth $75,000 and sell it days before death for $1 million, with taxes due on the $925,000 recognized gain. Or, the same investor can keep the property until death; the heirs receive a stepped-up basis to $1 million and then sell it for $1 million and pay no income taxes.

Although pyramiding to avoid capital gains taxes is a practical strategy, sometimes the sale of a property is unavoidable. As indicated, any gains made in such a sale are subject to income tax.

Principal residence

The income tax laws provide a special exclusion on the profits earned from the sale of private residences. Since 1997, taxpayers have been allowed to exclude from taxes up to $250,000 of the gain realized on the sale or exchange of a principal residence and up to $500,000 for a married couple filing a joint return. To be eligible to claim the exclusion, the residence must have been owned and used as the taxpayer's principal residence for a combined period of at least 24 months out of the 60 months before the sale or exchange. The months can be separated in time, as long as all 24 occur within the prior 60-month period. If a taxpayer is on qualified official extended duty in the Uniformed Services, the Foreign Service, or the intelligence community, she can suspend the five-year period for up to an additional 10 years. The full exclusion is available only if the owner did not use the exclusion on a prior home sale within a two-year period ending on the sale date.

If the sale of the principal residence is considered an *involuntary conversion*, such as a health-related move or a move necessitated by divorce, this benefit may be prorated. Thus, if a newly divorced couple has occupied the home as their principal residence for just one out of the past five years, then a partial exclusion of half of the capital gain is tax free.

Installment sale deferment

Capital gains tax can be postponed by the application of an installment sale plan, which is available to both residential and commercial property owners, provided the outstanding installment obligation at the end of the tax year is $5 million or less. For higher-installment obligations, special rules prevail. In general, dealers in real estate may not defer taxes under installment sales but must pay any tax on gains at ordinary income rates at the time of sale, even if payments will be received over many years. Dealers are persons or companies who have real estate as their stock-in-trade (e.g., subdividers who sell lots or builders/developers who sell houses).

The installment sale method of calculating taxes is optional. If elected, the seller may calculate the capital gains portion of each year's payments and pay capital gains taxes on only that amount received, instead of the entire capital gain on the gross sales price. The gross amount of recaptured depreciation is taxed in the year of the sale. Interest received in the payment year is taxed at ordinary income rates. See the following example to understand the mechanics of calculating taxable income with an installment sale.

A seller has an adjusted basis of $528,000 in property sold on June 1 for $985,000 with 100% financing at 6% interest, fully amortizing by monthly payments over 10 years. For purposes of this example, there are no selling expenses, which would ordinarily be added to the gross sales price. The seller has previously taken $122,000 in depreciation deductions during his ownership of the property. How much taxable gain is there during the first year if the seller elects the installment sale method of reporting income?

Adjusted basis	$528,000
Gross sales price	$985,000
Adjusted basis	$528,000
Depreciation to be recaptured	$122,000 (taxed in year of sale)
Add adjusted basis, selling expenses, and depreciation recapture to calculate the new adjusted basis for purposes of the installment sale.	528,000 + 122,000 = $650,000
Subtract the new adjusted basis from the gross sales price to arrive at gross profit.	985,000 – 650,000 = $335,000
Divide the gross profit by the sales price to calculate gross profit percentage.	985,000 / 335,000 = 0.3401, or 34.01%
Total monthly payments received (July–Dec)	$65,613.12 (calculated)
Interest portion of payments	$4,773.23 (calculated)
Principal payments received in first six months	65,613.12 – 4,773.23 = $60,839.89
Taxable capital gain received in first six months (principal payments × gross profit percentage)	60,839.89 × 0.3401 = $20,691.65
First-year taxable income	$122,000 recaptured depreciation (25% tax rate) + $4,773.23 interest income (ordinary income rates) + $20,691.65 (15% long-term capital gain rates)

Note: The gross profit percentage will remain the same each year unless the price is later reduced. The taxable capital gain will change each year because a smaller percentage of the annual payments will be interest, resulting in a larger number as taxable gain.

The installment sale provision in the tax law is intended as a relief provision for owners who can sell their property only by agreeing to accept payments in installments. A seller might receive less cash in the year of the sale than the tax required on the total gain. Therefore, the law allows tax payments to be made as installment payments are received.

IRS Publication 537 contains the rules and worksheets necessary to understand the calculations necessary to determine taxable installment sale income each year, including problems such as price reduction and foreclosure.

Exchanges

An alternative method for tax-deferred pyramiding can also be accomplished by upside trading or the property **exchange** technique. Section 1031 of the Internal Revenue Code provides for the recognition of capital gain to be postponed under the following conditions:

- Properties to be exchanged must be held for productive use in a trade or business, or for investment.
- Properties to be exchanged must be of like kind to each other; their nature or character must be similar.
- Properties must actually be exchanged.

The Tax Cuts and Jobs Act of 2018 eliminated the ability to use Section 1031 for personal property exchanges. It is now limited to only business or investment real property. All investment or business real estate is considered like kind to all other real estate except in the following instances:

- Real property with no land, such as a condo, is not like kind with raw law. The condo is like-kind with office buildings, shopping centers, apartments, and all other real property.
- Real property outside the United States is not like kind with property inside the United States.
- By definition, one's personal residence is not like kind with any other real estate because it is not used for investment or business purposes.

Improvements on the land are considered differences in the quality of the real estate, not in the type. Thus, a vacant lot can be exchanged for a store property, or an industrial property may be exchanged for a high-rise office building. Often, unlike property (called **boot**) is included in a real estate exchange and must be accounted for separately. Boot may include cash, jewelry, or other personal property. Since the value of the real properties being exchanged is often different, boot is used to equalize the values.

There are at least six basic mathematical computations involved in the exchange process:

1. Balancing the equities
2. Deriving realized gains
3. Deriving recognized gains
4. Determining tax impacts
5. Re-establishing book basis
6. Allocating the new basis

These computations are illustrated by the simple two-party exchange recorded in Figure 6.1.

Figure 6.1: Two-Party Exchange

Property A		**Property B**
Step 1. Balancing the equities		
$100,000	Exchange price	$150,000
− 60,000	Existing mortgage	− 80,000
40,000	Owners' equity	$70,000
+ 30,000	Cash required	
$70,000		
Step 2. Deriving realized gains		
$100,000	Exchange price	$150,000
− 70,000	Adjusted basis	− 90,000
$30,000	Realized gain	$60,000
Step 3. Deriving recognized gains		
(Recognized gain equals the sum of unlike properties.)		
0	Cash required	$30,000
0	Boot	0
0	Mortgage relief	+ 20,000
0	Recognized gain	$50,000
Step 4. Determining tax impacts		
(Taxable income is the realized gain or the recognized gain, whichever is less.)		
$30,000	Realized gain	$60,000
0	Recognized gain	50,000
0	Taxable gain	$50,000
(Note that Property B will pay income tax on $50,000. Property A will pay no tax.)		
Step 5. Re-establishing book basis		
$70,000	Old basis	$90,000
+ 80,000	New mortgage	+60,000
+ 30,000	Cash and boot paid	+ 0
+ 0	Recognized gain	+ 50,000
$180,000	Total	$200,000
Less		
$60,000	Old mortgage	$80,000
+ 0	Cash and boot received	+ 30,000
$60,000	Total	$110,000
$120,000	New basis	$90,000
Step 6. Allocating the new basis		
(Each party will decide which portions of the new basis to allocate to land and improvements to establish new depreciation schedules.)		

A two-party, like-kind property exchange will not qualify if

- the parties are related;
- either party sells the property within two years of the exchange; or
- a property in the United States is exchanged for a property outside the country.

For purposes of this regulation, related persons are immediate family members, lineal descendants, corporations in which the exchangers own more than 50% of the stock, two corporations that are members of the same holding group, and a grantor or fiduciary of a trust.

The two-year disposition rule is waived in the event of death or involuntary conversion.

It is not often that each of two potential exchangers owns property that is desired by the other. More frequently, exchanges involve three or more property owners. To effectively arrange these multiparty exchanges, the element of timing becomes an important aspect for consideration. The process requires two contracts: one between the first two parties that structure the exchange, and a second in which the third party buys the unwanted property. Each contract is conditional upon the closing of the other, and they must be closed simultaneously.

Deferred exchange

A federal court decision in 1979, *Starker v. United States* (602 F.2D 1341 (9th Circuit)), introduced the **deferred exchange** to expand the tax-free exchange provisions in the tax law. Section 1031 of the tax code was amended to include the deferred exchange, which, for the first time, allowed traders to set up an exchange for properties not yet available but to be found within certain time constraints.

Tax-deferred exchanges of like-kind real estate became popular when Congress amended the tax code to allow time-deferred exchanges. Tax-free *Starker exchanges* can be achieved, provided two time limits are met. The transaction is not truly tax free because taxes will have to be paid at some point in the future when the property is sold without another exchange. Despite that, it is common to call these tax-free exchanges. The tax-free exchange process is as follows:

1. The property to be received by A must be identified no later than 45 days following the date that A transfers property to B. One identifies the property via a written communication to a disinterested third party who acts as a qualified intermediary.
2. A must receive the exchange property from B no later than the earlier of (a) 180 days after A transfers to B or (b) the due date of A's tax return for the year in which the property is transferred to B.

Neither of these time periods can be extended; if they are not met, the exchange becomes a fully taxable sale.

One suggested solution to the relatively short time periods allowed in the delayed exchange is the reverse exchange developed by Louis Weller of Deloitte LLP real estate tax service of Los Angeles. A reverse exchange involves the acquisition by a property owner of a replacement property before the existing property is sold. An accommodating third-party buyer acquires the replacement property and holds it until the exchanger sells the relinquished property, at which time, a conventional exchange is complete.

The IRS provides a safe harbor for reverse exchange participants, answering such questions as whether an exchanger can fund the accommodating party's purchase or hold a fixed-price option on the replacement property.

Understanding 1031 exchanges is important to the real estate investor for the tax savings, and also to understand pricing anomalies. Recall that when an investor sells real property, he has a very short 45-day window within which to identify the replacement property for purchase. In an aggressive market, it might be difficult to find a suitable property to put under contract within the time limit. The investor might find himself in a bidding war, willing to pay a price significantly higher than market. That is because the increased purchase price is more than offset by the benefits of tax deferral. Other investors using such property as a recent comparable sale to help evaluate the value of their own properties being bought or sold might have misplaced confidence in such a purchase price.

Distribution to heirs

The ultimate capital gains tax shelter is to maintain ownership of investment property until death. At death, the property is appraised for inheritance tax purposes, and the deceased's heirs acquire title, with the new basis stepped up—increased—to the fair market value at the time of death. The old adjusted basis is no longer relevant, and the new owner starts with stepped-up basis. The heirs' depreciation deductions will be based on the stepped-up basis. Gain will be calculated using the stepped-up basis.

Although capital gains taxes can be avoided, certain estates are subject to the imposition of inheritance taxes. With the appropriate application of tax-free gift giving, even these taxes can be avoided.

Estate tax

The federal tax laws established exemptions for the values of estates subject to federal estate taxes. As of 2019, the exemption is $11.4 million per person. In addition, many states have estate tax. These state rates vary and should be reviewed in conjunction with investment planning.

Gift tax

With proper planning, investors may be able to distribute their entire estates by using tax-free gifts to avoid inheritance taxes.

The law provided gift exemptions of up to $15,000 for each donor per donee in 2019. Thus, a married couple could gift $30,000 tax free to each heir. The lifetime gift and estate tax exemption is $11.4 million. These exemptions are tied to inflation indexes and typically change annually.

SUMMARY

Active income is derived from wages, salaries, commissions, interest, dividends, and profits earned from year-to-year activities of businesses, in addition to other earnings. Ordinary income in excess of allowable deductions is taxed at the federal and state levels at progressive rates established by Congress and state legislatures.

Active income is sheltered to the extent of such allowable deductions as medical care, state taxes, moving costs, and charitable donations, if itemized. The net income from real estate investments is sheltered by operating expenses, interest charges, and depreciation deductions. Operating expenses include management and maintenance fees plus charges for utilities, advertising, property taxes, insurance premiums, bookkeeping services, and similar costs. Interest charges are deducted from a property's gross earnings before deriving the taxable income.

Current depreciation allowances are a 27.5-year straight-line rate for residential income property and a 39-year straight-line rate for nonresidential property.

Capital gains income is composed of profits (or losses) on noninventory assets held as investments for relatively long periods of time and then sold.

Losses from active trades or businesses can be used to shelter earnings from these activities, while losses from passive activities are limited to sheltering earnings from passive activities.

All nonpersonal service real estate rentals are considered passive activities unless owned by real estate professionals, and any losses are limited to the investment's income. The exception is a $25,000 excess loss carryover given to those individuals who earn less than $100,000 adjustable gross income and take a clearly defined active participation in a real estate investment in which they own 10% or more by value.

Investors often capitalize on their equity by refinancing and securing tax-free dollars from the new mortgage proceeds. Property equities grow through inflation and as a consequence of the regular repayment of existing mortgages. Funds secured from refinancing are not subject to income tax, even though this money may exceed the original price paid for the property. Thus, investors may refinance regularly and secure new cash assets that enable them to acquire additional properties and expand their investment portfolios.

Taxes on profits from real estate capital gains can be deferred through installment sales or the exchange process. When trading like properties, owners can carry their old book values over to the new properties, effectively deferring taxes on any gains. Depending on the terms of the transaction, an up-trader can usually shelter the entire gain, while the down-trader will have to pay taxes on the portion of the equity recovered.

DISCUSSION TOPICS

1. Check with a local real estate broker to review the benefits of a Starker exchange.
2. Using two separate properties, create a simple business plan to maximize deductions available to investors and dealers.

UNIT 6 EXAM

1. By definition, portfolio income includes all of the following *EXCEPT*
   A. stock dividends.
   B. oil and mineral royalties.
   C. investment sales profits.
   D. savings account interest.

2. Active income consists of earnings from all of the following *EXCEPT*
   A. wages.
   B. business profits.
   C. stock dividends.
   D. capital gains.

3. On improved income property, all of the following are allowable expense deductions *EXCEPT*
   A. interest charges.
   B. principal payments.
   C. maintenance costs.
   D. depreciation.

4. Stepped-up basis requires
   A. a gift inter vivos.
   B. a death.
   C. a like-kind exchange.
   D. a cost segregation report.

5. When an investment property purchased for $150,000 is refinanced with a new loan for $175,000, the $25,000 is
   A. taxed as portfolio income.
   B. taxed as active income.
   C. taxed as passive income.
   D. not taxed.

6. Under current tax law, long-term capital gains are
   A. limited to $25,000.
   B. taxed at 20% maximum.
   C. eliminated.
   D. applied only to commercial property.

7. The losses sustained when selling an investment property must first be deducted from any capital gains made in the year, with any excess losses
   A. allocated to shelter active income.
   B. marked off the books.
   C. carried forward to shelter any future capital gains at the rate of $3,000 per year.
   D. deducted as an operating expense.

8. Passive income is derived from which of the following?
   A. Interest on savings
   B. Dividends from stocks
   C. Income from rentals
   D. Royalties from oil leases

9. A commercial property was purchased for $100,000 with 20% allocated to the land. At a straight-line depreciation rate of 2.564% per year, what is the adjusted basis of this property at the end of the 10th year, allowing for rounding errors?
   A. $2,051
   B. $20,510
   C. $59,490
   D. $79,488

10. Recaptured depreciation is taxed at what rate?
    A. 15%
    B. 25%
    C. Applicable long-term capital gains rate
    D. Applicable ordinary income rate

UNIT 7 Time Value of Money

LEARNING OBJECTIVES

When you have completed this unit, you will be able to accomplish the following.

- Explain the concept of time value of money.

KEY TERMS

net present value (NPV) stabilized occupancy

INTRODUCTION

For purposes of many financial analysis models, one must be very comfortable with the concept of time value of money. One dollar received today is worth more than one dollar received a year from now. There are several reasons for that:

- $1 today can be reinvested and put to work, and will be worth more than $1 a year from now. $1 received in a year will be only $1.
- Inflation erodes spending power. $1 will buy more today than it will in one year.
- Today's risks can be evaluated more reliably than risks that might occur in one year. One dollar in hand is much less risky than a dollar that might or might not be paid a year from now. Increased risks generally drive down values.

TIME VALUE OF MONEY

There are mathematical tools for estimating the value today of a dollar to be received in the future. They are best understood by looking at a question we have all encountered through our own financial planning, or seeing commercials or advertisements. The question is always some version of, "If I put $500 per month into a bank account or investment that will earn 5% per year, and if all of my profits/interest are reinvested each month and also earn 5%, how much money will I have in 40 years when I retire?" In terms of financial analysis, we wish to find the future value (FV) of a periodic investment that will earn 5% per year, compounded monthly. The answer is $763,010.08. The process of money earning money, and then the original money plus the earnings all earn additional money, is called **compounding.**

Using Excel or a financial calculator, FV calculations need values for a present value, the value of periodic payments, an interest rate expressed in terms of the compounding period, and a time period expressed in terms of the compounding period. One must have at least a present value—the money originally invested—or the periodic payments. Both can be used, but at least one must be used. The compounding period is usually months, but could be years. For an investment compounded every month, 12% per annum interest would be entered as 1 (because it is 1% per month) and a 10-year term would be entered as 120. For an investment compounded only once a year, the rate would be 12 and the term would be 10.

A corollary of that question is, "If I were to win the lottery and receive $10 million, what lump sum amount would I have to invest today at 5% annual interest, compounded monthly, so that it would again grow to $10 million by the time I retire in 40 years?" (Presumably, the money not invested can be spent on a wide variety of impulse purchases and gifts.) In other words, if a dollar today is worth more than a dollar tomorrow, then something less than today's dollar will be worth one dollar tomorrow. The present value (PV) calculation tells us exactly how many dollars we must have today to have $10 million tomorrow, or 40 years from today. The answer is $1,358,987.89. One can win $10 million today, have a spending spree with $8,641,102.11, and *still* have $10 million at retirement age!

In financial analysis terms, the last question is, "What is the present value of $10 million to be received in 40 years if the discount rate is 5% per year?" The discount rate is the reverse of an interest rate. When we talk about today's money growing at a certain rate, we call it the interest rate. When we talk about going backwards from tomorrow's money to reach today's money, we call it the *discount rate.* If we can invest $1,358,987.89 today at 5% to have $10 million in 40 years, then the value of $10 million to be received in 40 years is $1,358,987.89, using a 5% discount rate.

PV calculations require a term, rate, and the future value. The rate is the discount rate selected by the investor.

Suppose we invested money in a very safe vehicle, earning only 1.5% per year? Our question would be, "What is the present value of $10 million to be received in 40 years, assuming a discount rate of 1.5%? The answer is $4,509,826.92. If the investment vehicle earned 12% interest, it would take only $84,283.12!

These few examples are the heart of the time value of money. Time has different values for different investments. Time is worth 5% per year, or 1.5% per year, or 12% per year in the previous examples. Choosing the correct value to put upon time is one of the greatest skills a real estate investor can develop.

The other important skill is predicting how much money can be put in the bank each month, to use the analogy of the previous question involving $500 deposits per month. What if, instead of depositing $500 a month from a paycheck, we deposited all of the net income from a rental house? Now we need to make educated guesses about how much money that will be each month for the next 40 years. That seems daunting. How can someone reliably predict rents and expenses 40 years into the future? They cannot. As a result, real estate financial analysis based on rental income rarely extends more than five to seven years in the future.

Net present value (NPV)

A concept that seems to cause confusion among novice investors is that of **net present value (NPV)**. Many use the terms *present value (PV)* and *net present value* interchangeably. The confusion is made worse because some financial calculators use a function labeled *NPV* to solve for present value.

Upon thinking about it, though, the word *net* has an important function. It indicates a sum left after netting two or more numbers against each other. If one calculates a PV of future cash flows, there is only one number—the PV. There is nothing to net. Income and expenses are netted against each other to arrive at net income, and then the present value of all the net incomes is discounted to one present value.

Usually, NPV calculations are used by starting with the acquisition cost, entering the periodic cash flows, and then also entering the investor's required rate of return. In that case, the net of the initial cash outflow (acquisition costs) and the PV of the future cash flows has three possibilities:

A property with an NPV of 0 is one in which the value of the future revenues is exactly equal to the current acquisition costs using the described discount rate. In other words, the property is being purchased for exactly its appraised value—or as near to the appraised value as can be in an imperfect world. This acquisition is easily financed with traditional methods.

- Zero, which means the investor paid, or will pay, an acquisition price that is exactly equal to the discounted value of all future cash flows, meeting pre-established and personal investment requirements, such as a 5% return on money. If we pay $1,358,987.89 for an investment that will earn 5% per annum, compounded monthly, and that will be worth $10 million in 40 years, then the NPV of that investment will be $0. We spent exactly the right amount of money today to earn the money we wanted tomorrow, assuming 5% growth.
- Some positive number, which means the sum of all the discounted cash flows (inflow) netted against the acquisition cost (outflow) is a positive number. This investment did, or will do, better than the investor's required return, which is 5% in the example. If we spend only $1 million to buy that same investment (which has a present value of $1,358,987.89 at 5%), then the net present value is $358,987.89. The positive number indicates we bought at a bargain. Again, using 5% compounding, our $1 million should have grown to only $7,358,417.32 in 40 years. We will actually receive $10 million. We paid a bargain price for our investment.
- Some negative number, which means the sum of all the discounted cash flows (inflow) netted against the acquisition cost (a negative number for outflow) is negative. The investor spent more than was warranted under the circumstances, using her investment criteria of a 5% return. If we spent $2 million to buy the same investment, then the net present value is $1,358,987.89 – $2,000,000 = ($640,101.22). At 5% compounded monthly, our $2 million should have grown to $14,716,834.64. Instead, we will receive only $10,000,000. We spent too much for our investment.

These simple calculations are the heart of the time value of money analyses for real estate investments. One must select the correct number for the value of time, and one must make reasonably accurate predictions about future income, expenses, and resale proceeds.

The value of time can depend on many different factors. It generally starts with the current rates on 10-year treasuries. Treasuries are the safest investment possible, and time has the lowest value. As risk increases, time becomes more valuable. This is logical. For those facing short-term death because of age or illness, the risk of death is fairly high. Time is valuable. Time is not so valuable to a 10-year-old healthy child. The risk of death, in the child's mind, does not even exist.

For any investment decision, one can ask the marketplace about the current value of time as it relates to that type of investment. The marketplace spokespeople include other investors, appraisers, and lenders. They do not create the market, but they know what the market is doing and can describe it in terms of a currently popular discount rate or a compounding rate employed by other investors. They can never be entirely certain of accuracy, however, because checking assumptions against performance requires long periods for the investment to mature and then check to see if it performed as anticipated. By the time one has collected two years of data, the market has changed. The market changes constantly, and one must always make educated guesses about the future.

As can be seen, there is no one right answer as to the value of time. Each investor must make her own decision. The other major component of time value of money calculations is the money. How much money will there be in the future, and when will it come in?

Alternative scenarios

Predicting future revenues, expenses, and property resale prices is not an exact science. The farther out into the future the prediction, the more peril of an incorrect prediction. One way to manage the process is to always make three sets of data assumptions: best case, worst case, and most likely case. The relevant financial analyses may then be performed on the three alternative sets of data. The results will then also reflect a best, worst, and most likely investment scenario. If the worst-case scenario will not support an investment decision to proceed, then the investor must do one of the following:

- Re-examine data and assumptions to determine if projections should be modified
- Recalculate the purchase price using a factor in the relevant model that accounts for risk (such as the capitalization rate or discount rate, explained later)
- Make a knowing decision to assume the risk of a possible worst case
- Identify early warning signs of an impending worst case, and make contingency plans for ways to rectify the situation

Not only is this exercise important for the investor, it is also relevant to the lender. Most investors do not provide such alternate scenarios to their potential lenders. Yet, many lenders perform the same calculations themselves. It is advantageous for the investor to present a worst-case scenario (assuming it still supports the investment decision) rather than allow the lender free rein to make its own adverse assumptions. Generally, the lender will use the borrower's worst-case assumptions. In addition, the investor who presents alternative scenarios to a lender indicates that he has thoroughly examined such possibilities, and therefore, has greater credibility in the loan application process.

DATA COLLECTION AND ASSUMPTIONS

Probably the largest obstacle for real estate investors regarding data collection is coming to grips with the fact that not all data is available online. It will almost certainly be necessary to make phone calls, visit with people, and drive the streets seeing what there is to see. None of it is difficult to find, however. A relatively small investment of time in data collection will yield much better results in financial analysis. The following areas are important to virtually all real estate investments. Additional information can be obtained from following units about specific types of investment opportunities.

Acquisition cost

This is the cost to acquire a property. Some models use the entire purchase price. Some look at only the investor's cash outlay and do not include borrowed money in the analysis.

Future capital expenditures

Raw land might need to be developed by clearing vegetation, leveling the soil to some degree, and installing infrastructure such as roads, utilities, and water/sewer. Other investments might need future rehab or major repairs such as a roof replacement. These cash outflows should be identified as to the approximate amount and timing.

Routine expenditures include maintenance, repair, insurance, taxes, legal, accounting, marketing/advertising, and leasing commissions and payroll, depending on property size and type.

Cost of money

Unless one is investing small or enjoys unusual cash liquidity, virtually everyone will need to borrow money. Even those who can invest without borrowing usually borrow anyway because of the power of leverage. Why tie up $1 million on a single investment when the same money can be used as $200,000 down payments on five different properties, with mortgage loans providing the balance of the purchase money? Yet, borrowing money means that the cost of borrowing must often be added to the other expenses of real estate , depending on the type of analytical model.

Market rents

Current market rents will need to be evaluated as a baseline and then assumptions made about future rent increases. The assumptions should be grounded in an analysis of the outlook for the general economy and related demographic trends, anticipated growth in competition that might limit rental rate growth, and existing or anticipated government actions that might help or hinder competition, among other things.

Unit sale prices

Subdivision developers and condo converters must determine the sales price of recent comparable properties in the marketplace and then project those values into a future when their own projects will be ready for sale. This can be affected by the same factors as are relevant to market rents.

Tax benefits

Investors should identify the tax benefits available from a property, especially if several competing projects are under consideration. If low-income housing tax credits are available, then the tax savings amount to additional profit. A property capable of cost segregation depreciation or bonus depreciation can generate early year tax sheltering to offset possible negative cash flows. In that manner, a property that might be unpalatable due to the investor's inability to carry early cash losses might be feasible because of the sheltering.

Operating expenses

Estimating operating expenses is relatively easy because the investor can be armed with a checklist of the most common operating expenses for that type of project. These can be obtained from reference books and online sources, and sometimes lenders. There are also rules of thumb in the local community for standard operating expense ranges as percentages of gross scheduled rents. Checking the investor's own numbers against the industry averages can provide an additional level of comfort. At a minimum, virtually all income-producing properties will have operating expenses that include property taxes, insurance, maintenance/repair, accounting and legal, and property management.

For purposes of financial analysis, property management expenses must be imputed, even if the owner self-manages. Maintenance/repair must also be imputed, even if the owner personally performs all the work. That is because (1) for resale evaluation, the prudent buyer must assume it will hire third-party maintenance and management, and he must evaluate the property during its own period of ownership, not just the seller's period of ownership; and (2) the investor's bank will order an appraisal, and the appraiser will impute those expenses to arrive at a property value, which will, in turn, determine how much money the investor will be able to borrow.

Resale expenses

The investor who anticipates sales of units, such as subdivision lots or condos, or who uses a financial model that takes into consideration the future sale of a property, must estimate all the expenses related to that sale. That could include a one-time paint-up/freshen-up to make the property more aesthetically attractive, plus adverting, marketing, sales commissions, and closing expenses. Some financial models consider all cash inflows and outflows, so it is important to account for all of them in the data collection stage.

Tax brackets

Investors must know their tax brackets for ordinary income and long-term capital gains to calculate after-tax cash flows. Some models need that information. In addition, investors who might be characterized as dealers (as discussed in the unit on income taxes) must remember to calculate self-employment taxes.

Time to lease-up

If the investor is buying a mature property, it will already be at **stabilized occupancy**. In other words, numbers of departing tenants will be roughly equal to the numbers of new tenants. For new projects, however, the investor must estimate how long it will take to reach stabilized occupancy.

Unit sales schedule

For things such as subdivision lots and condo sales, the investor will estimate how many units will be sold per month and how long it will take to pay off the development or conversion loan. Such loans are typically designed so that as each unit is sold, the lender will release it from the master mortgage, but only if most of the unit sales price is paid over to the lender. These terms are negotiated, but it would not be uncommon for a lot sale of $50,000 to result in $45,000 paid to the lender and only $5,000 paid to the developer. In that manner, the development loan is paid off rapidly from early lot sales, with the developer receiving 100% of the sales price for later sales.

Aside from the time necessary to pay off the development loan, investors will need to determine the length of time to sell out the project. This does not mean the time until 100% of the units are sold, but the time until a specific goal set by the developer has been reached.

That might be 75% of the units or 95% of the units. Each project and developer is different. The developer who chooses a 75% number might be thinking, "I know I can sell 75% of the units within the first 18 months. Yes, there will be sporadic sales over the next two to 10 years after that, but for purposes of my financial analysis, that will constitute the equivalent of an annuity. My decision whether to do this project or not will depend on activity during the first 18 months after completion."

As can be seen from the discussions here, time value of money analyses depend on the value of time, the length of time, and the amounts of cash inflows and outflows. The next section will examine some fairly simple analytical models that do not rely on time value of money and illustrate their shortcomings, and then conclude with time value of money tools.

SUMMARY

Investors must be aware of the concept of time value of money for purposes of many financial analysis models. One dollar received today is worth more than one dollar received a year from now. That is because of the loss of value over time due to inflation, and the fact that $1 invested today at a very modest 2% interest rate would be worth slightly over $1.02 in one year. It is more than $1.02 because interest will be earned every month, and that interest will then be reinvested to earn additional interest. Not so much when looking at a $1 investment, but with a $1 million investment, the power of compounding returns an extra $184.36 over and above the estimated $20,000 of interest.

NPV must be understood by investors. Usually, NPV calculations are used by starting with the acquisition cost, entering the periodic cash flows, and then also entering the investor's required rate of return. Investors must also be able to offer alternative scenarios, often best case, worst case, and most likely case. Data collection and making proper assumptions can be tricky for investors, since not all data is readily available online.

UNIT 7 EXAM

1. The time value of money is the present
   A. income.
   B. worth of future income.
   C. worth of past income.
   D. worth of past and future income.

2. The present worth of $5 to be received 15 years from today at a discount rate of 10% is
   A. $0.24.
   B. $1.20.
   C. $4.18.
   D. $2.40.

3. Income and expenses are netted against each other to arrive at
   A. net income.
   B. net present value.
   C. net future value.
   D. net expenses.

UNIT 8

Discounted and Nondiscounted Investment Criteria

LEARNING OBJECTIVES

When you have completed this unit, you will be able to accomplish the following.

- Perform financial analyses using a variety of commonly employed analytical tools.

KEY TERMS

- Annual Property Operating Data (APOD)
- capitalization of income
- capitalization rate
- cash on cash
- gross rent multiplier (GRM)
- income
- internal rate of return (IRR)
- net operating income (NOI)
- present value (PV)
- pro forma NOI
- recasting the financials
- revenue
- trailing 12

INTRODUCTION

Financial analysis of real estate investments intimidates many people, and yet it is both the easiest thing about investing and the most important. There are three components to financial analysis in this area. They are *gathering information, making assumptions about things to happen in the future*, and *performing some simple arithmetic*. For most of the arithmetic, one needs only the four-function (add, subtract, multiply, and divide) calculator app that is native to virtually all cell phones. Very few calculations are faster and easier with financial calculators, financial apps, or an Excel spreadsheet. The most common financial calculator is the Hewlett Packard HP 10bii, generally called the "Ten B 2." This unit will provide examples of solving problems using Excel and the 10bii and apps based on the 10bii. It is recommended that students download the app to follow along with the examples, then solve some of the unit question problems.

For purposes of this unit, in particular, it is important to remember the difference between revenue and income. **Revenue** means receipts only without any deduction for expenses. **Income** is what is left after one subtracts expenses from revenue. Cash flow means cash in and/or cash out. Borrowed money, depreciation deductions, and other noncash items are irrelevant to tools that evaluate cash flows.

Investment criteria and analytical tools fall into two major categories: discounted and nondiscounted. The former takes into consideration the time value of money. The latter does not. Nondiscounted criteria are usually fairly easy to calculate and typically examine only one year of revenue and expenses.

GROSS RENT MULTIPLIER (GRM)

The easiest analytical tool, and the one used by most unsophisticated investors, is called the **gross rent multiplier**. It is nondiscounted. It is a common tool for investors in single-family homes on up to four-plexes, and sometimes for small retail space, but rarely for any other properties. In some markets, one starts with the expected monthly rent of a property at 100% occupancy without any reductions for expenses. In other markets, one starts with the expected annual rent of a property at 100% occupancy, without any reductions for expenses. It is a matter of local custom only.

The investor then multiplies that figure by a number in common use in that area. For example, investors in community A might use monthly rent and a GRM of 100. If the monthly rent is expected to be $1,200, then the investor will multiply that to reach $120,000. That investor will make buying and selling decisions based on a perceived property value of $120,000. Investors in community B might use annual rent and a GRM of 8. For this same property, annual rent will be $14,400, which, if multiplied by 8, yields $115,200. That investor will make buying and selling decisions based on a perceived value of $115,200.

The GRM has the advantage of being very easy. The drawback is that it does not take into account differing expenses for different properties. The following table illustrates two different properties under consideration for acquisition. The GRM approach would seem to indicate the properties are equal from an investment standpoint. When examining the profitability of each one, however, it is obvious that one of them is the far better investment.

Figure 8.1: Comparing Profitability

	A: One-story brick home built in 1998 and sited on a ¼ acre lot	B: Two-story Victorian built in 1899 and sited on a 1 acre lot
Gross monthly rent	1,500	1,500
Gross rent multiplier	120	120
Indicated value	180,000	180,000
Annual gross rents	18,000	18,000
Annual property taxes	4,000	3,500
Annual insurance	2,200	4,700
Annual repairs and maintenance	1,000	5,100
Annual yard care	600	1,800
Annual property mgmt. fee	1,800	1,800
Annual legal & accounting	500	500
Net annual income	7,900	600

Based on only the information provided so far, any investor would prefer the property that generates $7,900 of cash flow over the one that provides only $600. Despite that, the GRM model predicts each property is worth exactly the same as the other. Another model, called the **capitalization of income** *approach*, is slightly more sophisticated because it also considers property expenses, not just the gross rents.

PAYBACK PERIOD

Another easy nondiscounted tool is the calculated payback period. Someone who invests $30,000 cash as a down payment for a rental house, and receives $6,000 a year in cash flows, has a five-year payback period. It does not take into account the time value of money and does not recognize that receiving $30,000 over the course of five years is worth less than the $30,000 spent for acquisition.

ROI

The cash-on-cash return on investment (ROI) analysis, also often called *CoC*, is used to decide whether a particular investment amount that will yield predictable returns is worth making. Depending on the size of the ROI, the amount of risk, and the uncertainty regarding viability of predictions, is the indicated return worth making the investment?

When establishing an ROI, the only absolute analysis is a triple-net lease with an AAA-rated corporation for a specified period. Here, the rental **income** would truly be a net amount because the tenant-corporation is paying all of the property's operating expenses, taxes, and maintenance. Because the tenant is so highly rated, the rental payment is a guaranteed income—all things being equal. Under these circumstances, the ROI can be ascertained with a high degree of certainty, with little left to guesswork.

The ROI analysis of other investments includes many educated guesses. The questions that permeate such analyses include, among others, "Will the tenant remain in business for the term of the lease?" "Will operating expenses rise?" "Will the tenant exercise the renewal option?" "Does the operating statement reflect accurate data on which an informed decision can be made?"

It has been customary to carefully examine the income and expense statement for one year's operation to discern what the cash flows will be. This analysis then becomes the benchmark for future years, with the investor hoping to offset any increase in operating expenses with commensurate increases in rent.

This is where the risk factor enters into the financial analysis. Is it worth buying this property to make a 10% return while being exposed to all of the risks and work the investment demands, should the return be 20%, 30%, or higher to make it worthwhile, or should the investor consider an alternative opportunity?

For example, consider an 18-unit apartment project generating $100,000 gross annual revenue. Total operating expenses, including a vacancy factor, reserves for replacements, property taxes, insurance premiums, utilities, maintenance, and management, are estimated to be 50% of the gross revenue. This leaves $50,000 for debt service and cash flow. The property is offered at $500,000 (a 10% **capitalization rate**) with $200,000 cash down and a loan for the balance for 30 years at 7.5% fixed interest. The mortgage payment will be $25,200 per year principal and interest. The building is booked for $400,000 for 27.5 years straight-line. The ROI analysis appears in Figure 8.2. It requires only addition, subtraction, and division.

Unit 8

Figure 8.2 calculates all the way out to after-tax ROI. Many investors stop at before-tax ROI. It is a matter of preference.

Figure 8.2: Return on an Investment of $200,000

1	$100,000	Gross annual revenue	This number provided in the example
2	– 50,000	50% operating expense ratio	Estimated annual operating expenses
3	50,000	Net operating income	Calculated NOI
4	– 25,200	Annual principal and interest	Reduce by mortgage payments
5	24,800	Net cash flow	Calculated annual cash flow
6	+ 3,000	Principal add-back	Add back principal to calculate tax deductions, which include interest, but not principal
7	27,800	Taxable before depreciation	Calculated taxable income before depreciation
8	– 14,500	Depreciation	Deduct depreciation
9	13,300	Taxable income	Calculated taxable income
10	× 0.32	Investor's tax bracket	Percentage for investor's tax bracket (2018 brackets)
11	4,256	Income tax	Taxes due, reduces cash flow
12	24,800	Net cash flow	Go back to net cash flow before deductions necessary to calculate tax liability, entered above in row 5
13	– 4,256	Income taxes	Subtract tax liability calculated in row 11
14	20,544	10.27% cash-on-cash ROI	$20,544 after-tax cash flow divided by $200,000 cash equity payment at acquisition = –.10272, or 10.27%
15	+ 3,000	Equity growth	Mortgage paydown, obtained from Row 6 as the principal amount of the mortgage payments during the year
16	23,544	11.77% broker's net ROI	Divide $23,544 by $200,000 initial cash investment to reach broker's net ROI of 11.77%
17	+ 10,000	2% market value growth	Estimated increase in value for first year of ownership
18	$33,544	16.77% bottom-line ROI	Add cash flow, plus equity increase due to mortgage payments, plus estimated increase in value for first year of ownership to arrive at $33,544. Divide by $200,000 cash acquisition cost to reach 16.77% bottom-line ROI

- Considering the facts presented in the example, should an investor buy this property? This is not an easy question to answer. It depends on as many variables as there are investors. For example, does the investor want to put $200,000 in this one project, or could two projects be purchased for $100,000 down for each? (Analyze this same investment with $100,000 cash down and observe the cash-on-cash ROI jump to 18.3% from 10.27%.) Other questions might include the following, among others: Is this property located in an area where the rents could be maintained and even improved? Are the improvements in good shape? Is the ROI enough to warrant taking the risk?

MARKET BREAKEVEN

Some investors look solely to market breakeven for their investment decisions. As long as an investment will break even at or near industry standards, such investors assume it is a good property. This is, of course, nondiscounted.

It is important to know when breakeven will be reached for comparable properties. Assuming standard 75% financing at market rates, most local lenders and appraisers will know market breakeven points. Apartments and shopping centers might average 80% occupancy; self-storage, 55% occupancy; and manufactured housing parks, 70% occupancy. By knowing these typical ratios in advance, the investor who calculates her own breakeven analysis will be alerted to potential problems if its numbers are dramatically higher or lower than local averages. When discussing occupancy levels, care should be taken to differentiate between physical occupancy and economic occupancy. Consult the following table to see the difference when evaluating a self-storage facility. Economic occupancy is always the preferred number for financial analysis and the one used by lenders.

Figure 8.3: Physical Occupancy and Economic Occupancy in a Self-Storage Facility

	Gross Rented Space	Gross Monthly Revenue
13 units, 10x20, renting for $240 per month each	2,600 square feet	$3,120
85 units, 10x15, renting for $200 per month each	12,750 square feet	$17,000
72 units, 10x10, renting for $145 per month each	7,200 square feet	$10,440
40 units, 10x5, renting for $90 per month each	2,000 square feet	$3,600
8 units, 5x5, renting for $50 per month each	200 square feet	$400
Totals	24,750 square feet	$34,560
Potential	30,000 gross rentable square feet possible, of which 5,250 feet are currently vacant	$50,000 gross potential rents possible at 100% occupancy
Occupancy rates	82.5% physical occupancy	69.12% economic occupancy

CAPITALIZATION OF INCOME

The *capitalization of income* model takes a snapshot of only one year of operating **revenue** and expenses. It is nondiscounted.

Subtracting expenses from the revenue yields a number called the **net operating income (NOI)**, which is expressed as an annual number. As a background to understanding this tool, assume a person invested $1 million in U.S. Treasuries at 3% per year interest. The investor would earn $30,000 in the first year. If we knew only that the investor spent $1 million and earned $30,000, we could calculate the interest rate: $30,000 / $1,000,000 = 0.03, which is the same as 3%. If, instead, we knew the investor could invest money at 3% and wished to earn $30,000, we can calculate how much money should be invested to earn that sum: $30,000 / 0.03 = $1,000,000. If the investor wants to earn $30,000 in its first year by purchasing Treasuries, and she knows that Treasuries are currently paying 3%, then the arithmetic says $1,000,000 of Treasuries must be purchased to meet investment goals. The capitalization of income analysis is not any more difficult than this example. In fact, it is exactly the same as the example just provided.

To illustrate the formulas using annual numbers:

investment × interest rate = interest earned	$1MM × 0.03 = $30,000
interest earned / investment = interest rate	$30,000 / $1MM = 0.03
interest earned / interest rate = amount to invest	$30,000 / 0.03 = $1MM

The real estate investor looks to property to earn money rather than CDs or Treasuries. Instead of *interest earned*, the cash flow from a property purchased for cash is called the *NOI*. Instead of *interest rate*, the investor looks at a percentage called the *capitalization rate*, usually shortened to *cap rate*. In a further short-hand, investors who talk about a capitalization rate of 6% usually shorten that to a *6-cap*. Quite simply, the cap rate is the percentage return the investor makes on his investment during one year of ownership. The model assumes the investor pays all cash for the property, even though that is usually not the case in the real world. New investors have trouble understanding why the model assumes a cash purchase price and why it looks at only one year of NOI. The answer is, financing terms should have no bearing on the inherent value of a property, and the one year window is the one used by this particular model. It is a relatively easy tool for evaluating properties and one employed by a large number of investors. There are other tools for making decisions based on several years or cash flows, or returns on cash invested, and other criteria.

Interest rates on CDs are usually very similar among competing banks. That is because all FDIC-insured CDs have exactly the same risk—none—and exactly the same number of management headaches—none. When the CDs mature, they will be worth exactly the same amount as on the first day of investment. There is nothing to differentiate any CD from any other CD, so they are equally attractive to all investors. That is why they all pay the same interest rate, with very small variations among banks.

Real estate comes with a very wide range of risk, management headaches, and resale profits. The possibility of large resale profits is part of a financial analysis model that will be examined later called the *discounted cash flow model*. The capitalization of income model takes into account only risk and management headaches. An investor who desired no risk and no management headaches would invest in Treasuries. As risk and management increase, the investor will want to earn more than the 3% of our example. How much more than 3% will depend on the amount of risk, the number of headaches, and marketplace pressure.

Assume an investor wants to earn a first-year 9% return, or cap rate, for a moderately risky property that will consume 10 hours a week of time. There is nothing magic about the 9% figure; it is just that investor's personal requirement under the circumstances. The investor is considering a small office building with an NOI of $30,000. If $30,000 has to represent a 9% return on the investor's money for the first year, then we divide $30,000 by 0.09 to arrive at $333,333. If the investor spends no more than $333,333, then he will earn at least 9% on its money. If the investor spends more, say $400,000, then the $400,000 investment will still earn only $30,000. When we divide the $30,000 earnings by the $400,000 investment, that results in 7.5%. If the investor pays $400,000 for the property, it will earn only 7.5% on its money for the first year. The cap rate is 7.5. As the cap rate goes down, the value of the property goes up. As the purchase price goes up, the cap rate goes down. That is because the investor spends more money to acquire the same annual earnings.

A trick to remember the relationship between cap rates and value is to imagine deciding among virtually identical houses with deferred maintenance issues. As the number of problems goes down, the value goes up. As the number of problems goes up, the value goes down. Cap rate goes down, value goes up. Cap rate goes up, value goes down.

The following is a table that illustrates the impact of cap rates on the valuation of a property with an NOI of $68,000.

Cap rate	6.0	6.5	7.0	7.5	8.0
Indicated value	$1,133,333	$1,046,154	$971,429	$906,667	$850,000

Evaluating a property using the capitalization of income approach depends entirely on correctly determining the NOI and choosing the correct capitalization rate. Capitalization rates change as market conditions change over time, by property type, and by part of town. Appraisers and lenders generally know market cap rates for different types of properties in the area. NOIs are simply a matter of arithmetic. Examine the following table in which an investor determines how much to spend for a property and what it will probably be worth after a few modest improvements. With the improvements, the investor can increase the rent, attract a less risky caliber of tenant, and enjoy fewer headaches. The decreased risk and fewer headaches translate into a lower cap rate. Remember, as the risk and headaches decrease, an investor is willing to spend more to buy a property. That can be expressed as the cap rate decreasing.

Figure 8.4: Evaluating Worth After Minor Repairs

	123 Elm	123 Elm after minor repairs and cosmetic improvements, slightly increased rent, and shopping for better insurance rates and management fees
Gross annual rents	$18,000	$18,600
Operating expenses	$7,200	$6,200
Net operating income	$10,800	$12,400
Cap rate	9%	8%
Indicated value	$120,000	$155,000

What does the previous table indicate?

- If 9% is the market cap rate for comparable properties, the investor should spend no more than $120,000 to purchase 123 Elm Street.
- If bought for $120,000, the investor might be able to spend as little as $5,000 in repairs and improvements, and thereby increase the value by $35,000 to $155,000. This property might be a good flip opportunity.
- If there is price competition among investors, one who knows how to do this financial analysis should be willing to spend as much as an extra $30,000 over the current indicated value because the $150,000 acquisition cost plus $5,000 worth of repairs and improvements would equal the $155,000 indicated FV.

The advantage of the capitalization of income method is that it is used by a majority of investors and lenders who deal in properties with values between approximately $200,000 and $3 million. As such, it is a type of common language among them. Higher-priced properties are often evaluated on an IRR, which will be discussed later. When a marketing piece for an investment says that the asking price is "$750,000 on a 6 cap," then everybody understands the asking price was determined by taking the NOI and dividing by 6% to arrive at $750,000. If an investor buys only properties based on an 8 cap, this property will seem to be outside its investment criteria. Based on the marketing information, this property must have an NOI of $45,000 ($750,000 × 0.06 = $45,000.) That NOI will support only a $562,500 purchase price by an investor who wants an 8 cap. If the investor obtains more information and recasts the financials, she might discover that the true NOI is $64,800. That NOI, divided by 0.08, equals $806,250. Now the $750,000 asking price is a bargain for that particular investor's personal requirements.

A useful tool for calculating operating expenses is the **Annual Property Operating Data (APOD)** form. Many versions exist on the internet in both generic and property-specific formats. The following sample is for an apartment complex.

Figure 8.5: Annual Property Operating Data (APOD) Form

5-Year Annual Property Operating Data

Date:

Prepared by:

Property:

	Year 1	Year 2	Year 3	Year 4	Year 5
INCOME					
Gross Scheduled Rent Income	219,600	224,190	229,868	237,487	246,103
Other Income	0	0	0	0	0
TOTAL GROSS INCOME	219,600	224,190	229,868	237,487	246,103
VACANCY & CREDIT ALLOWANCE	8,784	8,968	9,195	9,499	9,844
GROSS OPERATING INCOME	210,816	215,222	220,673	227,988	236,259
EXPENSES					
Accounting	1,400	1,442	1,485	1,530	1,576
Advertising	2,000	2,060	2,122	2,185	2,251
Insurance (fire and liability)	4,750	4,940	5,138	5,343	5,557
Janitorial Service	0	0	0	0	0
Lawn/Snow	0	0	0	0	0
Legal	0	0		0	0
Licenses	0	0	0	0	0
Miscellaneous	0	0	0	0	0
Property Management	15,400	15,066	15,447	15,959	16,538
Repairs and Maintenance	8,500	8,840	9,194	9,561	9,944
Resident Superintendent	0	0	0	0	0
Supplies	600	618	637	656	675
Taxes					
Real Estate	13,000	13,650	14,333	15,049	15,802
Personal Property	0	0	0	0	0

Figure 8.5: Annual Property Operating Data (APOD) Form (continued)

5-Year Annual Property Operating Data					
Payroll	0	0	0	0	0
Other	0	0	0	0	0
Trash Removal	2,400	2,472	2,546	2,623	2,701
Utilities					
Electricity	1,400	1,442	1,485	1,530	1,576
Fuel Oil	0	0	0	0	0
Gas	0	0	0	0	0
Sewer and Water	1,600	1,648	1,697	1,748	1,801
Telephone	0	0	0	0	0
Other	0	0	0	0	0
TOTAL EXPENSES	51,050	52,178	54,084	56,184	58,421
NET OPERATING INCOME	159,766	163,044	166,589	171,804	177,838

Often, the investor must evaluate past (historic) operating expenses on a property under consideration. This should be done with great care. Many times, the seller will provide the buyer with a profit and loss statement prepared by an accountant. One should remember that the accountant's job is to minimize tax liability. An aggressive accountant will write off some things as expenses that perhaps are more properly characterized as capital expenditures. For example, the line item *repairs* might indicate a figure that works out to $500 per unit. The buyer might be concerned about why this property requires so many repairs and if that condition will continue into the future. After asking questions, the buyer might discover that $400 per unit was to replace all the dishwashers, which is more properly characterized as a capital expenditure. Reasonable repair expenses in the future should be around $100 per month, based on historic information.

The process of carefully inspecting, and perhaps changing, some of the seller's profit and loss numbers is called **recasting the financials**. Some common areas that should be investigated for purposes of financial analysis include the following:

- Insurance expenses overstated because the seller's family health insurance, auto insurance, and perhaps life insurance has been included. Sometimes family members are carried on the payroll even though they have no responsibilities. These things have nothing to do with operating expenses of the property.
- Capital expenditures, such as appliance replacement, major roof repair, parking lot resurfacing, et cetera, listed as expenses, which is inappropriate.
- Revenue overstated because credit and collection losses are understated. This can be discovered by reviewing the balance sheet, and not just the profit and loss. If the buyer has $10,000 of rental income for the prior month, according to what tenants owe, but has collected only $6,000, then there should be an item on the balance sheet called *rent receivables* with a balance of $4,000. Large numbers in the rent receivables field of the balance sheet is a red flag regarding collection problems.
- Sometimes, owners will list gross scheduled rents as revenue, but enter rent concessions, such as discounts, as a marketing expense. A tenant could be in a $1,200 per month apartment, but paying only $1,000, with the $200 discount entered as a marketing

expense. The net income works out the same, but an investor who sees $14,400 a month of rental revenue for 12 apartments, and $2,400 per month in marketing expenses, might think to himself, "I will reduce marketing to $200 per month for my period of ownership, thereby improving the bottom line." That assumption would be incorrect. Some owners report revenue and expenses on an accrual basis and others on a cash basis. The investor must determine which method is being used. Accrual basis owners take money into income as it is earned, although it might not be collected until later. They also write off expenses as incurred, even though checks might be cut later. Cash basis owners enter revenue when it is received and expenses when they are paid.

A property with overstated expenses seems to be making a smaller profit than similar properties. The investor who takes financial information at face value might miss an excellent investment opportunity if she declined to purchase that property. A property with overstated revenues seems to be more profitable than it really is. The investor who takes those numbers at face value, and who buys the property, might be making a tragic mistake. One should always independently verify expenses and check totals against market-based estimates or averages.

Commercial lenders often take investor-provided financial information and then recast it themselves to fit within the fields of their computer-based underwriting models. Conversations with such local lenders about commonly recharacterized or disregarded revenues and expenses will assist with the investor's education. In addition, it will provide important insights into the thought processes of various lenders so that the investor can begin to develop profiles for which lenders might be appropriate for which projects. Further, being able to provide a potential lender with property information in the same format as the underwriting model virtually eliminates data entry or recharacterization mistakes that could make the difference between loan approval and denial.

Sales and marketing expenses

The rental property financial analysis model that relies on capitalization of income does not usually account for advertising, marketing, or leasing commissions. According to the CCIM Institute, which is the predominant association for commercial real estate brokers, such items are not operating expenses, but are considered sales expenses. Not all owners and brokers use the CCIM methodology, however, so this information must also be identified. An investor using the CCIM model must separately identify and place a dollar value on past and future sales expenses because these will decrease cash flow.

Manipulation of NOI

Aside from recasting the financials, there is another common manipulation of NOI that will yield differing values using the same cap rate. When asking the question, "What 12-month period does the NOI cover?" the possible answers include the following:

- *Calendar year NOI,* meaning January–December of the last calendar year
- *Trailing 12 NOI,* meaning the immediately preceding 12 full months
- *Pro forma NOI,* meaning a 12 month period in the immediate future
- *Stabilized occupancy pro forma NOI,* meaning 12 months after lease-up stabilizes

The most common NOI is for the prior calendar year because one usually has accounting financials for that time period. If the evaluation of price is being made in August 2018, the NOI for 2017 may no longer be relevant. Income might have increased or decreased significantly. Expenses might have also increased or decreased. The investor who receives last calendar year financials should also ask for the monthly raw data since the close of the last calendar year to see if there are any positive or negative trends. If an accountant has been involved in the preparation of financial reports, then the investor would ask to see the detailed trial balance report for the relevant time period. If there was no accountant, then the investor might have to rely on a check register and tenant rent payment history to prepare his own detailed financial information.

Trailing 12 NOI is probably the most useful, but generally not available except from owners of large projects. Those owners will most likely insist upon monthly P&L and balance sheet information. Smaller investors are prone to look at financial data only once a year when it is time to write a check to the IRS.

Pro forma NOI is an estimated net operating income for some point in the future. Sometimes it is the 12 months immediately after the purchaser buys the property and sometimes the next calendar year. Purchasers balk at pricing based on pro forma NOI, saying, "I am buying the property you have today, at the value today, not what it will be worth after I buy it and increase the NOI through my own efforts." Sellers will say, "I am not selling yesterday's NOI. The value of this property is the value in your hands, which is tomorrow's NOI." Both are correct, depending on circumstances. If the NOI will increase because of the buyer's better management skills and capital investments, then the seller should not be paid a price based on that increased value. If the NOI will increase merely because of average and typical rental increases, then the buyer is, in fact, buying future revenues, not past revenues, and should make her buying decision based on future revenues.

Stabilized occupancy pro forma is used to evaluate a price for property that will be developed or that is currently in lease-up. The true value of the property cannot be based on current revenues and expenses because those will change dramatically every month. Instead, the investor (and perhaps its lender) will project a date in the future when the property is expected to have reached stabilized occupancy of a predetermined percentage. The investor will then calculate an estimated value as of that date and subtract the cash shortfalls that will be incurred in the meantime. For example:

NOI at stabilized occupancy in seven months:	$62,300
Cap rate	7.5%
Indicated future value	$830,667
Negative cash flow until stabilized	($48,600)
Current indicated value	$782,067

In other words, after paying $782,067 to buy the property, and then injecting another $48,600 to cover temporary negative cash flow during lease-up, the investor will have a total of $830,667 in the property when it reaches stabilized occupancy. According to the investor's best estimates at the time of purchase, it will also be the value of the property at that time.

The weakness of the capitalization of income tool is that it depends entirely on a snapshot of only one year of ownership and considers only operating expenses, but not capital expenses. For a more sophisticated pricing model, we would use the *discounted cash flow model.*

Discounted cash flows (DCF)

A more sophisticated approach to estimating value of an investment is the **discounted cash flow (DCF)** method. It can consider many years of ownership income, plus fluctuations caused by capital expenditures, partial sales (such as selling off surplus land in an office development), and property resale after a specified period. Included in this approach is the recognition that income fluctuates from time to time and that properties are usually sold or traded at an appropriate time. Even more important, this method recognizes that monies to be received in the future are discounted to their PV by a rate that reflects an investor's required return on the investment. Essentially, then, the DCF analysis is an application of the principle of the PV of future income. In economics and finance, this future stream of cash is called an *annuity*. A series of straight rental payments over the lease term creates an annuity for a property owner-investor. The **present value** of this annuity is calculated by using the PV functions in Excel, or the 10bii.

FOR EXAMPLE

Assume a regular net annual cash flow of $5,000 under a 15-year lease with a projected future net sales price for the property of $150,000 at the expiration of the lease, and an investor-required 12% annual return rate.

Solving for the PV requires two different calculations. One is for the PV of the periodic income stream, and the second is for the PV of the $150,000 to be received in 15 years.

In Excel, use the PV formula to create the entry box shown here. One can enter numbers or field addresses. Solving for PV gives $34,054. This is the PV of the rental income stream.

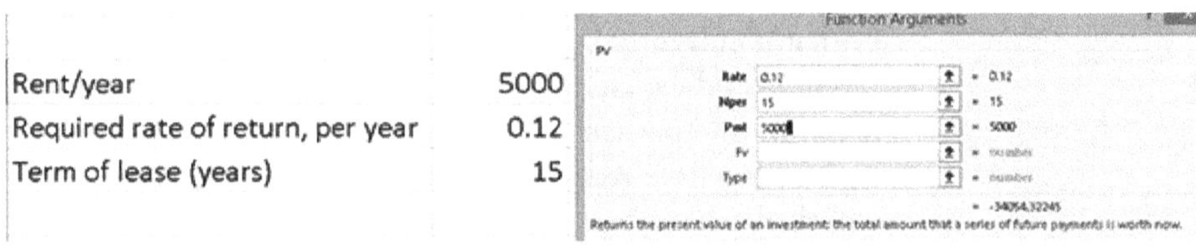

Rent/year	5000
Required rate of return, per year	0.12
Term of lease (years)	15

Next, solve for the PV of the $150,000 reversion amount due in 15 years. We know the rate (12% per year), the number of periods (15 years), and the FV of a single payment ($150,000). We do not use the PMT field because that is reserved for regular periodic payments. Because the $150,000 is a one-time payment, we use the FV field.

Reversion Amount	150000
Required rate of return, per year	0.12
Years until paid	15

Solving for PV yields $27,404. Adding together the PV of the rental income stream and the PV of the reversion results in $61,459.

In other words, an owner can invest approximately $60,000 in cash and earn 12% annually on this money if the $5,000 net annual cash flow remains constant for 15 years and the property is sold for $150,000 net cash at the expiration of the lease term.

Although rents can be fixed at a constant annual amount for the term of a net lease, the basic weakness in this analysis is trying to estimate the value of the property at a point in the future. Most investors use a capitalization rate for this purpose, as discussed earlier.

The PV analysis can also be employed to measure the value of a series of irregular cash flows developed by a stepped-up, or graduated, lease.

FOR EXAMPLE

Assume a 15-year lease with $4,000 net annual cash flows for the first five-year period, $5,000 for each of the next five years, and $6,000 annually for the final five-year period. Again, assume that the property will be sold for $150,000 net cash at the end of the lease term. The present worth of this investment is $59,014 at a 12% return rate, derived as in the previous example.

In Excel, we can find the PV of each of the years' cash flows and then add them together, or we can list each year's cash flow in a column—with the sales price (reversion) and the final year's net rent proceeds added together in one field—and then solve for the NPV of the entire column. Technically, we are solving for PV, not *net* present value, but the formula in Excel that solves for a series of irregular cash flows is the NPV formula.

The field entries and the formula box for NPV appear next:

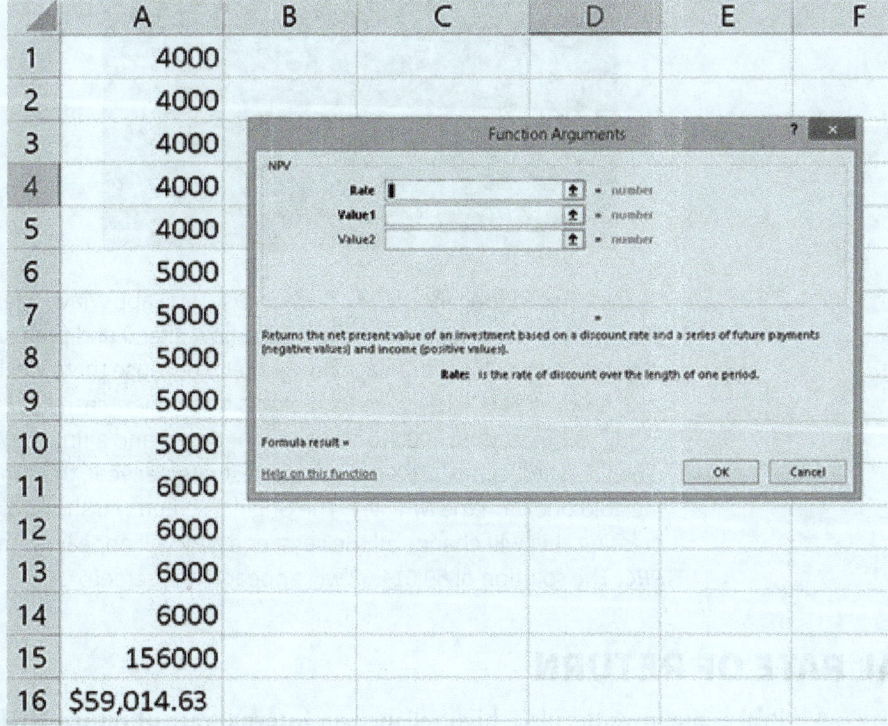

	A	B	C	D	E	F
1	4000					
2	4000					
3	4000					
4	4000					
5	4000					
6	5000					
7	5000					
8	5000					
9	5000					
10	5000					
11	6000					
12	6000					
13	6000					
14	6000					
15	156000					
16	$59,014.63					

The entry for ***Rate*** is 0.12 for our example because rents are received annually, not monthly, and a rate of 12% per annum return is specified.

In the Value 1 field, enter the range of fields to be included. In the example, it would be A1:A15

Field A16, the one containing the formula, will then solve for the PV of the income stream, $59,014.

Using a 10bii app, we would set up a list of numbers similar to the one used for Excel, except that the initial cash flow will be 0 and then so on through 156,000. Using the ***Cfj*** key, enter each of the cash flows, starting with 0.

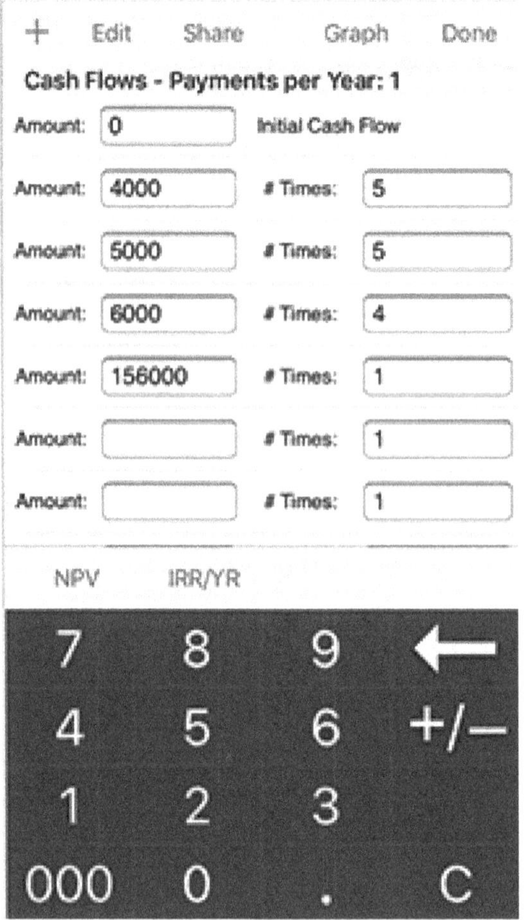

Or, instead of a long list of cash flows, most 10bii apps have a feature that will allow you to enter ***4000*** for the next cash flow after 0 and then ask you the number of times you will have this cash flow. Enter ***5*** because there will be five years of cash flows at $4,000 per year. Repeat this for the next cash flow at 5000, to be used five times, then 6000 to be used four times, and a final payment of 156000. When finished, enter ***12I/YR*** as the interest rate per year, then the ***shift*** key (usually the gold one) and the *NPV* key. The original screen will show this key as PRC, but pressing shift will change all the keys, and *NPV* will appear on the screen instead of *PRC*. The solution of 59,014.63 will appear in the screen.

INTERNAL RATE OF RETURN

Real estate investors place high reliance on **internal rate of return (IRR)** analyses in their decision-making. It is a discounted investment criteria. The IRR is a rate of discount at which the present worth of future cash flows is exactly equal to the initial capital investment. Rather than specifying the discount rate as we did in the prior example, we want to use the initial investment outflow of cash and all the inflows of cash and calculate the discount rate.

An investor, who estimates all future cash flows (including resale), discounts them all at 12% per year to PV, sums the PVs, and then pays exactly that number to acquire the property, has an IRR of 12%. The IRR is no more complicated, conceptually, than that example. It is simply a matter of changing the unknown and solving for the discount rate instead of the PV.

In the real world, we usually know the asking price, and the amount and timing of future cash flows, so the only remaining action is to calculate the correct levelized discount rate that will describe the relationship among those numbers.

The IRR analysis comes in two varieties: levered and unlevered. The names are related to the leverage concept just explained. Levered IRR is based on levered cash flow—or NOI less debt service—with a final cash flow of the property sale proceeds less the mortgage loan payoff. Unlevered IRR assumes no debt service or loan payoff. Comparing levered and unlevered IRR can help illustrate the power of leverage in a particular investment.

Calculating unlevered IRR begins with the amount of cash investment required. The analyst then takes the net returns projected over the term of the project, including net sales proceeds after an appropriate period, and searches for the appropriate interest rate that will discount these returns to zero. This is the project's IRR.

FOR EXAMPLE

Assume a $100,000 cash investment requirement, a $10,000 net annual cash flow for 10 years, and a cash reversion of $100,000 at the end of the lease period when the property is sold. The IRR is 10%.

$10,000 × 6.1446	$61,446	
$100,000 × 0.3855	$38,550	
Total:	$100,000	(rounded)
Investment:	$100,000	
NPV:	0	

If the project's time frame is shortened to five years, the IRR will remain 10%.

$10,000 × 3.7908	$37,900	CWA
$100,000 × 0.6209	$62,090	PWR
Total:	$99,990	(rounded $100,000)
Investment:	$100,000	
NPV:	0	

To solve for IRR in Excel, enter the cash cost to acquire an investment, and then below that, a series of annual cash flows, both positive and negative. If one purchased a vacant building and spent one year rehabbing it, then the first-year cash flow would be negative. After that, hopefully, each year's cash flow would be positive because there would be a tenant in place. For the last year of the period under consideration—usually five years in the future—the cash flow is a combination of the cash flows from rental plus the cash net proceeds at closing from a hypothetical sale of the property. In the field used to calculate the IRR, use the IRR formula, which will create a window as follows.

Unit 8

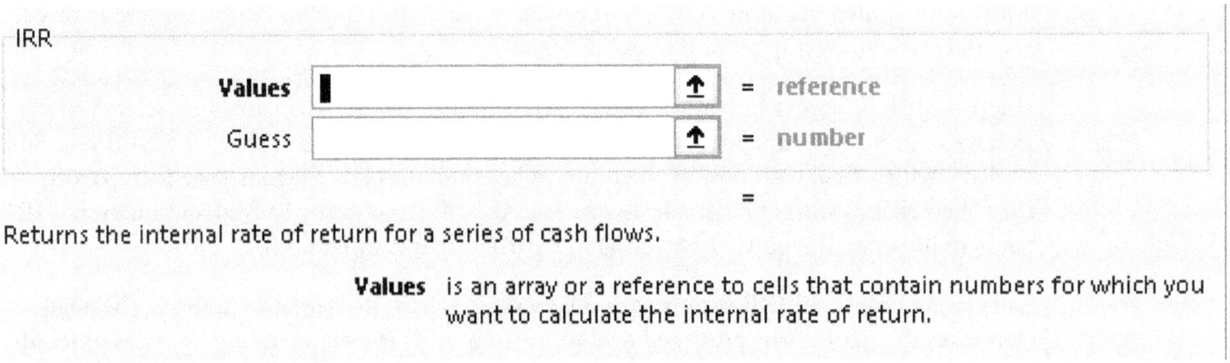

IRR

Values = *reference*

Guess = *number*

=

Returns the internal rate of return for a series of cash flows.

Values is an array or a reference to cells that contain numbers for which you want to calculate the internal rate of return.

The *Values* entry will contain the range of fields that contain the cash flow data, starting with cash for acquisition and ending with final year cash flow from operations plus cash net proceeds at closing. If the data appears in several places in a larger spreadsheet, *Values* would contain the fields with the relevant data, such as B12, C52, D18, and so on.

For the *Guess* entry, we enter a number that is a guess as to the IRR. Pick something reasonable, such as 10. Excel will then go through the iterations of guesses until it arrives at the correct number.

Using the 10bii app, you will enter a series of cash flows and then solve for NPV and for IRR. Usually, you enter the acquisition cash as a negative number and then press the *CFj* button to enter that initial cash flow. Most apps then bring up a screen that allow you to enter subsequent years' cash flows. When finished, press *Done*, then select a desired return such as 10%, and solve for IRR by pressing the gold key so that the IRR/YR function below the CST button (on the second row) becomes the dominant key. Press *IRR/YR* to solve.

The following figure shows two analyses of one investment: IRR and **cash on cash** (CoC) comparing cash flow before taxes to initial cash investment.

Figure 8.6: IRR and CoC comparing cash flow before taxes to initial cash investment

Purchase Price	500,000				
Cash investment	200,000				
	Year 1	Year 2	Year 3	Year 4	Year 5
NET OPERATING INCOME	50,000	52,000	54,040	56,121	58,243
Capitalization rate	10.00%	10.40%	10.81%	11.22%	11.65%
– Debt service, first mortgage	25,172	25,172	25,172	25,172	25,172
CASH FLOW BEFORE TAXES	24,828	26,828	28,828	30,949	30,071
Cash-on-cash return (CFBT/Initial Investment)	12.41%	13.41%	14.43%	15.47%	16.54%
PROJECTED SELLING PRICE, REAL ESTATE	500,000	520,000	540,400	561,200	582,400
Selling price based on capitalization rate of 10.0%					
ORIGINAL BASIS, Purchase Price of real estate (or new basis for property acquired in 1031 exchange)	500,000	500,000	500,000	500,000	500,000
ADJUSTED BASIS AT SALE	500,000	500,000	500,000	500,000	500,000
GAIN OR (LOSS) ON SALE, Real estate	0	20,000	40,400	61,200	82,400
PROJECTED RESALE PRICE	500,000	520,000	540,400	561,200	582,400
– First mortgage payoff, EOY	297,234	294,254	291,043	287,582	283,852
BEFORE-TAX SALE PROCEEDS	202,766	225,746	249,357	273,618	298,548
Internal rate of return, before tax	13.80%	18.76%	20.07%	20.51%	20.62%

Although the IRR is quickly reported via various software programs after making the appropriate entries, it is not the final answer to all investment questions. The IRR approach forces guesstimates of future net cash flows (it works best with a fixed net lease with an AAA-rated tenant) and net sales proceeds. It also has built-in value deceptions. For example, three different investments showing the same IRR may not be equal choices for every investor. One investment shows high initial yields, and another, high-end yields; the third is balanced over the project's holding period.

In other words, each investment must be analyzed individually to see how it fits into the overall strategy of a specific investor. Thus, to maximize the use of computational analysis software, the analyst should plug the IRR of the contemplated investment into the client's entire portfolio to see if the overall IRR is affected positively or negatively.

SUMMARY

The data collected in a financial study is used to estimate gross annual cash flows, operating expenses, depreciation allowances, and returns on investment. These mathematical analyses apply the concepts of interest, time value of money, and various measures of profitability, and they complement the information secured in the feasibility study.

Interest is defined as rent paid or received for the use of money. Thus, a deposit in a savings account earns the depositor interest, or rent. Similarly, an investment (deposit) in an income property will generate a yield (interest), called a *return on the investment*.

Because interest, or yield, is earned on money deposited or invested, those funds not currently available for investments are then worth less than their face amounts. How much less is a function of time and the rate of interest, or yield, desired by the investor. Thus, $100 to be received in one year is worth approximately $90 today at a 10% yield, or discount rate. The $10 difference is the lost earnings or opportunity cost for not having the $100 on deposit or invested for the year.

Many feasibility studies use a traditional approach for estimating returns on investment, while others use the DCF method, based on the concept of the present worth of money. Traditionally, gross annual earnings are reduced by operating costs, debt payments, and depreciation to arrive at a net income figure. Depending on the owner's tax bracket, this net amount is adjusted to develop a bottom-line return on the owner's cash investment. This traditional approach assumes that the income stream will continue into perpetuity.

The DCF method, on the other hand, identifies a finite period for rent flows and assumes that the property will be sold. Thus, the future net cash flows and property sales receipts are discounted at the investor's required yield rate to derive the present worth of the investment. When the discounted amount equals the investment amount, it is said that the property is generating the owner's required IRR.

DISCUSSION TOPICS

1. What happens to the ROI if an investor refinances a positive cash flow property and recaptures all of the original money invested?

UNIT 8 EXAM

1. An investor in the 28% bracket purchases a small multioffice property for $350,000 with a $100,000 cash down payment. The loan for $250,000 is payable at 10% interest for only 10 years. The property generates $50,000 annual gross income. Its operating expense ratio is 30%. The land is booked at $50,000 and the improvements at $300,000 with depreciation using the 39% straight-line rate.

   The annual cash-on-cash return on this investment is
   A. 3.6%.
   B. 10%.
   C. 28%.
   D. 30%.

2. A residential rental property has gross collected rents of $38,000 per month after vacancy and collections. Operating expenses are $13,300 per month. Mortgage money can be borrowed at 4.8% per annum. Comparable properties have sold recently on a 7 cap. Assuming a 20% down payment, what is the indicated value of the property, rounding to the nearest dollar?
   A. $3,752,228
   B. $4,234,286
   C. $4,726,771
   D. $13,588,818

3. Assume the same property and numbers as in the prior question. An investor desires to add a security system to each unit at a one-time cost of $5,700, plus $247 per month in monitoring expenses. The added security will increase revenues by $950 per month. How much would these changes increase the value of the property?
   A. It is unchanged
   B. $114,814
   C. $120,514
   D. $126,214

4. Which investment analysis tool fails to account for operating expenses?
   A. GRM
   B. IRR
   C. Capitalization of NOI
   D. CoC

5. Which investment analysis tool considers multiple years of cash flows?
   A. GRM
   B. IRR
   C. Capitalization of NOI
   D. CoC

6. What are the two most common financial calculation tools?
   A. Excel and Lotus 123
   B. Excel and 10bii
   C. 10bii and TI359
   D. TI359 and four-function calculator

7. Who would prefer to use pro forma NOI for valuation purposes?
   A. IRS
   B. Lenders
   C. Buyers
   D. Sellers

8. Which of the following analytical tools employs the concept of money tomorrow being worth less than money today?
   A. IRR
   B. Leverage
   C. CoC
   D. RFP

9. Which of the following takes risk into account?
   A. Profitability index
   B. Cap rate
   C. NOI
   D. Nominal rate

10. When analyzing the expenses incurred in operating a commercial investment property, which of the following is most often overlooked?
   A. Maintenance
   B. Reserves
   C. Utilities
   D. Management

UNIT 9

Applications to Property Tax

LEARNING OBJECTIVES

When you have completed this unit, you will be able to accomplish the following.

› Describe property tax considerations relevant to real estate investments.

KEY TERMS

ad valorem tax
appropriation
general real estate tax
special assessment
tax levy

INTRODUCTION

All states have some level of **general real estate tax** they collect, called an **ad valorem tax**. Ad valorem is Latin for "according to value." Ad valorem taxes are based on the value of the property being taxed and are specific, involuntary, statutory liens. The rates range from a current low in Hawaii with an effective rate of 0.32% of property value for homeowners, to a current high in New Jersey, at 2.31% of home value. The actual numbers vary over time, but usually Hawaii is the lowest and New Jersey the highest.

Real estate property taxes are a favored source of revenue for local governments because real estate cannot be hidden and is relatively easy to value. Property taxes pay for a wide range of government services and programs, including those of

- states;
- counties;
- cities, towns, boroughs, and villages;
- school districts (local elementary and high schools, publicly funded junior colleges, and community colleges);
- drainage districts;

- hospital districts;
- water districts;
- sanitary districts;
- transportation districts; and
- parks, forest preserves, and recreation districts.

RELEVANCE OF AD VALOREM PROPERTY TAX

Property taxes are typically a large fixed operating expense for commercial real estate owners, but also affect all investors to some degree. This expense impacts cash flows and is also relevant to valuation models that use cash flows as data. It will be necessary to determine current property taxes and anticipate how they might change in the future. Investors who see current or anticipated rapid growth in housing without comparable retail growth must worry about increasing property taxes. Such bedroom communities, as they are called, require large government expenditures for infrastructure such as roads and schools and expenses such as payroll and overhead for police and education. If the money will not come from sales taxes, it must come from increased property taxes.

Differing tax rates in different contiguous jurisdictions can determine the likelihood of nearby competitors, who might find the climate more or less favorable than that in the investor's jurisdiction. In addition, state and local governments often use property tax policies, such as exemptions for certain owners or activities, in order to promote public goals.

EXEMPTIONS FROM TAXATION

Most state laws exempt certain real estate from taxation. Such property must be used for tax-exempt purposes, as defined in the statutes. The most common exempt properties are owned by

- cities;
- various municipal organizations (such as schools, parks, and playgrounds);
- state and federal governments;
- religious and charitable organizations;
- hospitals; and
- educational institutions.

Some state and local governments offer real estate tax reductions through limited exemptions or waivers to promote public policies and goals. Senior citizens might receive complete or partial exemptions as a public policy of assisting seniors and also to eliminate opposition to tax increases for things such as school construction. Seniors, who typically do not have children in school, would be expected to vote against tax increases to fund such projects. If they are tax exempt, they are less likely to vote down such measures.

Other tax exemptions might be limited in scope, such as a limited percentage of tax reduction, or a limited time period for the reductions. Such examples include those for low income housing, industrial development, or retail development. Such exemptions are designed to encourage investment in the designated areas. Investors contemplating acquisition or development should investigate all potential exemptions because a reduction in ad valorem taxes will increase profitability and also affect value. Conversely, if exemptions are already in place, investors should research possible expiration dates that will cause future expenses to increase, sometimes dramatically.

Tax waivers

In addition to other economic incentives, city leaders may offer a new job-creating industry certain tax waivers. Property taxes may be waived for specified periods if a company agrees to purchase a plant instead of leasing it. Inventory taxes may be waived for the term of the lease or longer, depending on circumstances. Local sales taxes, income taxes, and state income taxes, in certain cases, may be waived for prescribed time periods to allow an infant industry an opportunity to mature.

Theoretically, these tax waivers—as well as the plant subsidies—will cost a community little, if any, money because of the incremental taxes that will be generated. The increased tax revenue will emanate from the income taxes of newly employed workers and the services they will use.

All local tax matters must be thoroughly researched and understood by investors in order to build the correct data model on which to calculate their analyses.

ASSESSMENT

Real estate is valued for tax purposes by county or township assessors or appraisers. This official valuation process is called *assessment*. Many local governments will request a completed income and expense form from the commercial property owner to assist with determining the value of the property.

It is extremely important to list every known expense as it relates to the property's operation. The assessors take into consideration these expenses when deciding the amount of property taxes that should be levied. A property's assessed value is generally based on the concept of fair market value, although most jurisdictions use mass appraisal techniques and artificial intelligence instead of individual appraisals. Land values may be assessed separately from buildings or other improvements, and different valuation methods may be used for different types of property. Most taxing authorities periodically reassess the subject property and establish appraisal criteria as part of the valuation process. Property is also likely to be reassessed upon transfer.

Tax assessment begins with the fair market value of property. That can be established through comparable sales or through analytical models that examine fair market rents. If a property changes hands in a distressed sale, the fair market value for tax assessment might be much higher than the purchase price. A landlord burdened with older long-term leases at below market rates will usually not be able to argue that his property is worth less than others. Fair market rents determine fair market value, not actual rents.

Owners of apartments with significant deferred maintenance or functional obsolescence often suffer disincentives to repair or upgrade their units because of ad valorem tax laws. Such increases in value will result in increased property taxes that might not be capable of being passed along to tenants in the form of higher rents. The landlord will have to absorb the higher expense and suffer a loss of profits and a resulting loss in value. From an economic standpoint, the better course might be to make no repairs or improvements. For that reason, communities that examine such market dynamics sometimes offer tax exemptions to remove that disincentive.

Taxable property includes fee ownership of all the rights to real property, as well as separate valuation and taxes for things such as mineral interests, life estates, and long-term leases. Business personal property is often the subject of ad valorem taxes and must be separately declared and assessed by the owner. Condo developments sometimes have units assessed to individual owners and common areas assessed to the condo association. In those jurisdictions, common area taxes are paid out of association dues. Other jurisdictions assign a pro rata share of the common areas to each unit owner. If the common areas are assessed with a value of $250,000 and there are 25 unit owners, then each unit owner will have an additional $10,000 added to their individual unit assessment for purposes of calculating tax liability.

Some states differentiate between current-use fair market value and highest- and best-use fair market value. Twenty acres of raw land on the very edge of population growth might be used as pasture for cattle. Land used for such purposes might be plentiful and sell for $5,000 an acre. Proximity to population centers is not important. If purchased to build a home improvement store and a few fast-food outparcels, it might command a purchase price of $20 per square foot. With 43,560 square feet in an acre, that works out to $871,200 per acre. Should the 20 acres be assessed at a value of $17,424,000 or $100,000? That is the difference between current-use and highest- and best-use valuation.

Jurisdictions that want to preserve family farms and open tracts of land or that have strong lobbyists for large landowners will employ current-use valuations so that property owners are not forced into sales because they cannot afford high taxes. Jurisdictions that want to encourage land sales to developers to increase property and sales tax revenues will choose highest- and best-use valuations. Small farms and owners of fallow land will be forced to sell because they will not be able to afford the property taxes.

For those governments that give tax breaks based on current-use valuations, many also have a tool called *rollback taxes*. Rollback taxes come into play when a use changes from a former current use—such as pasture land—to a highest and best use such as retail development. States have varying clawback periods ranging from one year to five years. When a property changes use, the tax assessor may look back at the allowed period of time, reassess the property at its highest and best use, calculate the taxes, and then add them to the next year's tax bill. If taxes have been $1,000 per year for the land, but will be $25,000 per year for the land after it is decided to use it for retail development, and if the clawback period is five years, then the first year's taxes will be $125,000. The next year's taxes will be $25,000, unless they increase more due to the construction of improvements.

Purchasers of raw land or underutilized land should always investigate the existence and potential impact of rollback taxes on their investment. The same situation might occur if tax incentives expire due to change of use from low-income housing to luxury housing for apartments, or tax incentives to attract new industry expire when that particular player ceases to use the property.

Assessment disputes

A property owner who believes that an error was made in determining the assessed property value may present their objections to a local board of appeal or board of review. In most jurisdictions, the board is called a board of equalization. Its goal is to make sure that all properties are assessed in such a manner that property owners equally bear the tax burden according to their property values, except for exemptions created for specific goals.

Disputes can usually be made only in certain times during the ad valorem tax year. That is to provide some degree of certainty about tax revenues for the year once the dispute period has passed. Owners who miss the window will have to pay taxes based on the current assessed rate and can then file a dispute for the next tax year.

Some owners decline to dispute the valuation. They knowingly make a decision to allow a high tax assessment and pay the increased tax liability. Usually this occurs with small investors of single-family rental homes or small apartments. Sales of such properties are rarely based on financial analysis. Instead, the buyers rely on instinct, anecdotal evidence regarding recent nearby sales, or the tax assessed value. An owner who successfully disputes a valuation and reduces it by $25,000 in order to save $250 a year in taxes might be shooting himself in the foot when a potential buyer wants to pay only the tax assessed value for the property.

TAX RATES

The process of arriving at a real estate tax rate begins with the adoption of a budget by each taxing district. Each budget covers the financial requirements of the taxing body for the coming fiscal year. The fiscal year may be the January through December calendar year or some other 12-month period designated by statute. The budget must include an estimate of all expenditures for the year.

The next step is **appropriation**, which means that a taxing body authorizes the expenditure of funds and provides for the sources of the funding. Appropriation generally involves the adoption of an ordinance or the passage of a law that states the specific terms of the proposed taxation. Some states require voter approval of any real property tax increase.

After appropriation or approval by voters, the amount to be raised from the general real estate tax is imposed on property owners through a *tax levy*. A **tax levy** is the formal action taken to impose the tax, usually by a vote of the taxing district's governing body.

The tax rate for each taxing body is determined by state law or computed separately. Unless the tax rate has already been determined by state law, the total amount needed for the coming fiscal year is divided by the total assessments of all real estate located within the taxing body's jurisdiction.

The actual tax rate may vary depending on the classification of the property according to the use of the property. Classifications typically include commercial/industrial, multiple dwelling, residential, agricultural, and business.

Some states offer discounts and monthly payment plans to encourage prompt payment of real property taxes. Penalties, typically in the form of monthly interest charges on overdue taxes, are added to all taxes that are not paid when due.

SPECIAL ASSESSMENTS

A **special assessment** is a tax charged on real estate to fund public improvements to the property, and it creates a lien for the amount of the assessment on the property. Property owners in the improvement area must pay for the improvements because their properties benefit directly from them. For example, the construction of paved streets, curbs, gutters, sidewalks, storm sewers, or street lighting increases the value of properties that benefit from them. The additional tax paid by the property owners of those properties covers the cost of the improvements. The assessments typically expire after a predetermined number of years. Investors should determine if any assessments have been approved, but not yet charged to properties, to obtain an accurate picture of future expenses.

PROPERTY TAX DEFAULTS

Property taxes result in a lien that has super-priority status in all jurisdictions. The taxing authority may foreclose its lien for unpaid taxes and pre-empt virtually all subsequent liens such as mortgages, judgment creditors, income taxes, and others. If there is an exception to that "virtually," it is because there are sometimes different priorities for local government liens such as improvement assessments or demolition liens. For all other creditors besides local government, lienholders may redeem from the tax sale by paying the taxes and interest plus ancillary costs as allowed by local law, but they may not foreclose their lien and eliminate the tax lien or tax sale. This issue is examined in more detail elsewhere in this material.

Other than possible investment opportunities, property owners should be aware of the super-priority of ad valorem tax liens for two reasons.

1. The sale of property or liens for unpaid ad valorem taxes jeopardizes a mortgage lender's lien position. At best, the lender will have to expend money to redeem from the tax sale. At worst, the lender could lose its lien position entirely and have no collateral. For that reason, nonpayment of property taxes is an important technical default in mortgage instruments. It can result in acceleration of the entire loan balance and foreclosure by the lender, even if all regularly scheduled loan payments have been made in a full and timely manner.
2. Tax sales are often overlooked by small investors who engage in DIY property research. Care should be taken to investigate the tax assessment records when buying property and determine that the taxes have been paid by the current owner. A tax auction might have occurred in the past, with current taxes paid by the auction purchaser, not the property owner. The specific workings of these matters vary by jurisdiction but must be understood and researched by investors.

ASSESSMENT DATA

Investors can find a wealth of information from local tax assessment offices. Many offices maintain parcel maps of all the real property parcels in the jurisdiction, plus information as to current past ownership of each parcel, nature and value of improvements, value of land, existence of exemptions, size of parcel and boundaries, zoning, and other information. Often, this information is available online in the form of Geographic Information System (GIS) maps. Researchers can generally click on subject parcels to obtain information on them and also click on nearby parcels to build a profile of the area.

SUMMARY

It is important for investors to understand property taxes so they can determine current property taxes and anticipate how they might change in the future. Investors may be able to benefit from tax exemptions and waivers. Investors who understand how assessment values are determined will be able to make strategic decisions regarding their properties and the uses of their properties. A **special assessment** is a tax charged on real estate to fund public improvements to the property, and it creates a lien for the amount of the assessment on the property. Property taxes result in a lien that has super-priority status in all jurisdictions.

UNIT 9 EXAM

1. Which of these types of property tax is based on the value of the property being taxed?
   A. General real estate tax
   B. Special assessment
   C. General assessment
   D. Ad value tax

2. County or township appraisers perform official valuations of properties through a process called
   A. tax rating.
   B. tax waivers.
   C. general taxing.
   D. assessment.

3. A tax charged on real estate to fund public improvements in a specified area are called
   A. general real estate taxes.
   B. special assessments.
   C. tax waivers.
   D. tax levy.

UNIT 10

Financing for Real Estate Investments

LEARNING OBJECTIVES

When you have completed this unit, you will be able to accomplish the following.

- List major sources of financing funds.
- Describe types and forms of real estate financing.
- List special provisions for investment financing.
- Describe different types of defaults and foreclosures.

KEY TERMS

acceleration clause
adjustable-rate mortgage (ARM)
assumable
bridge loan
caps
ceiling
commercial mortgage-backed securities (CMBS)
collateral
conduit loans
construction loan
contract for deed
debt coverage ratio
deed of trust
default
defeasance
defeasance option
deficiency judgment
draws
due-on-sale clause
exculpatory clause
forbearance agreement
foreclosure
four major food groups
graduated payment loan
hypothecation
index
interim
loan-to-value (LTV)
junior loan
lien
LIBOR
lock-out clause
mortgage
negative amortization
nonrecourse
note
partially amortized loan
recourse
sale-leaseback-buyback
senior loan
SOFR
split-fee financing
sponsor
subject to
take-out commitment
term loan
variable interest rate
wraparound loan

INTRODUCTION

The importance of finance in real estate investments is axiomatic. The profitability of most transactions is based primarily on financial arrangements designed to enlarge the returns on investments. The appropriate application of leverage may dramatically increase investors' profit margins but, often their risks, as well.

In its simplest form, real estate finance includes the pledge of real property as **collateral** to back up a borrower's promise to repay a loan. If a default occurs, the lender is legally entitled to force the sale of the pledged property to recover the balance owed.

In a broader sense, the financing relationship is described in terms of rights pledged as collateral for a loan. Borrowers hypothecate (pledge) their rights to a lender but continue to own and control the property throughout the term of the loan. In this relationship, the lender holds rights to the property, which can be perfected or enlarged into full legal ownership if the borrower defaults.

Hypothecation is a pledge of property as security for a loan, but with the borrower retaining ownership and control of the property. Car loans are common examples of hypothecation. Pawn shops are the opposite of hypothecations. In real estate, when one hypothecates a property, the borrower may acquire or continue occupancy and control of the real estate pledged as collateral for a loan. Thus, a borrower may live in, rent out, farm, and otherwise continue to use and benefit from property that is itself encumbered by the lien of a real estate loan. In some states, there are technical exceptions to the retention of ownership aspect of hypothecation. In California, Texas, and Wyoming, to name a few, borrowers transfer ownership of the real estate to a trustee, who holds title until the loan is paid in full. Upon full payment, the trustee transfers title back to the borrower. After default, the trustee transfers title to the lender in a nonjudicial foreclosure. Despite such technicalities, the borrower still enjoys what is called *equitable title* and has full control over the property, the right to use it, and the right to derive income from it.

The ability to hypothecate explains one of the basic attractions of real estate as an investment vehicle. An owner may control a large, valuable property with relatively little amounts of money. The process, called *leverage*, is the use of small amounts of money to control valuable properties through financing. It is similar to the physics concept of using a fulcrum and a lever to move very heavy objects with small amounts of force. Thus, with a 10% cash down payment, a purchaser might conceivably invest $10,000 and buy a $100,000 property if a $90,000 loan could be arranged. The interest paid on this loan is deductible as an annual expense against the investment's income.

Leverage gives investors a powerful tool for the potential accumulation of large estates in their lifetimes. In fact, many investors strive to apply leverage to the greatest extent possible to control many highly valued properties with a minimum amount of their own money. This approach also preserves an investor's liquid assets, which can then be used for necessary repairs or capital improvements or to cover short-term cash flow issues if a property is temporarily vacant.

A property purchased for $100,000 cash and later sold for $120,000 shows a 20% return on the investment: $120,000 – $100,000 = $20,000 profit / $100,000 invested = 20%. If this property were purchased using leverage with a $10,000 cash down payment and a mortgage of $90,000, it would show a 200% return on the investment: $20,000 / $10,000 = 200%. If it were purchased with a $20,000 down payment, the return would be 100%. If the investor had been able to buy the property with zero down, the return would be infinite.

Leverage couples high returns with high risks. Because large mortgages require large payments, rental cash flows need to be carefully maintained at levels adequate to meet these obligations. Any slight rental decrease could adversely affect a highly leveraged investor's safety position. In addition, in times of economic downturn, lenders might require that a borrower make large principal reductions if the property value drops below required LTV ratios. That is often difficult, and frequently results in foreclosure of properties that are otherwise able to meet their monthly debt service payments.

SOURCES OF FUNDS

Generally, our economy is based on the power of credit—using other people's money. The philosophy of buy now and pay later is precisely what real estate finance is all about. However, despite the pressures for increased use of credit in this country, the need for savings is also emphasized, because without savings, there is no credit. Most lending is based on savings accumulated through accounts and certificates at banks and savings institutions, premiums paid to life insurance companies, and pension and retirement fund contributions.

The inventory of lenders for real estate finance may be divided into two general categories: institutional and noninstitutional lenders. They are distinguished by the degree of responsibility exercised by the specific lenders in each category.

Institutional lenders

Institutional lenders, charged with demonstrating the highest degree of responsibility to their principals, include commercial banks, savings institutions, and life insurance companies. Displaying a generally conservative attitude toward real estate finance, these lenders, also called *financial intermediaries*, are charged with preserving the quality and quantity of their depositors' and premium payers' money. This responsibility is manifest in the careful screening of each loan applicant's credit and the studious examination of the collateral property's value.

Commercial banks

Originally designed to serve only the commercial checking needs of their customers, these banks now offer a full spectrum of checking and savings accounts, as well as other services, including real estate loans. However, they prefer to participate in relatively short-term loans to maximize their market position.

The short-term real estate mortgages that attract commercial banks include construction loans, home improvement loans, and equity loans. **Construction loans**, also called **interim loans**, are designed to finance real estate development projects during their construction stage. These interim loans are replaced by more permanent types of financing secured on new buildings once construction is completed.

The contractor for a new building requires regular funding during the course of construction to meet the payroll and purchase the materials necessary for the building process. However, because the contractor has no building to pledge as collateral for a loan at the outset of the development process, a lender cannot be expected to issue a check for the full amount of the loan until the collateral is constructed in the manner and quality specified in the plans.

To solve this dilemma, the interim loan is funded through a series of **draws**. Whenever a specified stage of construction has been completed to the lender's satisfaction, a portion of the entire loan is released to the contractor, providing the funds to pay for the services and materials used to date. Each time another stage is completed, another draw is issued, continuing until the building's completion when the final draw is paid.

The borrower makes monthly interest payments based on the amounts and dates of draw requests up through the monthly payment date. It is common for borrowers to have loan approval in a large enough amount so that the monthly payments can also be drawn down from the loan. These amounts also incur interest and result in the compounding of interest for a portion of the real estate loan. When construction is completed to everyone's satisfaction, the interim loan is usually replaced by a permanent long-term mortgage. In this manner, the increasing value of the collateral matches the growing balance of the loan as draws are issued, thereby protecting the lender.

In the event of a default during the construction period, the lender will foreclose on the collateral even though it is unfinished at that point. Because of this risk, some lenders require that borrowers obtain completion bonds from an insurance company as a condition of approving the construction loan. The cost is generally a percentage of the project budget. If the developer walks away from the project, the bond will pay someone else to complete the work. Besides the risk of default during construction, there is an additional risk that the investor will not be able to secure permanent financing, either through a deterioration of the borrower's creditworthiness or the markets in general, or through an inability to appraise the property for a sufficiently high value. To guard against that risk, many construction lenders require a **take-out commitment** from another lender, which contractually agrees to place permanent financing on the property. There is a fee for that, adding another cost that must be paid by the borrower.

Commercial banks are also active in the market for loans under $5 million with maturities of five years or less. Monthly payments are calculated as if the loan were fully amortizing over 20 or 25 years. Most borrowers must provide the bank with audited annual profit and loss statements and balance sheets, allowing the lender to monitor the financial health of the collateral. Some banks require monthly deposits into a special account to build up reserves for repair and replacement. This ensures funds so the collateral does not decline in value due to deferred maintenance issues caused by a lack of money. It also builds up cash collateral that can be seized by the bank—set off—in the event of borrower default.

Home improvement loans are another short-term lending activity commercial banks engage in, and these loans are of particular significance to those investors who purchase rundown properties for repair and resale. Issued to cover the costs of room additions, swimming pool installations, or other remodeling requirements, home improvement loans usually take a second mortgage position behind an existing first mortgage. Some loans available today include an amount specified for rehabilitation as part of the new loan.

Equity loans are a popular product for commercial banks because the interest on consumer loans is no longer deductible for income tax purposes. To replace the diminishing number of consumer loans, banks may promote loans on the equity that borrowers have accumulated in their houses to provide those borrowers with cash for personal spending. Home equity loans provide borrowers the benefit of deductible interest.

Savings institutions

Consisting of mutual savings banks, savings associations, and savings banks, these financial institutions provide many of the long-term loans for single-family, owner-occupied housing. Dealing primarily in conventional loans, these institutions invest most of their assets in real estate financing.

In the past, limitations imposed on savings institutions by federal and state regulating agencies restricted their service areas. Savings institutions invariably developed as neighborhood banks, with their lending capacity limited by the quantity of deposits they attracted. In today's real estate market, any limitations on area have been eliminated by participation in the secondary mortgage market.

The Federal Reserve System has emerged as the governing body for most of these lenders and has established a strong depositors' insurance program under the Federal Deposit Insurance Corporation (FDIC).

Life insurance companies

The nation's life insurance companies invest approximately 7% of their assets in long-term mortgage loans and participate predominantly in the financing of large commercial real estate developments. As of year-end 2017, mortgage loans represented $514 billion out of a total investment portfolio of $7.183 trillion, according to the National Association of Insurance Commissioners. Life companies must be able to depend on regular interest income in predetermined amounts. As a result, they usually insist on fixed interest rates, fixed terms of five, seven, or 10 years, prohibitions against prepayment during the first several years (lock-out clause), and prepayment fees for early payoff after the lock out. Instead of the fee, borrowers may elect the **defeasance option** by purchasing another investment with the same cash flow and offering that as a substitute to the lender.

Life companies look for loans in the **four major food groups**—multifamily, office, retail, and industrial. The minimum loan size is usually $5 million, calculated as no more than 55% to 58% of LTV. At one time, insurance companies typically funded large development projects, but today, their target market is a 1031 exchange with a large down payment. Most insurance companies work only through one or two mortgage brokers in a geographic area. Some, such as MetLife and Protective, still source loans directly from property owners, but they are a rare exception.

Noninstitutional lenders

Noninstitutional lenders act somewhat independently from principal depositors and premium payers. Included in these sources for real estate finance are retirement and pension funds, mortgage brokers and bankers, issuers of improvement district and industrial development bonds, real estate investment and mortgage trusts, and credit unions. These lenders retain a high degree of internal discretion regarding their investment decisions and are not regulated as closely as the institutional lenders.

Retirement and pension funds

Although federal legislation has imposed greater controls over the financing activities of these entities, they still are able to make many independent decisions regarding the kinds of real estate loans they issue. As a result, their autonomy allows them to participate in financing speculative land development projects as well as invest in more stable real estate ventures.

As with the institutional lenders, retirement and pension funds often invest in real estate financing through the services of mortgage brokers and bankers.

Mortgage brokers and mortgage bankers

Acting as representatives for their investors, mortgage brokers and mortgage bankers are important sources of real estate finance. These companies are not primarily responsible to depositors or premium payers but are directly accountable to their investors, who rely on these loan originators and servicers to underwrite new loans carefully and according to established lending standards.

Mortgage brokers differ from mortgage bankers in that they bring together borrower and lender, confirm the loan arrangement, charge the borrower a placement fee for their services, and move on to the next transaction. Mortgage bankers, on the other hand, not only originate loans and secure fees for these activities, they also service these loans by collecting payments, periodically inspecting the collateral, and supervising any necessary foreclosure actions. In effect, a mortgage banker becomes the lender's local representative, responsible for a loan from inception through satisfaction, whereas a mortgage broker primarily acts as a catalyst in the creation of a new loan.

Commercial mortgage-backed securities (CMBS), also called **conduit loans**, account for approximately 10% of commercial real estate debt, according to the National Association of REALTORS®. Such loans are originated through mortgage brokers. They are usually made for 10-year terms, at fixed interest rates, and are fully nonrecourse, meaning with no personal liability by the borrower. Generally speaking, there is a $5 million minimum loan amount, but larger sizes are preferable. Apartments, hotels, office buildings, factories, and shopping malls make up the bulk of CMBS collateral types. Loans are packaged into pools and then transferred to a trust. The trust then sells different tranches of bonds to large and institutional investors. Interest income to the trust is not taxable income because the trust enjoys conduit tax treatment—hence, the popular name *conduit loans*. Instead, income is taxable to bondholders when distributions are made to them.

Real estate bonds

Many communities finance municipal, industrial, and housing developments with the issuance of bonds. These debts are repaid from property taxes, rental receipts, and mortgage payments collected from tenants and owners of the various properties.

Individual subdivision developers may also be eligible to finance the installation of off-site improvements, including sewer and utility lines, street paving, sidewalks, and similar items, by issuing improvement district bonds. In some areas of the country, these bonds are the specific obligation of the property owners within the district. In other areas, these bonds can become general obligation bonds.

Real estate investment and mortgage trusts

REITs and REMTs are sources of funds for real estate finance. Acquiring their money through the sale of beneficial interests to the public, these trusts make loans for construction mortgages as well as permanent long-term mortgages on improved income properties. Acting mainly through the services of mortgage brokers and bankers, the trusts provide the extra flexibility in loan placements often vitally needed for the completion of complex realty projects.

Credit unions

Although credit unions are primarily active in financing personal property acquisitions for their members, their increasing popularity is allowing them to expand their investments to include short-term and long-term real estate loans.

Private loan companies

Private loan companies range in size from the individual entrepreneur and mom-and-pop operations to large national franchise organizations. These companies deal primarily in junior loans, lending second mortgages on homeowners' equities. They make loans from their own funds or from money borrowed from their commercial banks.

Private real estate loan companies usually charge higher interest rates than other lenders in an attempt to offset the risks inherent in their junior lien positions. They also impose relatively high loan placement fees. Many states have developed laws regulating the lending activities of private lenders. Besides requiring these companies to be licensed and post performance bonds, these laws limit the amount of fees that can be charged by these lenders for their services.

Individuals

When other financing is not available, the sellers of property often have to provide the funds necessary to close the transaction. Arrangements for seller financing are usually made directly between the buyer and seller.

Some seller financing involves first mortgages, usually when the property is owned free and clear. More often, it involves junior financing when the seller carries back a portion of the equity as a second mortgage. In this arrangement, an escrow collection service is usually established. The buyer is then required to make regular monthly payments to the escrow, adequate for both senior and junior loans. The escrow company then forwards these payments to the respective lenders, keeping accurate records of each transaction.

Frequently, buyers of single-family homes need to borrow money for the down payment and closing costs from their parents or other family members. In some cases, the donors are requested to cosign the new first mortgage documents to add their financial resources as additional collateral to help the buyers qualify for the new loan.

To balance and manage an investment portfolio more efficiently, real estate investors should be fully acquainted with all the various mortgage loan opportunities in their specific geographic areas, including lender attitudes, loan costs, and availability of funds.

According to the National Association of REALTORS® Commercial Real Estate Lending Trends of 2017 report, top sources of capital were the following:

- Local/community banks 32%
- Regional banks 26%
- Private investors 10%
- National banks ("Big Four") 8%
- Credit unions 6%
- Life insurance companies 3%
- REITs 2%
- CMBS 1%

- Gov't-sponsored enterprises 1%
- International banks 1%
- Public companies 0.5%

LOAN COMMITMENTS

Investors seeking mortgage loan money usually solicit written quotes for various lenders' important underwriting criteria and loan terms. By preparing an RFP, Request for Proposal, the borrower can elicit comparable information from each lender and be in a position to make an apples-to-apples evaluation of financing options.

Cost of money

In its simplest form, *cost of money* means the interest rate charged for the loan. Rates can be fixed for the entire term of the loan, adjust periodically to reflect changes in market conditions, or even adjust daily, as in the case of construction and development financing.

The quoted interest rate might not reveal a complete picture of the cost of borrowing, however. Investors must inquire about additional requirements that will add expenses to the mortgage relationship. Examples include origination fees, appraisals, underwriting fees, legal fees, mortgage insurance, and nonstandard title insurance riders. Such additional charges are a matter of negotiation and can often be capped at a *not to exceed* number. This is usually wise with a legal expenses requirement, which could surpass many tens of thousands of dollars on a large transaction.

To calculate the cost of money, the investor must add the total of all interest payments over the life of the loan, plus any additional charges related to the loan, and then calculate an effective interest rate by amortizing that sum over the life of the loan. In the following example, each lender has a five-year loan, with monthly payments calculated based on a 25-year amortization. Lender 1 has $2,000 in up-front fees and a higher interest rate. Lender 2 has a lower interest rate, $10,500 of fees, and is willing to add the fees to the loan instead of requiring the money up front. Review the following example to see why Lender 1 is a less-expensive loan than Lender 2.

Figure 10.1: Example Comparison of Two Loans With Different Terms

	Lender 1	Lender 2
Nominal interest rate	6.25%	6%
Up-front fees	$2,000	$10,500
Loan amortization	25 years	25 years
Loan balloon	5 years	5 years
Total interest, five years	$104,409	$103,068
Balloon payment	$315,878	$324,205

Debt coverage ratio

There is a basic difference between lending for homeownership and for investment purposes. In lending for home ownership, the income to repay the loan comes from the individual borrower. This is why lenders are concerned with the borrower's credit standing and job history. Commercial lending differs in that the funds to repay the loan come not from the individual borrower, but from the property. It is the NOI of an investment property that is used to repay the loan. This is why lenders are as concerned with the property's operating statement as with the individual borrower.

Commercial property lenders require that the NOI from the property cover the debt service (principal and interest payment) a specified number of times. For example, a lender may require that the NOI cover the debt service at least two times per year. This means that if the debt service is $100,000 per year, then the NOI must be at least $200,000. This ratio of NOI to debt service is called a **debt coverage ratio** *(DCR)* or sometimes a *debt service coverage ratio (DSCR).*

The lender must have a comfort level that, even if vacancies or expenses increase temporarily, the property will still have sufficient cash flow to make the mortgage payments. The very cautious lender in the example, who desires a DCR of 2.0, demands that average monthly NOI be twice as much as the mortgage payment. Said otherwise, the total of the monthly mortgage payment can be no more than half of the annual NOI. Because NOI is relatively fixed and not easily capable of increase, the lender's requirement effectively caps the amount of any loan. Average DCRs are in the range of 1.1% to 1.25%.

FOR EXAMPLE

Assume NOI of $6,000

DCR of 2.0 means annual mortgage payments cannot exceed $3,000

Assume a loan at 6.25% per year on a 30-year amortization

Solve for maximum loan possible with annual payments of $3,000

Excel: Use the PV formula with a monthly interest rate of +0.0625/12, a term of 360 months, and monthly payments of +3000/12 to solve for PV. The answer will be $40,603.06

Financial calculators are similar. This problem requires a PV calculation. We are asking for the PV of a loan at 6.25% interest that, using a 30-year amortization, will result in monthly payments that add up to $3,000 per year.

Using the capitalization of income valuation method used in the prior unit and a relatively modest cap rate of 8%, an NOI of $6,000 should yield a value of $75,000. ($6,000 / 0.08 = $75,000) Most borrowers would expect they could borrow at least 75% of the value of the property, or $56,250. Instead, this particular lender's DCR requirements result in a maximum loan of $40,603.06. In other words, borrowers shopping for money should ask about interest rates, LTV, and DCR requirements.

In reality, it is rare to see a DCR that high. Common DCRs often vary between 1.2 and 1.7. Using a 1.2 DCR means that the NOI must be at least 120% of debt service, also expressed as 1.2 times the debt service, or 20% more than the debt service.

Using the previous example, assume a different lender with all terms the same as the first, except Lender 2 has a DCR requirement of 1.2 for these types of loans. The maximum annual loan payments can be $5,000, calculated by dividing the $6,000 NOI by 1.2 to arrive at $5,000.

Note: When in doubt, if choosing the right calculation, always select a very easy example before using the actual numbers. Fortunately, our problem is also a very easy example. We can immediately see that if the mortgage payments are $5,000, then the NOI is 20% higher (an additional $1,000) to arrive at $6,000.

Solving for the PV of a loan at 6.25% interest, amortized over 30 years, with one year of monthly payments no more than $5,000, we arrive at $67,671.76 as the maximum loan amount. It seems the investor can borrow significantly more money with Lender 2 than with Lender 1. But, when considering the LTV requirements of Lender 2, we still have the same $75,000 value calculated on the NOI and a cap rate of 8%. Using that ratio, the maximum loan size will be $56,250.

After looking over their various underwriting criteria, lenders will make a loan that is no larger than their most conservative requirement.

Figure 10.2: Comparing DCR Requirements

	LTV Ratio	LTV $ Max	DCR	DCR Max $	Loan Approved
Lender 1	75%	$56,250	2.0	$40,603.36	$40,603.36
Lender 2	75%	$56,250	1.2	$67,671.76	$56,250.00

Lenders have different DCRs for different loans. Investors should always ask, "What would be necessary to receive a more generous DCR requirement? If I pledged a CD as additional collateral, would that justify a lower DCR, thereby increasing the amount of money that can be borrowed?" There might be other actions that could result in more favorable terms, such as providing a guarantor or using a bank lockbox for receipt of rent payments.

Loan-to-value ratio (LTV)

Most lenders will not loan more money than the value of the property securing the loan, unless the borrower also pledges additional collateral such as CDs or other property. To ensure that a potential foreclosure and sale of the property will pay off the loan balance, lenders will advance only a certain percentage of the value of the real estate. The balance, or equity, is money the borrower has at risk. It is commonly referred to by the Warren Buffet phrase "skin in the game." Equity makes it harder for the borrower to simply walk away from an investment with cash flow problems because the borrower would lose all of its equity.

Different types of commercial lenders have different average LTV requirements. The most common one is that 75% of the appraised value of the real estate will be the maximum loan size. Some are willing to go as high as 80% LTV. For properties to be constructed or built, the value will be determined as of some future date. Construction loans use value as of the issuance of a certificate of occupancy. Multiunit development loans, such as apartments, self-storage, and shopping centers, typically select a future date at which the parties expect the project to have reached certain occupancy levels. That is because a property with tenants in place will almost always appraise at a higher price than a vacant one. The lender will order its own third-party independent appraisal, but the expense must typically be paid by the borrower, even if the loan fails to fund.

Recourse

The borrower's personal liability for loan default is often an important consideration in loan terms. Many commercial loans are full **recourse**, meaning the lender can foreclose and then pursue the borrower for any balance still due on the loan, or it can decline to foreclose and simply sue the borrower for the full amount. At the other end of the spectrum are the **nonrecourse** loans for which the borrower has no personal liability at all. There is a wide variety of middle grounds, including full recourse for only a limited number of years, limited recourse of an amount not to exceed a certain dollar amount, or a certain percentage of the balance due. These are generally matters of negotiation that depend on the borrower's financial strength, the value of the collateral, and the competitive marketplace among lenders.

Underwriting

Despite making a loan commitment, the fine print at the bottom of the document will usually contain the phrase "subject to underwriting." It means that the lender is willing to honor the terms of the commitment, provided the borrower and the property meet minimum standards designed to manage risk.

Income property loans

When making loans on apartment, commercial, and industrial income properties, lenders must evaluate many variables. In addition to the property's value and the credit characteristics of the borrowers, the lenders must consider the possibility that they may wind up managing the property in the event of a foreclosure.

Following guidelines established by Fannie Mae for purchase of commercial loans, lenders will carefully examine the ability of the income from the property to support the debt service required to amortize the loan. Thus, the amount of the loan will be established as a function of the property's NOI and down payment, and debt ratios will be adjusted accordingly.

To qualify for an income property loan, the following items will require examination:

- Personal financial statements
- Property income statements
- Appraisals and feasibility studies
- The borrower's management track record

Because of the reliance on the borrower's management track record, it creates opportunities for investors with cash to partner with cash-poor, but management-experienced, persons on a project. This arrangement is so common that there is a name for the experienced person, who is called the **sponsor.** Loan underwriting requirements make the sponsor as valuable a member of the team as the person with the liquid assets and borrowing power.

FORMS OF REAL ESTATE FINANCE

When property is pledged as collateral for a loan, three basic forms are used to establish the desired lender-borrower relationship—depending on the area of the country. The basic forms are the note and mortgage, deed of trust, and contract for deed.

Note and mortgage

In this form of finance, the **note** is the actual contract for the repayment of the debt, while the **mortgage** is the pledge of real estate to secure the promise to pay. A note by itself is legal evidence of a debt and stipulates the conditions of the loan and the terms of repayment. A mortgage always needs a note to be legally enforceable, and it describes the collateral and rights being pledged.

This form of financing requires that the borrower-mortgagor pledge the property and all the rights therein to a lender-mortgagee in exchange for a loan. The borrower retains legal fee simple ownership, while the lender secures an equitable interest in the collateral—an interest that can be expanded into a full legal fee simple interest if the borrower defaults. Often, the borrower also executes an assignment of rents agreement. In the event of loan default, this document allows the lender to demand tenant rent payments directly to it and not to the borrower.

Because borrowers retain legal fee simple title, foreclosure requires a court order authorizing the lender to sell the property at auction and apply the proceeds to the debt balance. With one exception, states that use a mortgage instrument as security must all engage in judicial foreclosure. Depending on jurisdiction, the judicial foreclosure process can take up to 18 months to complete. The one exception is Alabama, which uses an instrument called a *mortgage*, but which transfers legal title to the lender, with only equitable rights remaining in the borrower. Those rights include the right to treat the property as if the borrower owned it, in all respects, and the right to reacquire full legal title when the loan is paid in full. Because lenders in Alabama already enjoy technical legal title, foreclosure is by simple sale on the courthouse steps and does not require a court order.

Some states have post-auction redemption rights, allowing the borrower to recover the property upon payment of statutorily prescribed sums of money. This is called the *statutory right of redemption.*

Deed of trust

The note and deed is used to establish a **deed of trust** financing relationship parallel to the note and mortgage, with one exception. With the deed of trust, the borrower-trustor deeds the legal fee simple interest in the collateral to a third-party trustee to hold in trust, subject to the lien of the lender-beneficiary. When the loan is paid in full, the trustee reconveys the property to the trustor. State laws vary regarding the use of the deed of trust. In California, for example, it is not absolutely necessary for a note to accompany the trust deed. In Washington, the trust deed arrangement is worded so that the property vests in the trustee only in the event of a default.

The deed of trust financing arrangement acts to shorten a borrower's redemption period from as long as one year, under a note and mortgage, to as little as 90 days under the trust deed. In the event of a default, the trustee is empowered by the terms of the trust agreement to sell the collateral at public auction after having followed the letter of the law. This procedure includes provisions for adequate notice to all concerned parties.

As with a mortgage, any proceeds from a foreclosure auction sale must first be applied to pay any government property tax liens or special assessments and the costs of the sale. The remaining funds are then distributed first to the senior lender, then to all junior lienors, and finally to the trustor.

The deed of trust is currently being used in the District of Columbia and the following states:

- Alaska
- Arizona
- California
- Colorado
- Georgia

- Idaho
- Mississippi
- Missouri
- Nevada
- North Carolina
- Tennessee
- Texas
- Virginia
- Washington
- West Virginia

Contract for deed

Also called a *land contract*, *bond for deed*, *agreement of sale*, or *contract of sale*, a **contract for deed** is a form of financing used primarily between individual lenders and borrowers, not with banks or savings institutions. A contract for deed is not accompanied by a note but is a single complete agreement, granting physical possession to the buyer-borrower-vendee at the same time that it establishes the financing agreement with the seller-lender-vendor. The *bond for deed* phrase is still used today to describe a seller financing with deferred title transfer, but it is an archaic format that is virtually never used in modern times. In the traditional bond for deed, the seller secured a bond that named the buyer as the beneficiary. If the buyer made all the payments, but the seller failed or refused to convey good title, then the bond would pay a predetermined sum of money to the buyer. It was a method of protecting buyers.

Contracts for deed are usually employed in situations where the seller of a property is helping the buyer complete the purchase by carrying back a loan for a portion of the seller's equity in the property. In such a case, a contract for deed is executed between the buyer and seller for the amount of the seller's equity. The legal fee simple interest remains in the name of the seller, while the buyer secures an equitable title in the property as well as its possession and control. When the terms of the loan contract are met, the seller delivers a deed to the buyer, the recording of which is evidence of the loan's satisfaction.

Some pitfalls of the contract for deed form of financing include

- providing for transfer of title on seller's demise before contract's satisfaction;
- providing for protection of title in case of litigation against seller; and
- determining priority of intervening liens.

Maintaining legal title in the collateral during the term of the loan gives the seller certain foreclosure powers not available in either the mortgage or deed of trust forms. Basically, the buyer's redemption periods are dramatically reduced, sometimes to as little as 30 days. Certain states, fearful that this foreclosure power may be used arbitrarily or capriciously, prohibit or seriously inhibit the use of contracts for deed as a form of financing.

TYPES OF REAL ESTATE FINANCE

The three forms of finance—the note and mortgage, deed of trust, and contract for deed—may be used to serve the particular needs of the principals in a real estate transaction. Generally, the mortgage and trust deed forms are used by institutional lenders and are designed to be in a **senior loan** position, with priority over any and all intervening liens. The contract for deed can also be a senior loan when the seller-vendor owns the property free and clear and carries back such a contract. However, most land contracts are established as junior loans.

A **lien** is a legal claim against real or personal property, whereby the property is made the security for the performance of some act, usually the repayment of a debt. A lien can be either voluntary, such as a mortgage, or involuntary, such as a tax lien.

A mortgage loan becomes a voluntary lien as of the precise time of its recording at the office of the recording official of the county in which the property is located. The property's recorded history will be carefully reviewed before the granting of a new loan, and all prerecorded encumbrances will have to be satisfied. This procedure establishes that the new lender's rights are superior to the rights of any subsequent lienholders. Thus, the legal doctrine of "first in time, first in right" acts to protect a lender's senior lien position.

Senior loans

The institutional lenders described previously—commercial banks, savings institutions, and life insurance companies—are required by their licensing and regulating agencies to practice the highest possible degree of financial responsibility. They are totally prohibited from placing their customers' funds in jeopardy when making investment decisions. Consequently, the real estate financing activities of these lenders are normally limited to senior mortgages and deeds of trust. They usually adopt a conservative approach to lending, including a scrupulous analysis of a borrower's credit and a thorough evaluation of the property to be pledged as collateral.

In the event of a foreclosure, these lenders will seek to recover any funds still unpaid through the sale of the collateral. To exercise their responsibility, these lenders must be in senior lien position against the subject property at all times. The creation of any intervening liens jeopardizes a lender's chances of recovery at a foreclosure sale and constitutes a breach of the loan contract. Generally, senior loans are conventional, insured, or guaranteed loans.

Conventional loans

Although many conventional loans are insured by private mortgage insurance companies, some do not have any insurance or guarantee by a third party. On these uninsured conventional loans, complete reliance is placed on the borrower to meet all obligations when due.

To offset the risk implicit in this arrangement, a conventional lender will not only conscientiously qualify both borrower and property, but it will also require that a borrower have a prescribed amount of personal funds invested in cash in the property. This equity investment provides the lender a safety cushion in the event of a default.

The amount of this equity cushion establishes the **loan-to-value ratios (LTVs)** employed by lenders to determine the amounts of the loans to be made. Historically, lenders required that a borrower pay 50% of a property's value as a cash down payment, and then a loan for the balance would be issued. These equity requirements gradually diminished from 50% to 33% to current requirements of between 20% and 25%, thus allowing a conventional mortgage to be placed at about 80% of a property's value. This equity requirement acts to protect lenders by tying borrowers to their property ownership. A borrower who has invested personal funds of 20% to 25% is less likely to undermine the value of the property or walk away from it. Periodic decreases in the loan balance each month, coupled with a possible rise in the property's value due to inflation and physical improvements, increase an owner's equity from the very first payment. Therefore, a conventional senior first mortgage should be unlikely to go into default. In the recent past, however, many areas in the U.S. suffered substantial drops in value, causing borrowers to choose to walk away from the property (and their loan obligations), leaving lenders to assume massive losses.

Junior loans

Most real estate transactions are finalized when a buyer secures a new senior loan for the major portion of the property's value, with the balance paid as a cash down payment. Sometimes, however, a buyer will require additional financing in the form of a second mortgage or contract for deed to offset the burdens of heavy front-end cash requirements. These **junior loans** are sometimes established between the individual parties to a real estate transaction, with the seller carrying back a portion of the equity in the form of a second mortgage.

Alternative types of finance

The three basic forms of real estate finance—the note and mortgage, trust deed, and contract for deed—are employed as either senior or junior loans. The structures of these instruments are somewhat flexible, and therefore, reasonably adaptable to fit various contingencies. In addition, these instruments can be specially designed to finance unique real estate situations such as the wraparound, the sale-leaseback, and the joint venture.

Wraparound encumbrances

A useful form of junior loan is the **wraparound loan**, also called an *all-inclusive loan*. The unique feature of a wrap is that it creates a new loan that encompasses any existing loan without disturbing the legal priority of the underlying encumbrance. The wraparound loan became very popular in the early 1980s when many property owners had long-term loans at fixed interest rates of 6% or less, but current mortgage rates were 17% or higher. Due to deregulation of the banking and savings and loan industries, those institutions were paying 12% or more on deposits, but earning only 6% on loans, which were then wrapped into the creative partial seller financing arrangement called *the wrap* for short. Lenders began putting due-on-sale clauses into their debt instruments, making the entire principal balance due on a loan if a property were sold. Federal courts upheld the clauses, and wraps became largely a historic footnote in consumer mortgage lending, but still exist in commercial lending, especially with the prevalence of lockout and **defeasance** clauses.

The wrap cannot be used to bypass a due-on-sale clause. If the lender learns about a nonapproved wrap, it can accelerate its loan and demand payment in full. Typically, the wrap can be drawn at a higher rate of interest than the underlying encumbrance.

FOR EXAMPLE

Assume that a property is to be sold for $100,000, with a $10,000 (10%) cash down payment made by the buyer and a $90,000 wraparound mortgage carried back by the seller at 10% interest. The seller's existing mortgage has a $70,000 balance, which is payable at 8.5% interest. Thus, the seller has $20,000 equity in the wrap and will be earning a full 10% on this amount plus a 1.5% override on the first mortgage balance. This results in an effective annual earning rate of 15.25% [$20,000 × 0.10 = $2,000 + ($70,000 × 0.015 = $1,050) = $3,050 / $20,000 = 0.1525, or 15.25%].

Obviously this yield, being as high or higher than that offered by many alternative investments, may go a long way to relieve the reluctance of a seller who must carry back a junior loan to complete a sale of a property.

A wrap can assume any of the three major financing forms—a mortgage, deed of trust, or contract for deed. It can be designed to incorporate any and all of the special clauses to be discussed later in this unit. Because of its relative simplicity, it allows for great flexibility in its design.

Sale-leasebacks

Another useful tool of real estate finance, the sale-leaseback is used primarily in large-project real estate transactions. In this situation, the owners of a property sell it to investors and, simultaneously, lease it back, usually for long periods of time—often from 30 to 40 years. The rents established in the lease are based on a fair and prearranged return of the investment over the lease period. Thus, the investors are purchasing a guaranteed return on their investment while insuring its recovery.

The advantages of this form of finance to the seller-tenant include the immediate use of the cash proceeds from the sale and the opportunity to deduct the entire rental amount as an operational business expense. This deduction is particularly advantageous because the rent is based on the value of the land and the buildings. If the seller were to retain ownership of the property, only depreciation on the buildings would be allowed as a deductible business expense. Thus, the sale-leaseback technique is used most effectively with properties already fully depreciated.

An additional advantage for the seller-tenant in this arrangement is that the obligation for the lease appears on the firm's balance sheet as an indirect liability, whereas a mortgage is considered a direct liability that adversely affects the firm's debt ratio in terms of obtaining future financing.

When the lease includes an option for the tenant to repurchase the property at the end of the lease term, it is called a **sale-leaseback-buyback**. However, care must be taken to establish the buyback price for a fair market value at the time of sale, otherwise the arrangement is considered a long-term installment mortgage, and any income tax benefits that might have been enjoyed during the term of the lease will be disallowed. The buy-back option is an important tool for the tenant because it effectively re-establishes a new depreciable basis when the property is repurchased.

Joint ventures

Also of great value as an investment financing tool for acquiring real estate is the *joint venture*. This technique is a form of equity participation that teams lenders, who advance most or all of a project's funds, with the developer, who contributes time and expertise, as partners and co-owners. Some joint-venture participation arrangements can be expanded to include the landowner and the construction contractor, as well as the financier and the developer.

A variation of this arrangement is **split-fee financing**. Here, the lender purchases the land under the project and leases it to the developer, while, at the same time, financing the improvements to be constructed on this leasehold. The land lease payments are established at an agreed-on base rate plus a percentage of the profits from the building's revenues. Under this arrangement, the lender-investor benefits by receiving a fixed return (interest) on the loan investment, a flexible return on the land investment, and possible residual benefits when the lease expires and clear ownership of the property is acquired. The developer has the advantage of high leverage and a fully depreciable leasehold asset.

Bridge loans

Sometimes an owner will need interim financing during a period of significant cash flow shortage, a period of expansion, or when property #1 has not yet been sold, yet the equity is necessary to invest into property #2. **Bridge loans** bridge the gap between the current borrowing capacity of the investor and the property, and the future borrowing ability of the investor and property. As such, they are always short-term arrangements designed to have very high returns to the lender in return for the high amount of risk assumed. Bridge loans typically carry high interest rates, high up-front fees, and often, a significant share of the profits until the bridge is taken out, including a share of resale profits and/or refinancing proceeds.

SPECIAL PROVISIONS FOR INVESTMENT FINANCING

Creative financing arrangements

The variety of possible loan terms and conditions is virtually inexhaustible, complementing the quality of high personal control usually acquired in real estate investments. Some special financing clauses of particular importance to investors include prepayment arrangements, due-on-sale provisions, assumption privileges, exculpatory clauses, and what are often called creative financing arrangements.

Prepayment clauses

Prepayment provisions in a real estate loan may include the right to pay the debt in full before it is due, to impose penalties for any prepayment, to completely restrict prepayments for some designated time period, or various combinations of these terms.

Prepayment privileges

In the absence of any reference to prepayments in a loan contract, a borrower may satisfy the balance of the debt at any time without restriction or penalty. Some loans include a provision stipulating the total prepayments that may be made in any one year without penalty. Such a clause establishes a partial prepayment privilege.

Prepayment penalties

Normally, a lender will not want a high-interest-rate loan to be repaid prematurely. Hence, controls are established on prepayments of high-yield loans. One form of control is the inclusion of a prepayment penalty clause in the loan terms. This clause imposes a penalty—also called a *defeasance penalty*—on any prepaid sums, thereby compensating a lender for any loss in earnings due to early repayment. These penalties generally range from 3% to 5% of the loan balance. In extreme cases, these percentages could be applied to the original loan amount. Some states have laws restricting such penalties.

Lock-out clauses

Some loans include a clause that prohibits any prepayment for a specified time period, often for as long as 10 years. This stringent form of control, called a **lock-out clause**, is placed on very high-yield loans to preserve a lender's earning position.

Often, combinations of prepayment conditions are incorporated into a single loan. For example, a loan could restrict any prepayment for a certain time period, then allow proportionate prepayments to be made annually, and then finally allow the balance of the loan to be repaid without restriction at the expiration of a specified term. Any deviations from the agreed-on formula would result in the imposition of penalties.

Due-on-sale clauses

Lenders usually include a **due-on-sale clause** in their loan contracts. Also called a *call clause* or *transfer clause*, this provision stipulates that a borrower may not sell, transfer, encumber, assign, convey, or in any way dispose of the collateral property or any part thereof without the express written consent of the lender. The due-on-sale clause goes on to state that if any of the forgoing events should occur without the lender's consent, the loan balance then becomes due in full immediately, with true jeopardy of foreclosure if not so paid.

The due-on-sale clause had its roots in a time of rapidly rising interest rates and the lenders' desire to obtain payoff of older loans, and then reinvestment at higher rates. Today, it is still employed even though interest rates are stable and justified as a measure to protect a lender from default by a subsequent buyer of the property who assumes the original loan. Studies have shown that fewer defaults and foreclosures occur against original borrowers than against second or third owners—a testimony to the credit-underwriting procedures of most lenders.

Thus, in an assumption of an existing loan, the due-on-sale clause subjects the credit of a potential new owner to the rigorous scrutiny of a credit analyzer. If the buyer's credit ability is found to be lacking, some adjustments in the loan provisions will be suggested. If these adjustments are not acceptable to the parties involved, the lender simply calls in the balance of the loan, requiring the parties to seek financing elsewhere.

A lender's imposition of this call power can seriously affect the easy salability of an encumbered property. The legality of due-on-sale clauses was challenged and, after conflicting high court decisions in many states, they were ruled legally enforceable by the U.S. Supreme Court in 1982. However, the case ruled upon, *Fidelity Federal Savings and Loan v. de la Cuesta*, pertained only to federally chartered savings associations and banks. Consequently, Congress passed the Garn–St. Germain Depository Institutions Act, which clearly stated that all due-on-sale clauses are enforceable for all real estate loans.

Assumption vs. subject-to provisions

In the absence of a due-on-sale clause, existing financing is **assumable** by the buyers. A buyer who assumes an existing mortgage agrees to sign the note and accept responsibility for repayment of the balance of the loan. In fact, the purchase of a property and the assumption of the existing loan legally place the buyer in the same liability position as the original makers of the note and mortgage and all intervening owners who had assumed the same loan. In other words, a lender can look to any and all persons who have assumed the loan for repayment and, in the event of a default, hold them all personally liable for complete satisfaction of the balance of the loan.

To avoid the imposition of this personal liability when buying a property with an existing mortgage, and in the absence of a clause prohibiting such an approach, a purchaser may stipulate in the contract that the purchase is being made **subject to** the existing loan balance. This approach effectively eliminates this particular buyer's contingent personal liability in the event of a future default. Only the original borrower and any intervening assumers are liable.

Exculpatory clauses

An effective technique used to minimize a borrower's personal liability is to create a nonrecourse loan with the inclusion of an **exculpatory clause** in the contract. This clause is designed to limit a borrower's personal liability exclusively to the property being pledged as collateral, thus eliminating any possible attachment of other assets in the event of a default. Most exculpatory clauses are included in construction loans but may be added to real estate loans between individuals. They can be fully exculpatory, fully recourse only up to a certain percentage of the balance, or fully recourse until a certain loan anniversary and then nonrecourse after that. These are all matters of negotiation between the borrower and the lender and typically depend on the competitive lending environment. Typically, only loans in excess of $5 million are nonrecourse, due largely to the bargaining strength of the borrower.

Acceleration clauses

Virtually all real estate loans contain an **acceleration clause** that allows the lender to immediately accelerate the loan payment schedule and demand payment in full. It is commonly used when there has been several months of payment default and is legally necessary as a predicate to foreclosure. Otherwise, the lender would be limited to suing for past-due payments, as each one became due and then past due. It is also used in conjunction with the due-on-sale clause. Other acceleration events include loss of a large and important tenant without replacement for some period, the DCR dropping below pre-established requirements for a stated period, decline in value of the property, death of a key member of the management team, or anything else that might cause the lender to deem itself insecure. Thus, any unforeseen event that might jeopardize the borrower's repayment ability, or the value of the collateral, can be used to accelerate the loan.

Alternative financing arrangements

Under most circumstances, a real estate loan is paid in regular monthly payments of principal and interest over a specified time period. This system is called *amortization*. Every payment is a function of the interaction between the loan amount, rate of interest, and time of payments.

Economic conditions causing a lack of money for real estate loans and relatively high interest rates on what money is available stimulate many innovative forms of finance. These alternative financing techniques include variable-payment schedules as well as variable interest rates. They attempt to satisfy both a lender's desire to generate earnings and the borrower's desire to structure affordable payments. The following are some of the more popular forms of creative financing.

Variable-payment schedules

Under a loan contract, payments can be arranged to reflect the specific needs of the parties thereto. For example, some borrowers require lower payments in initial loan periods, while others prefer to pay higher amounts during the early years. In the first instance, persons with limited earnings could enjoy the privilege of lower payments for a few years, whereas in the second instance, higher wage earners might choose to repay their loans earlier in anticipation of retirement.

Most variable-payment schedules are designed as **graduated payment loans**, also called *escalating loans*, with lower early payments and later payments that gradually increase to reflect a borrower's improving economic status.

When a portion of the interest is deferred in addition to the principal, the loan amount owed will increase from payment to payment. This is called **negative amortization**, and unless some provisions are made for the payments to increase to include some principal and interest, the final payment will be higher than the original face amount of the loan. Negative amortization has fallen into disfavor, and as a general rule, should be avoided. It is now illegal for most consumer real estate loans to contain such provisions.

Most loans are designed to amortize the amount owed over a prescribed period. When payments are varied to reflect the needs of the loan participants, both interest and principal can be adjusted. To the extent that the principal portion of the payment is deferred, an interest-only amount can be derived. Under this arrangement, the amount owed remains constant over time, and some provision must be made for this balance to be paid in full as a balloon payment at a specified stop date. This loan is then called a **term loan**. On the other hand, a **partially amortized loan**, where the payments are based on a longer amortization schedule, requires that a balloon payment be made at the earlier agreed-on stop date. Most commercial loans have payments calculated as if the loan fully amortized over 25 or 30 years, but with a balloon in five, seven, or 10 years.

Variable interest rates

Most real estate loans are arranged to be repaid over relatively long periods of time at fixed interest rates. This procedure has proved to be somewhat less than efficient because interest rates fluctuate over time—sometimes quite dramatically.

As a result, a number of lending institutions include **variable interest rate** clauses in their mortgages. Also called an **adjustable-rate mortgage (ARM)**, this technique involves the development of a formula for interest computation based on an acceptable measuring unit called an **index** (such as U.S. Treasury Bill rates), plus a fixed margin rate, as an indication of current interest rates. If the index moves up a point, then the interest rate on the loan will be adjusted upward 1%. Likewise, if the index drops, so will the loan's interest rate. Another common index for commercial loans is **LIBOR** (pronounced "lie-bore"), or the London Interbank Offered Rate. Starting April 9, 2018, LIBOR is being phased out in favor of the newly created Secured Overnight Financing Rate (**SOFR**, pronounced "so-fer"). The SOFR index is based on the interest rates banks charge each other for overnight loans. Examples of quotes for proposed ARMs are "Wall Street Journal Prime plus 1 (meaning 1%)" or "SOFR plus 100 basis points." One hundred basis points is the same thing as 1%.

Obviously, there are faults in this program. Any substantial change in the index could result in chaotic conditions for both the borrower and the lender. To offset the potential problem of drastic changes in interest rates, certain conditions are usually included in the contract to limit the amount of rate variability. For example, in some contracts, the interest change is limited to a maximum of 1% at any one time (**caps**), and then the new rate must remain fixed for at least three years. Others have a **ceiling**, or limitation, on how high the interest rate may be raised over the life of the loan. These types of limitations, or any variation thereof, allows for a smoother transition between payment changes.

A *participation mortgage* allows a lender to participate in the income stream of an income property, as well as secure a share in the growing value of the property being financed. Normally, a lender will reduce the interest rate on a new loan in exchange for the share in the profits. Ownership remains in the borrower's name, but the note recites the partnership agreement.

A *buy-down mortgage* allows the seller, builder, buyer, buyer's parents, or any third party or combination of parties to make a lump-sum payment to the lender at the time a loan is originated. In exchange, the interest rate is lowered, making the payments more affordable.

A *rollover loan* is another effective technique for adjusting payments and interest. Long-term payout schedules are established, but three-year, four-year, or five-year stop dates are included. This forces the borrower to refinance accordingly and allows the lender to adjust interest rates and payment amounts.

Zero-percent financing (ZPF) features loans at no interest. Offered by sellers who agree to carry back these loans to sell their properties, only principal payments are required until the loan amount is satisfied. The IRS imputes an interest rate on these transactions, both to the borrower and the seller, allowing the borrower a commensurate income tax deduction while charging the seller-lender tax on the imputed interest. The interest rate imputed is the current U.S. Treasury Bill rate, adjusted twice a year.

A slight variation on this theme is the *growing equity mortgage (GEM)*, where the borrower increases the principal portion of the payment regularly, reducing the loan term substantially.

The *biweekly mortgage* is an illustration of the GEM. By making half the loan payment every two weeks, the borrower makes one full month's extra payment per year. This entire amount is applied to the principal and acts to reduce the amortization period. Thus, a 30-year loan with this repayment method is reduced to 22 years.

A *lease-purchase-option* is still another form of creative financing. Here, a lease is designed to include the terms and conditions of a purchase option at the expiration of the lease period. Often, portions of the rental payments are credited to the purchase price. If the rental payments are considered option payments, a seller can postpone income tax impacts until the option becomes due. If the option is exercised, the payments are treated as capital gains. If the option is not exercised, the payments are considered ordinary income (*Koch v. Commissioner of IRS*, 67 T. C. 71, (1976)).

DEFAULTS AND FORECLOSURES

The basic responsibilities of the parties to a real estate financial contract are clear-cut. In exchange for money loaned, a borrower is obligated to

- repay the loan according to the conditions stipulated;
- preserve the value of the collateral; and
- protect the priority lien position of the lender.

In the event the borrower breaches any of these obligations, the lender can exercise the power of the acceleration clause and insist that the loan balance, plus accrued interest and costs, be paid immediately and in full.

Defaults

A **default** is the breach of one or more of the conditions or terms of a loan agreement. When a default occurs, the acceleration clause found in all loan contracts is activated, allowing the lender to begin foreclosure proceedings.

Payment delinquencies

The most common default is the nonpayment of principal and interest when due. Although most loan payments are due *on or before* a specified date, most lenders respect a reasonable grace period—usually up to 10 days. Delinquencies of longer than 10 days usually result in a reminder phone call or letter, and a continuing lack of response will generally trigger the foreclosure process.

Property tax delinquency

The nonpayment of property taxes is a technical default under most real estate loans. Because the collection of property taxes represents the life's blood of state and local government, statutes are enacted to preserve that income. Virtually all states have specific laws stating that property taxes have a super-priority over other liens, even if those liens were created before the current year's property taxes came due. As a result, property taxes represent a priority lien over existing loans. Consequently, if a tax lien is imposed, the lender's position as a priority lienholder is jeopardized. The collateral property may be sold for taxes (free and clear of all liens in some cases), eliminating the lender's safe lien position. Because of the potential loss of the lender's collateral in a tax sale, virtually all realty loans include a clause that stipulates the borrower's responsibility to pay property taxes in the amount and on the date required.

Due to federal regulations, most residential loans include monthly payments of principal and interest, plus a pro rata portion of the annual real estate taxes and insurance. Such loans are called *budget loans* or sometimes *PITI loans*, for principal, interest, taxes, and insurance. The tax portion of the borrower's payment is then held by the lender in escrow until due. In accordance with the Real Estate Settlement Protection Act (RESPA), only one-twelfth of the taxes may be collected each month. When the tax bill arrives, the lender must pay the bill in the full amount even if the escrow account has insufficient funds. This could happen if the property taxes increase but the lender fails to increase the monthly payment due from the borrower. Very few commercial loans are set up as PITI loans.

Other property liens

Defaults also occur when a borrower allows federal, state, or city income tax liens to vest against the property. In some jurisdictions, construction (mechanics' and materialmen's) liens also take priority over pre-existing loans, and a borrower is in default if these liens are recorded against the collateral property.

Hazard insurance premiums

Nonpayment of hazard insurance premiums also constitutes a default because the protection of the value of the collateral is paramount. Often, the insurance premium is included in the loan payment. In accordance with RESPA, only one-twelfth of the premium may be collected each month.

Neglected property maintenance

Finally, a borrower is considered in default if the property is allowed to physically deteriorate to the point where its value falls below the balance of the loan.

Foreclosures

If any of the stated defaults occur, most lenders would rather work out the problems of a loan with the borrower before entering the **foreclosure** procedure. For example, if the monthly payment is delinquent, some provision for a moratorium on a portion of the payment, or even on the entire payment, might be offered to solve the problem in the short run. Such arrangements are generally informal for residential loans, but memorialized by a **forbearance agreement** for commercial loans. Forbearance agreements spell out the borrower's new responsibilities and the lender's agreement to forbear from further collection activity if the agreement is met. Generally, the borrower must pay the lender's legal fees for drafting the agreement and a separate fee for the agreement itself. The forbearance fee is the price tag for an agreement to not foreclose and is usually a percentage of the loan balance. It is rarely negotiated, because at that point, the borrower has very little negotiating power. If this is not successful, or if any of the other reasons for default are not curable, then formal foreclosure is the only alternative.

Voluntary conveyance of deed (deed in lieu of foreclosure, also called deed in lieu)

To avoid the complications and expenses of pursuing a formal foreclosure, a defaulting borrower may voluntarily convey the property to the lender. This strategy puts the collateral into the hands of the lender quickly and efficiently, and avoids borrower liability for additional expenses related to foreclosure. It usually does not preserve the borrower's credit rating, however, because deeds in lieu of foreclosure are reported as such to credit reporting agencies. They do not affect credit as much as a foreclosure because the deed in lieu indicates the borrower's willingness to work with a lender to reduce losses. Some lenders may not accept a voluntary conveyance, especially in those states that allow intervening liens to remain on the property after a deed in lieu.

Short sale

In a distressed economy, lenders are more likely to be creative to avoid taking property back. Instead of a foreclosure, the lender may agree to a short sale—that is, a sale from the delinquent owner to a new buyer at less than the loan balance. If the debt is nonrecourse, the deemed sales price is the amount of the debt. If the debt is recourse, then the difference between the debt and the short sale price will be considered cancellation of debt income, and the short sale price minus the property's adjusted basis will produce gain or loss that is taxable in some circumstances. Some lenders do not forgive the balance after a short sale, and the borrower remains fully liable.

Judicial foreclosure and sale

If the voluntary conveyance procedure is not possible, as in cases of abandonment, then more formal procedures are followed. The most common foreclosure method under a note and mortgage format is the *judicial procedure*. A complaint is filed in the court for the county in which the property is located, and a summons is issued to the mortgagor and all other lienholders indicating the foreclosure action.

Simultaneously, a title search is made to determine the identities of all parties having an interest in the collateral property, and a lis pendens is filed with the court, giving notice to the world of the pending foreclosure. Notice is sent to all parties involved, allowing them to defend their positions. If they do not do so, they will be forever foreclosed from any future rights by judgment of the court.

After the appropriate number of days required by the jurisdiction for public notice, a foreclosure suit is held before a presiding judge, and a sale of the property at public auction is ordered by means of a judgment decree.

A public sale is necessary to establish the actual market value of the property. If the proceeds from the auction sale are not sufficient to recover the outstanding loan balance plus costs, the lender may, in most states, sue on the note for a **deficiency judgment**, which allows the lender to try and recapture any losses from the borrower's other assets. Nonrecourse loans cannot have a deficiency judgment.

Power-of-sale foreclosure

Under a deed of trust, the foreclosure process is the power-of-sale method of collateral recovery. In the event of a default, the beneficiary (lender) notifies the trustee of the trustor's (borrower's) default and instructs the trustee to foreclose.

Notice of default is recorded by the trustee at the county recorder's office, and a public notice is placed in the newspaper stating the total amount due and the date of the public sale, usually 90 to 120 days from the recorded default.

Strict foreclosure

Under a contract for deed, some states allow a strict foreclosure process to prevail when the borrower's equity is small. Designed to protect lenders under low down-payment transactions, strict foreclosures can take place in as little as 30 days when the borrower has paid less than 20% of the purchase price. Strict foreclosure, when allowed, is usually nonrecourse.

Redemption periods

A defaulted borrower has certain redemption rights under the law. In the judicial foreclosure process, the borrower can sometimes bring the payments current, plus interest, legal fees, and penalties, before the auction sale and redeem the property. This is called *equitable redemption.* In some states, the borrower has the right to pay the loan in full, plus interest and expenses, for a certain period (varies from state to state) after the auction sale and redeem the property. This is called *statutory redemption.*

Under the power-of-sale procedure, the borrower has the right to pay the balance in full before the sale date to preserve ownership.

SUMMARY

The funds for financing real estate emanate from savings, both personal and corporate. These savings are held in the form of deposits in banks and savings institutions, and as premiums paid for life insurance policies and into retirement and pension funds.

Basically, the funds for financing real estate investments originate from the financial institutions in this country—the banks, savings associations, and life insurance companies. Either directly or through their correspondent mortgage bankers or representative mortgage brokers, these intermediaries provide most of the money for short-term construction or home improvement loans; owner-occupied, single-family home mortgages; and large-project, long-term financing, respectively.

Operating under a system of hypothecation where the borrower pledges the subject property as collateral to back up a promise to repay a loan while still retaining possession and control of the property, the loans issued adopt the form of a note and mortgage, deed of trust, or contract for deed. Under the note and mortgage, the borrower-mortgagor has the longest periods of equitable and statutory redemption if the lender-mortgagee forecloses. These redemption periods are shortened somewhat in the deed of trust format, which requires that a borrower-trustor transfer the property's title to a holder-in-due-course trustee, who will maintain this title in trust for the lender-beneficiary. In the contract for deed or land contract format, the buyer-borrower-vendee does not receive title to the property from the seller-lender-vendor until the terms of the contract are met, thus developing the possibility for even shorter redemption periods.

The mortgage, trust deed, or land contract can be used as either a senior or junior loan. A *senior loan* is a lien in first priority position, with no other liens allowed to exist or be created to jeopardize this protected position. The institutional lenders participate in the senior loan market.

Junior loans are also sometimes used with increasing frequency by individuals to arrange for the financing of the disparity between a new or an existing senior mortgage and the price of the property being transferred. One of the more flexible types of junior encumbrances is the *wraparound contract,* which encompasses existing liens. When the wrap is drawn at a higher interest rate than the underlying mortgage, the wrap holder can effectively raise the yield.

Among the variety of special provisions that may be included in a real estate loan contract, those that are of primary importance to investors are the lock-out, right-to-sell, assumption, and exculpatory clauses. Often, mortgages are established at interest rates high enough so that a lender may enjoy this yield for a prescribed time period. To ensure this continuity, the borrower is prohibited from repaying the loan before the number of years stipulated in the agreement.

In addition, a popular technique for lenders seeking to control their yields is the *due-on-sale provision.* Here, the borrower must inform the lender in writing of the possible sale of all or a portion of the collateral property and obtain the lender's permission before the sale can be consummated. In this process, the lender may adjust the terms of the loan to reflect more readily current money market conditions.

Investors may avoid any extended personal liability obligations when purchasing a property by arranging the terms to include the words *subject to* rather than *assume and agree to pay* when accepting responsibility for an existing loan. This format limits the investor-buyer's personal liability to the collateral property, thus protecting other assets from attachment in the event of foreclosure and a subsequent deficiency judgment.

This same limitation can be created by designing an exculpatory clause into the format of a new loan secured when purchasing a property.

Real estate loans can be established with an almost infinite variety of terms and conditions, each loan being the final manifestation of the bargaining positions of the participants. Thus, payment schedules, interest rates, stop dates, balloon payments, discounts, placement fees, and loan amounts reflect the status of the money market at the time a loan is originated. And a borrower, given the personal control intrinsic in real property ownership, can refinance property periodically to provide the cash flows necessary to pursue the highest possible profit potentials.

Creative financing techniques, incorporating any number of versions of variable interest rates and variable-payment schedules, currently are available to finance real estate purchases. Variable-payment arrangements allow lenders and borrowers to manipulate both interest and amortization rates. Variable interest rates protect lenders from holding low-interest loans when rates are rising sharply. They are generally indexed to government securities rates or other published rates not susceptible to manipulation.

The participation mortgage and its variations, including the equity participation mortgage, allow the borrower-buyer to pay lower interest rates or payments in return for allowing the lender-seller a share in the property's appreciation over a specific number of years. The rollover loan allows lenders to periodically alter interest and payment terms, whereas zero-percent financing eliminates interest and acts as an inducement to buy. The growing equity mortgage allows for regularly increasing proportions of principal in monthly payments, thereby reducing the term of the loan. The lease-option treats monthly payments as rent with an option to buy at the expiration of the lease period.

A borrower is in default when regular payments are delinquent, property taxes are not paid, income tax liens are allowed to become liens, hazard insurance premiums are neglected, or maintenance is ignored. If the borrower does not or cannot cure these problems in a reasonable time and does not give the lender a voluntary deed in lieu of foreclosure, then a formal foreclosure procedure is pursued.

Judicial foreclosure is used under a note and mortgage format. Here, a lis pendens is filed and a judgment is sought to sell the collateral property at a public auction. If the auction does not produce enough money to satisfy the balance of the debt plus costs, the lender may secure a deficiency judgment. Under a trust deed, the power-of-sale foreclosure allows the lender to record notice of default and schedule a public sale in 90 to 120 days. Some states allow strict foreclosure under a contract for deed when the borrower's equity is low and can be wiped out in as little as 30 days.

Some states provide a time before the foreclosure auction under a judicial sale to bring the payments current. In addition to this equitable right of redemption, some states allow an additional period after the sale, called a *statutory period of redemption*, to redeem the property by paying the balance of the loan in full. Under the trust deed, the borrower must pay the balance in full before the auction sale to maintain ownership.

A *DCR* is the number of times a property's NOI can pay the debt service. By using the DCR, an investor can calculate the most a lender will lend on a property and then add to that the most the investor can invest of the investor's own funds to receive the desired rate of return. By this calculation, investors know the very most that they can pay and still meet the desired goal.

DISCUSSION TOPICS

1. Check the interest rates, placement rates, and terms of real estate loans available in your geographic area to finance real estate investment property.
2. Examine the laws in your state covering the redemption periods allowed to a defaulted borrower under the various real estate financing forms: mortgage, trust deed, and land contract.

UNIT 10 EXAM

1. An adjustable-rate loan includes all of the following clauses *EXCEPT*
   A. fixed monthly payments.
   B. an index.
   C. a cap.
   D. a ceiling.

2. A basic difference between a deed of trust and a note and mortgage is
   A. the redemption period.
   B. the interest rate.
   C. the length of loan.
   D. the size of loan.

3. A coverage ratio
   A. protects the lender from possible defaults.
   B. establishes the amount of down payment.
   C. establishes the amount of insurance required.
   D. usually exceeds more than 3 to 1.

4. When assuming the balance of an existing loan,
   A. the original borrower and the new borrower are jointly liable on the loan.
   B. the original borrower is relieved of any further personal liability on the loan.
   C. the new borrower does not incur any personal liability on the loan.
   D. the new borrower is buying the property subject to the terms of the loan.

5. All of the following refer to a real estate financing transaction *EXCEPT*
   A. agglomeration.
   B. collateralization.
   C. subordination.
   D. hypothecation.

6. The real estate loan form under which the lender maintains legal ownership is
   A. a deed of trust.
   B. a note and mortgage.
   C. a contract for deed.
   D. a certificate of title.

7. A negative amortization loan includes
   A. a principal-only payment.
   B. an interest-only payment.
   C. a less than interest-only payment.
   D. a principal-plus-interest payment.

8. A wraparound financial encumbrance implies all of the following *EXCEPT*
   A. an existing underlying encumbrance.
   B. a possible override profit.
   C. an all-inclusive loan.
   D. a priority lien position.

9. A seller under a sale-leaseback arrangement benefits from all of the following *EXCEPT*
   A. immediate cash receipts.
   B. release of liability under the existing assumed mortgage.
   C. tax-deductible rent payments.
   D. continued possession of the property.

10. With a $60,000 wrap loan payable at 10% interest-only around an existing $50,000 loan balance at 8%, the wrap holder's annual yield is
    A. 8%.
    B. 10%.
    C. 20%.
    D. 56%.

UNIT 11

Residential, Land, and Commercial Investments

LEARNING OBJECTIVES

When you have completed this unit, you will be able to accomplish the following.

- Summarize the essentials of land investment, including feasibility studies, types of single-lot investments, the concept of acreage, and evaluating land.
- Explain the options available and the implications of the Fair Housing Act when investing in residential properties.
- Describe the types of office investments and the important provisions of the Americans with Disabilities Act (ADA).
- Compare the types of commercial investment opportunities and pitfalls.
- Describe the characteristics and types of industrial real estate investment.
- Explain the options available when investing in special real estate.

KEY TERMS

- air rights
- Americans with Disabilities Act (ADA)
- anchor tenant
- assemblage
- big box
- build out allowance
- build to suit (BTS)
- business park
- c-stores
- central business district (CBD)
- common areas
- conciliation
- condominium
- congregate care center
- community shopping center
- Comprehensive Environmental Response, Compensation, and Liability Act (CERCLA)
- conversion
- cooperative
- corner of Main and Main
- credit tenant
- discount
- factoring
- Fair Housing Act
- Fannie Mae
- franchise
- Freddie Mac
- functional obsolescence
- general obligation bond
- Ginnie Mae
- going dark
- gross rent multiplier
- growth management
- hobby tax rules
- homogeneous tenancy
- horizontal regime
- incremental taxes
- incubator industrial building
- industrial development bond
- industrial park
- infant industry
- International Council of Shopping Centers (ICSC)
- Interstate Land Sales Full Disclosure Act
- land banking
- labor-intensive
- leasehold
- location
- loft building
- Low-Income Housing Tax Credits
- mall
- manufactured home
- mineral rights
- naming rights
- neighborhood shopping center
- net lease
- office park
- off-street parking
- plottage
- potentially responsible party (PRP)
- property tax lien
- proprietary lease
- railroad spur
- real estate mortgage investment conduit (REMIC)
- recognition clause
- regional center
- release clause
- repossession
- retirement community
- revenue bond
- rezoning
- royalty income
- secondary market
- securities
- self-storage
- sharing the market uplift
- spot zoning
- strip
- strip center
- subordination clause
- super-regional center
- surplus land
- tax credit
- time-share
- topography
- tranche
- warehouse building

INTRODUCTION TO INVESTING IN LAND

There are numerous and diverse investment opportunities in real estate, including land, residential developments, office buildings, shopping centers, industrial projects, and manufactured-home parks. In this portion of the book, the principles presented in the prior units will be applied to an examination of these various types of investments.

Of all the forms of real estate ventures, investment in vacant land probably provides the greatest opportunity for creativity and profit. It is also no doubt the riskiest real estate investment. Ranging from the simple purchase of an improved lot in a subdivision by an individual who wishes to build a home, to the more complicated accumulation of hundreds of unimproved acres to hold for future development and subdividing, to the acquisition of a tract of land in anticipation of rezoning for a more intensive use, land is the real estate developer's and speculator's playground.

This lesson examines methods for estimating the profitability of investing in vacant lots and acreage as a portion of an investor's total property ownership portfolio. The goal of most land buyers is to own the right property in the right place at the right time to command the highest possible return on an investment. Depending on an individual's investment strategy, vacant land can provide a viable alternative to the ownership of improved income property.

Raw acreage presents the investor with an opportunity to diversify holdings, earn high profits, and offset the risks of loss from other investments.

However, high profits are inevitably balanced by high risks, and vacant land investments are probably more affected by uncontrollable outside events than any other type of real estate. Furthermore, land is not depreciable for tax purposes, and a beginning investor is well-advised to start a portfolio with an improved income property. In this way, the investor can maximize profits through the use of the tax shelters that improved property provides. When income taxes have been somewhat minimized through investment tax shelters, the investor is in a stronger financial position to speculate with vacant land.

ESSENTIALS OF LAND INVESTMENT FEASIBILITY STUDIES

Whether the investor in vacant land is a speculator or a developer of buildings, the property's location and physical quality will have a significant impact on the success of the investment. Timing strategies, farming losses, development costs, and community attitudes also affect the land investor's potential profits.

Property location

Primarily, the **location** of land determines its potential future growth in value. Although some enterprising promoters have earned large profits from the sale of parcels of relatively isolated land, well-situated property is more likely to increase in value. For example, land lying within a three-mile area on either side of a major highway connecting two neighboring communities is almost certain to increase in value over time. Generally, communities tend to grow toward each other, developing increased demand and higher values for intervening properties. As a rule, the closer to the highway a parcel of land is situated, the higher its potential value.

Similarly, the purchase of raw acreage at the periphery of a community by an investor who wishes to hold the land for appreciation requires an educated prediction of the direction in which the city will expand. An incorrect estimate of future growth patterns will result in the investor's waiting longer than expected for profit realization. As the waiting period increases, the time value of money affects the average annual rate of return.

This relationship of location to value is equally applicable to single lots and large tracts of land. For example, a lot purchased on a major arterial street in anticipation of future rezoning for a more intensive use may prove to be an extremely profitable investment if the neighborhood grows in that direction. The reverse is also true. Another example is a lot that is located on the exterior boundary of a subdivision that overlooks a large, vacant parcel of land. If the lot is to be used for the construction of a home, then the development of a shopping center, office building, or other commercial activity on the larger parcel may diminish the lot's value. To a large degree, the value of land is based on what can be built on that land.

Property features

The physical features of vacant land, such as **topography** (changes in elevation due to hills and valleys) and soil composition, are as important as location in terms of future profitability. A parcel of land's physical features may be economically advantageous to one owner and disadvantageous to another. For example, sloping foothill land is inefficient for farming but desirable for high-priced homes with attractive views. Likewise, unimproved acreage near a large city may be less useful for cattle grazing than for development as a suburban bedroom community.

Purchasers of single lots within a city must also be aware of the physical characteristics of their land. A lot's location, contours, drainage, soil quality, and rezoning potential affect its value. Interior subdivision positions are essential to the buyer of a house lot, while railroad tracks and highways are significant features of an industrial parcel. Retail and office developments require access to major traffic arteries with high traffic counts, while apartment and manufactured-home dwellers seek public transportation facilities and neighborhood serenity.

Timing

Buy low and sell high is axiomatic to any investor seeking a profit, and proper timing has a great deal to do with both of these accomplishments. Timing is a particularly important factor in real estate investments because, by their very nature, these investments are long term. In fact, real estate is often considered to be a nonliquid investment. Often, it is easy to buy real estate but quite a bit more difficult to sell it; in some unfortunate instances, it can become impossible to even give away.

Land speculation requires a greater awareness of timing than many other real estate investments because most land does not produce income during the holding period. It is held by the investor pending a rise in value. The longer this interim holding period, the lower the investment's annual yield will be.

In addition to the land's initial purchase price, the investor must make cash expenditures for mortgage payments, property taxes, liability insurance, water control, and vegetation control. Sometimes there are local improvement assessments and, in the case of subdivision lots, homeowners' association dues. Unless the property can be leased for some income-generating activity, vacant land requires constant financial support during its investment life.

Depending on a lot's location and characteristics, some owners will seek to minimize their holding costs by renting their properties as parking, mobile home, or used-car lots during the waiting period. Owners of larger parcels have found it desirable to develop farm or ranch operations while waiting for the property to appreciate in value. Leasing the land to tenant-farmers on a profit-sharing basis will often produce enough tax-sheltered income to carry an investment.

Farming losses

Although we have passed from a primarily agricultural society to a highly industrialized one and are now in an era of services and informational systems, many parcels of land in this country are still used for farming and ranching. When these activities are the main occupations of their owners, the income acquired is treated as active income for tax purposes.

Some land investors attempt to lease the land to a farmer or rancher to generate cash flow and keep the taxes low while they wait for the land to increase in value. Other investors may seek to engage in farming or ranching activities themselves to take advantage of those tax deductions and credits. Unfortunately, those who are not clearly defined as active farmers or ranchers will come under IRS Code Section 183, which limits the deductions that can be taken by any individual or S corporation (active or passive) that is involved in these activities as hobbies. Deductions are limited to gross income. Any excess losses are not allowed to be carried forward to future years, but are lost forever. The IRS has additionally qualified the differences between farming and ranching for a profit or for a hobby based on the following criteria:

- The activity must be currently and clearly pointed to making a profit.

- The owners/operators must have experience in the activity.
- Considerable personal time and effort must be expended in the activity.
- There must be legitimate hope for value appreciation.
- The owner's or operator's other activities must be limited.
- A continued series of annual losses cannot be tolerated.
- Occasional minimum profits are not acceptable.
- The activity must be the owner's or operator's main source of income.
- Farming and ranching solely for enjoyment makes it a hobby.

The IRS is strict about enforcing these **hobby tax rules** in an effort to close the tax loopholes that became prevalent in the 1970s and early 1980s. Some farming and ranching enterprises had been designed for large operating losses to allow their investors the opportunities for abusive tax shelters.

Opportunity costs

Whereas mortgage payments and property tax cash outlays during the holding period are fairly obvious expenses, opportunity costs for the equity invested in the land are all too often ignored. While the interest paid on a debt can be easily identified as a cost for maintaining the investment, the interest not earned on the cash invested in the property must also be included as a holding cost. The rationale for this practice is based on the present-worth principle. If this money were invested, it would generate a profit. Therefore, the money not earned on the capital invested should be considered carrying costs.

For most real estate investors, the opportunity cost on invested capital forms the basic measuring unit for determining their investment acquisitions. If, when sold, a property cannot develop a return on the investment that substantially exceeds the loss of earnings during the holding period, then this money should be left on deposit or invested more profitably elsewhere.

Community acceptance

An investor in vacant land must become acutely aware of the legal and political attitudes of local governing bodies. Local government may have a direct effect on the future development of a specific parcel of land. Some communities have passed **growth management** legislation that requires developers to have their infrastructure (streets, sewers, sidewalks, utility lines, and so forth) in place before they offer their properties for sale. Others require insurance company-issued bonds that will pay local government to complete infrastructure in the event the developer fails to do so. There may be other barriers to development. For example, if a community practices a no-growth policy, it may be difficult, if not impossible, to secure the cooperation necessary to have subdivision plans approved, or necessary utility services installed.

The FV of land often depends greatly on the availability of gas, electricity, high speed internet, and sewer services. Some communities control their growth by refusing to issue permits for the installation of these utilities. Because a local moratorium on gas or sewer installations can destroy the timing strategy for a particular development, an investor in land should carefully select those parcels that can be developed with as few potential difficulties as possible. In the long run, growth management may result in ever-increasing prices for developments and serious shortages of land for housing.

Land investors should be cognizant of the time involved in securing concurrency—a meeting of the minds regarding appropriate land use. In addition, they should be aware of the cost of impact fees charged by various government agencies for expanding pertinent access roads and utility services or to cover increased wear and tear on existing roads due to increased traffic.

SINGLE-LOT INVESTMENTS

The opportunities for single-lot investments include those individual parcels purchased for residential construction and those that have the rezoning potential for more intensive, and therefore more profitable, uses. In the first instance, the investor acts as a developer, albeit on a small scale. In the second, the investor is a speculator seeking to profit from the gain in value of the rezoned lot.

Residential lots

Many people purchase a lot in anticipation of building a house on it in later years. By acquiring a homesite at current costs, such a buyer hopes to profit from its growth in value over time. Simultaneously, many of these buyers, unable to purchase a lot for cash, enjoy the opportunity to make affordable payments over time so that the debt on the lot will be paid in full before construction. The free and clear land then becomes the equity necessary to secure a mortgage on the building.

Speculative lots

In addition to residential lots purchased for future use, investors also buy strategically located vacant lots in anticipation of a rise in value and profitable resale. Generally, these speculative lot purchases are based on the possibility of a successful rezoning of the property for a more intensive use than single-family residences. Often, subdivision developers will be forced to purchase a seller's entire property, even though only part of it is suitable for home building. The excess, or **surplus land**, can often be purchased, rezoned, and sold for a higher price. Included in this inventory are lots physically suited for multifamily apartment projects and office structures, as well as commercial and industrial developments.

Rezoning residential land to a more intensive use usually raises the value of the property—sometimes quite dramatically. For example, in one community, when a 600-foot block of residential property was rezoned to retail commercial use, its value changed immediately from $200 per front foot to $500 per front foot. No physical changes were required to make the land more usable, nor was any additional money invested.

Successful rezoning requests are based largely on the subject property being located in an area of use compatible with the use being sought by the property owner. Good land-control practices usually prevent any **spot zoning** and require that the applicant prove conformity to the general land-use plan.

When purchasing vacant lots with possibilities for growth in value, an investor must make a careful examination of the community to identify potential areas of expansion. Once these neighborhoods are discovered, a meticulous search should be made to discover the particular vacant parcels of land that have rezoning potential.

Lease vs. resale

It is important for investors who purchase lots for resale to carefully evaluate their personal financial positions before selling. It may be more advantageous to lease, rather than sell, the property. The practice of leasing land to another, who then builds improvements on it, is called **ground leasing.**

A lease develops certain advantages for both the landowner and the tenant. The owner benefits by securing an income stream into the future. In addition, at the expiration of the lease, the reversionary rights to the land are retained, as well as any improvements made thereon by the tenant. Long-term land leases also provide the landowner with an asset—the lease—that can be capitalized on. By pledging the lease as collateral, the landlord can secure tax-free cash, which can be used to purchase additional investments, from a lender. Thus, the landlord continues to own the leased land and can expand the investment portfolio accordingly.

The primary benefit to a land-leasing tenant is leverage: the leasehold interest acquired under a long-term land lease can be pledged as collateral for a mortgage to construct a new building. With a loan sufficient to pay for the costs of construction, the developer may be able to leverage 100% and avoid investing personal funds in a project. In addition, the rent paid by the tenant for the use of the land is considered an operating expense in the year that it is incurred. Thus, by paying rent on land rather than owning it, a tenant is effectively gaining the benefits of depreciating the land over the life of the lease. Remember that land is not specifically depreciable. Care should be taken by the tenant to ensure that its lease is superior to any mortgage originated by the property owner. This is usually done via a **subordination clause** in an existing mortgage, whereby the lender agrees that its mortgage is subordinate to the rights of the tenant. If there is a foreclosure of the land, the tenant will be able to continue in place, though making rent payments to the new owner

Build to suit (BTS)

In an attempt to convert a vacant lot into income-producing improved property, owners sometimes advertise that they will construct a building on a lot that will satisfy the particular requirements of a potential tenant. On the signing of a long-term lease and the construction of the building, the landowner becomes a landlord in the traditional sense. At the expiration of the lease, the landlord continues to own both the land and the vacant building, which can be rerented or converted to a new use.

Build to suit (BTS) generally refers to industrial, warehouse, office, or fast-food-restaurant facilities constructed for single users and designed specifically to meet individual needs. The user may agree either to purchase the property when construction is completed or become a tenant under a relatively long-term lease.

The BTS market is currently fueled by the rapid growth of high-tech firms and life science businesses, as well as possible shortages of commercial space in some areas of the country. Property owners may not be willing to sell the **corner of Main and Main** (meaning a highly desirable parcel in the central business district), which will only increase in value over the years. If a retailer wants that location, it will have no choice but to enter into a BTS arrangement with the owner.

The difference in economic positions between an owner of a vacant parcel of land and an owner of a vacant building is of critical importance to an investor in deciding whether to BTS. In the first instance, the property owner pays relatively low property taxes and faces no continuing property maintenance problems. In the second, the owner's taxes are higher because they are based on the value of the building as well as the land. In addition, the building requires continuous care, repair, and protection.

Because the economic position of a building owner is more vulnerable than that of a vacant lot owner, the landowner who solicits a tenant on a BTS basis will negotiate rather firmly for a lease that will completely satisfy investment requirements over the term of the initial lease period. The rent will be arranged to develop an acceptable return on the investment as well as a timely return of the investor's cash outlay. BTS leases are typically with only the most credit-worthy tenants. Otherwise, if the tenant defaults, the landlord might find himself with a building that has such distinctive architectural details that it is not suitable for any other tenant.

ACREAGE

Investors in raw acreage can be classified as either speculators or developers, as can purchasers of small lots. A land parcel can be bought for resale as a single unit or for subdividing into either improved or unimproved lots. In the former situation, the investor acts as a speculator, holding the land for growth in value and then selling the tract intact.

When raw acreage is subdivided, the investor who sells the land in small parcels after few or no improvements have been made is speculating in land promotions, whereas the subdivider who improves the raw acreage with roads, sewers, water, and other utilities and amenities before selling lots is a land developer.

Land is often worth more as one wholly integrated and cohesive unit than it is as a number of individually owned separate parcels. This concept is called **plottage**. To apply this principle of ownership, a major farming or ranching enterprise would seek to control as many adjoining acres as possible to attain more efficient production. Similarly, the total of the individual values of lots in a block could be worth less than the value of the entire block as a single site for a large shopping center. However, in this case, the value increase is a function of a change in use, as well as the efficiency of single ownership, called **assemblage**.

Plottage can have a reverse effect on the value of acreage for speculators and developers. When quantities of land are accumulated for investment purposes, the total value of the individual smaller parcels is usually less than the value of the total property when finally acquired. However, if the speculator or developer decides to subdivide this wholly owned property, the sum of the sales prices of the individual lots often greatly exceeds the value of the property as a single unit. This concept will be examined later in a discussion of conversion of rental apartments into condominiums.

Acreage for resale in one unit

In regions of the country where the land is fertile, very little acreage speculation takes place. Productive land is usually held by individual farmers, timber companies, or ranchers. Upon the death of the owner, the land is passed to family heirs. Speculation in acreage is most common in areas of the country where the land is relatively unproductive.

The value of land is not based merely on its productive capacity. Depending on intended use, location can become the key factor in determining value. Land speculators are not as concerned with soil fertility as they are with locational advantages or disadvantages that will affect the future desirability of the land for developers or builders. Accessibility to nearby major highways and communities; availability of water, gas, and electricity; and proximity to natural and manmade amenities such as nearby lakes, woods, golf courses, or ski slopes all increase the profit potential of investments in raw acreage. News that a car manufacturing plant will locate in a community will usually drive land speculation prices in a dramatic manner.

Speculators in unimproved land range from the small investor, who buys five to 40 acres located on the periphery of an expanding community, to the large investment syndicates, which purchase thousands of acres to hold for future resale. Regardless of the size of the investment, however, the philosophy is always to buy right to net a large profit.

Large profits are often less than they appear to be. For example, throughout its holding period, raw acreage requires the payment of such basic carrying charges as property taxes, interest, and opportunity costs. Although taxes on vacant acreage are relatively low, the compounding effects of opportunity costs must be included when analyzing the feasibility of an investment in acreage. Remember, there is usually no cash flow to provide offsetting income during the years between purchase and sale.

Assuming a property tax rate at a cost of 1% per year plus an opportunity (interest) cost of 9% per year, the value of the land will have to increase at least 10% annually just for the investor to break even when the property is sold. When an investor's desired profit rate and an appropriate percentage ratio to cover money needed for the costs of a sale (for example, commissions, title policy premiums, legal fees, income taxes) are added to this 10% rate, required annual increases in property value of 15% to 20% are often required.

This rate of increase means that the property must double in value every five to seven years if the costs of investment plus a profit are to be earned. For example, even if the value of the land increases 100% over a 10-year holding period and the property owner sells for an amount twice what was originally paid, the annual rate of return is only 10% (100% / 10 years = 10% per year). At a 10% value increase annually, the investment may not yield an amount of return adequate to cover both carrying costs and anticipated profits. Thus, it is vital that an investor make an effort to identify future value-growth patterns by carefully investigating trends in local property values.

EVALUATING LAND

The evaluation of raw land depends to a great degree on its future, rather than its present, use. Thus, an investor must be able to predict the type of eventual use as well as the time when this use will become feasible, which isnot an easy task.

The most popular basis for evaluating land is the comparative approach, whereby similarly zoned parcels of land that sold recently are said to establish the value. This is after adjustments have been made for location, size, and date of sale.

A more comprehensive approach is advisable because the existing zoning of the land may not be its highest and best future use. The time value of money also must be considered. Careful attention should be paid to an opinion of future use by analyzing the area's demographics, employment centers, and traffic counts. This information would form a basis for projecting the number of acres that are in demand for each use classification (i.e., residential, business, industrial, and so forth).

In addition, a careful forecast should be made of when the property will be ready for development. The factors to consider in this analysis include supply, demand, availability, growth patterns, and distance from existing development. Some effort should be made to project building costs and rents to estimate what a developer might pay for the land in the future.

Finally, to derive the PV of the land, an appropriate investment return must be established. When improved properties are being sold for close to a 10% capitalization rate on an all-cash basis, raw land requires that the investor double this figure to account for the increased risks involved. Thus, a 20% annual return requirement should be applied to project the future sale price.

FOR EXAMPLE

Suppose a 15-acre tract of raw land is available for sale to an investor who anticipates its use as a neighborhood shopping center within five years. The present commercial rents in the area average $12 per square foot, and a 5% annual inflation factor is anticipated.

If the land were ready for immediate development, its value would be worth approximately half the anticipated rents or, in this case, $6 per square foot. At 5% annual growth, the land will be worth $7.66 (rounded) per square foot in five years. For an investor who requires a 20% annual return, the price for the parcel today will be $3.08 (rounded) per square foot:

$6 × $(1.05)^5$ = $7.6577 per square foot, five years

$7.6577 × 0.4019 = $3.0777 or $3.08 PV

Subdividing for speculation: land promotions

Some land-promotion projects are the consequence of speculation in raw acreage. The promoter buys a large tract of vacant acreage, divides it into smaller parcels, and resells these smaller, usually unimproved, lots to buyers scattered throughout this country as well as others.

These lots are marketed through various promotional plans and advertising media. One of the more common marketing methods is to invite prospective buyers to a free dinner during which salespeople extol the virtues of the property through lecture and film. Often, these dinners are followed by an offer of a trip to the site, with any costs for traveling reimbursed by the promoters after purchase of a lot. Generally, the various large companies involved in such land promotions follow a format of marketing the individual lots as second, or retirement, homesites.

The financing designs of both the original purchase of raw acreage by the promoter and the subsequent sales of lots to individuals are the most important elements in this form of real estate investment. A purchase of land for use in a sales promotion usually requires the seller of the raw acreage to carry back a substantial portion of the sales price as an installment land contract or purchase money mortgage. Thus, after the promoter makes a cash down payment, usually about 5% to 10% of the purchase price, the landowner will accept a lien on the acreage involved for the remainder of the sales price. This balance is to be paid by the promoter on some regular amortization schedule. Under a land contract, the seller retains legal title to the acreage until the terms of the contract are met—usually the requirement that the balance be paid in full.

Most land-promotion property is sold to subsequent small-lot owners with any underlying financial arrangements left intact. As a result, each individual sale is made subject to the lien of at least one existing encumbrance, the installment contract, or purchase money mortgage between the promoter and the seller of the acreage. The existence of an underlying encumbrance poses a serious threat to the purchaser of an individual lot if the promoter does not make payments as required. The small-lot owner may be financially hurt in a subsequent foreclosure of the master lien. To offset this problem, most legitimate promoters will secure a **recognition clause** in their original financing agreement in which the vendor or mortgagee agrees in advance that if the promoter should default during the term of the agreement, the lender will respect the rights of subsequent lot owners and honor their contracts.

Alternatively, a **release clause** may be inserted in the land contract under the terms of which individual lots may be released from the master lien after a certain percentage of its balance has been paid by the vendee.

The sales of lots to individual purchasers are generally designed as installment land contracts. Most buyers of these promotional lots make small cash down payments, and the balance is carried back by the selling company to be paid in regular monthly installments. Frequently, the seller's signature is not notarized, and, consequently, the contract is unacceptable for recording purposes at the appropriate county office.

A promoter hopes that the initial sales campaign will generate enough individual sales to quickly develop the cash flows necessary to meet the required underlying contract payments. Sometimes it takes a few years to reach this breakeven point, and the promoter must be prepared to meet payments and operating costs with other funds. A promoter can offset a cash shortage either by selling the individual contracts secured through early sales, a process called **factoring**, or by pledging these contracts as collateral for a bank loan to meet operating expenses. Once a breakeven point has been met, however, continued sales will generally result in substantial profits.

Because they recognize the complexities and possible pitfalls for the consumer, and because of some past dishonesty in this form of land promotion, both federal and state regulatory agencies carefully supervise such programs. All interstate land sales must conform to the requirements of the federal government's Interstate Land Sales Full Disclosure Act. The promoters must prepare and distribute to all prospective lot purchasers a full disclosure report describing the subject property and the complete financial arrangements of the transaction. In addition, many states require that the promoter post bonds in amounts adequate to complete any promised improvements to the land, such as roads, golf courses, clubhouses, and lakes, before granting the promoter permission to market the lots (see *Case Study 11.1*).

CASE STUDY 11.1 1,280-Acre Land Promotion

The profit potentials in a land-promotion program can be illustrated by examining the case of a two-section (1,280-acre) parcel of land, to be subdivided into 1,920 half-acre lots. This assumes a 75% efficiency factor, meaning 75% of the original 1,280 will be available for lots, and the other 25% will have to be used for roads, entrance, and common areas such as parks, greenbelt, or walking trails. These lots will then be marketed within the state in which the property is located.

The purchase price of the raw acreage is $1,000 per acre, and it is estimated that it will cost an additional $500 per acre to improve the land with roadways and basic utilities. An additional $500 per acre will be needed for interest charges, carrying costs, and promotional fees. The sales price of the half-acre lots will average $3,000 each, with 10% of the total sales to be received as cash down payments. This money will be allocated for sales commissions and closing costs. The land contracts to be secured from the sales will be discounted and sold by the promoter for 75% of their face value. It is anticipated that the project will take three years to complete. The financial analysis is as follows.

Costs:	
1,280 acres @ $1,000 per acre	$1,280,000
1,280 acres improvements @ $500 per acre	+ 640,000
1,280 acres carrying costs @ $500 per acre	+ 640,000
Total costs:	$2,560,000

Income:	
1,920 half-acre lots @ $3,000 each	$5,760,000
Sales and closing @ 10%	– 576,000
Sales contracts face amount	$5,184,000
25% discount	– 1, 296,000
Net cash receipts	$3,888,000
Less costs (above)	– 2,560,000
Net profit before taxes	$1,328,000
28% taxes (active income)	– 371,840
Net profit after taxes	$956,160
Return on total investment ($956,160 / $2,560,000)	37.35%
Average annual return (37.35% / 3 years)	12.45%

Note that this case includes discounting the contracts in an amount of $968,000, a substantial sum of money. If the promoter were to hold the receivables, the returns would increase dramatically. However, the face amount of those receivables would not be immediately available for reinvestment, nor would the discounted sum. Thus, an opportunity cost would have to be applied for the loss of earnings during the contracts' holding periods, offsetting, to a great degree, the higher profits.

However, note that the returns in this analysis are based on the full amount of the investment, assuming that they are paid in cash. More realistically, considering a leveraging investor, the cash expended over the three years would include only the $1,280,000 costs for land improvements and carrying charges plus a portion of the purchase price represented by an acceptable down payment such as 10%, or $128,000. The balance of $1,152,000 is carried back by the seller of the raw acreage and is paid over time by the receipts collected from the subsequent individual land contracts.

Therefore, the face amount total of the sales contracts, $5,184,000, must be decreased by the $1,152,000 owed to reflect the promoter's equity before discounting. The difference is $4,032,000, and a 25% discount ($1,080,000) will result in a $2,952,000 cash flow before costs and income taxes. Applying the more realistic cash investment figure of $1,408,000 ($1,280,000 + $128,000 = $1,408,000), the returns are now as follows:

Total gross income	$7,680,000
Sales and closing costs	– 768,000
Sales contracts face amount	$6,912,000
Less underlying encumbrance	1,152,000
Promoter's equity in contracts	$5,760,000
25% discount	– 1,440,000
Net cash receipts	$4,320,000
Less costs (adjusted)	1,408,000
Net profit before taxes	$2,912,000
28% taxes	– 815,360
Net profit after taxes	$2,096,640
Return on cash invested ($2,096,640 / $1,408,000)	148.90%
Average annual return (148.90% / 3 years)	49.64%

Thus, leveraging doubles the bottom-line return of this investment.

Interstate land sales regulations

The Department of Housing and Urban Development (HUD) engages in the regulation of interstate land sales. HUD's activities, in connection with the **Interstate Land Sales Full Disclosure Act**, are of particular significance for those investors contemplating large-scale land sales promotions.

Authorized under Title XIV of the Housing and Urban Development Act, the interstate land sales law is administered by the HUD's Office of RESPA and Interstate Land Sales. This law requires that anyone engaged in the interstate sale or leasing of 25 or more improved lots register the offering with HUD and make available to each prospective lot purchaser or lessee all facts pertinent to the legitimate use of the land. The terms and conditions of any financing in existence at the time of the sale or lease must be stated and the existence of any other liens revealed. The probability for completion of promised off-site improvements such as paving, parks, golf courses, and marinas must be given.

In addition to this data, the disclosure must also provide information about distances to nearby communities over paved or unpaved roads; provisions for placing contract payments into a special escrow fund set aside for the purchase of the property; the availability of recreation facilities; the availability of sewer and water services or septic tanks and wells; the present and proposed utility services and charges; the number of homes currently occupied; soil and foundation conditions that could cause problems in construction or the use of septic tanks; and the type of title the buyer will receive.

A buyer is protected in several ways against failure to comply with the provisions of the full disclosure requirements. If a prospective buyer has not been furnished a property report before signing, the contract may be canceled and a refund obtained. Furthermore, the buyer must receive a property report at least 48 hours before a contract is signed and must have seven calendar days after for a cooling off period. If the buyer wishes to cancel the contract during this period, a full refund of any payments will be made. If the disclosures are not made at all, the buyer has extended time periods within which to cancel. At one time, aggressive borrowers' attorneys claimed the act applied to condominium sales, then used it to set aside condo purchases that became undesirable after the 2008 crash. Developers argued that the act was intended to protect unsophisticated purchasers of modest means and was never intended to protect wealthy individuals who could afford second homes in resort areas. In 2014, Congress amended the act to specifically exclude condominium sales.

Criminal penalties of up to five years imprisonment, a fine of up to $5,000, or both may be imposed if a developer willfully violates the law, makes an untrue statement, or omits any material fact required in the statement of record or in the property report. In addition, the purchaser may sue for damages not to exceed the purchase price of the lot, plus any improvements made thereto, and reasonable court costs.

Complementing HUD's requirements, a number of states have enacted their own interstate land sales regulations, as well. Administration of such state laws is usually placed in the office of the state real estate or land commissioner. In Nebraska, for example, a developer wishing to sell land located in other states must file an application for permission to sell with the Nebraska Real Estate Commission. The developer must pay a filing fee commensurate with the number of lots in the subdivision and post a bond to guarantee the timely completion of the off-site improvements promised in the sales.

Before granting approval for interstate land sales in Nebraska, the director of the commission or a deputy visits the land at the developer's expense to verify personally the facts presented in the application.

Both the federal Interstate Land Sales Full Disclosure Act and the various state laws regulating such sales have been developed to curb the fraudulent activities of unscrupulous promoters of vacant land. Although land promoters invariably earn relatively high profits, the purchasers of these lots often can barely recover their investments.

Subdividing for development: land bankers

Speculation in acreage places an investor in a somewhat passive role while waiting for values to rise to the point where profitable sales can be made. On the other hand, development of acreage into subdivisions requires that an investor play a more active role to effectively market the inventory of lots. Often, investors or builders purchase raw acreage situated on the boundary of an expanding community; improve the property; subdivide it; and sell lots or build houses, apartments, offices, or shopping centers on the land.

Every action of the subdivider creates value for the property, including zoning, repairing the land, installing the infrastructure, subdividing the land into lots, and constructing houses.

A developer who improves raw land for construction purposes and maintains an inventory of lots as a function of this ongoing business is called a **land banker**. Besides the purchase price of the unimproved acreage, the costs of **land banking** include property taxes, interest, off-site and on-site improvements, engineering, site development, plat acceptance, sales commissions, insurance, and costs incurred because of timing constraints. The skills, risks, and responsibilities required of the land banker-developer make this a very specialized segment of real estate investment.

To begin the development process, a land banker purchases a parcel of raw land—usually 160 acres or more—and prepares plats and maps of the property designating street locations, lot sizes, and the general plan for the entire proposed development.

These plats, usually drawn by licensed civil engineers, are submitted to the appropriate community regulating agencies for approval of design and zoning. After meeting local government requirements, including submission of a full environmental impact study, the subdivider will proceed to physically prepare the land and sell lots to both individuals and builders.

Depending on the amount of acreage involved in the development, the resulting subdivision may follow the style of surrounding neighborhoods or may acquire a distinct character of its own. Many large-scale developments include land designated for the location of a school or a park, including a swimming pool, tennis courts, clubhouse, and, perhaps, even a golf course.

Most well-planned subdivisions include a set of restrictions itemizing the type, design, and quality of the improvements to be constructed on the lots therein. These subdivision restrictions are recorded and become covenants that run with the land so that each lot buyer and subsequent homeowner must observe these restrictions. Their enforcement becomes the responsibility of the neighborhood association formed after the project is completed. The restrictions are designed to create an economic and physical homogeneity within a neighborhood—a condition important for maintaining property values. By restricting lots to residential construction, incompatible uses are eliminated. By requiring a minimum square or cubic footage for each house, an economic floor is created, limiting the neighborhood residents to those who can afford to purchase a home of the specified size.

Many builders do not have the financial capacity, expertise, or inclination to become involved in land development. Such builders prefer to leave this type of real estate investment opportunity to those with proven skill in the field. Smaller builders are usually content to purchase lots from a developer-land banker, either singly or in packages of from five to 50 lots, depending on their needs. The prices paid for these lots reflect the developer's cost of acquisition, preparation, and desired rate of return on the investment. For smaller builders, this technique of land acquisition is much less costly and demanding than an active entry into the field of subdividing.

SUMMARY OF INVESTING IN LAND

This lesson examined some of the opportunities for investing in vacant land. Depending on a property's location, quality, purchase price, holding costs, and appropriate timing, profitable speculative land investments can be acquired to enhance an investor's portfolio. Because most land holdings do not produce regular income, they are recommended for the investor who has accumulated numerous improved income properties that will provide cash flows needed to carry the investment.

Land investments provide speculative opportunities that may generate relatively high profits, depending on specific circumstances. Primarily, the location of the land determines the amount and timing of its future growth in value.

Investors must be aware of the opportunity costs and the initial purchase price when estimating the profitability of purchasing raw land. In addition, careful attention must be paid to the physical attributes of, and political attitudes toward, a specific land parcel and the area in which it is located. These inputs must be positive to generate the required growth in value within a reasonable time frame.

Single-parcel investments include residential lots purchased for the construction of a home at some future time, as well as speculative lots for resale.

More pertinent to the accumulation of a diversified real estate investment portfolio is the purchase of residential lots with rezoning potential. The rezoning of a parcel of land to a more intensive use often substantially raises the property's value. It is not unusual for values to double or triple when a property is rezoned from residential to commercial use. In the long run, it sometimes is more profitable to lease these rezoned parcels for new construction rather than sell them. The rental income developed from leasing establishes an annuity for the landowner.

An alternative to leasing vacant land is to construct a building on the property and thus convert the speculative quality of the investment to a more permanent income stream. Care must be taken when erecting a single-purpose building, which may be difficult to rerent when the initial lease expires or if the tenant defaults.

In addition to single-lot investments, many people speculate in vacant acreage in anticipation of profits through growth in value. Some investors purchase acreage to hold until it increases in value to a point where the property can be sold profitably in one unit, while others purchase acreage wholesale for subdivision purposes and then make a profit by selling the smaller parcels at retail prices. It must be clearly recognized that investing in vacant land is probably the highest risk of any real estate investment.

DISCUSSION TOPICS

1. Investigate the political attitude in your area regarding encouragement of growth, no growth, or planned growth, and examine the implications of this attitude for real estate investors and developers.
2. Find a vacant site that is for sale on the periphery of your community and analyze its PV using the information in this lesson. How does your appraisal compare to its asking price?

INTRODUCTION TO INVESTING IN RESIDENTIAL PROPERTIES

More people invest in residential property than in any other form of real estate. Residential investments include ownership of a single-family detached house, an apartment unit in a cooperative or condominium complex, and multiunit apartment buildings ranging in size from duplexes to high-rise complexes, also called *elevator buildings*.

This lesson includes an examination of the various types of residential property investments, including management responsibilities and cash-flow analyses. A case describing the profit possibilities in the conversion of a 100-unit apartment complex into a condominium association of individual ownerships is presented to broaden perspectives on the field of residential property investment.

SINGLE-FAMILY DETACHED HOMES

Free-standing houses on single lots compose the greatest number of individual investments in the real estate inventory. According to the National Association of REALTORS® (NAR), 64.2% of American families own their own homes, steadily increasing after a 50-year low in 2016. Included in this inventory are detached single-family homes, condominiums, townhomes, and manufactured housing on owned lots.

In recent decades, suburban areas have been dominated by the single-family detached house. This is changing to townhomes and condominiums that offer housing with less maintenance and lower costs. Condominiums have a median cost of approximately $231,700 according to an April 2018 study by the NAR. This compares with a similar size single-family house costing a median of $259,900, based on higher lot costs. This emerging market appeals to

- divorced buyers who want to be near their children;
- young professionals with no children;

- empty-nest couples seeking freedom from maintenance responsibilities; and
- senior citizens wanting to live near their children.

Owner-occupied homes

Technically, owner-occupied homes do not meet the full criteria for a real estate investment. They are not income-producing properties and, therefore, are not eligible for the complete range of deductions allowed for income properties. Only property taxes and interest paid for mortgages on an owner-occupied home are deductible expenses for income tax purposes. Additional deductions allowed for income property include maintenance costs, insurance premiums, and depreciation of the improvements. Most owner-occupants, however, consider their houses as investments. For many people, buying a home is the only real estate purchase they will make, and if they buy low and sell high, it will come closer to an *investment* in the complete sense of the word.

The owner-occupied home has proved to be a successful means of enforced savings for many people. A commitment to long-term mortgage payments generally results in the accumulation of equity, which provides the basis for the measurable inheritable estates of many owners. Frequently, homeowners find that they have relatively large equities in their properties—equities that may be capitalized to acquire additional real estate holdings. Furthermore, interest deductions may be taken on home equity loans.

Owner-occupied houses have also historically proven to be hedges against inflation for those who wish to expand or improve their accommodations. Although the costs of new construction have been rising, owners of existing houses have historically secured enough funds from the sale of their older homes to enable them to purchase new homes.

Under current tax laws, owner-occupants can sell their homes every two years and never pay any taxes on the profits. For many, this is an investment strategy that can build significant value over the years, ending with a large debt-free home at retirement age that can then be sold tax free. Part of the proceeds will be used to purchase a smaller home or condo, and the balance is added to the investment portfolio.

Affordable housing

The availability of affordable housing is an important social issue. Personal crises may force America's working poor to leave the safety and comfort of their homes and live on the streets. Entire families are sometimes dispossessed and wander around looking for jobs and shelter. There is a shortage of affordable homes and apartments for low-income and no-income people. Cutbacks in national welfare programs have exacerbated the problem, while state and local agencies scramble to provide temporary shelters to preserve the health and safety of the poor.

Low-income housing tax credits

One of the more socially redeeming current tax shelters is the tax credit available to owners and developers of low-income housing. Low-income housing developed for the purpose of obtaining these credits has created more than 3 million affordable homes since the 1986 passage of the U.S. Tax Reform Act. The **Low-Income Housing Tax Credits** (LIHTC, often pronounced "lie-tech") program gave state and local LIHTC-allocating agencies the equivalent of $8.7 billion in annual budget authority in 2017 to issue tax credits for the acquisition, rehabilitation, or new construction of rental housing targeted at lower-income households.

A **tax credit** is directly deductible from income taxes. Thus, it is a 100% tax benefit, unlike other tax benefits such as operating expenses, which are deducted from income. For example, a $100 deduction at a 28% tax rate is worth only $28, whereas a $100 tax credit can save the same taxpayer a full $100.

The program begins with the federal government deciding the total dollar volume of LIHTC for the year and then allocating that money among the various states based on their gross population. Each state has its own housing finance authority (HFA), which receives the tax credits. The HFAs then review applications for the tax credits and decide those projects to which they will be granted, and in what amounts. Depending on the state and that state's perceived current needs, there might be a preference for new construction or for rehab and renovation of existing housing. Developers who are awarded LIHTCs often use them to attract investors, to whom the tax credits will be disbursed in proportion to their investment size. In this manner, tax policy is a vehicle for social policy in favor of increasing the supply of affordable housing.

LIHTCs provide an owner/developer with credits over a 10-year period on the following bases:

- New construction and rehabilitation—a credit of 9% of costs is allowed each year for the construction or rehabilitation of each qualifying low-income housing unit. To qualify, the costs must exceed $6,000 per unit or 20% of the adjusted basis of property purchased for rehabilitation.
- New construction and rehabilitation financed with tax-exempt bonds or other federal subsidies—a maximum credit of 4% is allowed each year, including projects financed with Farm Service Agency loans.
- Costs of acquiring existing housing—a maximum credit of 4% is allowed each year. To qualify, the property must not have been used for low-income housing within the previous 10 years.
- Targeting requirements—to receive these credits, at least 20% of the units in a project must be occupied by individuals who earn 50% or less of the area's median income, adjusted for family size, or at least 40% of the units must be occupied by individuals who earn 60% or less of the area's median income, adjusted for family size. Units may not be used on a transient basis, thus eliminating hospitals, retirement homes, hotels, and so on from these credits. According to Fannie Mae, there is an oversubscription for LIHTCs each year, and they are now allocated by lottery in some states because of the demand.

Homes for rental income

To qualify as an investment in the fullest sense, a house must be rented. Generally, single-family house rentals generate only enough funds to cover the mortgage payments and minimum maintenance costs. The owner of a detached house rarely secures cash flows that exceed breakeven requirements, unless the owner bought low and performed significant renovations. Thus, any vacancy, even for a short time, seriously erodes the profit potential of this type of rental income property.

FOR EXAMPLE

Consider an investment house valued at $150,000 purchased with $30,000 cash and a loan for $120,000, payable at 6% interest. Assuming a rent of $1,000 per month, this property will experience a 4% ROI.

$12,000.00	Gross annual income
− 4,800.00	40% operating expenses ratio
7,200.00	Net operating income
− 7,200.00	Interest only @ 6%
(0)	Cash flow
4,320.00	Depreciation ($120,000 × 0.036)
(4,320.00)	Loss (tax shelter if qualified)
× 28%	Tax bracket
$1,209.60	Tax savings (4% ROI)

An owner of a rental house must be personally responsible for the constant maintenance of the property to ensure its continuous rental appeal. Maintenance of a single-unit dwelling is costly, time-consuming, and inefficient in comparison with larger apartment projects. The need for personal involvement of time and effort and the requirements of maintaining a one-to-one relationship with tenants seriously inhibits the popularity and profitability of this form of investment. Many companies will not accept single-family homes in their management portfolios, so finding third-party management can be difficult.

Some single-family-house investors have entered into partnerships with their tenants on an equity sharing basis. The investor purchases the property and, instead of rent, the tenant makes the loan payments and maintains the property. Then, at some specified time in the future, they either refinance or sell the property and share in the profits, if any.

For those who are able to personally repair and rehabilitate older, worn-down properties, higher profits are possible. By purchasing dilapidated houses at bargain prices, these investors can receive benefits in at least three ways:

1. An income stream that often shows a positive return on a small amount of invested capital
2. An immediate growth in property value as a result of the repairs made, and as a result of this, added value
3. An expanded base for refinancing and continued investment pyramiding

Single-family investment homes are generally bought and sold at prices based on the **gross rent multiplier** (GRM). If the current market multiplier is 100-times monthly rent, then a house that rents for $1,000 per month will be valued at $100,000. The GRM model is very inaccurate for properties with exceptional expenses such as an older home with constant maintenance needs. It has the advantage of being very easy to remember and calculate, and therefore, appeals to unsophisticated investors.

Homes for resale

Because of the increasing costs of constructing new homes, speculation in buying and selling older houses is a popular form of real estate investment. The anticipation of growth in value has attracted investors to buying homes, leasing them, and then selling them for profit. The rental income during the intervening years helps reduce the carrying costs of the investment.

Some investors pyramid their holdings by constantly buying and repairing older homes for resale at higher prices. Profits from the sales are used to purchase more properties for rehabilitation.

Gentrification

Many communities are expressing a growing interest in the renovation of buildings in areas that are or were considered to be low income. This redevelopment pushes up land values, rent, prices, and so on. That, of course, is good for property owners, but not so good for tenants who generally need to move because of higher rents. This results in gentrification, the upgrading of neighborhoods, and the displacement of low-income residents.

Homes for rezoning

Generally, the most profitable detached-house investments include those located on potentially rezonable lots. Depending on location and physical attributes, these houses can often be renovated after **rezoning** and leased rather than sold. Frequently, these older homes are particularly attractive to certain tenants who are able to capitalize on the architectural charm of such buildings to enhance their business activities. For example, law offices, antique shops, and real estate offices enjoy a *home office* environment when located in older houses.

Conversion of homes to apartments

A unique investment opportunity is the conversion of large, older, but sturdily built houses into several rental units. Many mansion-sized homes built on the periphery of older, central, downtown areas and passed over by a city's growth have fine conversion possibilities. Often, the quality of construction of these houses is such that new partitions, bathrooms, and kitchen facilities can be installed quickly and efficiently for a relatively small cash outlay.

These apartments are usually in demand because of their proximity to downtown work areas and their old-fashioned charm. The spacious rooms with high ceilings found in such buildings appeal to many people who will pay higher rents to enjoy this environment.

In the past, many of these grand old homes were purchased and razed by builders of high-rise apartment and office buildings. Now, community planners are encouraging conversion of the remaining properties into apartments or offices and requiring the retention of their historic architectural styles. Income tax laws assist with such goals by allowing charitable deductions to owners who place façade easements on their historic buildings and then donate those easements to qualifying historic organizations. With a façade easement in place, current and subsequent owners must maintain the exterior architectural integrity of the building.

THE FAIR HOUSING ACT

The rules and regulations of the Civil Rights Act (Title VIII—Fair Housing, effective December 31, 1968, as amended) are of significance to investors. The **Fair Housing Act** and its amendments are designed to eliminate discrimination in the sale or rental of housing based on race, color, religion, sex, national origin, disability, or familial status. Individual investors who own three or fewer single-family homes, and who do not use real estate licensees to assist in the sale of the home(s), are exempt. Ownership in an LLC or corporation does not qualify as individual ownership. In addition, owners of multifamily homes of two to four units who live in one of the units and who do not use a real estate licensee to assist in the rental of the units are also exempt. HUD takes the position that discrimination on the basis of race was outlawed by the 1866 Civil Rights Act, which contains no exemptions at all. As a result, all investors are prohibited from discriminating on the basis of race.

These exemptions do not indicate that the government approves of discrimination under any circumstances. Investors are strongly advised to avoid any and all discriminatory situations.

The original act was expanded in 1988 to include protection against discrimination for persons with disabilities and families with children. The law extends fair housing protection to persons with physical or mental disabilities. However, it specifically excludes persons who would pose a direct threat to the health and safety of others.

The law stipulates that apartment buildings with four or more units must be accessible to those in wheelchairs. In buildings with no elevators, only the first-floor units are covered by this provision. All doors and hallways in the building, as well as in individual units, must be wide enough to allow passage by wheelchairs. Light switches, electrical outlets, and other controls also must be wheelchair accessible. Bathroom walls are required to be reinforced to accommodate the installation of grab bars, and kitchens and bathrooms must be designed to allow free mobility for individuals with disabilities.

The law also covers families with children under the age of 18, including pregnant women. All-adult communities are banned, except those that operate specifically for persons who are at least 62 years of age. Housing in which at least 80% of the units are occupied by at least one resident who is 55 years old is also exempt, if approved by HUD.

Although the Fair Housing Act is a federal law and is under the jurisdiction of HUD, its implementation is generally left to the individual states, which have inaugurated their own open-housing regulations. These state laws are usually broader in scope than the federal law, and many include prohibitions against discrimination in financing and appraising of real property as well as in leasing and selling. Any state fair housing law must have at least the same seven protected classes as the federal law.

When a problem occurs under the open-housing laws, a complaint is filed with the local commissioner, who investigates accordingly. The commissioner attempts to solve the dilemma amicably and without litigation in a process called **conciliation**. If a suit is necessary, it is initiated by the plaintiff in the appropriate state or federal court. In addition, the U.S. Attorney General's office may bring an action for injunctive relief in the federal court having jurisdiction over the dispute. The plaintiff has the burden of coming forward with evidence of discrimination, and the defendant then has the burden of showing a nondiscriminatory reason for its actions. Then plaintiff may then present evidence that the nondiscriminatory reason was a sham.

Defendants found guilty of violating the act can be fined up to $16,000 for a first offense and $65,000 for subsequent offenses. They are also typically ordered to take part in fair housing education, as well as engage in aggressive advertising and marketing campaigns to indicate their compliance with the law to overcome the chilling effect of past violations. Violators who refuse to obey the order of the court are held in contempt and fined or sent to prison for up to six months. Those found guilty of bringing false charges or complaints with willful intent to falsify are subject to five years imprisonment or a $10,000 fine.

For more information on these laws, see Figure 11.1.

Figure 11.1: Federal Fair Housing and Credit Laws

Legislation	Race	Color	Religion	National Origin	Sex	Age	Marital Status	Disability	Familial Status	Public Assistance Income
Civil Rights Act of 1866	•	•								
Fair Housing Act of 1968 (Title VIII)	•	•	•	•	•					
Housing and Community Development Act of 1974	•	•	•	•	•			•		
Fair Housing Amendments Act of 1988								•	•	
Equal Credit Opportunity Act of 1974 (lending)	•	•	•	•	•	•	•			•

MULTIUNIT APARTMENT RENTALS

Rental apartments are a popular form of living unit in this country. Ranging in size from a single small room above a garage to the numerous duplexes, triplexes, and giant apartment structures found in all major communities, rental units vary widely in price, design, amenities, and profitability.

After decades of fulfilling the American Dream of owning a home, the pendulum is swinging back to favor apartment living. Renters have become older, more affluent, and more educated. In recent years, as homeowners have experienced layoffs at work, houses have been foreclosed upon in record numbers, and credit has been negatively affected, more people are moving into rental properties. After the recent economic downturn, the apartment market is growing, and multihousing starts are up. According to a report by REIS, multifamily vacancies were at 4.9% at the end of 2018 and expected to increase slightly due to continued apartment construction. Rents have increased by 1.5% per year from 2017 to 2018, lagging behind the inflation rate. According to the National Association of REALTORS®, increasing housing inventory and demand will keep rent growth sluggish for the foreseeable future. New designs and locations in downtown areas are spurring the increasing popularity of apartments in those areas. The aging roadway infrastructure means that commute distances from suburban areas typically exceeds two hours of daily commuting, making urban rental units more attractive.

Duplexes and triplexes

Probably the most effective starter for a real estate investment portfolio is a duplex or triplex apartment building. A beginning investor can occupy one unit while renting the other(s). In this manner, the owner-landlord is on the premises to minimize maintenance responsibilities. Generous loan programs designed for homeowners can be used to purchase duplexes, triplexes, and even fourplexes, provided the owner lives in one of the units. One example of investing in a triplex is outlined in *Case Study 11.3*.

CASE STUDY 11.3 Triplex Profitability Analysis

This property consists of a brick building containing three two-bedroom, two-bath apartments, each renting for $1,400 per month. They are unfurnished except for stove, refrigerator, carpets, and drapes, and the tenants pay their own gas and electric bills. Operating expenses, including an amount for vacancy, total 40% of the gross annual income. The property is available for $400,000 with $50,000 cash and a 15-year carryback at 8.64% interest-only payment. The following is a return analysis:

$50,400	Gross annual income
− 20,160	Operating expenses (40%)
30,240	Net operating income
− 30,240	Debt service ($100,000 @ 8.64% interest only)
0	Cash flow
− 7,272	Depreciation ($200,000 × 3.636% annually)
(7,272)	Loss
× 28%	Tax bracket
2,036	Tax savings (rounded)
+ 20,000	Growth in value (5% annual average)
$22,036	Bottom-line return (44.07% on $50,000 investment, rounded)

This analysis shows the effect of a breakeven cash flow. It is difficult to generate any strong positive cash flows with smaller investments without making larger down payments or financing at lower-than-market interest rates. Note that eliminating an amount for growth, this investment's yield is only 4.07% ($2,036 / $50,000 = 0.0407), not enough to attract an investor. Thus, the smaller property has to be purchased at a price low enough to allow the inclusion of a growth factor.

Another advantage for the owners-tenants of a duplex or triplex is the development of a tax shelter for the premises as investment property. This technique requires that the owners pay a fair market rent for their apartment, as well as collect rents from the other tenants. By including this rent in the reported annual income, the entire property becomes eligible for allowable deductions as income property, including maintenance costs, property taxes, insurance premiums, utilities (when applicable), and depreciation. Thus, the owners may be able to shelter the entire income from the investment.

Multiunit Apartment projects

The number of apartments in any one project might be 10, 50, 100, or even 1,000 units or more. Depending on the nature of the specific rental complex, there are varying degrees of management responsibility that reflect the size and scope of the project. However, regardless of size, basic financial principles of rental property are essentially the same, with the only significant difference being the amount of money involved. One example of investing in a large apartment complex is outlined in *Case Study 11.4*.

CASE STUDY 11.4 100-Unit Apartment Complex Profitability Analysis

Now examine the economics of a 100-unit apartment complex. The apartment mix and monthly rental schedule are as follows.

10 efficiency apartments @ $1,250 per month	$12,500
20 one-bedroom apartments @ $1,350 per month	27,000
60 two-bedroom apartments @ $1,500 per month	90,000
10 three-bedroom apartments @ $1,650 per month	16,500
Total monthly rent:	146,000
Total annual rent:	1,752,000
Income from other sources (laundry, parking, etc.)	27,000
Gross annual income	$1,779,000

Operating expenses, including a vacancy factor, are estimated to be 45% of the total gross income. The property is evaluated at $9 million, with $2 million allocated to the land and $7 million as the building's basis for depreciation. An investor in the 35% tax bracket may purchase this property with a $1.8 million cash down payment to a new $7.2 million first mortgage payable at 8% interest-only, due in full in 15 years. Here is a first year's profitability analysis of this investment:

$1,779,000	Gross annual income
– 800,550	Operating expenses (45%)
978,450	Net operating income
– 576,000	Debt service ($7,200,000 @ 8%)
$ 402,450	Net cash flow
– 254,520	Depreciation ($7,000,000 @ 0.03636)
$147,930	Taxable income
$402,450	Net cash flow before taxes
– 51,776	Taxes (35% bracket)
$350,674	Net cash flow after taxes
/ 1,800,000	Investment
19.48%	Cash-on-cash ROI

Note the absence of any principal add-back in this analysis because of an interest-only mortgage. Note also the absence of a growth factor. Its inclusion would raise the bottom-line yield substantially. However, unlike smaller properties, which generally follow the market values closely, larger properties invariably lag behind. In this case, the value of $9 million will probably remain constant for a while, depending on the local economic circumstances. In deciding to purchase this property, an investor would concentrate on the almost 20% ROI as the measure of profitability.

COOPERATIVES

A number of people wish to combine the economic benefits of home ownership with the carefree attributes of apartment living. While home ownership provides an inflationary hedge through value growth and equity buildup plus the tax shelters of property tax and mortgage interest deductions, living in an apartment minimizes a tenant's maintenance responsibilities and usually provides a compatible community environment. In addition, apartment living often provides tenants with a pool, sauna, marina, golf course, and tennis courts—amenities most people cannot afford on their own.

The **cooperative** apartment ownership format provides an investor with an opportunity to marry the best of two housing concepts: ownership and tenancy. As with the condominium, which will be examined later in this lesson, the cooperative provides an individual investor with the capability of being an owner and simultaneously enjoying the tenancy of an apartment, maximizing both the economic and the social benefits that accompany this arrangement.

History

A cooperative is a union of members formed for the achievement of a mutually satisfactory goal. The benefits of goal attainment are shared by the members in direct proportion to the labor and capital contributed to the cooperative enterprise. A real estate cooperative involves the joining together of people for the purpose of owning real property—usually an apartment building.

The concept of community housing is as old as humanity, dating back to the group sharing of a tree or cave. There are records of shared ownership housing dating back to Babylon and ancient Rome, but the concept saw its modern genesis in 19th century Great Britain. Then, as now, the right to share in the living accommodations was contingent on membership in the group.

Today, property control is a function of our laws defining the rights of ownership. Cooperative ownership as a legal means of holding title to property dates back to the 1880s in the United States. Until the end of World War II, however, cooperative ventures in this country were somewhat limited. It wasn't until the postwar period, when mortgage financing and all types of housing were in short supply, that cooperative corporations were organized on a large scale to combat high rents, especially in Chicago, Los Angeles, New York, and Philadelphia. The cooperative has been eclipsed in popularity by the **condominium**.

Ownership design

Cooperatives fall into two general categories: those that are publicly assisted and those that are private. Publicly assisted cooperatives are designed to serve lower-income groups through rent and mortgage interest subsidies and FHA loans. FHA Section 213 provides up to 97% insured financing for eligible cooperative enterprises. FHA Section 221(d)(2) provides up to 100% insured financing for up to 40 years at below-market interest rates to solve certain pressing inner-city housing shortages. Section 236 provides direct mortgage interest subsidies for low-income cooperative developments.

Private cooperatives can be designed as either trusts or corporations. A trust cooperative places legal ownership of the property in the name of a trust company, which then issues beneficial participation certificates to purchasers of units in the cooperative. Ownership of this certificate includes the right to lease a specific unit, subject to the cooperative's rules and regulations. Officers of the trust retain the responsibility for maintaining and managing the cooperative.

Most cooperatives are organized as private corporations. This ownership form is probably the most efficient in design because it provides for the election of directors by the apartment owners-shareholders. These officers of the corporation then assume the responsibilities for management. At the same time, the individual shareholders are immune from direct personal liability for corporate obligations.

A corporate cooperative vests ownership of the property in the name of a corporation. Stock in this corporation is issued and sold to apartment buyers in denominations proportionate to the value of the apartments available for lease. Buyers select a specific apartment, purchase a corresponding amount of stock in the owning corporation, and execute a **proprietary lease** with what is now their own company. The lessees are then subject to the rules and regulations established in the corporate charter and bylaws.

Under the terms of a proprietary lease, the specific unit is inseparable from the entire ownership format. The amount of rent to be paid is a function of the proportionate share of the apartment's value, compared with the total value of the project. For example, assume a 200-apartment high-rise cooperative with an overall value of $8 million. An owner of a $40,000 apartment (stock is issued to the owner in this amount) has a 0.5% obligation for operating costs ($40,000 / $8,000,000 = 0.005). If costs equal $100,000 for the year, this apartment owner'tenant's contribution for operating costs is $500, or $41.66 per month ($100,000 × 0.005 = $500 / 12 = $41.66).

Financing

Developers of cooperatives secure the land for the project by purchase or lease; construct the apartment building, usually in the form of a high-rise or group of high-rise structures; and offer the apartments for sale. The purchaser is sold stock in the corporation that owns the structure in an amount commensurate with the value of the apartment chosen.

The stock may be purchased for cash or on terms. If cash is paid, then the lease for the subject apartment is developed at a rent reflecting the tenant's proportionate obligation for operating costs, as described earlier. These costs include property taxes, insurance premiums, and maintenance expenses. If the stock is purchased on terms, after an acceptable down payment has been made, the buyer will execute an installment contract with the corporation to include an appropriate amount for principal and interest, in addition to the proportionate operating charges.

Tax benefits

Most privately developed cooperatives allow their shareholders to benefit from any gain in the sale of their individual stock. However, government-sponsored projects limit the amount of profit a shareholder may earn to the original purchase price of the stock plus any principal paid on the mortgage and any capital improvements made to the individual apartment. Under the provisions of Section 216 of the IRS Code, a cooperative shareholder may deduct from taxable income the money paid for proportionate shares of the property taxes and interest paid on the corporation's indebtedness. Furthermore, if professionals or businesses use the cooperative property for the production of income, they are also eligible for depreciation allowances.

To qualify for these deductions under Section 216, 80% of the cooperative's income must be derived from tenant-owner rentals. Hence, a project designed to allocate space for rental income other than that from the tenant-owners' units, such as street-level offices or retail shops, must observe the 20% limitation on such income to preserve the individual shareholder's tax benefits.

Current trends

Cooperatives as a form of apartment ownership currently appear to have the greatest appeal to high-income individuals who wish to control their environments completely. By forming a closed corporation and limiting the sale of its stock, a cooperative can legally circumvent the open-housing laws. If a cooperative requires only cash purchases be made (thus eliminating any delinquent mortgage payment problems) and strictly enforces the buy-back provisions in its bylaws, it can be designed to serve the interests of people who desire a completely homogeneous and carefully controlled economic and social environment.

All other forms of community housing must be offered for sale to the general public. For this reason, most middle-income cooperatives have been converted to condominiums to avoid the problems of delinquent rental payments and subsequent mortgage foreclosures. However, government-sponsored, low-income cooperatives are still being promoted as a means of raising housing standards in the central areas of many large cities.

CONDOMINIUMS

The condominium, a natural alternative to the cooperative, is based on the individual ownership of space in a multiunit building, be it an apartment, store, office, or other real property. Unlike the cooperative, the condominium-ownership design removes the risk of reliance on others who might fail to make mortgage payments, and consequently, jeopardize an entire project.

History

Although present to a small degree in early Rome, condominiums did not become popular until medieval times when they effectively solved housing shortages in the walled cities of Europe. The condominium concept, as developed in the middle-European countries, became called coproprietary ownership and assumed varying degrees of importance through the centuries.

The idea was transported to South America by the immigrants of the early 1900s. Years before the United States accepted this form of ownership, many other countries, including Belgium, Brazil, Chile, Germany, Italy, and Mexico, had developed statutes recognizing and defining the condominium **horizontal regime** as a legal proprietorship.

With passage of the 1961 National Housing Act, condominiums were legally recognized in this country for the first time. Section 234 of this act provided FHA mortgage insurance for apartments to be built in densely populated areas of Puerto Rico, which was suffering from a severe housing shortage. High-rise structures were constructed and individual mortgages arranged under FHA terms for individuals who wished to purchase their own apartments. The concept, however, showed slow acceptance by mainland developers. By 1968, only California, Florida, Michigan, and the District of Columbia had constructed any significant number of condominiums.

During the early 1970s, *condomania* spread throughout the nation. A national housing shortage, coupled with an easy money market, gave rise to an apartment building boom that used the condominium format as a selling technique. In 1972, however, adverse national publicity concerning the abuses perpetrated by some unscrupulous developers slowed the condo boom considerably. There were reports of condominium developers who retained the legal ownership of the land under their projects plus the amenities constructed thereon, such as the swimming pool and clubhouse, and then charged apartment owners extraordinary land rents and exorbitant amenity-use fees. These reports quickly dampened the public's enthusiasm for condominium ownership.

As a result of purported and proved abuses, new laws controlling condominium construction and management have been adopted by most states. Currently, condominiums have matured into an efficient and viable form of property ownership that offers investors great flexibility in designing their realty holdings.

Ownership design

Condominiums can be established for any type of real property, not just for apartment buildings. Other applications of this ownership form include marinas, called *dockominiums*, office space, and warehouse space, to name a few. The organizational design, however, is essentially the same for all condominium developments.

Most states have enabling legislation that establishes the legal structure under which a condominium can be developed. Among other stipulations, these statutes include provisions for

- recognition of divided ownerships transferable by existing title documents;
- establishment of a binding declaration of bylaws among the participants that cannot be voided or altered without mutual consent;
- limitations on developer self-dealing and other control issues while the developer still owns the majority of the units, and thus a majority of the votes;
- restrictions against further partitioning of the property described in the condominium regime; and
- establishment of separate property tax assessments on each clearly defined unit.

The organization of a condominium requires that the developer first file a declaration of condominium and a master deed with the appropriate local government registration office. Then, each purchaser of a condominium unit secures an individual deed to an apartment, which defines a fee simple ownership plus an undivided legal interest in all **common areas** of the condominium structure.

Financing

In effect, a high-rise condominium is a vertical subdivision, with each floor representing a block, and each apartment or office space, a lot. Likewise, low-rise condominium structures are horizontal subdivisions with the improvements joined together by common walls, eliminating the side yards. Thus, a developer generally secures funds for a condominium development from sources that normally provide money for subdivision site improvements and construction financing, such as commercial banks or mortgage bankers. A condominium apartment buyer generally secures a loan from a lender in the home mortgage field, similar to a buyer purchasing a single-family detached house.

A real estate lender views a high-rise condominium apartment as a *house in the air* or a cube of space circumscribed by walls. The individual apartments are collateral for specific loans, and their values are determined much like the values of individual houses. In the event of a default, a lender can foreclose on the collateral and assume an ownership role with all of the associated duties and obligations until the apartment can be resold. Thus, all of the normal realty lending activities apply to the financing of condominium property.

Condominiums are accepted by the FHA and VA for their insurance and guarantee programs. Moreover, they are considered by these federal agencies to be important vehicles for the provision of needed housing for low-income and middle-income individuals.

Tax benefits

Because a condominium unit is considered to be a basic form of real estate, all of the tax benefits accruing to property owners also apply to condo owners. Deductions for property taxes and mortgage interest are available to the owner-occupant, while operating costs and depreciation allowances are deductible if the apartment is rented as income property. If an owner wants to sell the unit, any profits secured from the sale do not have to be shared with a corporation (as in cooperative ownership) and can be postponed through the use of an installment sale or like-property exchange.

Current trends

The condominium form of ownership is likely to continue in importance, retaining its position in the housing market and as a viable ownership alternative for singles and childless couples.

In addition to apartments, the condominium format can be applied to office and commercial buildings, as well as industrial and factory-built home parks. Even single-family detached houses are being constructed around condominium-area amenities such as golf courses or marina facilities. In this type of condo development, the purchaser receives a deed to the house and underlying lot plus an undivided interest in the amenities. A regular fee for the use of these facilities is assessed by the managing association and charged to the subdivision homeowners, establishing a private club atmosphere. Sometimes only the house is purchased, with all landscaping, exterior painting, and roof replacement performed on a regular schedule by the condo association.

Retirement and recreational developments have also used the condo format—many very successfully. Retirement communities have burgeoned all over the country, primarily in the warm-weather states. These developments, which cater to the tastes and physical abilities of the owners, are usually composed of a mixture of single-family detached homes and condominium apartments. Other retirement villages consist entirely of condominiums. The larger factory-built home projects, in which each person owns a lot in common with the other lot owners, provide for shared ownership and use of the common-area roads, pool, and clubhouse.

Recreational condominium projects also have become successful as members of our society have become more affluent and acquired more leisure time. Ski areas, ocean and lake resorts, and golf courses increasingly catch the eye of the astute investor-developer as potential building sites.

Securities rule

Careful attention should be paid to second-home investment condominiums that are purchased with a money-back guarantee and lock-in management agreement with the selling agency. The Securities and Exchange Commission (SEC) has interpreted that these purchases are not considered real estate per se, but rather, securities that their promoters and developers must register for SEC supervision. If this interpretation prevails and the investments are not real estate, then the IRS may disallow any realty tax benefits. Consequently, investors in this area of real estate would have to prove that they were taking the risks normally associated with investment activity to be eligible for income property allowances.

Time-sharing

An innovative ownership format that is a spinoff of the recreational condominium concept is the **time-share**. Here, a condominium unit can be designed for multiownership, with each owner having a specific period of use. Consequently, in theory at least, 26 persons could jointly own one condominium apartment and each use it for two weeks of the year.

Expanding on this theme, the joint owner of a mountain condominium apartment could trade the time allocation with the owner of a seaside condominium. Through the services of an association of time-sharing owners, this approach has been further extended to include foreign country condominium owners. A two-week stay in a Monaco condominium is possible in exchange for the use of an Atlantic City apartment.

Time-sharing can be for a specific period or in perpetuity. The time-share owner will have annual assessments for property expenses.

CONVERSIONS TO CONDOMINIUMS

One of the more creative real estate investment opportunities is the **conversion** of rental properties into condominium ownerships. Depending on market conditions at the time of conversion, as revealed by a feasibility study, an owner of an apartment, office, or commercial building can file the appropriate documents to declare the existing property a condominium and proceed to sell the individual apartments, office units, or stores. The basic market of potential purchasers of the converted units is the tenants occupying the building.

The most successful conversions are of properties that are successful rentals. People want to be there and will buy. The least successful conversions are those of problem properties. A conversion will not attract buyers to an unattractive property.

Some investors are engaged solely with conversions as profit-making ventures and travel the country purchasing property specifically to convert into condominiums. In land use, the principle of agglomeration is reflected by combining small parcels to make one large, more valuable property. These investors apply the agglomeration principle in reverse—when converting to individual units, the sum of the parts exceeds the value of the whole. Other investors use this technique as a means of securing a final gain for the sale of their property when all the depreciation has been used up. Still others use conversion as a means of selling their property to avoid rent ceilings placed by local government agencies. These ceilings quickly dry up rental cash flow because property taxes, utility charges, and maintenance costs continue to rise unabated. In many cities, there are restrictions on condominium conversions, such as lottery procedures and minimum rental vacancy requirements. City planners sometimes desire to maintain the pool of affordable rental housing by restricting conversions.

Case Study 11.5 provides an overview of converting a large apartment complex into condominiums.

CASE STUDY 11.5 Problem Analysis: 100-Unit Apartment Conversion

A conversion analysis measures a property's value as an ongoing rental operation against the potential total value to be derived from the sale of the individual units, be they apartments, offices, stores, or other types of space.

Examine the economics of the conversion of a 100-unit apartment complex to a condominium-ownership format. The property includes 100 apartment units situated in 10 separate, individual, wood-frame, and stone-faced buildings, clustered around a swimming pool and clubhouse. In addition to its garages and storage facilities, the property is surrounded by high hedges and tall trees that effectively isolate it from the adjoining neighborhood. This feeling of unity is enhanced by the rustic alpine decor complementing the rolling eight-acre terrain. The project is 20 years old and fully depreciated by its owner. It includes one-bedroom, two-bedroom, and three-bedroom apartments, all with fireplaces, kitchens with built-in appliances, and individual central heating and cooling units.

The buildings include a total of 150,420 square feet, of which 40,420 square feet are the hallways, laundry rooms, and storage spaces—leaving 110,000 square feet as the rentable area. Market rents for this property are estimated to be an average of $0.35 per square foot per month. Thus, the gross annual rent from the apartments is $462,000 (110,000 square feet × 0.35 = $38,500 × 12 months = $462,000). Together with $8,000 as additional annual income from laundry machines and separate garage rentals, the property generates $470,000 total annual gross income. Assuming total operating expenses of $212,000, including vacancies, the NOI before debt service is $258,000 ($470,000 – $212,000 = $258,000).

In this example, the $258,000 NOI indicates a market value of $2,580,000 for the property as a rental investment. This amount is derived from an application of the income-approach appraisal technique, using a 10% capitalization rate. A capitalization rate may be interpreted as that rate of return from a particular investment with which an investor is satisfied. Thus, an investment of $2,580,000 will develop a return of $258,000 at a 10% rate ($2,580,000 × 0.10 = $258,000, or $258,000 / 0.10 = $2,580,000).

This value can be compared with the total amount that could be secured from the sale of the individual apartments as condominiums. There are various appraisal methods to estimate the sales value of converted condominium apartments. One is the market approach in which an estimate of value is derived by comparing the subject property to similar properties recently sold. Another appraisal method is the cost approach, which estimates the total costs for rebuilding the property today and then deducts an amount for depreciation commensurate with the subject property's loss in value over time. The income approach provides an estimate of a property's value based on the capitalization of its net income stream, as applied above.

In appraising the value of the apartments as individual units, a combination of the market and cost approaches develops a factor of $60 per square foot of living area as a proper comparison unit. This amount reflects the current depreciated value of all of the improvements, including the value of the land. Thus, the total amount of money that can be secured from the sale of the individual apartments is estimated to be $6,600,000 (110,000 square feet of living area × $60 = $6,600,000).

Estimating a 40% sales cost factor, including required renovations as well as commissions, title examination and insurance fees, escrow, legal, and mortgage-placement charges, the net proceeds from the sale would equal $3,960,000 ($6,600,000 × 0.40 = $2,640,000 and $6,600,000 – $2,640,000 = $3,960,000).

The difference in the value of the project as a rental operation versus its potential net sales income is $1,380,000 ($3,960,000 – $2,580,000 = $1,380,000). Thus, the owner stands to make a substantial profit on such a conversion.

Procedure

The conversion procedure involves filing the necessary legal documents to secure approval from the appropriate local government agencies, as described earlier. Then a marketing strategy is designed to reflect the current local demand for the type of space being offered for sale. This plan includes a price schedule of the individual units as a function of their size and location within the complex. In addition, a program for financing the individual sales with local lenders must be developed in advance.

Many conversions, especially of older apartment buildings, require extensive renovation and modernization of improvements to comply with current building codes and to provide for the government's disability requirements. Structures with more than three floors may require the installation of elevators, and others may need their stairwells remodeled to meet current fire protection standards.

When extensive repairs must be made, care should be taken to minimize disturbance of the present tenants to preserve rental cash flow during the conversion period. One of the greatest risks of the conversion technique is the possible mass exodus of tenants and the elimination of rental income before sales commence. A converter should be prepared to meet this financial contingency with adequate capital reserves and a sound marketing plan.

A natural, often readily available, market for the converter-investor is the tenant who already occupies the property involved. An honest and forthright approach is required when notifying tenants of the conversion decision. A tenant's alternatives are relatively simple—purchase the unit and retain possession or be prepared to move when the unit is sold.

Often, the harshness of the buy-or-move alternative can be softened by a new lease for six months or a year to enable the tenant to find other quarters. More effective from the converter's viewpoint, however, is to arrange the purchase terms specifically for the tenant-occupant so that little cash is needed and the required mortgage payment approximates the present rental amount. Thus, the tenant can become an owner with little change in financial position. This approach can overcome some of the sales resistance from tenant-occupants, but experience has shown that only 30% to 50% of current tenants choose to become owners.

Midconversion difficulties

Aside from the expected difficulties encountered with condominium organization and renovation, some conversion projects undergo extraordinary problems during the marketing period.

At some point in the sales program, a mixture of tenants, resident owners, and nonresident owners may all share an interest in the same project. Problems may arise, such as inconsistent payment of rent and association dues, ignored rules, and noninvolvement of resident owners.

The converter must consider the solution to these problems at the outset, establish a clear and concise set of rules and regulations, and devise a set of enforceable penalties to back them up. As this is a complicated process, conversion programs should be closely supervised by competent lawyers, accountants, and property managers.

SUMMARY OF INVESTING IN RESIDENTIAL PROPERTIES

This lesson examined the alternatives available for investments in residential properties, including single-family detached homes, multiunit apartment projects, cooperatives, and condominiums.

More investments are made in residential properties than in all other forms of real estate combined. The most common ownership is the single-family detached home. An owner-occupied home, however, does not fully fit the technical description of an investment because it does not generate income. Still, a homeowner does consider a house as an investment and profits from it through property tax and mortgage interest deductions, as well as through possible growth in value.

To qualify as an investment in the fullest sense, a house needs to be rented. House rentals usually generate only enough income to cover the minimum maintenance expenses plus mortgage payments. Detached houses situated in areas with rezoning potentials are more profitable. Here, the rental income generated during the holding period before rezoning acts to develop a return on an investor's initial cash outlay, and the expected increase in property value reflects potentially large profits.

For investment purposes, duplex, triplex, and larger multiunit apartment projects provide investors with many tax-sheltered, profit-making opportunities. Because it involves a large degree of personal commitment to management, residential rental apartment ownership requires more of an owner's time and effort than do most other forms of realty investment. Depending on the size of the project, these responsibilities can be delegated to professional management firms.

Single apartments in a multiunit building may be owned by individuals who join together in cooperatives or condominiums to enjoy the positive attributes of apartment living while minimizing the responsibilities of home ownership. The benefits of apartment living, with friends and activities close by, appeal to a large segment of our population.

A cooperative is based on a corporate format in which individual shareholders execute proprietary leases for apartments suitable to their needs. The corporation owns the property, but the shareholders can benefit from deductions for their proportionate payments for property taxes and interest.

In a condominium, a specific apartment is owned in fee simple by an individual, who also acquires a joint ownership interest, together with the other apartment owners, in the areas common to the overall project. Such common areas include the land, parking areas, hallways, elevators, interior walls, and roof.

Condominium owners are responsible for the costs of maintaining their individual apartments, including principal and interest, property taxes, and insurance premiums involved in the apartments' ownerships. Owners are also responsible for contributing to the maintenance costs of the common areas on a proportionate basis relative to the value of their apartments compared with the value of the overall project. Building and liability insurance may be part of the condominium association fee.

In both forms of single-apartment ownership, the cooperative and the condominium, an owner may occupy the apartment and enjoy the facilities provided or may sell or rent the apartment as desired but must observe the rules, regulations, and bylaws of the specific project. In each case, the administration of the property is the responsibility of an association whose membership comprises entirely of apartment owners.

Another investment alternative is the conversion of improved income properties to condominium ownerships. Applicable to apartments as well as office buildings, shopping centers, and other commercial uses, the condominium conversion technique enables an owner to capitalize to the highest degree when selling the property. Rather than offer the property for sale as an operating rental project, an owner can create a condominium regime and offer each apartment, office, or store for sale to individual buyers. This strategy often develops profits in excess of the value of the property as an operating rental project.

Because of the many complexities involved, including the financing arrangements and usual renovations required by local building inspection agencies, professional advice from lawyers, accountants, building contractors, and real estate brokers should be sought by a converter before conversion plans are undertaken.

DISCUSSION TOPICS

1. Investigate the occupancy rates of somewhat comparable apartments in the community, as well as the rental rates. Discuss the factors that seem to allow some properties to enjoy lower vacancy rates.

INTRODUCTION TO INVESTING IN OFFICE BUILDINGS

The nation's business activities are oriented to an office environment. Each profession, government agency, financial institution, corporation, or business needs an office to house its service activities. The largest industrial firms require a main office in which to centralize their management operations, in addition to branch offices located in each city in which plants manufacture their products. The General Services Administration of the U.S. federal government is the world's largest lessee of office space. It is responsible for providing the housing for government activities, which range from post office operations, to the parks service, to the space program, in addition to the myriad of activities in between.

In the fourth quarter of 2018, overall vacancy remains relatively high at 13.1%, according to Statista, and is expected to remain flat through 2020. A significant number of office space construction projects starting in 2017 for Manhattan, San Francisco, Seattle, and Washington, D.C., mean those markets will suffer temporary oversupply, but absorption is expected to be rapid. These same low vacancy rates, however, are forcing tenants to explore new, untapped real estate markets. Tightening market fundamentals are also driving landlord confidence across most markets.

Downtown areas—also called the **central business district (CBD)**—include the most significant concentrations of premier office space. The growing influence of "smart buildings" that can accommodate modern technology and provide adequate heating, ventilation, and air-conditioning systems means that existing buildings increasingly suffer from **functional obsolescence**. This often justifies new construction in office markets that seem to have adequate supplies of space. Data centers and network operational centers are becoming more popular real estate investments.

The characteristics of a suitable location in the central city include adequate parking, an aesthetically pleasing ambience, and proximity to government entities, transportation, lodging, restaurants, retail businesses, and other office buildings. In the suburbs, there should be an absence of adverse influences or activities and access to good roads, transportation, air service, parking, and other office buildings.

The factors considered to be essential in deciding on the location of a company's headquarters were derived from a survey of the top executives from 400 nationwide organizations. Listed in descending order of importance, those factors are

- large functional space,
- quality of community life,
- room to expand,
- efficient access to market(s),
- low cost,

- good business climate,
- community image,
- available qualified labor supply,
- social climate, and
- college and university availability.

This lesson examines the varied investment opportunities in this segment of the real estate market.

TYPES OF OFFICE INVESTMENTS

Office building owners range from the individual owner-occupant to the large corporate conglomerate. Most central city, multistory office buildings are owned by large institutional investors that have the financial capability to support the investment over the initial years when cash returns are limited. The smaller office building owner, unable to compete with the corporate giants, has turned to the suburban market for profitable office investments. These outlying developments range from converted old houses to modern preplanned **office parks**.

Office space is generally classified as Class A, Class B, or Class C, according to general guidelines established by BOMA. They take into account market place, location, finishes, amenities, transportation, parking, and public perception. Class A space is the most desirable, proceeding downward to Class C space. Class A office space in Manhattan might require the most expensive luxury finishes and art work, as well as the newest buildings with the best views. In the capitols of states with small populations, it might be an historic building with virtually no modern amenities but with a prestigious address near legislative offices. Each market is different, and even submarkets differ widely. Local commercial real estate brokers should be consulted for area perceptions of office space classification.

Low-rise office buildings

Owning a small office building is similar to owning a small apartment building in terms of constant tenant turnover and management responsibilities. Although office tenants generally fulfill their lease commitments, small offices tend to be difficult to rent on long-term leases.

A prime location is not an overriding factor for many tenants of low-rise office buildings. Consequently, profitable investments can be made in office units located on secondary streets, enabling an investor to offer somewhat lower rents. In fact, many large-parcel developments are designed to attract high-rent tenants to the more prominent street-front exposures, with smaller offices constructed toward the rear areas of the lot. Of course, appropriate access and **off-street parking** facilities must be provided, not only to satisfy zoning requirements, but also to attract tenants.

Owners of low-rise office developments are usually able to pass the responsibility for interior maintenance to their tenants while retaining the obligation for all major repairs and exterior care. The degree of these responsibilities is a function of the size of the project. For example, the tenant in a one-office home conversion normally accepts most of the maintenance tasks; if the house contains four offices, the owner of the building usually maintains the exterior and provides office-cleaning services, whereas the tenants are responsible for interior maintenance, repairs, and decorating.

Neighborhood offices

The most popular forms of low-rise office investments are usually found in smaller projects designed to serve neighborhood needs. The conversion of old homes into offices is a much-favored technique in this category. The charm of spacious, high-ceilinged rooms, the generous use of fine woods, and the period-piece quality of decor appeals to many business and professional tenants. When these homes are located in relatively accessible areas of a neighborhood, they attract lawyers, accountants, smaller insurance companies, and real estate brokers. Frequently, the architectural beauty of these converted offices adds a special uniqueness that holds tenants for comparatively long time periods.

Other types of neighborhood offices include those situated above street-level stores that front on main thoroughfares with a high volume of pedestrian traffic. These locations appeal to dentists, optometrists, lawyers, and others who cater to an established clientele but who do not require the more impressive and expensive premises of the retailer. A modern variant of this type of office space is the small, mixed-use commercial center constructed around an inner courtyard containing some artistic focal point, such as a fountain or sculpture. In this design, the retail shops occupy the ground-floor spaces, while the offices are located at balcony level, with entrances facing the courtyard.

Medical office buildings

Among the more profitable low-rise office investments are clinics housing a number of medical practitioners, such as doctors and dentists, who have joined together to offer services from one centralized location. Depending on the size and scope of the clinic, a pharmacy and a laboratory might also be included on the premises.

Although clinic designs vary, most include the doctors' offices as complete, self-sufficient units. Others are developed around the theme of a central reception and waiting room. Here, participating doctors share the costs of a central filing and billing system, as well as a pool of receptionists, nurses, and medical technicians.

The additional plumbing, parking, and special electrical requirements involved in clinic construction, including ceiling-to-floor partitions and a larger-than-normal number of interior doors greatly exceed the costs of other forms of office construction. Therefore, the rents are higher and the leases are longer than for standard office space. As a result, many doctors have formed groups to develop clinics that they themselves own, often as condominium units.

Homogeneous tenants

Other nonmedical groups may also be joined together in mutually beneficial relationships. For example, executive office suites could be offered to insurance agents, real estate brokers, mortgage bankers, title insurance companies, lawyers, and accountants who could form a homogeneous tenant grouping in the financial center of a neighborhood office development. A beauty salon, barber shop, physical fitness studio, and health food retailer would also make a complementary group.

A variation of this approach uses the same theme to attract a group of tenants offering the same service. Thus, a lawyer's building or an insurance building can be developed, where a person seeking these special services can choose from a number of practitioners who are all housed in the same structure.

These **homogeneous tenancies** lend themselves to central receptionists, common electronic services, photocopying facilities, telephone answering services, and other shared office amenities. Such systems are especially attractive to both newly licensed professionals and thrifty old-timers. This central design enables a tenant to choose considerably smaller office space than would be necessary if the centralized services were not provided. Consequently, the rents can be commensurately less, although a contribution of a proportionate sum of money for compensation of those who staff the central services would be stipulated in the lease agreement.

Mixed-use buildings

Investors often design buildings that are established to attract a number of different types of tenants. For example, consider the construction of a building that would provide underground parking, street-level retail spaces, office accommodations on floors 2 through 10, and apartments above.

High-rise office buildings

In most metropolitan areas, the largest amount of office space is contained within skyscrapers constructed to house a single institutional tenant, a group of tenants, or both. The financial ability to carry negative-cash-flow investments for a number of years has probably made high-rise offices the exclusive investment prerogative of major corporations.

Often, a large company erects an office tower, occupies some of the space for its own operations, and leases to others the area it does not immediately require.

Usually, the management strategy for these large developments includes the opportunity for the major tenant to expand into the leased space as the need arises. Other large corporations construct their own wholly occupied high-rise towers in strategic mid-city locations to enjoy the advantages of centralized services. These companies often incorporate unique architectural designs to establish publicity value, such as the shape of the Transamerica Pyramid in San Francisco.

Case Study 11.6 provides a five-year analysis for a high-rise office building.

CASE STUDY 11.6 Five-Story Office Building

The property is located at the intersection of two heavily traveled major arteries. It is a new, glass-walled, five-story office building containing 50,000 total square feet—40,000 of which is rentable space. The other 10,000 square feet include the entry lobby, hallways, elevator shafts, bathrooms, storage space, and utility rooms. A paved parking area surrounds the building. The rents vary from floor to floor but average $10 per square foot of rentable area per year. Operating expenses are 35% of the gross rents, including vacancy and reserves. The total cost of the project is $2.5 million, and the investors can secure a first mortgage for $1.75 million (70% of value) payable at 10% interest only for 15 years. This requires a $750,000 cash investment. Depreciation is established at an annual straight rate of 2.564% (39 years straight-line), which is applied to a book basis beginning at $2 million. The land is booked at $500,000. All leases are established for five years, at which time, the property will be sold. The following tabulation shows a profit analysis of this project, including its sale. All rents and operating expenses are kept constant for the five-year analysis:

I. Annual Income	
$400,000	Gross annual income
– 140,000	35% operating expense ratio
260,000	Net operating income
– 175,000	Debt service (10% interest only on $1.75 million)
$85,000	Gross income before depreciation
– 51,280	Depreciation ($2 million @ 0.02564, 39 years straight-line)
$33,720	Taxable income
× 0.34	Tax bracket
$11,465	Income taxes
85,000	Gross income before depreciation
– 11,465	Income taxes
$73,535	Cash-on-cash ROI 9.8% on $750,000 investment

II. Sale at End of Five Years	
$3,000,000	Net sale price
– 2,243,600	Adjusted book basis ($2,500,000 – $256,400)
756,400	Gross gain
× 0.15	Maximum capital gain tax
$113,460	Income taxes
642,940	Net profit
/ 5 years	Holding period
128,588	Annualized gain (rounded)
/ 750,000	Investment
17.00%	Annualized yield on gain
+ 9.80%	Cash-on-cash annual ROI
26.80%	Bottom-line annualized ROI

Note that this analysis does not consider the time value of money.

Office parks

The congestion of downtown areas and the inconvenience this crowding creates in terms of traffic and lack of adequate parking facilities often hamper efforts to provide efficient services. Many inner-city companies, following current migrational trends, have settled into buildings located in suburban office parks.

In addition to quick accessibility from suburban home to suburban office, many office parks offer additional amenities to attract tenants. Some provide recreational, cultural, or dining facilities within the complex, in addition to a preplanned and well-maintained ambience, to serve tenants and their clients. Full-range indoor gymnasiums, pools, tennis courts, and health club facilities, as well as quality restaurants, are available in some modern office park projects.

Rental achievement requirements

In the development of many new commercial real estate projects, including high-rise office buildings and office parks, the financing pattern requires that the investment's breakeven point be met by advance lease commitments from credit tenants. A **credit tenant** is one that is large enough, and financially strong enough, to be rated as investment grade. Some projects require national credit tenants, and others are satisfied with regional credit tenants. Before issuing a construction loan, an interim financier will insist on the developer securing an agreement from a permanent lender to issue a long-term mortgage at the completion of construction, the proceeds of which will take out the interim mortgagee.

Although many permanent loan financiers, such as insurance companies, will readily issue such standby commitments for economically sound developments, they will only fund their commitments when the buildings are completed according to the approved plans and specifications. In addition, and as a condition of the loan under a rental achievement clause, these lenders require enough advance leases to be secured by the developer to meet at least the investment's fixed expenses of property taxes, insurance premiums, basic maintenance costs, and mortgage payments.

Thus, an investor involved in the development of a new project must solicit leases before the completion of construction. Whereas the developer of a shopping center may only need advance commitments from a few basic major tenants, an office building developer usually needs to secure leases from numerous individual tenants to meet the lender's rent-up requirements. Most office building managers need to produce leases for approximately 80% of full occupancy to reach a breakeven point—a relatively arduous task.

Office condominiums

The office condominium concept, long used by doctors and dentists in their clinics, has won widespread interest around the country as other tenants seek to become owners. This desire results from rising rental rates for all types of rental space. To guarantee a controlled cost, many office tenants are becoming office owners.

Ownership of an office condominium is similar to ownership of a residential condominium. A prescribed space is owned in fee simple, together with an undivided ownership of the common areas. These common areas include the land under the building, the parking area, the entry hall and other hallways, bathrooms, utility and storage rooms, and the roof. The individual owners belong to an association that is responsible for maintenance of the common areas plus enforcement of the adopted rules and regulations. Each owner contributes a proportionate share of the common-area costs as the association fees, which are adjusted by the board of directors to reflect annual fluctuations.

One of the advantages of condominium office ownership, in addition to controlled occupancy costs, is the possibility of equity growth through mortgage principal paydown plus increasing value. Although owners are allowed to deduct interest, property taxes, association fees, maintenance, and depreciation, they forfeit rent as a deductible expense, so these benefits are minimized somewhat. Still, an owner, unlike a tenant, can participate in the building's management policies.

Probably the most serious problem facing a condominium office owner is the limitation on future expansion because it may be impossible to acquire adjoining, already-owned offices. Under these circumstances, the only alternative may be to sell and move.

Conversion to condominiums

An office building owner may find it desirable to convert the investment into a condominium. By using the concepts of conversion previously discussed for the apartment project, the tenants can be given the right to purchase their offices before the project is offered for sale to the public. *Case Study 11.7* is an example of such a conversion.

CASE STUDY 11.7 24-Unit Condominium Office Complex

As part of a larger park development, the developers set aside three acres on which 24 condominium office suites were constructed. These garden units are arranged around a central courtyard, with each office having a private entrance. This arrangement has given the complex an aspect of separation from the other buildings in the project. The units are of contemporary design, one and two stories in height, and include modules of 1,200, 1,500, 2,400, and 4,800 square feet. Each is self-contained, with separate heating and cooling facilities, as well as individual bathrooms and utility meters.

The land under the condominium project is held under a 99-year lease rather than in fee simple. This **leasehold** arrangement—a feature of the sales package—created an unusual marketing problem for the developers. Although it allowed for a lower initial purchase price, it also required overcoming predictable customer resistance to the nonownership ramifications of the leasehold.

Each purchaser of a condominium office suite automatically becomes a member of the association organized to manage and maintain the common areas and supervise the condominium bylaws. The member's voting rights are based on the percentage of space purchased in relation to the overall building area of the complex. The association establishes the fees to be paid by its members for common-area upkeep. These fees are shown in the following tabulation:

	1,200 sq. ft.	**1,500 sq. ft.**	**2,400 sq. ft.**	**4,800 sq. ft.**
Janitorial services	$45.60	$57.00	$91.20	$182.40
Insurance	7.20	9.00	14.40	28.80
Ground lease	129.60	162.00	259.20	518.40
Land taxes	26.40	33.00	52.80	105.60
Common-area services	16.80	21.00	33.60	67.20
Accounting fees	14.40	18.00	28.80	57.60
Total monthly payment	$240.00	$300.00	$480.00	$960.00

After the appropriate renovation, filing of condominium papers, arrangement of financing, sales promotion, and closings, an office building can be subdivided into individual, private office ownerships that include an undivided interest in the common areas. These common areas are the roof, elevators, hallways, entry area, utility and storage rooms, and the land under the project, including the parking areas. Similar to apartment condominiums, the new owners would form their own association, responsible for the upkeep and taxes on these common areas. As with apartment condominiums, an office condominium owner is responsible for the principal, interest, property taxes, insurance, and maintenance of the specific office space plus a proportionate share of the expenses for the common areas.

This raises the problem of what would happen if some unit owners lost their properties through bankruptcy. The other unit owners would have to meet the property tax, maintenance, and insurance premium liabilities. This could put all of them in jeopardy. Careful attention must be paid to all contingencies and provisions made for a real estate condo conversion.

THE AMERICANS WITH DISABILITIES ACT (ADA)

Much like the Fair Housing Act, investors must also be aware of the **Americans with Disabilities Act (ADA)**. The most pertinent provisions for investors are contained in Title I, which deals with employment, and Title III, which contains requirements concerning public accommodations. Modifications to a property that may be required under this law are the responsibility of both the owner and the tenant. However, the cost of the modifications may be paid as negotiated in the lease.

The following information was obtained from the Department of Justice's website www.ada .gov/cguide.htm.

The ADA prohibits discrimination on the basis of disability in employment, state and local government, public accommodations, commercial facilities, transportation, and telecommunications. It also applies to the United States Congress.

To be protected by the ADA, one must have a disability or have a relationship or association with an individual with a disability. An individual with a disability is defined by the ADA as a person who has a physical or mental impairment that substantially limits one or more major life activities, a person who has a history or record of such impairment, or a person who is perceived by others as having such impairment. The ADA does not specifically name all of the impairments that are covered.

ADA Title I: Employment

Title I requires employers with 15 or more employees to provide qualified individuals with disabilities an equal opportunity to benefit from the full range of employment-related opportunities available to others. For example, it prohibits discrimination in recruitment, hiring, promotions, training, pay, social activities, and other privileges of employment. It restricts questions that can be asked about an applicant's disability before a job offer is made, and it requires that employers make reasonable accommodation to the known physical or mental limitations of otherwise qualified individuals with disabilities unless it results in undue hardship. Religious entities with 15 or more employees are covered under Title I.

Title I complaints must be filed with the U. S. Equal Employment Opportunity Commission (EEOC) within 180 days of the date of discrimination, or 300 days if the charge is filed with a designated state or local fair employment practice agency. Individuals may file a lawsuit in federal court only after they receive a right-to-sue letter from the EEOC.

Charges of employment discrimination on the basis of disability may be filed at any U.S. EEOC field office. Field offices are located in 50 cities throughout the U.S. and are listed in most telephone directories under "U.S. Government." For the appropriate EEOC field office in your geographic area, contact:

(800) 669-4000 (voice)
(800) 669-6820 (TTY)
www.eeoc.gov

Publications and information on EEOC-enforced laws may be obtained by calling:

(800) 669-3362 (voice)
(800) 800-3302 (TTY)

For information on how to accommodate a specific individual with a disability, contact the Job Accommodation Network at:

(800) 526-7234 (voice)
(800) 781-9403 (TTY)
http://askjan.org

SUMMARY OF INVESTING IN OFFICE BUILDINGS

This lesson examined various aspects of office building ownership, including a review of the various types of offices available to an investor.

Typically, an office building investor will make careful market studies before becoming involved in a specific project. Not only will the existing trends in supply and demand for offices be examined, but more particularly, the segment of the office market that pertains to the building under consideration will be scrutinized. Primary consideration will be given to the demand for space by new businesses in the area as well as to the expansion and movement of existing tenants.

The widespread popularity of low-rise office buildings provides investors with innumerable opportunities to participate in this form of real estate ownership. Ranging from the converted house to the modern office park, these offices can be leased to small and large companies alike. Many small offices are found above stores along major arterial streets, as well as in spaces allocated for this use within the arcades of large shopping centers. The most popular forms of low-rise office investments are found in smaller projects designed to serve neighborhood needs.

Some specialty small-office groupings are designed as clinics and house a number of medical practitioners. These homogeneous tenants complement each other's activities through referrals and cooperation. Other homogeneous tenancies include the complementary services of professionals such as financiers, lawyers, and insurance agents.

Most high-rise office buildings are found in the central areas of cities, although some communities allow skyscrapers in other sections as well. Sometimes, a high-rise structure is designed around a single major tenant that owns the entire building. Other high-rise office structures enjoy a mixed use, with some located in preplanned, suburban office parks. The modern office park also includes such amenities as on-site parking and recreational and dining facilities.

The ADA has an impact on the rental industry, and investors should be familiar with its provisions. A disability under this federal statute is defined as "a physical or mental impairment that substantially limits one or more major life activities."

DISCUSSION TOPICS

1. Secure an inventory of the tenants in a nearby office park and analyze their mix on the basis of the services they offer and percentage of the total space they occupy. If possible, also secure the schedule of rents paid and compare these charges with the rents for similar office space available outside an office park environment.

INTRODUCTION TO INVESTING IN COMMERCIAL REAL ESTATE

The retail real estate market includes strip store buildings, **neighborhood shopping centers**, **community shopping centers**, regional shopping centers, factory outlet malls, the e-commerce shopping alternatives, fitness centers, fast food, and restaurants. It includes any property that provides goods and services to consumers.

As of 2019, the condition of the retail real estate market has improved substantially in contrast with recent years. New supply is at an historic low, partially because market rents have not generally justified new construction and because financing has remained relatively constrained. This leaves opportunities for upside potential via increased occupancy and rents. Furthermore, the improved housing market has led to an improved retail environment. With home prices recovering and financial markets making strong gains, household wealth has risen to more than $100 trillion as of the first quarter of 2018. Also, the annual expansion in retail sales has levelized to stability at 4% per annum, indicating that retail activity has achieved a rate consistent with job creation and income growth. All of this points to further boosts to the continued strengthening of the retail real estate recovery. Even with e-commerce edging out brick and mortar for many products, there is still a strong demand for retail space, with a trend toward experiential and immersive shopping, also called *retailtainment.*

STRIP CENTERS

In most American cities and towns, small store buildings line both sides of the community's busiest streets. These stores offer commodities and services of every nature and description and serve the neighborhood, as well as the entire city, with their wares. Like the smaller apartment and office buildings previously described, **strip centers**, also called *strip malls* and *convenience centers*, are found everywhere. According to the **International Council of Shopping Centers (ICSC)**, strip centers accounted for 12% of the market in 2018 and have a trade area of less than one mile. With such a small trade area, it is easy to see why there are so many of them in American communities.

Their general availability and rectangular design permit great flexibility for a variety of tenant uses. The relatively simple installation of carpeting, draperies, and partitions can convert a standard 20-by-60-foot module into an inviting office. The attachment of a counter and the appropriate stoves, refrigerators, tables, and chairs would create a restaurant in this same space. Shelves and display counters might transform it into a dress shop, pants store, or family shoe center, while chairs and booths could make it into a barber shop or beauty salon. Strip centers may contain art galleries, flower stores, jewelry shops, and boutiques—among other things—and offer continuing tenancies and unlimited conversion possibilities. Most strip centers have a standard tenant mixture called a *six pack*, which varies according to neighborhood, but is fairly consistent among area neighborhoods with the same demographic base.

Appeal to small investors

It usually costs very little more to purchase two-store or three-store buildings than it does to buy a duplex, triplex, or small office structure. Primarily because of the longevity of commercial tenants and fewer management responsibilities than residential rentals, these opportunities are attractive to the small investor. Mortgage loans are relatively easy to secure on this type of investment. A typical strip center is a 5,000- to 30,000-square-foot building designed with bay sizes of 20 feet wide by 60 feet deep. Most small tenants will require only one bay of 1,200 square feet, but interior partition walls can be demolished for larger requirements. In most instances, space is not subdivided into anything smaller than

20-by-60-foot units. By constructing the shell of a building and attempting to rent it before completing the interior, a landlord may also attract tenants who require special installations. A liquor store owner, who would need the special plumbing and electrical installations associated with a walk-in cooler, and a barber, who would require appropriate unique plumbing, are two such tenants.

CASE STUDY 11.8 **Strip Center Development**

This block-long property consists of 600 feet of frontage on a major thoroughfare and is 150 feet deep to a 20-foot alley. The investors rezoned the parcel to commercial—it had been apartment zoning—by inviting adjoining neighbors to participate in its design. They quickly eliminated any fast food, gas stations, or all-night markets to control noise and traffic. The architecture was to conform to the neighborhood, and no unsightly signs or disturbing lights were erected. The alley was paved, and a seven-foot wall was built on the house side of the alley to help buffer noise. All stores were set back from the main street a distance of 40 feet to allow for front parking.

The 43,200-square-foot building was designed to be built in nine stages of 60-by-80 feet each, starting from one corner. The building code required a 30-foot setback at each corner to allow for traffic visibility. The 60-foot modules were designed to be rented in multiples of 20 feet, with the tenants choosing the space they needed. Once the construction started, the buildings filled quickly and took nine months to rent. The final tenant mix is as follows:

Shoe store	100 feet
Ice cream parlor	40 feet
Bicycle shop	80 feet
Lamp shop	40 feet
Candy store	60 feet
Barber shop	40 feet
Carpet shop	60 feet
Beauty shop	40 feet
Real estate office	40 feet
Insurance office	40 feet

NEIGHBORHOOD SHOPPING CENTERS

A *neighborhood shopping center* is designed to provide for the sale of necessary goods (food, drugs, sundries) and personal services (laundry, dry cleaning, barbering, shoe repairing) for the daily needs of the people in the immediate neighborhood. This type of center is usually situated on a four-to-10-acre site and normally serves a trade-area population of 5,000 to 40,000 persons within a three-mile radius. According to the ICSC, they account for 30.8% of the industry's gross leasable area (GLA.)

Tenant mix

The neighborhood center usually has as its major tenant a supermarket, national drug-discount store, or both, which will occupy approximately 30% of its 30,000 to 100,000 square feet of gross leasable area. Other tenants may include a general merchandise store; clothing, shoe, and furniture stores; financial offices; and other service businesses.

The grouping is arranged on a readily accessible site and offers ease of shopping through adequate off-street parking facilities and agreeable surroundings. Often, the supermarket adjoins the drugstore, with common entry into both establishments. The other stores are generally arranged in a straight line that doglegs toward the streets, with parking spaces in front of the building. Thus, shoppers may drive directly to the store of their choice, park briefly while completing their purchases, and pull away quickly and efficiently. When compared with the inconvenience of the curbside parking required around strip stores, neighborhood centers have made serious inroads into the strip store's ability to compete for the shopper's dollar.

There is a trend developing in neighborhood shopping centers where the drugstore is becoming a stand-alone building on an outparcel located in a corner of the property. Several of the newer shopping centers are moving away from the attached-buildings format to one, two, or up to five separate stores in a perimeter with parking available in front of each group.

Condominium conversions

More than any other type of shopping center, neighborhood groupings lend themselves to conversion to condominiums. The sale of individual store buildings would probably produce more profit than selling the center as a whole to a single investor.

The beginning legal procedure is the same as that for an apartment or office conversion. Then the tenants can be approached to purchase their own store buildings and receive an undivided interest in the common-area parking spaces as well.

Case Study 11.9 provides an overview for a neighborhood shopping center.

CASE STUDY 11.9 Neighborhood Shopping Center

This 10-year-old center contains numerous shops, medical suites, and office spaces arranged around a centrally landscaped mall. It is connected to the residential area it serves by major arterial streets with traffic lights that control ingress and egress. The tenant mix is intended to provide the surrounding residential neighborhood with basic everyday needs. Its anchor tenants are a national chain food market and drugstore. The complete tenant mix of the center is listed below.

	Square Feet		Square Feet
Food market	25,000	Interior decorator	2,500
Drugstore	13,000	Bank	2,500
Sporting goods	5,000	Sewing center	2,500
Motorcycle dealer	5,000	Savings association	1,500
Hardware store	5,000	Dry cleaner	1,500
Medical offices	4,500	Carpet store	1,500
Insurance broker	4,250	Real estate broker	1,500
Shoe store	3,600	Florist shop	1,200
Liquor store	3,600	Women's wear shop	1,200
Restaurant	3,600	Gift shop	1,200
Men's shop	3,000	Small shops (10)	6,850

COMMUNITY SHOPPING CENTERS

In addition to the convenience goods and personal services offered by the neighborhood center, a community shopping center provides an even wider range of facilities for the sale of large appliances, furniture, apparel, and related services.

Designed around one or more major department or variety stores as the **anchor tenants**, also called *magnet stores*, plus a supermarket and other retail and service stores, a community shopping center has a gross leasable area ranging from 125,000 to 400,000 square feet, needs 10 to 30 acres or more, and serves a trade-area population of 40,000 to 150,000 people located up to six miles from the center. According to the ICSC, they account for 25.4% of the industry's gross leasable area.

Tenant mix

A community shopping center devotes approximately 20% of its space to a supermarket, 30% to a major general merchandise tenant, 25% to other clothing and shoe retailers, and the balance to other kinds of merchandisers and service businesses.

This type of center is midway between the neighborhood and the regional shopping center and incorporates a little of both in its design. Some community shopping centers include a major national department store plus a locally prominent department store, positioning them at either end of a group of stores occupied by smaller tenants. The two anchor tenants create foot traffic that is attracted into the connecting local tenant stores by window displays, signs, and other promotional devices.

Community shopping centers are usually designed with the stores lining a central **mall** area. In warm-weather states, this mall is generally uncovered, but in most inclement-weather areas, the mall is either covered or enclosed completely and temperature controlled for customer comfort. Whereas the neighborhood center's format encourages a quick shopping trip, the community shopping center's design is such that the customer is enticed into spending more time visiting from shop to shop and making impulse purchases in the process.

Because these centers are larger in size than neighborhood centers, many overlapping types of businesses are represented. This situation offers a customer the opportunity to compare prices and quality on similar articles in a number of competing stores. The intent is to convince shoppers that the center can serve most of their needs—all they have to do is seek out the appropriate vendor to achieve satisfaction.

Community shopping centers do not grant tenants the same exclusivity for their lines as do neighborhood centers. Thus, there may be a number of men's clothing establishments, dress shops, and shoe stores in one community shopping center. However, to prevent unusual shifts in lines of merchandise, it is necessary to include in each lease the general types of products or services the store will be allowed to carry. Each store is thus limited in the type of business to be conducted, and the landlord can maintain an appropriate tenant mix.

In this regard, management is always concerned that tenants generate the type of traffic flow that will provide all of the businesses in the center with customers on a continuous basis. The owners of a successful center enjoy the opportunity of carefully choosing tenants from a list of those waiting for openings to occur, thus ensuring the symbiosis that a successful center requires.

On the other hand, the management of centers with high turnovers and a number of vacancies are often reduced to accepting tenants who do not generate traffic, just to fill their spaces. These tenants include those that rent space for warehousing their merchandise, those that need office space, recruiting centers, places of worship, and other nonretail vendors.

A serious problem for investors in shopping centers occurs when retailers close their shops at various centers, with some companies going bankrupt. Those that close because it is less expensive to pay rent on the closed store than to continue to operate create a special problem for the center's management. When the leases contain a clause specifying that the tenant has to remain open and continue its business on 100% of its premises, the landlord has the right to obtain specific performance of this provision. This covenant of continuous operation, also called a **going dark** clause, is designed to create the ambience of a successful center and ensure that the needs of the shoppers are met, regardless of retailer difficulties.

REGIONAL AND SUPER-REGIONAL SHOPPING CENTERS

The largest of the shopping center designs is the **regional center**, providing general merchandise, apparel, furniture, and home furnishings in full depth and variety. At least one national, full-line department store is the major drawing power, with most regionals having two, and some even three such tenants to establish the magnetic nodes for the foot traffic between shops. Regionals range in scope from 400,000 to 800,000 square feet of gross leasable area on at least 30 acres of ground and serve a trade area of 150,000 to 400,000 or more people. This trade area may extend upward of 15 miles, depending on the accessibility of highways. Regionals are, in effect, a wide assortment of downtown stores, all collected under one roof and with controlled free parking, offering the suburban customer convenient, full-line shopping facilities. According to ICSC, they comprise 4.7% of the industry's GLA.

Some regional shopping centers, called **super-regional centers** or megacenters, are part of a larger, overall land plan that includes being buffered by office towers and apartment buildings that create a self-contained consumer market. However, there is a limitation on the size of the center itself—a limitation imposed by a shopper's ability to walk a certain distance, especially with packages in hand. Consequently, regionals are relatively compact in design and offer a basement and second floor as an alternative to lateral expansion. This requires vertical transportation facilities, usually in the form of staircases in the common areas. Elevators and escalators are often located within the stores themselves and act as subtle enticements to shoppers to do some impulse buying. They make up 10.2% of the industry's GLA.

Tenant mix

Unlike the other centers, the regional usually has no food market, although various packaged grocery items are found in its many stores. Rather, 50% of the center is occupied by general merchandise stores, 15% by clothing and shoe retailers, 10% by other dry-goods shops, and 25% by service and related businesses, including food court vendors. Many regionals include an auditorium that is available for special community meetings as well as for promotional efforts. Recreational facilities, such as movie theaters, are often available.

Building design

To achieve the greatest interplay among the stores, a regional center is usually designed around a mall area with the major national tenants located at either end. The inclusion of a third major tenant requires a central location opening on the mall, while a fourth major is positioned directly across and facing the central area.

When the key tenants have been assembled, the other tenants—large and small—are strategically located where they will be most appealing to the pedestrian traffic flow in the mall. Some types of businesses have special locational requirements. For example, a drugstore and a dry cleaner need to be immediately accessible from the parking area. Furniture stores require many square feet of display area, which is expensive if on the main floor. Thus, a typical furniture store layout would include a main floor entry, an attractive display room in a basement, a second-floor area, or a dogleg wrapped around the rears of adjacent smaller stores. Some stores have co-location site selection requirements, such as a bath products store that must always be within three spaces of a women's lingerie store.

Specialty shops and those that feature high-quality, high-priced lines will normally be grouped near the department store featuring this type of merchandise, while the popularly priced stores are grouped in immediate proximity to their complementary department store. Stores that specialize in convenience goods are located as close as possible to the parking area. Supplementary stores, such as those that offer hardware, electrical repair, and home furnishings, are usually located close together. Gasoline stations, repair shops, auto supplies, garden nurseries, outdoor furniture, and other stores of this nature are usually located at the exterior of the center or even in separate buildings.

Some regionals are designed around an open mall, but most have enclosed malls to provide a comfortable shopping environment that is heated in the winter and cooled in the summer. Sculptural displays or fountains usually highlight important mall areas, while many benches for resting are conveniently located along the preplanned pedestrian routes.

Specialized-purpose retail

Once a major industry of 9,000 stores representing more than 500 manufacturers, factory outlet malls are currently a dying breed. Only a few enjoy continued good business, while the others appear to be suffering from the competition of the burgeoning e-commerce market and the large, warehouse-type stores and clubs such as Walmart, Home Depot, Sam's Club, and Costco. In addition, it appears the merchandise in the factory outlet malls is no longer the bargain it used to be and, in many instances, is higher in price than similar merchandise in local stores, especially if one waits for the frequent sales.

Lifestyle centers cater to upscale consumers with above-average disposable income. There is typically dining and entertainment in an outdoor setting, with extensive use of art work, landscaping, and music throughout the center. They attract shoppers from a radius of 8 to 12 miles. Tenants are fairly homogenous and will usually include such names as Williams & Sonoma, Eddie Bauer, Orvis, and Ann Taylor, to name a few.

Power centers typically have several anchors in a similar category, such as discounters, with very few small tenants. They have a trade area with a radius of 5 to 10 miles.

Theme/festival centers are leisure and tourist-oriented locations, such as New Orleans' Jax Brewery or San Francisco's Ghirardelli Square. They are most often located in or near city centers in older buildings that have been adapted to retail use. Tenants are heavily weighted toward entertainment and dining, with some smaller specialty stores. Because of the tourist component, their typical trade area is a 25 to 75 mile radius.

Airport retail space is located within a commercial airport. Tenants include travel-related retail and dining.

Big box stores, so named because they are shaped like a large one-story box, typically buy their own land, sell it to a REIT or a subsidiary, and then lease it back. Examples of big box stores are Lowes, Walmart, and Costco. Investment opportunities for such properties include land speculation and assemblage. Most big boxes post site selection requirements on their websites to encourage investors to find opportunities to present to the local commercial brokers representing the stores.

Modern **self-storage** is now considered a retail use. The industry has evolved from first-generation space with all outdoor units, and the only security was the padlock on the rollup door. Second-generation space added perimeter fencing, and third-generation space added air-conditioning for some units and individual door alarms for others. Fourth-generation space moved entirely inside multistory buildings, and fifth-generation space has attention to energy efficiency, disaster resistance, biometric security features, and a more complete retail experience for a wide variety of moving and storage needs. The rule of thumb for site selection is any parcel of land from which the investor can see a branch bank and a McDonald's. The industry's trade association, the Self-Storage Association, estimates annual revenues at $38 billion as of the first quarter of 2018, with a total estimated inventory of 2.3 billion square feet.

E-COMMERCE COMPETITION

The recent recession and the wave of e-commerce in recent years have redefined the retail market equation. The days of the suburban mall anchored by a mid-market department store are fading, and investors should anticipate a tremendous revolution in retail trends over the course of the next decade. Issues shaping retail trends include the consolidation and emergence of super-chain stores, the rise of both budget and premium brands, and a transformation of physical retail, driven by mobile technologies in our always-connected world—a world that is transforming the retail experience for consumers.

Dying malls

Analysts estimate that up to 25% of this country's existing 1,100 malls are obsolete or nearly so and will close in the next five years. These malls are being hurt by faltering department stores, competition from no-mall discounters such as Walmart, and growing e-commerce networks.

Lee Schalop, an analyst with the Bank of America, reports that 20% of these *D* malls need to be refurbished, converted to other uses, or demolished entirely. A growing trend has been to convert these malls to other uses such as government service centers, office complexes, medical malls, or entertainment parks (for example, Netpark in Tampa, Florida). Great opportunities are available to investors that find new and innovative uses for these properties. Communities that relied on sales tax revenues from dying malls are highly motivated to provide incentives and low-cost loans for investors seeking to repurpose them to other uses. Experts predict that what is likely to emerge over the next several years is a retail landscape with somewhat fewer regional malls than exist today.

SUMMARY OF INVESTING IN COMMERCIAL REAL ESTATE

In most American cities and towns, small store buildings line both sides of the community's busiest streets. Housing all forms of retail businesses and services, the strip store building offers a small real estate investor a viable alternative for investment dollars. The flexibility of the store module allows a property owner to create new uses relatively inexpensively to meet the demands of an ever-changing market. Thus, a store that would house a pizza vendor for one period may be easily converted into a real estate office for the next.

Neighborhood, community, and regional shopping centers appeal to investors with financial capacities for larger projects. Neighborhood shopping centers are designed to cater to the everyday needs of residents in the center's immediate vicinity. With a food market and a drugstore as basic tenants, the neighborhood center also provides shopping facilities for other necessary goods and personal services.

The community center, on the other hand, expands the number of tenants to include department and variety stores, as well as the convenience goods tenants found in the neighborhood arrangement. This enlarged tenant mix allows the community center to serve a market area of up to 150,000 people.

The regional center provides the greatest variety of comparison shopping by housing a number of purveyors of the same types of products. Regionals are generally composed of at least two nationally prominent department store tenants that anchor each end of a mall area. With dozens of smaller tenants lining this mall, the shopper is able to choose goods and services from competing shops.

E-commerce is transforming the retail market equation, and investors must anticipate a major shift in retail trends over the course of the next decade.

DISCUSSION TOPICS

1. Investigate what rent-up requirements the permanent lenders in your area demand before they will issue a standby loan commitment on a new community or regional shopping center.
2. Choose a neighborhood shopping center in your area and compose a feasibility study on its conversion to condominium ownership. Compare the value of the center as a single investment entity to its total value as a condominium conversion.

INTRODUCTION TO INVESTING IN INDUSTRIAL PROPERTIES

The technical and legal expertise required to develop industrial property makes it one of the more complicated types of real estate investments. The developer must not only guarantee the industrialist labor pools, utilities, and transportation facilities, but also satisfy the rigorous regulations of government agencies concerned with zoning, licensing, and environmental controls. It is no longer possible to simply convince a prospective industrialist to move to a new community; purchase a parcel of land near a freeway, railroad, or airport; and quickly construct a building. Now, the industrial developer must be concerned with the adequacy of the available utilities and waste-disposal provisions, as well as with the various impacts the project will have on the environment, both local and regional.

THE INDUSTRIAL REAL ESTATE MARKET

The success of the e-commerce market is reshaping the industrial space market in many parts of the country. Demand is rising, for both new and converted buildings, to warehouse products being sold with the promise of 24-hour to 48-hour delivery. Properly located properties in space near airports remain in high demand. For example, Trammel Crow Company, in partnership with the AMB Property Corporation (a REIT), constructed an air cargo center at the Portland International Airport in Oregon that directly accesses the landing strips. Called *high throughput* buildings, the air cargo is unloaded at one end and immediately transported to waiting trucks at the other end. Another such facility is located at the Dallas/Fort Worth International Airport.

Other technology firms throughout the country require customized industrial space to satisfy their unique e-commerce needs. Consequently, commercial real estate investors are increasingly factoring in the influence of technology, collaborating increasingly with potential and existing tenants at the design stages to understand tenants' technological needs and incorporate those needs as an integral part of a building's design.

Land-use patterns

Most industrial developments have in common the basic locational dilemma of isolation from the residential areas of a community. A concern for the health of citizens has led community regulatory agencies to require that industrial activities that create noise, smoke, and waste be isolated in designated areas, preferably as far away from homes as possible. As a result, transportation facilities must be available to provide workers with easy access and allow for ease in receiving raw materials and shipping finished goods. Isolation also creates the problem of securing the utility services needed for manufacturing, including facilities for electricity, natural gas, water, and waste disposal.

Attracting new industry

Despite the no-growth attitudes of political leaders in some cities throughout this country, many others actively seek to attract industry. Because they recognize the numerous economic benefits that stem from new employment opportunities, many expanding communities offer special incentives to induce manufacturers and other employers to relocate, sometimes called a *beggar-thy-neighbor* policy.

Subsidized plant locations

One technique uses the community's taxing power to float **industrial development bonds** and then uses the proceeds to purchase land and build the plants required by new firms moving to the community. The payments on these bonds are made by the city from taxes collected for this purpose (general obligation bonds) or from the rents collected from the industrial tenants (**revenue bonds**). In either case, a community can adjust the charges to prospective employers and thereby provide economic incentives for locating in that particular area.

Tax waivers

In addition to low rents, city leaders may offer new industry-certain tax waivers. Property taxes may be waived for specified periods if a company agrees to purchase a plant instead of leasing it. Inventory taxes may be waived for the term of the lease or longer, depending on circumstances. Local income taxes, as well as state income taxes in certain cases, may be waived for prescribed time periods to allow an **infant industry** an opportunity to mature.

Theoretically, these tax waivers—as well as the plant subsidies—will cost a community little, if any, money because of the **incremental taxes** that will be generated. These extra taxes will emanate from the incomes of the newly employed and the properties they will require for housing and peripheral services.

Economic feasibility

In addition to industrial developments sponsored directly by community leaders, usually under the direction of an industrial development board, individuals and corporations also invest in industrial properties. The objective of an industrial developer is to match a particular property with a specific firm. This process requires a detailed study of local market conditions as well as the tenant's needs.

Locational preferences

When selecting plant sites, industrial firms will be looking to minimize transportation costs in the acquisition of raw materials and the distribution of finished goods. In addition, production costs will be analyzed in terms of wages, rents, taxes, and other necessary expenses. In a highly competitive market, the site offering the lowest costs will be chosen.

The special characteristics of a firm determine, to a large extent, where it will locate. Market-oriented companies that rely on a large consumer population will locate close to these customers. A bottler of soft drinks is an example of this type of industry. A firm that depends on heavy or bulky raw materials will elect to locate near these resources to minimize transportation costs; for example, a steel mill should be located near supplies of iron ore or coal deposits. A labor-oriented firm requires a location that will attract the types of workers required for its activities. Thus, a research company would seek a site near a university, but a manufacturing plant might prefer a location closer to a large market of semiskilled laborers.

Local market conditions

An industrial firm that anticipates a move into a new area requires precise data concerning the economic base of the community and its demography. Data describing the available labor force, its skills, educational levels, and turnover ratios will be accumulated. In addition, an industrialist will require firsthand knowledge of the political attitudes of the community leaders and the degree to which they will cooperate in establishing a new plant. Sources of income and property taxes, tax rates, assessment policies, municipal services, and zoning ordinances are all vital inclusions in the evaluation of a community.

Much of this information can be obtained from public sources such as the Census Bureau, property tax rolls, and local employment agencies. Other data can be gathered from development groups, municipal agencies, utility companies, and research bureaus maintained by universities and local banks.

CHARACTERISTICS OF INDUSTRIAL REAL ESTATE

The term **industry** includes all activities involved in the production, storage, and distribution of tangible goods. Industrial property includes the plants, lofts, and warehouses located throughout the country, and the construction of these facilities requires vast amounts of investment capital. Many manufacturers feel their own funds are more productive when used in the operation of their industry. Consequently, industrial real estate is generally investor-owned, with the manufacturer assuming a tenant's role. Frequently, a sale-leaseback-buyback ownership agreement is used.

Building characteristics

Industrial buildings are classified as general purpose, special purpose, or single purpose, depending on their adaptability.

- *General-purpose buildings* have a wide range of alternative uses. These properties can be adapted for light manufacturing or assembly plants, or simply used as warehouses.
- *Special-purpose buildings* have certain physical characteristics that limit the scope of their use. For example, only a few industrial enterprises require heavily insulated cold-storage facilities. Other special purpose buildings use overhead cranes, loading docks, clean rooms, and fire/explosion suppression systems.
- *Single-purpose buildings* are suitable for only one use, such as a steel mill. These single-purpose properties are difficult, if not impossible, to convert to other uses. Institutional buildings such as theaters, churches, and government structures should not be considered special-purpose property because they are not used for industrial purposes.

Because of the specific purposes of some buildings and the unusual size of others, industrial property is considered a slow turnover commodity in the real estate market. This poor liquidity increases an investor's risk and requires that an industrial property owner seek out an experienced and knowledgeable tenant. The value of this type of property is closely intertwined with the profitability of the firm that occupies the premises. If the tenant is unsuccessful, the building will be vacated and difficult to rent.

More so than in any other form of real estate investment, an industrial tenant's installation of heavy equipment and machinery will ensure the longevity of the tenancy. In fact, the cost of installing expensive and bulky equipment often forms the basis for the observable inertia of large manufacturing firms that remain in one location for several generations. Although this longevity is favorable to an investor's yield, functional obsolescence can sometimes place the operating firm at an economic disadvantage in competing with companies that have located in modern, more efficient plant facilities.

When industrial firms locate in outlying areas, they tend to prefer single-story buildings because of the efficiency of manufacturing operations made possible by this design. A single-level plant lends itself to greater flexibility in the use of open areas and promotes the efficient flow of goods through the building. The expediency of a horizontal floor plan, which allows for greater ease in the handling of materials, as well as for an assembly-line arrangement for the use of machinery, gives the one-story industrial tenant a competitive edge in the marketplace.

Land characteristics

Industrial property development requires land that is properly zoned, includes a sufficient amount of square footage for buildings and off-street parking, and has access to utility facilities and major transportation arteries adequate to serve the prospective enterprise.

Utilities

One of the important variables for an industrial developer to consider is the availability of electricity and natural gas. In the future, perhaps only lands that are now serviced or can be serviced with these utilities will receive permission to be improved for industrial use. Where these utilities are available, their costs must be included in the feasibility analysis of a major project. Utility charges are becoming an important part of an operations statement because their increasing costs can seriously erode the profits from an otherwise potentially successful investment.

Not only must basic utilities be available for an industrial development, but waste-disposal facilities must also be provided. The treatment of solid and liquid wastes is now an essential concern of every industrial developer. Proof must exist, to the satisfaction of all concerned public and prviate parties, that appropriate provisions are being made for the disposal of wastes without disturbing the natural environment. The recent emphasis on control of polluters has placed new industrial developments under the careful scrutiny of zoners, planners, air and water quality-control agencies, and environmentalists of every order.

Compounding the problem of sewage disposal is the isolation required for activities that create the greatest amount of waste. Whereas clean industry can locate in towns and on existing sewer lines, heavy industry is relegated to more distant areas where no sewage disposal facilities exist. Faced with this problem, industrial developers of outlying properties must often provide their own disposal systems, usually at high installation costs. Septic tanks and leaching fields are generally not adequate to service a manufacturing plant, so a treatment pond must be constructed, along with sewer lines to transport the waste over a substantial distance. Just imagine the clamor of property owners that adjoin such a malodorous pond!

Railroad spurs

Generally, industries produce products in large volume and require facilities for the receipt of bulk raw materials, as well as for the shipment of finished goods. Other than companies dealing in relatively small, expensive items that justify the costs of air freight, many manufacturing operations require a plant location adjoining a **railroad spur**. The railroad cars can then be available at dockside for efficient loading and unloading.

Most railroad companies will cooperate in constructing a spur line to a new plant to serve a potential shipper. Allocations for the costs of such installations are based on the anticipated volume of business—that is, the higher the volume, the more likely the possibility that the railroad company will absorb the costs. Often, a developer will have to pay for the installation of a spur line, but in the case of an industrial park, railroad service may well provide the marketing attraction necessary for a successful sales effort.

Highway access

In addition to railroads, many industries rely on trucks to transport goods into and out of their plants. Every industrial plant design includes provisions for loading docks and an adequate area for the turning radius of 18-wheelers to serve truck traffic. Smaller companies, lacking access to an adjoining railroad spur, often deliver their products by truck to a railroad siding, where the merchandise is transferred to a railroad car for shipment to the customer. The reverse process is used when goods are received. Thus, easy access to a major highway is also considered an essential factor in most decisions concerning an industry's location, with an ideal site being one that is situated between a railroad and a major highway. Highway access must also be considered for employee commuters.

Harbor facilities

Despite the efficiency of the railroad and trucking systems in providing shipping facilities for manufacturing activities in this country, most of the major metropolitan cities have well-developed seaports. The harbor facilities found at the various river, gulf, Great Lake, and ocean port cities are a reflection of the vast amount of goods being transferred by water in national and international trade.

Water routes are used primarily by shippers of heavy or bulky items from materials-oriented industries. Internal waterways provide an inexpensive means for transporting sand, gravel, coal, ore, and other cargo of this nature. Towed by tugs, fully laden barges of these raw materials are delivered to their users up and down the navigable rivers of the country.

Storage areas often are constructed at strategic points on the periphery of a community where the materials can be dumped from barges and held in anticipation of shipment inland by truck or rail.

Harbor facilities are receiving increased attention from the federal government. Many harbors, like the one at Port Brownsville, Texas, have been deepened and enlarged to meet growing needs. Communities along the northern and southern boundaries of the United States have experienced increased activity in exports and imports to and from Canada and Mexico as a result of the North American Free Trade Agreement, enacted in 1994 and now called the United States-Mexico-Canada Agreement.

Labor supply

A feasibility study of an industrial development should include a careful analysis of both the quantity and the quality of the available labor supply. Whether an industry requires the extensive use of machines or an intensive use of workers, an available pool of potential employees—trained or trainable—is essential to its success.

In addition to the personnel needed for a **labor-intensive** industry, the strength of their unions is also an important consideration in industrial location decisions. A brief glance at the burgeoning industrial South and the relatively diminished industrial North illustrates industrialists' efforts to move away from powerful labor unions. Of course, there is no way to escape the impact of unionization because workers tend to join together for mutual benefits, and unions continue to emerge in each new geographic location.

An interesting pattern of commuting habits evolves when the labor supply is analyzed in terms of white-collar and blue-collar workers. Many labor-intensive manufacturing enterprises are restricted to the outlying areas of a community. This situation requires that blue-collar workers travel from their homes, usually in the central city areas, out to the plants. At the same time, central city areas have evolved into financial, government, and office centers that require the services of white-collar workers, who must travel from their suburban homes into the center of the city. This, of course, results in rush-hour traffic jams.

Lease characteristics

An industrial lease usually takes one of two forms: gross or net. Both forms contain many of the provisions already discussed in the units on residential, office, and commercial properties, including a description of the premises, lease term, rent, security deposit, use of premises, and the legal responsibilities and remedies of the parties. However, the conditions of an industrial lease involving taxes, insurance, maintenance responsibilities, and other legal factors are highly individualized, and each lease must be negotiated specifically between the individual owners and tenants.

Mainly because of the high costs involved in establishing a manufacturing operation, most industrial leases are designed to run for long periods of time. As a result, these long-term leases are established on a fully net basis. Unlike a gross lease in which the landlord pays the property taxes, insurance premiums, and maintenance costs, the fully **net lease** requires that the tenant pay these expenses in addition to the basic rent. Thus, an owner of an industrial property is guaranteed an agreed-on return on the investment over the term of the lease period.

Of course, there are innumerable variations of the basic gross and net leases. For example, a tenant may be required to pay only incremental property taxes and insurance premiums, with the landlord obligated to pay the costs for these items that existed when the lease originated. A tenant may be required to contribute a specified sum to offset any increase in maintenance cost or be obligated to pay an escalating base rental amount as a result of the fluctuations of the consumer price index—one measurement of inflation over the lease period. Other variations can be designed to reflect the special relationships that exist between specific parties to an industrial lease.

As in most decisions to invest in real estate, competent legal advice should be sought in the preparation of the documents required in each transaction.

Environmental concerns

Particularly important with industrial properties are the various environmental concerns that may arise. Of special importance to investors is the **Comprehensive Environmental Response, Compensation, and Liability Act (CERCLA)** of 1980. Under this statute, the cost of environmental cleanup may fall to any **potentially responsible party (PRP)**. PRPs include the property owner, previous owners, property managers, and anyone who produced, transported, or installed the hazardous material, even if they were not aware of the environmental problems.

An *innocent landowner* defense does exist but only for an owner who used reasonable diligence in looking for problems before acquisition of the property and no problems were found. This reasonable diligence entails a Phase I Environmental Assessment, and if this report shows no problems, then a purchaser may assert the innocent landowner defense.

A Phase I assessment includes basic research to determine whether or not there may be a problem. This includes a title search, interviews with those familiar with the property, and a review of any previous records on the uses of the property. Should a possible problem be discovered (i.e., the property was once used by a dry cleaner or as a gas station), then a Phase II assessment is performed.

A Phase II assessment is designed to confirm the presence and extent of an environmental problem and may include soil, air, and water testing. Once the presence and extent of the environmental problem is identified, then a Phase III Environmental Assessment is completed.

The Phase III assessment is the final step before the actual cleanup begins. The Phase III assessment details how the environmental cleanup is to be performed.

More information concerning environmental issues and regulations may be found online at www.epa.gov.

TYPES OF INDUSTRIAL INVESTMENTS

Industrial activities range from upholstering living room chairs to the manufacture of air cargo planes, and include the entire spectrum in between. The upholsterer can work in a room behind a retail furniture store; the plane manufacturer requires acres of space. Thus, large or small, industrial activities are usually housed in some form of improved real estate.

Industrial parks

A popular form of industrial property development is the **industrial park**, which offers many advantages to both industry and the community.

Industry benefits by having a choice of readily available sites, usually located on the outskirts of the community, at relatively reasonable costs. Operating economies, such as a common sewage facility, can be realized, and amenities can be offered that will give the park a prestigious atmosphere. With properly designed subdivision restrictions, tenants and owners alike may enjoy protective covenants that enable them to control their environment and provide opportunities for them to interrelate.

An industrial park benefits a community because of its ability to attract new industries. As a result, the community can expand its economic and tax base, provide more efficient use of municipal services, and exercise control over isolated industrial operations.

One form of industrial park is designed as a land banking operation and is usually developed either by a railroad on land earmarked for large shippers or by a community-sponsored organization empowered to expand the industrial base. Raw acreage is subdivided into lots, improved with street and utility installations, and offered for sale or lease. Often, an active campaign is mounted to entice manufacturers to move into the area from another community.

Another form of industrial park is developed by an individual owner-investor who offers a complete package of land and building to a prospective buyer or tenant. The user can specify the design of the construction, usually a form tailored to specific needs, and the industrial park owner thus acts as a land banker, holding lots until they are needed.

In either case, an industrial park is a preplanned subdivision designed to satisfy the needs of industrial users and provide the lot sizes, utilities, road installations, and restrictions essential for an efficient and prestigious operation.

One basic rule for all industrial park developments is to provide as much flexibility as possible in the layout plan. This can be accomplished by effective block planning and stage development. Block designs should include parcels of differing dimensions that can be used separately or combined to satisfy special requirements. Stage development specifications restrict activities to one area at a time, preclude checkerboarding of the entire park by haphazard locational decisions, and allow for flexibility in future development.

Restrictive covenants prepared by the developer are established to ensure compatibility among occupants and between the park and the community in which it is located. Again, flexibility is required to avoid any unreasonable impositions that might be unacceptable to potential occupants. Most restrictions prohibit any uses that might prove offensive, such as those generating excessive odors, smoke, or noise. Some restrictions establish minimum site sizes, site coverage, building setbacks, designated parking and loading areas, outdoor storage limitations, landscaping responsibilities, construction design, sign control, and other provisions peculiar to a specific park.

Besides planning homogeneous landscaping, the developer should also weigh the value of providing restaurants and other amenities conducive to attracting tenants to larger parks. Some industrial developments might include a clubhouse with sleeping facilities, as well as showers, saunas, a swimming pool, a gymnasium, exercise equipment, and meeting rooms.

Industrial park management, although demanding at the outset, does not require a great deal of effort once the park is established. Tenants usually execute long-term net leases or purchase their own properties. In the latter case, the owners usually form an association similar to that of a condominium association to solve mutual problems. In a tenancy situation, as discussed previously, the terms of the net industrial lease usually require the tenants to assume responsibility for paying property taxes and insurance and for maintaining their individual properties.

Industrial park properties have had a relatively flat level of inventory and rent growth in the past several years.

Manufacturing buildings

In addition to industrial parks, there are numerous free-standing industrial buildings housing all forms of manufacturing activity and located on individual plots of land in various areas of a community. A typical investment for the small, limited partnership is an **incubator industrial building** of 5,000 to 25,000 square feet. Designed to house new companies during their start-up periods, these buildings are located on numerous available lots throughout a community. A variation on this theme is the **business park**, increasingly popular in the Southwest. These parks are patterned after the industrial park but include retail, office, manufacturing, and storage facilities in one cohesive unit.

Historically, most manufacturing operations were located in the central area of a community, with housing developing along major streets in a radial pattern from these job nuclei. Many of these older manufacturing establishments, called **loft buildings**, are currently obsolete, made so by technological improvements and the need for greater operating efficiency. A tall building housing a single manufacturer and designed so that various operations are carried out on different floors causes vertical transportation problems that most manufacturers prefer to avoid. Currently, a one-story building that permits horizontal traffic flow is preferred for most manufacturing operations.

The operational dictates of manufacturing, therefore, require that large industrial plants move to the periphery of communities where ample land is available at reasonable costs. This movement often results in the abandonment of many older buildings in central city areas. Depending on their physical condition, some are converted to other uses or destroyed in urban renewal projects.

Despite the general movement to the suburbs, some loft buildings continue to house the activities of manufacturers for whom moving would be unprofitable or who can still operate with relative efficiency in the old vertical manner. An example of this is the garment manufacturing industry, which continues its production in the old loft buildings of New York City. For the most part, however, the loft is becoming obsolete, with virtually no new construction in this style having taken place within the past two decades. The vacant spaces in many loft buildings have been filled by tenants who require inexpensive storage areas or unusually large office spaces at rents much lower than those available in competing office buildings.

Warehouse buildings

Throughout the country, there is a proliferation of **warehouse buildings** designed to provide enclosed storage facilities for goods and merchandise of all types and descriptions. Individuals and businesses alike use these warehouses to store goods for extended periods, as well as facilitate the transshipment of smaller lots of merchandise from a larger initial bulk quantity.

In addition to privately owned industrial warehouse buildings, the large warehouses of major furniture-moving companies, like Bekins and Mayflower, can be found in many American communities. These storage facilities are offered for rent to the general public, and customers may pick up and deliver their own goods, as well as hire the transfer company for these services. The managers of these warehouses charge a fee for every entry to either add or remove goods held in storage.

The wide-span, open-bay design of these warehouse buildings allows most items to be placed into standard-sized containers and efficiently stacked by forklift trucks, with the high ceilings allowing maximum use of the interior warehouse space. Thus, rents are based on the number of cubic feet occupied by the goods and are imposed as a monthly charge.

Conversions of lofts and warehouses

Old lofts and warehouses are regaining popularity with real estate investors. From abandoned lofts in downtown areas to older warehouses in the suburbs, innovative and economically successful conversions to other profitable uses are taking place. Not only is loft space being converted into low-cost offices, but downtown buildings are also being transformed into interesting and desirable apartments. High ceilings and large rooms become effective marketing attractions for rentals and have led to remarkable success for this type of enterprise.

While upper floors are used for offices or apartments, the ground-floor space is usually converted into specialty restaurants and retail stores. Here, the unfinished look of exposed bricks and pipes is blended into a counterculture decor that appeals to the customer's sense of adventure. Some cities have had entire areas redeveloped into new and unusual uses that attract throngs of visitors. The Quay in Kansas City, Haymarket Square in downtown Boston, Old Town in Omaha, and much of downtown Cleveland are just a few of these rejuvenated areas. At the same time, individual large, old warehouse buildings are becoming community focal points after their conversion to other uses. Such remodeled structures may house spaghetti or steak houses, such as Denver's Larimer Square Spaghetti House or the Spaghetti Factory in downtown San Diego. An old chocolate factory is the cornerstone of the famous Ghirardelli Square on the San Francisco Embarcadero, which houses numerous small shops and boutiques catering to the tastes of thousands of daily visitors. Another example of a successful conversion is the Trolley Square Shopping Center in Salt Lake City, once the stables and trolley barn for the old street transportation company. Creative investment opportunities are available everywhere for the alert developer.

SUMMARY OF INVESTING IN INDUSTRIAL PROPERTIES

This lesson examined the unique qualities and characteristics of industrial property as an alternate method of real estate investment. The technical and legal expertise required to develop industrial property makes it one of the more complicated types of investment. In addition to satisfying the plant design and locational requirements of a potential tenant, the industrial property developer must also meet the increasingly stringent environmental controls and other regulations of local government agencies.

Despite the number of communities committed to no-growth policies, many cities are still actively seeking to attract new industry to their environs. These expanding communities establish industrial property development agencies empowered to offer new employers subsidized plant locations and tax waivers to entice them to their cities.

Basically, the possibility of more economical operation is what attracts a firm to a new site. Suburban and rural locations provide inexpensive land for one-story construction but also present problems in securing utility connections and waste-disposal services. Adequate transportation facilities and the quantity and quality of the labor supply also affect locational decisions. In addition, a knowledgeable potential tenant will analyze the community's tax base, zoning ordinances, and political attitudes toward industry before making a move.

Many industrial buildings are designed as general-purpose structures with a wide range of alternative uses. These buildings provide an investor with flexibility for reuse if a tenant leaves, thus reducing risk. Special-purpose or single-purpose industrial structures designed for a specific firm require long-term leases from highly creditable tenants to offset an investor's risk. Generally, industrial real estate is considered nonliquid because of the many unique physical requirements for development.

In addition to the zoning, utilities, and labor inputs essential to develop industrial property, adequate transportation facilities must be readily accessible. Railroad spurs and sidings, as well as major highways, are usually prerequisites for a successful industrial investment. Often, a railroad company will pay for the installation of a spur track to a new industrial tenant in anticipation of new shipping business. Just as often, an industrial park developer will have to pay for construction of a spur track into the subdivision to attract new tenants.

Most industrial leases are drawn for long time periods and are designed on the basis of net rents. A net lease requires that a tenant pay property taxes, insurance, and maintenance costs in addition to a base rent. Thus, because the cost of these items is absorbed by the tenant over the term of the lease, the landlord's yield is preserved. Often, an escalation clause is included in a long-term net industrial lease to offset the effects of inflation.

Industrial investments include industrial parks, manufacturing buildings, warehouse buildings, and the conversion of old lofts and warehouses into new and profitable uses. Industrial parks are preplanned subdivisions that house all forms of commercial activities, including manufacturing, storage, distribution, sales, service, and research and development. One kind of park is designed only for the sale or lease of lots, whereas another may include a lot and building in a package deal. In either case, the park generally is designed around a set of restrictive covenants that specify the types of uses allowed as well as the architecture of the buildings. Industrial park management is active at its inception and usually becomes passive once the park is established.

Old loft buildings are generally obsolete but are still being used to house the activities of businesses for whom moving would be unprofitable or for tenants who desire inexpensive bulk storage or office space. Warehouse buildings are designed to provide enclosed storage facilities for goods and merchandise for extended periods of time. Tenants pay for the use of space in these buildings by the cubic foot and must also pay a fee each time the goods are moved. Self-storage facilities, on the other hand, provide enclosed storage in the form of individual bins that remain under the complete control of the tenant during the term of occupancy.

Conversions of old lofts and warehouses into new uses, such as restaurants, offices, apartments, and shopping centers, are a promising source of real estate investment opportunities.

DISCUSSION TOPICS

1. Determine what, if anything, is being done in your community to entice new industry to locate there.
2. Research the economic results of the multiplier effect of a new industry coming to your town. Estimate how it would affect your community if the new enterprise hires 500 people.

INTRODUCTION TO INVESTING IN SPECIAL REAL ESTATE

In addition to the more traditional forms of real estate investment—land, houses, apartments, offices, commercial properties, and industrial developments—there are numerous opportunities to participate in profitable ventures in specialized real estate. This category includes manufactured-home parks, motels, amusement parks, and golf courses. Other alternate forms of real estate investment are **franchises**, **mineral rights**, **air rights**, and real estate securities. This lesson examines these and other diverse opportunities.

MANUFACTURED-HOME PARKS

An important category in real estate investment is the development of land for manufactured-home parks—for both renting and selling space. Renting a space in a park is similar to renting an apartment, whereas the purchase of a condominium manufactured home lot parallels the purchase of a residential lot in a subdivision.

The successful development of manufactured-home parks, both as rentals and as condominiums, is attracting investors to this form of realty venture. Their growing interest is based on three interrelated phenomena: a dramatic increase in the costs of constructing more traditional housing, our population's increasing longevity, and the effective vesting of numerous pension and retirement programs. **Manufactured homes** appeal to people who cannot afford the costs of more traditional housing, as well as to a large segment of retired people attracted by the amenities that the various parks provide. In many cases, the receipt of both pension and Social Security benefits allows retirees to move to warm-weather states where manufactured-home parks are found in abundance.

Manufactured homes, originally called mobile homes, were originally regarded as minimal-quality housing. Since 1976, this type of housing has been regulated by the Department of Housing and Urban Development under its Manufactured-Home Construction and Safety Standards. The standards are similar to those established for site-built housing and, as a result, manufactured homes have not only become more durable and safer, but their appearance has significantly improved. Modern manufactured housing is often entirely compatible with site-built housing and may well be the most affordable housing on the market today.

In some cases, the establishment of a manufactured-home park is an interim use of land while the owner waits for development to move into the area. It may also be an answer to a shortage of affordable homes, providing a viable alternative for low-income and moderate-income occupants. The cost of housing in a manufactured-home park is frequently 20% to 30% less than the cost of conventional housing elsewhere in a community.

Location and design

The land for manufactured-home parks is invariably located in relatively isolated areas of a community because this form of real estate development has not generally been favorably accepted by either land planners or owners of more traditional housing. In many communities, these parks are considered to be undesirable developments, a stigma traceable to the growth of a myriad of trailer parks after World War II. These trailer parks jammed up to 20 units on one acre, and they became havens for transients. They developed into slum-like environments detrimental to the values of surrounding properties. With the advent of the modern, well-landscaped, preplanned manufactured-home park, featuring only seven to 10 units per acre, this negativism is largely being overcome in a growing number of communities.

Because many parks are located on outlying parcels of land, the initial outlay of funds required for site acquisition may be relatively small. However, improving this property with roads, utilities, concrete pads, and amenities is a costly investment, much of which can be financed through local banks or savings institutions. The FHA also provides special mortgage insurance for manufactured-home park financing. The design of a manufactured-home park can follow a horizontal grid pattern, a herringbone layout, or a series of concentric circles or half circles around a centrally located office or clubhouse, as shown in Figure 11.2. The grid pattern places the units in a horizontal position, with each pad parallel to all others. A more efficient design is the placement of units at an angle to the street, herringbone style, which allows the homes to be more easily maneuvered in and out of position.

Figure 11.2: Designs of Manufactured-Home Parks

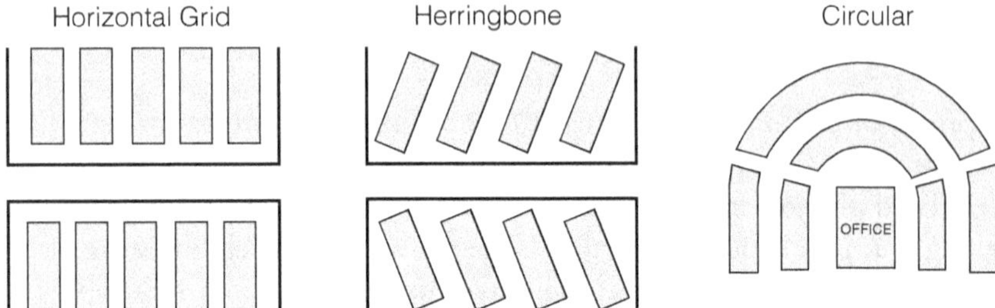

Most new parks provide occupants with special amenities, including swimming pools, clubhouses, tennis and shuffleboard courts, laundry rooms, and storage facilities. Many modern parks also include a separate parking area for travel trailers and other recreational vehicles.

Spaces for rent

The rent for spaces in a manufactured-home park depends on the location of the park, the size of the unit, and the amenities included in the project. Some parks require leases for specific terms; others operate on a month-to-month basis. The tenant is usually responsible for moving the unit into place and setting it up. Most quality parks insist that a front patio and cabana be installed as a condition of the lease. These improvements are required to create an atmosphere of unity and permanence in the park.

The financial success of a rental park is largely a function of the managerial skills of the owner or manager. The availability of well-planned social activities and the constant maintenance and cleanliness of a park often make the difference between whether it suffers chronic vacancies or enjoys full occupancy. Some parks are so popular that they maintain a list of potential tenants waiting to move in as soon as a vacancy occurs.

The profitability of a rental park is based on the same variables that exist in other improved-property investments. However, the deductions for depreciation are limited to the improvements made to the land: utility installations, concrete pads, the clubhouse, laundry rooms, and storage buildings. When compared with other improved income property, this lack of depreciation shelter, plus the high degree of personal involvement required in management, inhibits investment in this form of real estate. In effect, a manufactured-home rental park is considered a business venture more than a real estate investment.

When rental spaces are in short supply in a particular community, local manufactured-home dealers sometimes develop new parks to provide unit spaces for customers. Occasionally, dealers enter into joint ventures with landowners for such purposes.

Sometimes, rental-park owners have the opportunity to acquire ownership of the units from tenants who wish to dispose of their holdings or from executors of the estates of deceased owners. These units can be rented by the park owner, and the income can be sheltered by appropriate depreciation deductions.

Spaces for sale

Another approach to manufactured-home park development is the sale of individual lots. This is an increasingly popular application of the condominium concept in which a buyer secures a deed to a lot plus an undivided interest in the common areas. The lot is described in legal terms and is an identifiable portion of land lying within the park area. The common property includes the roadways, clubhouse, and amenities.

After acquiring a suitable site, a developer subdivides the land into a prescribed number of lots according to an officially approved plan. These lots, fully improved with concrete pads, sewer and water connections, and other utilities, are then sold to individual owners. The development includes a set of bylaws that call for the establishment of an association of lot owners to manage the common areas and enforce the covenants, conditions, and restrictions of the park.

Manufactured-home dealers engage in condominium park developments and sell package deals that include both lot and unit for one price under a single financial arrangement.

Manufactured-home sales

More than 22 million people live in manufactured housing in the United States. Manufactured-home sales account for approximately 9% of single-family home sales. Fannie Mae now treats loans for manufactured homes in the same manner as site-built homes. Mortgage loans on manufactured homes must meet criteria specific to the industry, but obtaining loans to purchase modular and manufactured homes is no longer the onerous exercise it once was. With average prices for new units at $70,600, they are an attractive alternative to site-built single-family homes.

New manufactured-home communities are designed to accommodate larger, contemporary units on no more than five sites per acre, together with various on-site amenities appealing to the local market.

DIVERSE REALTY INVESTMENTS

It is often difficult to distinguish between real estate as an investment and real estate as a business. A clear delineation exists when one person owns the real estate and another operates a business on the property. Here, the real estate is clearly its owner's investment, and the businessowner pays rent. However, there are diverse investments that involve real estate as a part of the business itself—for example, hotels, motels, amusement parks, golf courses, housing for the elderly, medical buildings, **repossessions**, and **property tax liens**.

Hotels and motels

Commercial hotels

Commercial hotels are designed to serve the individual business traveler. They contain some meeting space and food services. They enjoy strong weekday demand but suffer low weekend occupancies. Traditionally, commercial travelers are the backbone of the lodging industry, paying full rates for their accommodations with expense accounts, thus minimizing price resistance. The advent of new technologies such as video communications and telecommuting may alter the need for business travel and have an adverse effect on the commercial hotel business.

Convention hotels

Convention hotels contain extensive meeting space that attracts the meeting and group market segments. Most cater to both commercial and convention guests. These properties require specialized management expertise. Convention hotels are affected by general economic conditions and may be threatened to some degree by emerging video conferencing technology such as webinars. The high costs of developing new convention hotels will limit new supply growth and protect existing properties.

Resort hotels

Catering to vacationers, resort hotels provide good long-term investment opportunities, particularly in areas that are not too seasonal. People will continue to take vacations regardless of new technologies, and business is good in resort hotels because of increased leisure time and expanding two-income families.

All-suite hotels

All-suite hotels offer guest rooms larger than those found in traditional hotels, as well as limited meeting and public space. This expanded space appeals to business travelers and their families and has been effective in attracting travelers, filling rooms during weekdays as well as usually slow weekends.

Extended-stay hotels

Extended-stay hotels are lodging facilities with kitchens, living areas, and bedrooms that resemble apartment buildings. They cater to travelers who intend to stay in one area for a longer time—a week or more. Thus, these hotels do not experience weekend occupancy declines. These properties often achieve occupancy levels reaching 80% and enjoy special operating efficiencies brought about by lower guest turnover.

Motels

The motel industry emerged as a result of our mobile society's demands for convenient temporary housing along the nation's major highways. Development of land for motel construction is considered a real estate investment, and the operation of the motel itself is a business venture. When the operator of a motel also owns the real estate, the charges for mortgage interest, property taxes, insurance premiums, maintenance costs, and depreciation become deductible expenses on the operating statements of the business, and the income from the operations is considered active.

Hotel-condos

Hotel-condo hybrids are upscale luxury hotels that sell some of the units as condos. The owners enjoy the investment aspects of owning real estate coupled with the amenities of a full-service hotel. Many luxury hotel chains such as Ritz-Carlton, Hilton, and Four Seasons have embraced this concept. These properties are often a second home for the owners, and the hotels will assist in leasing the units when the owner is absent. Often, the hotel and unit owner will split the rental income produced.

Amusement parks

The amusement park as a real estate investment is enjoying continuing popularity throughout the country. Based on the successes of Disneyland and Knott's Berry Farm in the Los Angeles area, theme amusement parks have emerged in all parts of the nation. Just a few examples of these enterprises are Disney World, the three SeaWorld properties in the United States, Silver Dollar City, Worlds of Fun, Six Flags, and Cedar Point.

An amusement park development requires a high level of technical expertise, beginning with the choice of its theme and continuing through design and the construction of its various attractions. Many larger parks incorporate peripheral complementary real estate developments into their overall designs. Often, hotels, motels, shopping centers, restaurants, and, occasionally, houses and apartments are made part of the park development.

Golf courses

Although golf courses as business enterprises are sometimes located in isolated areas, they are more often developed as an integral part of a centrally located municipal park or new subdivision. There are a number of golf courses that are designed as private clubs, with membership and greens fees, along with concessions and pro shop income, providing the cash flows necessary for financial success.

The construction of a golf course is a complicated, highly technical undertaking. The success of such a project is largely a function of its location, site suitability, and challenging layout. Most large courses are designed by professional golfers who act as consultants to the developers.

The acreage needed for a golf course is determined to a great extent by what type of course is planned. Normally, 120 to 180 acres of gently rolling land is considered adequate for a regulation 18-hole course, while approximately 70 acres are needed for a 9-hole course. Par 3 courses can be constructed on 30 to 45 acres if the fairways are designed in parallel.

The costs of constructing a golf course vary greatly, depending on the terrain and natural setting. These costs include the price of the land; its preparation; the installation of fairways, greens, and sprinkler systems; and the acquisition of necessary equipment. Course maintenance costs have increased dramatically over the past several years.

Senior housing

Two types of senior housing are popular real estate investments: retirement communities and **congregate care centers**.

Retirement communities

This special form of community is designed to cater to the growing retirement market. The **retirement community** stresses lifestyle amenities, recreation, shopping convenience, comfort, minimum maintenance, and a high degree of security. Blended into a well-planned unity, retirement developments include single-family dwellings, condominiums, garden apartments, townhomes, shopping centers, and recreation facilities. Some larger projects include golf courses, swimming pools, clubhouses, hobby shops, medical clinics, and convalescent centers.

Congregate care centers

A special form of senior housing—the congregate care center, which includes assisted living facilities and nursing homes—is emerging as an important real estate investment alternative. Designed in the format of an apartment hotel or complex, these developments provide housing, food, maintenance, and health care within one facility. At least 70% of all people over 65 will require long-term care during their lifetime, and more than 40% will need a nursing home facility.

According to the NIC Investment Guide, a report from the National Investment Center for the Seniors Housing & Care Industry (NIC), demand for senior housing and care is driven by a combination of age, frailty, wealth, income, and desire to live in a senior housing community. The most prominent trend is the growing senior population resulting from the baby boom. As of 2018 census estimates, 19.39% of the U.S. population was 75 years or older. The level of seniors in this age group will continue to grow at a steady pace through 2020. An important factor contributing to demand for senior housing is increased life expectancy. Recent emphasis on healthy living, combined with advances in medicine, has led to seniors living longer, thus increasing the length of time they stay in a senior housing community.

These trends warrant the attention of real estate investors as they consider their investment options.

Medical buildings

Specialization has long been the custom within the medical profession, but specialization of facilities for doctors' offices has not kept pace with the need. Private investors may participate in providing real estate facilities for medical practitioners under FHA Title XI (mortgage insurance for constructing or rehabilitating group-medical-practice buildings) and Title XV (mortgage insurance for new or rehabilitated hospitals owned by nonprofit organizations). Doctors generally prefer locations close to major medical facilities in buildings that can provide complementary, as well as peripheral, medical services.

Medical buildings are generally more expensive to build than conventional offices because of parking, water, and electrical requirements. Successful medical developments require special consideration of doctors' unique needs. Proper planning includes constant consultation with architects and the doctors themselves on how best to design the complex. Large, multidoctor facilities produce maximum tenant interest and better use of the land. The larger projects offer a greater potential patient-referral system, based on a proper mix of tenants as well as on such auxiliary facilities as a pharmacy and a clinical pathology lab.

Convenience stores

There are more than 150,000 convenience stores, also called **C-stores**, in the United States. They typically sell fuel, snacks and drinks, food staples such as breakfast foods and some canned goods, small sizes of pet foods, and hot food such as pizza and chicken wings. The modern trend is to sublease part of the space to a national chain fast food company such as Subway, Dunkin, or Taco Bell. Investment advantages include the ability to build on relatively small parcels of land, stability of national credit tenants with long-term leases, ability to easily sell to investors nationwide who are seeking 1031 exchange opportunities, and accelerated 15-year depreciation under the right circumstances.

Distressed properties

There are numerous opportunities for real estate investments through the acquisition of distressed property. The classic definition of the fair market value of property is what a knowledgeable buyer would pay a willing seller who is not operating under pressure or distress. When a seller is operating under some distress, property can be purchased for less than fair market value, often at dramatic discounts.

Examples of distressed sales include foreclosure auctions, banks disposing of previously foreclosed real estate, bankruptcy auctions, sales for nonpayment of real estate taxes, and government seizures such as those by the IRS, DEA, and others. Often, owners who lose their property in such manner have redemption rights—the right to reacquire their property at a predetermined amount, plus interest. They may or may not have to compensate the new owner for improvements or repairs after the distressed sale. Such sales may or may not eradicate other liens against the property.

While it is not common, sometimes a second position mortgage lender will foreclose, leaving the property subject to the lien of the first mortgage holder. In that case, the investor will have to pay the first mortgage or face loss of the property. If preforeclosure notices are not sent in the proper manner to the IRS, an IRS lien can remain on the property after foreclosure, even if the IRS lien was filed long after the mortgage being foreclosed.

In a short sale, a borrower owes more than the current fair market value of the property. Despite that, lenders are usually willing to accept less than full payoff, but still release their liens, because it might generate more money than a foreclosure and subsequent sale. The lender is under pressure to monetize its collateral as quickly as possible and minimize the risk of additional market value decline. A short sale can result in purchases 10% to 20% below current market value, but can be tricky if there are junior liens. That is because all lienholders will need to release their liens at closing on the short sale, otherwise they will remain on the property and place the purchase in jeopardy.

Properties acquired as a result of nonpayment of property taxes generally require some period of seasoning. Most states auction tax liens only. The successful bidder wins the right to a return of its principal and a certain amount of interest if the owner redeems. If the owner does not redeem within state-specific deadlines, the investor may then foreclose its lien and acquire full ownership. Other states sell tax certificates that include additional rights besides interest income, such as possession rights, and that later mature into full ownership if not redeemed.

Stigmatized properties can also be distressed properties. They have some type of reputation problem that chills the market and enables a bargain purchase. Whether there is an actual problem or not is usually irrelevant. Such properties include those reputed to have structural problems, hazardous waste, or supernatural phenomena. Residential properties that have been the scene of a violent death are often stigmatized. An investor may need assistance from engineers and/or attorneys to evaluate such properties.

Careful consideration should be given to the legal ramifications of acquiring good title to distressed properties. The rewards can be great, but the risks can also be commensurate. The services of a knowledgeable real estate attorney or title company are strongly recommended. In seeking out leads to these opportunities, investors usually contact the various local banks and savings associations, as well as community lawyers, bankruptcy trustees, and real estate agents. Perusal of the local newspapers can also alert investors to foreclosures and tax delinquencies. There is a great variety of online sites for government-seized real estate. In many states, foreclosing lenders must file a notice in the real estate records before commencing their foreclosure proceedings, thereby providing early leads to investors. Investors interested in distressed properties often specialize because of the many potential pitfalls that must be learned and avoided. Despite that, the returns can be phenomenal, which is why it remains a popular strategy.

ALTERNATE INVESTMENT OPPORTUNITIES

A number of investments that are not classified as real estate, per se, are definitely real estate oriented. These alternate investment opportunities include franchises, mineral and air rights, and dealing in real estate securities.

Franchises

Franchises have become such an integral part of our economy that it is difficult to recall a time when this type of cooperative business arrangement did not exist.

Real estate investors often negotiate with franchise owners when arranging leases. A franchise is created when a franchisor grants to a franchisee an exclusive right to engage in the distribution of services or goods under a prescribed marketing plan or system. The operation of the business then follows this plan, using the franchisor's trademark and designated operating format to provide uniformity among all franchise members. Among the many nationally known franchises are McDonald's, Kentucky Fried Chicken, U-Haul, Midas, and Orkin.

Although some franchise operators prefer to purchase land and develop their own buildings, others prefer to be tenants. A lease for property designed to house a franchise operation is usually a three-party agreement among the landlord, the franchisee, and the franchisor. The building frequently reflects an easily recognized architectural design and is built from plans provided by the franchisor. Many of these buildings are designed for only a single purpose; therefore, to offset the risks involved, a developer usually requires a lease that generates enough rental cash flow not only to yield a return on the investment, but also to return the developer's entire cash outlay during the initial lease period. Any renewals can be negotiated at rents appropriate to the market, depending on specific circumstances.

Mineral rights

In this country, an owner of real property is legally entitled to control the minerals, natural gas, oil, and water that lie below the surface of the land. When minerals are removed from the ground, they assume the quality of personal property and can be sold separately from the real estate itself. Because minerals, natural gas, and oil have value, whenever the existence of a substantial quantity of these commodities is discovered in a specific location, a market for their exploitation is developed. Dealers in mineral rights are very active in some areas of the country such as Arizona, California, New Mexico, Montana, Oklahoma, Texas, and Wyoming, where some land is purchased and sold primarily on the basis of its mineral content.

Often, owners of mineral-bearing lands retain the rights to these minerals when they dispose of the real estate. This allows them to sell or lease their mineral rights to others engaged in the mining business. Generally, the retention, or reservation, of mineral rights is accompanied by some specified surface access for their removal. In the absence of the opportunity to enter the surface of a property for direct vertical excavation or drilling, the owner or lessee of the mineral rights may be forced to arrange for vertical descent on an adjoining property and then make a lateral underground approach to the minerals.

Owners of mineral rights receive income in one of three ways: by selling the rights, by leasing the rights, or by selling the minerals themselves. Selling the rights yields a one-time payment, whereas leasing the mineral rights provides **royalty income**, which may continue for the term of the lease. For example, the owner of oil rights might receive a royalty per barrel of oil extracted, and the owner of copper rights might receive a royalty per pound of refined ore over the duration of the excavator's lease.

Investors are attracted to mineral exploration for the tax shelter it offers. Operating expenses, deductions for mining activities, and generous depletion allowances are available under current income tax laws.

Air rights

Although dealing in air rights has, until now, been unheard of in many parts of this country, as the cost of urban land continues to rise, the air is becoming a new arena for real estate investments. The sale or lease of air rights offers an investor a vastly expanded opportunity for constructing high-rise buildings on strategically located sites in central city areas.

The use of the airspace over a specific property often implies the presence of an existing building or other improvements, such as roadways or railroad tracks. Thus, any contract involving the construction of a new building into the air will require an agreement with the base-property owner concerning the surface area to which the edifice will be affixed.

Some developments are anchored by huge columns that straddle the existing building and support a platform on which the new construction is erected. Other buildings are constructed on a platform supported by a central core, much like a golf tee. This core is constructed in the center of the existing building with access to the street through a hallway. The core contains the utilities and elevators that serve the offices or apartments built in the airspace above.

Other uses of airspace include the construction of buildings over roadways in which the streets become tunnels through these structures. Properties developed over Riverside Drive in New York City illustrate this technique. The Merchandise Mart in Chicago is an example of a building constructed over railroad tracks.

Airspace can sometimes be a vital part of a real estate investment that, for its success, depends on an ongoing, uninterrupted view of a lake or ocean where the rents are a function of this view. Owners of such properties might be well-advised to ensure this view by either purchasing or leasing the airspace over adjoining properties that might be used for other buildings. A case in point is the Lake Point Tower in Chicago, which was constructed near, but not quite at, the very end of a strip of land extending into Lake Michigan. Developers purchased the tip of the land and erected a high-rise building that effectively blocked the view from the existing structure.

Water rights

Water rights have become increasingly more important. Who owns the water and who has the right to use it? These issues are controlled by state law and will vary greatly. Real estate development has been halted in some areas due to lack of water. Developers must include research of available water supplies into any feasibility studies. Some investors profit by buying and selling water rights. Property values, especially in some of the western states, may be affected significantly by the water rights that are appurtenant to the land. Private entities assemble water rights to sell to municipalities that are sometimes miles away from the source of water.

Real estate securities

Although not technically real estate investors in the truest sense of the word, dealers in real estate **securities** are actively participating in the market by providing the funds necessary to complete most realty transactions. Lenders who originate most of the senior mortgage loans often sell these securities in the **secondary market** through the services of **Fannie Mae**, **Ginnie Mae**, and **Freddie Mac**.

Dealing in real estate securities offers an investor a viable alternative to the responsibilities that accompany the more active management role associated with traditional real estate investments. A lender assumes a passive role in the operations of a realty venture but still participates as a sort of partner, collecting a portion of the profits in the form of interest. Even more attractive to those who enter this field, the payments do not stop until the loan is repaid, despite the fluctuations of the rental marketplace. Thus, a lender can anticipate receiving a steady income stream in the future—an income that develops a return on the investment commensurate with the risk involved. If the borrower does not fulfill the contractual obligations, the property that is the collateral for the loan reverts to the lender.

Junior securities

In addition to the activities of the secondary mortgage market in dealing with the purchase and sale of senior mortgages, there is a growing demand to use money for trading in junior real estate securities. Because of the rising cost of land and the expenses connected with its preparation, as well as increasing construction costs and the climbing prices for used properties, a second or third mortgage, or a land contract, is often the only way a property can be financed. Generally, the seller ends up carrying back a junior loan to facilitate the sale of the property.

By its very nature, junior finance is a relatively high-risk investment. *Junior* means second in priority behind an existing first mortgage lien; thus, there is a greater risk of loss in the event of a default. In a foreclosure, the senior mortgagee is paid first, and then the junior lienholders receive their payments from any excess funds secured at the property's auction.

However, junior financing instruments can be made more secure. Junior lenders often insist on the inclusion of a *cross-defaulting clause* in their contracts, whereby the borrower will default if he defaults on any other obligation. Wraparound contracts can be established with payments routed through a collection agency or a trustee to ensure the loan's close supervision. Property subject to a contract for deed can be placed into a trust, eliminating much of the inherent risks.

Generally, returns required for junior loans are secured by negotiated interest rates, substantial placement fees, or discounting.

Discounting

Discounting raises the yield of a receivable for its buyer without affecting the terms of the loan contract. When a real estate loan is originated at a 9% nominal (contracted) interest rate and sold to a securities dealer for its face value, the purchaser earns a true 9% return on the investment. If, however, the current market interest rate is lower than 9%, the contract will be sold at a premium—an amount higher than its face value—which has the effect of reducing the yield to more closely reflect the current market conditions.

More commonly, however, a mortgage is sold at a **discount**—an amount less than its face value—to raise the yield for its purchaser. The amount of the discount is a function of the mortgage buyer's yield requirements, the contract's interest rate, and the term of the loan.

FOR EXAMPLE

Examine a mortgage for $10,000 with interest-only payments at the rate of 9% per year, due in full in five years. A securities purchaser who requires a 12% return on the investment will pay exactly $8,918.57 for this contract.

$900.00	Annual interest-only payment
× 3.604776	Factor for PWA @ 12%, five years
$3,244.30	Present worth of annuity
$10,000.00	Reversion at end of five years
× 0.567427	Factor for PW of $1 @ 12%, five years
5,674.27	Present worth
+ 3,244.30	Present worth of annuity
$8,918.57	Present worth of contract

Real Estate Mortgage Investment Conduits (REMICs)

Real estate mortgage investment conduits (REMICs) are an ownership entity that can hold mortgages and issue multiple classes of ownership interests in the form of pass-through certificates, bonds, or other securities. The overall goal of this entity is to simplify the structure of the secondary mortgage market. Even more important, however, the income from a REMIC is considered passive rather than portfolio. Thus, it may be used to offset passive losses.

Under a REMIC, mortgages are pooled in various categories called **tranches** and sold to investors requiring specific yields for specific risks. For example, one tranche may include only fixed-rate loans, while another, only variable-rate loans. Another may pool only long-term loans, while another, only short-term loans.

All of the tranches offer pass-through services, where interest-only, principal-only, or a combination of both is passed through to the holder of the securities. Various arrangements can be made with receipts, as well. For example, payments can be passed through as they are received, or they can be paid on a guaranteed basis, whether the REMIC receives them or not. The prices of the tranches are reflective of the risks and yields expected.

The most recent innovations in this program are *interest-only (IO)* and *principal-only (PO)* **strips**. Strips can be either highly speculative or act as a hedging vehicle, depending on when the loans in the pool are paid in full. IO strips decrease in value when interest rates fall, and refinancing induces accelerated prepayments of existing loans. Thus, the holders will receive less interest. However, PO strips will increase in value under these same circumstances because their holders will receive principal payments at a faster rate. In the event of rising interest rates, the reverse is true.

SUMMARY OF INVESTING IN SPECIAL REAL ESTATE

This lesson examined the opportunities for private investment in manufactured-home parks and such diverse realty projects as hotels, motels, amusement parks, and golf courses, as well as alternate ventures into franchises, mineral rights, air rights, and mortgage securities. All of these investments are somewhat removed from the more standard real estate opportunities and, as a result, require special skills and knowledge to ensure success.

Manufactured homes appeal to a growing segment of the American population because of increased costs of more standard housing, increased life expectancies, and the effective vesting of many pension and retirement funds. Despite its increasing importance, many community planners frown on this form of property development because of the notion that a "trailer park" is detrimental to property values and places undue strain on city services. Despite this handicap, most modern manufactured-home parks are designed to provide a comfortable and secure residential environment, with some parks offering relatively luxurious accommodations at reasonable rates. These parks include such amenities as swimming pools, clubhouses, meeting rooms, organized social activities, and other provisions for tenant comfort and entertainment.

An alternative land development program involves constructing a modern manufactured-home park and selling the spaces to individual owners in a condominium format. The owners join in an association for their mutual benefit, much as they do in condominium apartment developments.

Hotels, motels, theme amusement parks, and golf courses may be considered businesses as well as realty investments. As a result, the land involved is very much a part of the business activity. Hotels and motels serve the traveler's need for short-term housing accommodations. The investment opportunities in this form of real estate run the entire gamut, from small mom-and-pop operations to luxurious resorts. Amusement parks are specialized investments that require high levels of technical and managerial skill to ensure success. These same requirements are essential to any golf course investment if it is to succeed.

Anticipating an aging baby boom population, some investors are concentrating on developing senior housing. Some seek the security of long-term medical tenancies, while others like to speculate in buying repossessions from institutional lenders.

Some real estate investors deal with franchises when leasing property for the operation of special businesses. Franchises are designed to direct the operation of a business so that it follows a prescribed marketing plan under a recognized trade name and property design.

Trading in mineral rights often results in substantial royalties on precious minerals, natural gas, and oil removed from under the land. Some investors deal only in buying and selling the rights to minerals and never become involved in the excavation or drilling process themselves.

A market in air rights is emerging in this country as a result of the increasing costs of urban land. As a result, the sale or lease of air rights offers an investor expanded opportunities to participate in this form of real estate. Dealers in air rights must make arrangements to control a portion of the surface if they anticipate constructing a building.

Dealing in mortgage securities offers an investor a viable alternative to the responsibilities that accompany the ownership of real estate. In effect, a mortgagee is, to a limited extent, a partner with the owner of the property and collects a portion of the profits in the form of interest on the loan, despite the fluctuations of the marketplace.

Real estate mortgages are created by lenders, both large and small, and the securities they originate are often sold in the market. Senior loans are traded in the secondary market through Fannie Mae, Ginnie Mae, and Freddie Mac. Junior loans are sold to securities buyers who normally require discounts to enhance their yields.

DISCUSSION TOPICS

1. Discuss with the planning and zoning officials in your area their attitudes toward the desirability and location of constructing new manufactured-home rental and sales parks. Did you discern any prejudice in their remarks, and if so, do you think the prejudice is valid?
2. Examine the deed to your property (or any property). Are your mineral rights reserved by the government or by a private individual?

UNIT 11 EXAM

1. An analysis of the profitability of a vacant land investment includes all of the following *EXCEPT*
   A. income lost from unrented vacant land.
   B. price and terms paid for initial purchase.
   C. carrying costs, including interest and property taxes.
   D. opportunity costs on equity invested.

2. Excess loss carryover is disallowed by the IRS for
   A. wheat farmers.
   B. horse ranchers.
   C. cow ranchers.
   D. hobby farmers.

3. Of the following, the property that will generally develop the highest rental rate is
   A. an existing vacant store building.
   B. a newly constructed garden apartment.
   C. a new store building constructed to suit a specific tenant's needs.
   D. a new store constructed as a speculative investment.

4. Under the Interstate Land Sales Full Disclosure Act, a buyer of a lot in a nationally promoted subdivision has how many days after signing the purchase agreement to cancel the deal?
   A. Zero days
   B. Three days
   C. Five days
   D. Seven days

5. Investors generally consider a single-family home purchase to
   A. be a speculative and specialized activity.
   B. be a desirable investment alternative.
   C. require little expert knowledge.
   D. need little advance financial planning.

6. An investment in an apartment building is considered economically feasible if it
   A. breaks even.
   B. returns a profit on the investment.
   C. returns a profit and the initial investment.
   D. can be converted to a condominium.

7. The conversion of a rental apartment project to a condominium includes all of the following procedures *EXCEPT*
   A. evicting all the present tenants.
   B. bringing the structure up to the current building code.
   C. filing legal documents for government agency approval.
   D. arranging financing for the apartments sold.

8. The formation of a condominium requires the filing of a declaration of intentions including provisions for all of the following *EXCEPT*
   A. recognition of divided ownerships.
   B. establishment of a binding set of bylaws.
   C. creation of a single master mortgage.
   D. restrictions against further partitioning.

9. For most small, low-rise office building investments,
   A. financing is usually difficult to secure.
   B. rents are generally higher than for larger projects.
   C. major arterial locations are not of prime importance.
   D. securing tenants is generally a difficult task.

10. High-rise office developments are generally designed for all of the following *EXCEPT*
    A. to serve the community.
    B. as institutional, owner-occupied buildings.
    C. to serve the neighborhood.
    D. as an office park complex.

11. Under the Americans with Disabilities Act, *disability* is defined as
    A. any impairment of any kind.
    B. a physical impairment that substantially limits one or more major life activities.
    C. a physical impairment that substantially limits any life activities.
    D. a physical or mental impairment that substantially limits one or more major life activities.

12. Which of the following statements is *FALSE*?
    A. Strip stores provide neighborhood shopping services.
    B. Neighborhood shopping centers provide their customers with necessary goods and services.
    C. Community shopping centers service a trade-area population of over 400,000 persons.
    D. Regional shopping centers are constructed on parcels of land containing at least 30 acres.

13. Which of the following types of shopping centers does *NOT* usually include competitive stores selling the same merchandise?
    A. Large and small shopping centers
    B. Neighborhood centers
    C. Community centers
    D. Regional centers

14. The small investor is attracted to strip store buildings for all of the following reasons *EXCEPT*
    A. affordability.
    B. ease of financing.
    C. off-street parking convenience.
    D. convertibility to other uses.

15. Which of the following is expected to transform the retail market over the course of the next decade?
    A. General mall
    B. Strip store shops
    C. Community centers
    D. E-commerce

16. The demand for industrial space depends to a large degree on all of the following *EXCEPT*
    A. the condition of the business cycle in the overall national economy.
    B. the supply of available and proposed industrial space.
    C. the number of new housing starts.
    D. local and regional economic conditions.

17. From an industry's point of view, the benefits of locating in an industrial park include all of the following *EXCEPT*
    A. immediate site readiness.
    B. symbiosis with other firms in the park.
    C. operating economies.
    D. unrestricted site uses.

18. From a community's point of view, the benefits of encouraging the development of an industrial park would include all of the following *EXCEPT*
    A. economic-base expansion.
    B. tax-base expansion.
    C. limiting urban sprawl.
    D. efficient use of municipal services.

19. Revenue bonds issued to develop industrial properties are repaid from
    A. taxes imposed on local property owners.
    B. incremental taxes earned from increased values.
    C. rents charged to new industrial tenants.
    D. inventory taxes charged to new tenants.

20. Which would *NOT* be an industrial property use?
    A. Building for assembly of automotive parts
    B. Warehouse space
    C. Hazardous waste-disposal facility
    D. Steel mill

21. When you own your own space in a manufactured-home park, you are in
    A. a cooperative.
    B. a condominium.
    C. a rental park.
    D. an RV park.

22. Depreciation deductions in a manufactured-home park that leases vacant spaces can be taken on all of the following *EXCEPT*
    A. concrete pads.
    B. tenants' manufactured homes.
    C. the recreation center.
    D. blacktop roads.

23. Which of the following relationships is *FALSE*?
    A. Convention hotels—large meeting rooms
    B. Commercial hotels—strong weekend demand
    C. Resort hotels—vacationers
    D. Extended-stay hotels—kitchen apartments

24. Knott's Berry Farm, Silver Dollar City, and Six Flags refer to
    A. new communities.
    B. theme amusement parks.
    C. recreational condominiums.
    D. urban renewal projects.

25. The retention of mineral rights in a parcel of land is called
    A. an agglomeration.
    B. an amalgamation.
    C. a reservation.
    D. a restriction.

Use Figure 11.3 to answer questions 26 and 27. Note that answers are rounded.

Figure 11.3: Annual Compound Interest at 12%

Period	PW $1	PWA $
1	0.8928	0.8928
2	0.7972	1.6900
3	0.7118	2.4018
4	0.6355	3.0373
5	0.5674	3.6048

26. What will a 12% investor pay for a new, 8%, four-year, $5,000 interest-only second mortgage?
    A. $4,200
    B. $4,392
    C. $4,460
    D. $5,000

27. What will a 12% investor pay for a two-year-old, 8%, five-year, $5,000 interest-only second mortgage?
    A. $4,375
    B. $4,400
    C. $4,519
    D. $5,000

UNIT 12

Managing the Investment Property

LEARNING OBJECTIVES

When you have completed this unit, you will be able to accomplish the following.

- Differentiate between the management needs of different types of investment properties.

KEY TERMS

- Building Owners and Managers Association (BOMA)
- common-area fee
- common-area maintenance (CAM)
- escalation clause
- eviction
- graduated lease
- Institute of Real Estate Management (IREM)
- lease
- move clause
- option
- percentage clause
- rental concessions
- sinking fund
- sublease
- tax clause
- tenant mix

INTRODUCTION

Management considerations vary depending on the type of investment property. It is important for real estate professionals to understand these differences and apply their knowledge according to the type of property they are managing.

An important feature of residential real estate ownership is the landlord-tenant relationship established when a house or apartment is rented. While these relationships are usually amicable, unpleasant circumstances occasionally do arise. The necessary commitment to active management, including the resultant interpersonal relationships, inhibits many investors from participating in residential rental ownership.

This unit also investigates the management requirements common to most office buildings, large or small, as well as managing different retail spaces.

MANAGING APARTMENTS

More than any other type of real estate investment, apartments require the greatest amount of management participation in terms of physical maintenance and continuing tenant goodwill. The responsibilities increase with the number of apartments owned.

The National Multi Housing Council (NMHC) reports that the attraction and retention of high-caliber individuals as apartment managers is a top priority for investment apartment owners. About half of the more than 300,000 apartment property managers are employees of real estate agency and management firms. Another 40% are self-employed, and the remainder work for agencies of state and federal governments.

Apartment property managers fall into two general groups: on-site and off-site managers. *On-site managers* are responsible for the day-to-day operations for a single project. Their duties include maintenance, dealing with tenant requests and complaints, and showing vacant apartments to prospective tenants. They keep records of income and expenditures and submit regular reports to supervisors or owners.

Off-site managers exercise supervisory authority over on-site personnel at a number of properties. They act as the liaison between the on-site manager and the property owners. They market vacant space and establish rental rates.

Apartment management companies have created access to online credit scoring to facilitate the leasing process. In addition, they have established web pages offering apartments available for online viewing and leasing, with tenant portals for online payments, maintenance and repair requests, and general communications. Most management software also includes owner portals for management reports, leasing activity, and other data.

Leases

The formal document that stipulates the length and the terms of a tenancy is called a **lease**. A lease is a legally enforceable contractual agreement between a landlord and a tenant. In exchange for a tenant's promise to pay the rent on time and to maintain the property in good condition, the landlord grants the tenant possession of the premises and guarantees the tenant's rights to the peaceful use of the property for the duration of the lease term (see Figure 12.1).

As important as the term of the tenancy may be, the investor's prime concern is the rent that the tenant is to pay for the use of the property. Rental payments by tenants are the owner's major source of income. Most leases require that rent be paid on some regular, fixed-amount basis—usually monthly. Although most apartment leases are established for one-year periods, some larger, more expensive complexes use leases of longer duration. In these cases, rent might be payable on a graduated basis. For example, a three-year lease for $21,600 could be paid at the rate of $500 per month for the first year, $600 per month for the second year, and $700 per month for the third year. This technique enables a tenant to offset the costs of moving and furnishings in the earlier period of the lease. It also raises the rent gradually, allowing an easier absorption of higher charges in the later periods.

A lease includes a promise to pay a certain sum of money as rent over a specified time period. Probably more animosity is generated over broken leases than any other aspect of the landlord-tenant relationship. Invariably, tenants lose their jobs, are transferred, become ill, get divorced or married, or purchase a house, but the binding legal nature of a lease inhibits and prohibits a tenant's freedom to change housing to suit current needs. A formal lease stipulates the monthly rental amounts and other terms in a written agreement, whereas an informal,

Figure 12.1: Residential Lease

RESIDENTIAL LEASE

DATE OF LEASE	LEASE TERM		RENT PER MONTH	SECURITY DEPOSIT
	BEGINNING DATE	ENDING DATE		

THIS RESIDENTIAL LEASE AGREEMENT ("Lease") is made between the following parties:

NAME:______________________________ NAME:______________________________

ADDRESS OF PREMISES:

"LESSEE"

BUSINESS ADDRESS:

"LESSOR"

SECTION ONE. RENT

1. Lessee will pay Lessor (or Lessor's authorized agent) the amount of____________Dollars ($________) per month, in advance, as monthly rental for the Premises for the term of this Lease. Total rental for the initial term of this Lease shall be ___________ Dollars. Lessee's first monthly rental payment is due on or before ____________, 19__, and each subsequent payment will be due on the _____ day of each month following for the term of this Lease. Payments will be made at the Lessor's address as stated in this Lease, or at any other address Lessor may specify in writing to Lessee.

2. Installments of rent that are not received by Lessor as required by this Lease are considered late. Late payment of rent constitutes default under the terms of this lease. If full payment is not received by the Lessor within ____ days of the date of default, Lessee agrees to pay to Lessor an administrative fee of____________Dollars ($_________). Lessee will pay Lessor a charge of____________Dollars ($__________) for any check returned to Lessor for insufficient funds. Lessor may require that any rent payment be made in the form of a certified check, money order or cashier's check.

3. Failure by Lessee to make any payment of rent, or any other fee or charge, under this Lease constitutes a default. In the event that Lessee fails to make any payment within _____ days after receiving written notice of Lessor's intention to terminate this Lease, Lessor may terminate this Lease and any and all unpaid rent for the full remaining term of this Lease shall then become due and payable. In the event of termination, Lessor shall be entitled to:

A. Immediate possession of the Premises.
B. Immediate payment of any unpaid rent or other charges.
C. Recovery of any damages incurred due to Lessee's default, including but not limited to the cost of reletting the Premises, lost rental under this Lease and the cost of collections.
D. Court costs and reasonable attorney's fees as permitted by law, arising due to Lessee's default.
E. Any other remedy as provided by the law of the State of _______________.

4. Lessor's rights and duties under the terms of this Lease are cumulative, and the exercise of any one or more of them does not prohibit Lessor from the exercise or use of any other right or remedy provided by this Lease or by law.

SECTION TWO. SECURITY DEPOSIT

1. Lessee has paid Lessor a Security Deposit in the amount of_________ Dollars ($__________) as set forth above, to secure his or her performance of all the covenants, agreements and terms of this Lease. The Security Deposit is subject to the following conditions:

A. Lessor may use, apply or retain any or all of the amount of the Security Deposit for the payment of any rent due from Lessee; for any administrative, maintenance or other charges set forth in this Lease; any damages or expenses incurred by Lessor arising from Lessee's failure to comply with any of the terms of this Lease (including but not limited to expenses incurred in reletting the Premises).

B. If, during the term (or any extension of the term) of this Lease, Lessor is obligated to use all or any part of the Security Deposit in accordance with the terms and conditions of this Lease or any other law or agreement, Lessor shall notify Lessor of the expenditure, in writing, within _______ days of its being incurred, and provide along with such notice an itemized list of the charges and expenses, including the reasonable cost of Lessor's own time and labor. Lessee shall have _____ days in which to deposit with Lessor a sum equal to the amount used, to ensure that the full amount of the Security Deposit is maintained with the Lessor at all times during the term of this Lease.

C. The use of all or any part of the Security Deposit by Lessor shall not be Lessor's sole remedy in the event of Lessee's default. If the costs of Lessor's expenses and/or damages incurred exceed the total amount of the Security Deposit, Lessee shall pay any excess. LESSEE MAY NOT APPLY THE SECURITY DEPOSIT AS RENT.

E. During the term of this Lease, and during any extensions of this Lease agreement, the Security Deposit shall be held in a/an:☐ interest-bearing ☐ non-interest-bearing [*check one*] account. *Parties initial here:* _______ _______

F. When Lessee has performed all obligations required under this Lease, has paid all rent and any other charges, and has surrendered the Premises, its keys, passes and any other documents or fixtures in the same condition as they were provided at the beginning of the term of this Lease, reasonable wear and tear excepted, Lessor shall return to Lessee any remaining amount of the Security Deposit, together with a fully itemized list of all charges deducted from it, with documentation, within ____ days of the termination of this Lease and the surrender of the Premises.

G. In the event Lessor's interest in the Premises are sold, transferred or assigned, Lessor shall notify Lessee of the change in ownership and the name and business address of the new lessor. Lessor shall transfer the Security Deposit to the new lessor or owner and be released from all liability to Lessee.

Figure 12.1: Residential Lease (continued)

SECTION THREE. TERM OF LEASE AND EXTENSIONS

The term of this Lease shall be _____ year(s). This Lease will be automatically extended on a month to month basis, on the same terms and conditions as agreed to in this Lease, unless either party gives the other _____ days written notice of his or her intent not to extend the Lease at the end of the term. In the event that this Lease is extended, _____ days prior notice shall be required to terminate it. Such notice must be received by the non-terminating party no later than the _____ day of the month, and Lessee's tenancy shall terminate on the last day of that month.

SECTION FOUR. CONDITION OF PREMISES

Lessee has examined the condition of the Premises, and acknowledges that the Premises are received in good condition and repair except as otherwise specified in this Lease. Lessee is responsible for all day-to-day maintenance of the Premises as defined in the Rules and Regulations, including maintaining all devices and appliances in working order.

SECTION FIVE. USE OF PREMISES

1. The Premises are leased to Lessee exclusively, and shall be used strictly as a residence and for no other purpose. The Premises shall be occupied only by Lessee and any children born to, adopted by or placed under Lessee's legal care and/or guardianship. A violation of any condition of this lease by any guest of Lessee shall be construed as a violation by Lessee.

2. The Premises may not be assigned or sublet by Lessee without the prior written consent of Lessor. Lessee shall not undertake any modification or structural change to the Premises without the written consent of Lessor.

3. Lessee shall not use or allow the Premises to be used for any unlawful or disorderly purpose. The Premises may not be used in any way that represents a material detriment to the health or safety of others. Lessee shall comply with all applicable laws and any Rules and Regulations established by Lessor. Lessee shall be provided with a printed copy of the applicable Rules and Regulations at the time this Lease is signed. Lessor has the right to immediately terminate this lease based on any such violation.

SECTION SIX. ACCESS

Lessee shall permit Lessor, or Lessor's duly authorized agent or representatives, unrestricted access to the Premises at all reasonable times for any necessary purpose, including but not limited to inspection, maintenance and exhibition.

SECTION SEVEN. PETS

No pets of any kind may be kept in or around the Premises for any purpose. This provision does not apply to companion animals trained and certified to assist a person with a disability.

SECTION EIGHT. UTILITIES AND MAINTENANCE

1. Lessor will ensure that hot and cold running water are supplied to the Premises for Lessee's use at all times. Lessor will provide reasonable heating of the Premises at all times between the months of ___________ and __________, as required by law. Lessor shall provide reasonable air conditioning to the Premises between the months of _________ and _________, or as provided by law. Lessor shall not be responsible to Lessee for any failure to provide water, heat or air conditioning due to causes beyond Lessor's control or for periods when any necessary systems are under repair.

2. Lessor covenants to maintain the Premises and all grounds and public areas appurtenant to the Premises, in good repair and tenantable condition. Lessor certifies that the Premises contains all smoke detectors and other devices required by law, and that all such detectors or other devices are in good working order. Lessee is responsible for maintaining such systems.

4. Should the Premises be damaged by fire or other casualty, Lessor may either (A) repair the damage within a reasonable time, not to exceed _____ days from the date Lessor is notified in writing of such damage, or (B) terminate this Lease by providing Lessee with written notice. Should such fire or other casualty impair Lessee's occupancy, Lessee may vacate the premises and provide Lessor with written notice, within _____ days of so vacating, of the intent to terminate this Lease. Such termination will be without penalty to Lessee. If such damage is caused by Lessee's own fault or negligence, or that of Lessee's agents, guests, visitors, servants or licensees, Lessee shall continue to be liable for all rent and charges during the remaining unexpired term of this Lease unless specifically released by Lessor.

SECTION NINE. SUBORDINATION, SEVERABILITY AND LAW

1. This Lease is subordinate to all mortgages, deeds of trust or other instruments now or later affecting the Premises.

2. If any provision of this Lease is or should become prohibited under any law, that provision shall be made ineffective, without invalidating any remaining provisions. The governing law of the jurisdiction in which the Premises are located is incorporated into and supersedes this Lease by reference, and the parties agree to be bound by such law.

SECTION TEN. MISCELLANEOUS

The words "Lessor" and "Lessee," as used in this Lease, are construed as including more than one lessor. All terms and conditions of this Lease are binding on and may be enforced by the parties, their heirs, assigns, executors, administrators and successors. This Lease represents the entire agreement between Lessor and Lessee. Neither party is bound by any representations made by any party that are not included in this Lease, except that the Rules and Regulations of the Premises and Lessee's Application are included by reference.

ADDITIONAL COVENANTS, TERMS, CONDITIONS AND AGREEMENTS: [*if none, write "NONE"*]

LESSEE:______________________**(SEAL)**	**LESSOR:**______________________**(SEAL)**
Date: _____________	**Date:** _____________

but still legally enforceable, monthly arrangement may be made through an oral commitment between the parties, or even an exchange of electronic communications such as emails or text messages.

Investors in areas with large concentrations of military personnel must consider the Service Members Civil Relief Act in calculating rental income. Under the act, military personnel may cancel their leases without penalty or loss of security deposit if they receive orders to relocate. The service member must give written notice to the landlord and proof of the relocation orders. Cancellation is effective as of the last day of the month following the month of notice. Tenants are allowed to waive the benefits of the act in their leases, but inclusion of such a clause could make the investor significantly less competitive than other landlords in the area. Care should be taken to investigate average turnover rates among military tenants, rather than rely on the efficacy of a one-year lease.

The absence of a lease would disturb many tenants because under such an arrangement, the landlord has the power to arbitrarily adjust the rents and conditions of occupancy. Some tenants, however, are relieved at the lack of a lease and are willing to risk a rent raise in exchange for the freedom of being able to move when desired. Most landlords observe a no-rent-raise policy for a year as an operational strategy because they also run the risk of tenants moving to a competitor's project. In the absence of a lease, tenants should still be required to sign an agreement to observe the rules and regulations of their occupancy.

Deposits

Most states, under statutes governing landlord-tenant relationships, stipulate that the landlord may collect a deposit under a lease, but that deposit must be maintained in a separate account with any accruing interest belonging to the tenant. This creates a bookkeeping chore. Some states limit the maximum amount of the deposit to a specific multiple of the monthly rent.

To avoid these problems, many smaller residential project managers eliminate front-end deposits and require the first and last months' rents in advance. Larger projects collect deposits and account for them as prescribed by law.

Evictions

Although the laws governing **evictions** for nonpayment of rent vary throughout the states, the following rules generally prevail:

- When a tenant neglects or refuses to pay rent when due, or when a tenant violates any provision of the lease, the landlord may reenter and take possession or commence an action for recovery of the leased premises. Some states require a *Notice of Default and Opportunity to Cure* letter that allows statutorily mandated time periods for the tenant to cure her default. If not cured within the time period, the lease can be terminated. Other states simply require a notice of termination with no cure period.
- The eviction or unlawful detainer suit is generally filed in a court of limited jurisdiction in the state, with shorter time limits and more informality than the regular courts that hear jury cases.
- After successful completion of the eviction lawsuit, there is generally an order issued from the court to local law enforcement to assist with tenant turnout, should that be necessary. In some states, a tenant who refuses to vacate after an eviction order is held in contempt of court. In other states, law enforcement is present to enforce the peace, while the

landlord's employees or third-party moving company moves all personal property to the curb.

- Some states allow for a landlord's liens on the tenant's personal property. Other states prohibit this.

Provisions for amenities

Depending on the size of the project, residential rental properties often include some amenities besides the normal landscaping and architectural style of the construction. In fact, the ability to enjoy a swimming pool, sauna, clubhouse, tennis court, putting green, ski slope, marina, beach, or golf course is what many apartment dwellers now seek for the amount of rent they pay. Whereas a tenant might not be able to afford these amenities in a detached house, the availability of these facilities is often a deciding factor when renting an apartment in a specific project.

Many apartment complexes are designed to attract individuals with similar tastes, such as retirement villages, ski resorts, golf and tennis groupings, and similar special-interest rental developments.

The maintenance and management of these amenities generates problems and costs for the project's owners—costs usually passed along to the tenants in the form of higher rents or user fees. The larger rental projects capitalize on their amenities by providing professional recreational directors who oversee organized, planned functions within the project. Ranging from dances to bingo games, these activities bring the tenants together and encourage friendships, which, in turn, act to create that sought-after longevity of tenancy so important for continued successful rental operations. Many of the more active apartment complexes find that they have lists of people waiting to move in at the first opportunity, rather than the sporadically vacant apartments found in less well-organized projects.

Apartment projects are generally bought and sold based on the capitalization of income model or the DCF model.

MANAGING CONDOMINIUMS

The bylaws of each condominium regime include a provision for the establishment of an association of owners to supervise the management of the project. Included in this management responsibility is care of the common areas, as well as enforcement of the project's rules and regulations. Each condominium unit owner receives a vote in the association, and the group elects a board of directors to assume the responsibilities of management. Larger condo projects hire professional third-party management to ensure continuity and impartiality.

In addition to supervising the personnel and services necessary for the maintenance of the property, the board develops the association's annual budget; including the amounts required for property taxes, insurance premiums, and operating costs for the common areas; legal and accounting fees; and third-party management. The board submits this budget to the general membership for approval, and its adoption forms the basis of a special assessment charged to each condominium unit owner, or monthly homeowners' dues, depending on the project's structure.

This common-area assessment fee is based on the ratio of a particular unit's purchase price to the total original value of the project. Thus, the owner of a $40,000 apartment in a $2 million project will have a constant assessment ratio factor of 2% ($40,000 / $2,000,000 = 0.02), which will be applied to the annual operating expenses to determine the proportionate share. A common-area operations budget of $30,000 would require a contribution of $600, or $50 per month, from this owner ($30,000 × 0.02 = $600 / 12 = $50).

In addition to collecting the monthly common-area operating fees from the association's members, most condominium managers impose an additional charge to accumulate reserves in anticipation of major repairs and replacements. To assess the owners for their proportionate contributions to this **sinking fund**, which is deposited separately into an interest-earning savings account, the useful lives of the major components of the common areas are analyzed. The sinking fund charges applied in a high-rise project would normally be greater than those for a low-rise apartment building because of additional maintenance responsibilities—such as the roof and elevator(s)—in the former structure. In a low-rise, while individual owners might be responsible for repairs to the roof, there are no elevators to maintain.

Condominium investors should examine all bylaws and recently proposed changes to the bylaws to ensure the investment objectives are possible. Some condos prohibit long and/or short-term leases, for example. Some require payment of a portion of resale profits to the homeowners' association. Some have move-in/move-out impact fees. In addition, several years of financial data should be evaluated, with particular regard to the method of paying for future capital repairs. The investor who buys a unit in a project without a sinking fund may be forced to pay a large assessment for roof repair or replacement. A project with large amounts in accounts receivable for unpaid dues or assessments may be in serious financial decline.

MANAGING OFFICE BUILDINGS

Whether investors in office space are large companies involved in high-rise projects or private developers investing in low-rise or midrise buildings, they have similar management responsibilities. A profitable venture requires a careful market study to determine the demand for the subject space in terms of existing rentals and future needs. Rental policies and procedures that will initially attract new tenants and still remain flexible enough to keep these tenants for long periods of time must be established. Included in the marketing of office space are *viable rental schedules* within the terms and conditions of leases.

Market analysis

Before any investment in office property, the availability and character of neighboring competitive properties should be ascertained. The direction and degree of future trends are more significant than the present status of the market. Primary consideration should be given to the demand for space by new businesses in the area, the expansion rate of existing tenants, and the number and types of tenants who desire to move from their present locations.

To gain more definitive perspectives, the investor should study the market for office space segmentally according to age, condition, location, facilities, and amenities. An overall market vacancy figure of 5% may include a more specific 10% vacancy rate for new office space and a 2% rate for a city's central business district. Market information is available from local newspaper reports, the local chamber of commerce, private research firms' monthly reports, and the local units of the **BOMA** and the **IREM**. BOMA's website is www.boma.org, and IREM's is www.irem.org.

The relocation of tenants from older structures to newer properties should be examined carefully to approximate the degree of movement from one to the other. An estimate can then be made of the potential attractiveness of a new structure, and new uses for older buildings may be discovered. For example, older space vacated by tenants moving to new quarters is often occupied by businesses that have relatively little customer contact. For these firms, a prestigious location is less important than convenience of layout and reasonable rent. Once the demand pattern for an area is identified, a rent schedule for a specific property within that market can be established.

Establishing a rent schedule

As with most rental properties, the charge for the use of space is probably the most significant factor, not only in attracting tenants, but also in establishing the profitability of the investment. Depending on the economic stability of the area in question, the condition of the market for the particular investment under consideration, the quality of the building, and the services provided, a realistic rent schedule should be prepared and administered forthrightly by the property owner or manager. Rental rates that are unrealistically high result in vacancies and serious cash-flow shortages, while rates that are too low minimize the investment's profit potential.

Generally, office rent schedules are established on a base rate plus extra charges for special services. Primarily, a tenant is concerned with the interior space allocated for use, although the building's location, its condition, and the availability of amenities are also considered when the rent is negotiated. As a result of the primary concern with space, office rents are usually established as a certain dollar amount per square foot of usable space. Thus, a base rate of $12 per square foot per year will result in a rent of $1,000 per month for an office with 1,000 square feet of interior space (1,000 square feet × $12 per foot = $12,000 gross annual rent / 12 months = $1,000 rent per month).

Rent is affected by many elements, including the competitive market, the location of the subject property, the quality of the building, the services provided by management, and the inclusion of partitions, floor coverings, air conditioners, utilities, parking facilities, and similar extras. In addition, a rental rate is influenced by the location of the office within the building itself—lobby and top-floor locations usually command the highest rates.

Because the determination of rent is based on the space used by the tenant, the areas used for an entry lobby, hallways, stairwells, elevator shafts, bathrooms, storage bins, and the like are considered nonproductive in terms of generating cash flows. The charges for their use are built into the base rate in the lease contract. As a result, an office building is described as having a specific degree of efficiency. For example, if a certain building has 10% of its overall square feet included in these nonproductive areas, it is said to be 90% efficient, whereas a building with 20% of its space used as hallways and so forth is considered to be 80% efficient.

Applying the efficiency factor that exists for a particular building allows an investor to estimate the number of rentable square feet available and establishes a basis for making an economic analysis of an investment's potential profitability. For example, an 80% efficient structure containing 50,000 total square feet has only 40,000 rentable square feet to which the rental rate is applied to determine the possible gross annual income from this investment.

It may appear as though a highly efficient building would generate a commensurately high gross annual rent, but this is not always the case. For example, a building with 10% of its total area devoted to nonproductive space may have narrow hallways and a small, unimpressive lobby. Although the efficiency rate for this structure is higher than that of a building with a larger lobby and wider hallways, the rental rate might be lower, reflecting a less prestigious building. Thus, the achievable gross rents would be less than those for a comparable structure with a lower efficiency factor.

Net leases

Often rents are established on a net basis, a double-net basis, or even a triple-net basis. A net lease would have the tenant pay a proportionate amount for property taxes, insurance, and utilities, in addition to the base rent. A double-net lease would include the tenant also paying for maintenance costs. A triple-net lease would include the tenant paying for all operating costs, and sometimes even the interest payments on the lessor's mortgage on the property, in addition to the base rent. These net leases are popular with investors who want to establish a fixed, steady stream of income without having to handle the problems associated with management and maintenance. The use of the terms *net*, *double-net*, and *triple-net* are not used consistently in the industry. It is prudent to clarify in any conversation or lease exactly what the parties mean when using these terms. Exactly what expenses will the tenant be expected to absorb? Among the expenses often included in a net lease are **common-area maintenance (CAM)** charges. CAM charges often include fees to cover maintenance costs on items shared by all the tenants, such as parking lots, atriums, public restrooms, hallways, and the like.

Marketing office space

Marketing office space requires a systematic and continuing program to attract prospective tenants and maintain their occupancy after they have moved in. Generally, new tenants are interested in getting a rental bargain, while at the same time, acquiring increased office and building efficiency, economy of operational expenses, and a dignified and convenient location that complements the enterprise involved.

Managers often display great zeal and ingenuity in seeking new tenants. Care, however, must be taken to qualify new applicants regarding their financial ability, current needs, and future growth potential.

One of the most common methods to attract tenants to an office project is hiring a broker appropriate for the area. This broker may use signs placed on the property, advertisements in local newspapers and regional editions of national magazines, and promotional brochures distributed electronically or by direct mail to all businesses in the geographic area. The use of social media has also expanded in this arena.

On-site leasing centers are often included in larger projects to centralize the activities involved in renting available space and to house the management staff. The objective of an on-site manager operating out of a leasing center is to present the building's features with sophisticated audio and visual productions, and thereby, create the appropriate environment for effective lease negotiations and closings.

Rental concessions

In the quest for new tenants, landlords and their agents often devise creative means of generating interest in their project. A popular technique is to offer certain **rental concessions** to make leasing office space in a new building a prestigious move, as well as a decided bargain.

Although it appears that simply decreasing the rent for the office space is the most effective rental concession, in reality, the owner of an office building is often precluded from doing so by the terms and conditions of a mortgage loan. Because a net market rent is used to substantiate the granting of a mortgage loan in the first place, any reduction of the scheduled rent would reduce the value of the entire project. As a result, landlords do not reduce rent per se, but offer other concessions—for example, a free rental period that allows the tenant time to get settled and adjust to the new office. However, any concessions that seriously erode the net rental income are often not tolerated by the lenders, who monitor such things through a requirement for annual profit and loss and balance sheet statements from their borrower.

Additional concessions may be granted by a landlord in return for a lease commitment from a new tenant. These could include the installation of partitions, carpets, drapes, and fixtures, as well as the inclusion of utilities costs and janitorial services in the rent rate for a certain period. Landlords often have a **build out allowance** for new tenants, quoted as a certain dollar amount per square foot of leased space. The build out allowance money can be used to customize the space for the tenant's needs and aesthetic demands. First-generation space, which is space that has never been used, will be in need of lighting, wiring, partition walls, doors, and flooring, among other things. The build out allowance for first-generation space is generally much larger than for second-generation space, which requires less work. Other landlords offer no build out allowance at all, using this tenant expense as a method of screening out those who are not financially strong and able to pay for their own space completion or renovation.

Another attractive concession is the **naming rights**, or *branding rights*, for an office building. Wells Fargo Plaza in Houston, Texas, is not owned by Wells Fargo; it is owned by MetLife. Building branding can be a very important component of lease negotiations. Companies that do not occupy enough space to justify branding rights will try to obtain building pylon rights. That is the placement of their company name on the sign at the main roadway entrance to the building, listing some of the more substantial tenants. Assigned parking places, usually allocated as a certain number per 5,000 square feet of rented space, are another important bargaining point. The investor, of course, would prefer to offer concessions such as these that have high value to a tenant and virtually no cost to the landlord.

One of the more intriguing concessions employed by lessors of new multistoried office buildings is the owner-developer's assumption of the responsibility for a new tenant's remaining obligation on an old lease. Rental agents of new office space often use the telephone listings of businesses in a given area to cold canvass and solicit new tenants. In the presentation, the agent indicates that the management of the new building will assume responsibility for the old lease. Thus, depending on the success of this form of solicitation, a developer may become obligated to pay the rent on a number of newly assigned leases.

The alternatives for managing surplus space until its lease expires include keeping it empty or minimizing the carrying costs by subleasing it at any rent obtainable. Often, the developer offers the landlord a buy-out settlement based on a cash payment in exchange for the cancellation of the lease. In any event, the developer's responsibilities are relatively short-lived when compared to the long-term investment in the new office project.

Lease agreements

Generally, a standard lease agreement is used in renting office space. Depending on individual circumstances, however, special clauses may be included to satisfy the specific requirements of the parties involved. Leases will vary greatly across the country due to the fact that landlord-tenant law is based upon state, not federal law. All leases, including a standard lease, should be carefully reviewed by each party's legal counsel.

Tax clause

As a result of constantly increasing property taxes in many areas of the country, a **tax clause** is becoming a common requirement in office leases, including those drawn for relatively short time periods. A tax clause stipulates that the tenant will pay any increase in taxes over the base year, in addition to the contract rent.

Escalation clause

Paralleling the rising taxes across the country is the dramatic increase in utility charges, often to the point of eliminating a landlord's profits on the investment. To offset this problem, most office leases are now designed to pass utility costs on to the tenant. This can be accomplished by installing individual meters for each office—an expensive and often impossible task. More likely, a lease will be arranged with an **escalation clause** so the rent can be adjusted annually to reflect increasing expenses for utility charges. Either the rent can be increased by some specific factor, say 5% per year, or the tenant may be obligated to pay a proportion of the overall increased utility cost, in addition to the base rent—much like is done under a tax clause.

Services included

Office leases often provide for the tenant to receive certain special services for which additional rent is paid. These services can include utilities, as previously mentioned, as well as resale of telecom and bandwidth, janitorial, and maintenance care. In certain office arrangements, the services of a central receptionist, access to photocopying facilities and conference rooms, and so forth are included in the lease agreement.

Assignment and subletting

No doubt, one of the more controversial clauses in an office lease is the provision that the tenant be allowed to assign or sublet space in the event of a change in circumstances. In effect, this is an escape clause for the old tenant that obligates the landlord to accept the new tenant. In some cases, depending on the market for office space in a particular area, a tenant may be able to **sublease** a unit for a rent higher than that stipulated in the original lease, and thus, make a profit on the landlord's investment. Often, leases require that these tenants provide the landlord with 50%–100% of any excess rent the tenant may collect from the subtenant. This is called **sharing the market uplift**. To provide protection against the assignment or subletting of space to a tenant not acceptable to the landlord, an office lease often includes the provision that the landlord's written permission must first be secured, with such permission not to be unreasonably withheld.

This is an example of the type of issue that should be reviewed in any lease. Some states' laws presume that a lease may be assigned or sublet at any time unless the lease says otherwise. If so, then the lease may require that the landlord receive some, or even all, of any additional rent collected from a subtenant. Other states, such as Texas, will only allow a tenant to assign or sublease with the landlord's written consent.

Move clauses

No landlord wants to lose a large tenant prospect merely because it does not have enough contiguous space in the building to accommodate that tenant's needs. The same rationale applies to a current tenant who must expand or relocate. As a result, virtually all office leases have move clauses. They allow the landlord to move the tenant to comparable space in the building, as needed. The interpretation of what is comparable often gives rise to litigation between the parties. Tenants should try to negotiate elimination of the move clause, or at least define what is and is not, comparable. Tenants should also include notice time limits to give them time to notify their clients and customers of the move, and a provision that the landlord pay all expenses of moving, notification, and creation of new stationary, business cards, and related material. They should also negotiate for prominent placement of a "we've moved!" sign at the building entrance for some preagreed period. Landlords, of course, should be conservative in addressing such demands and also place dollar caps on the expenses to be borne by the landlord.

MANAGING NEIGHBORHOOD SHOPPING CENTERS

Percentage leases

Neighborhood centers are generally located at the intersection of major streets on corners of land designated for this use when the raw acreage was originally subdivided. Sometimes a neighborhood center is constructed off the corner on a parcel of land situated in the middle of a block but facing a major thoroughfare. This off-corner location acts to relieve the traffic congestion normally associated with a major intersection and improves the accessibility to the parking area.

Wherever the center is located, its development creates a small monopoly for commercial tenants wishing to capitalize on the consumer traffic that it generates by its very existence. A landlord can secure a bonus from tenants who want to locate in the center. This bonus is achieved in the form of a percentage lease in which a tenant agrees to pay a fixed minimum rent plus or against a specified percentage of the gross business. The minimum rent develops a basic return on the property owner's investment, and the percentage override ensures the owner a share in the tenant's success as a result of locating in the center.

For example, a supermarket may execute a lease with a minimum rent imposed as a function of the number of square feet occupied, plus 1% of the gross sales above a designated amount. A dress shop may lease space on the basis of a minimum rent against 4% of the gross, or a jeweler might agree to a 10% overage. Figure 12.2 shows a sample shopping center lease agreement.

Noncompete clauses are often used with retail centers. Landlords may promise not to lease to any firm that competes with the tenant, and the tenant may promise not to open another location within an agreed distance of the center, so as to not draw away potential business from the current location.

MANAGING STRIP STORE BUILDINGS

Most strip center leases are designed to run three to five years, with **options** to renew included to protect the tenant. Once a tenant has established a clientele in a neighborhood, the lease is likely to be renewed indefinitely. Most leases include noncompetition clauses that prevent the landlord from renting to a competitor in the same center.

Short-term strip center leases usually designate fixed rental terms and include renewal options, providing for rent increases to offset rising operating expenses—utilities, property taxes, insurance premiums, and maintenance costs. Although commercial tenants will often accept the responsibility for minor interior maintenance, major repairs and exterior upkeep usually remain the landlord's domain. With this in mind, a financial analysis of a strip center investment should include reserves for replacement of the roof and HVAC and for parking lot resurfacing, plus other major property components.

Figure 12.2: Retail Premises Lease

Lease Agreement for Shopping Center Property

Shopping Centers, Inc.

Retail Premises Lease

Between SHOPPING CENTERS, INC., LESSOR and

____

LESSEE

This LEASE is made and entered into this ________ day of ________, 20 ____ by and between

SHOPPING CENTERS, INC., a ________________________ corporation, hereinafter called LESSOR, and

____

____

hereinafter called LESSEE.

WITNESSETH: That for and in consideration of the rentals hereinafter provided, and the covenants and agreements hereinafter contained, LESSOR leases unto LESSEE the following described premises, which premises LESSOR warrants it has good right to lease, to wit:

referred to hereinafter as "Leased Premises." A diagram of said premises, for purpose of reference and illustration only, is attached hereto and made a part hereof as "Exhibit A."

The Leased Premises are part of LESSOR'S property known as "BIG REGIONAL SHOPPING CENTER," and in which center other retail space is leased by LESSOR to other LESSEES. All areas in the Center other than retail space, including but not limited to, walks, parking lots, open areas, public facilities, etc., are designated "common areas" as used in this lease. All common areas are under the complete and exclusive control of LESSOR.

LESSOR and LESSEE further covenant and agree as follows:

1. TERM OF LEASE. This lease shall be for a term of ______________________________

(______) years, commencing upon the ________ day of ____________, 20 ______, and ending ______ day of ______________, 20 ______.

2. RENTAL. LESSEE agrees to pay to LESSOR, its successors and assigns, as rental for said Leased Premises, the following:

(a) Base Rent. LESSEE shall pay, as base rent, the sum of ______________________________

DOLLARS ($ ________) annually, in twelve installments of ______________________________

DOLLARS ($ ________) on the first day of each month during the term of this lease.

LESSOR acknowledges the receipt of ____________________________ DOLLARS ($ ______) as advance payment of the first and last months' rent for the above term of this lease, and as earnest money assuring LESSEE will enter into possession as agreed under the terms of this lease.

Figure 12.2: Retail Premises Lease (continued)

Lease Agreement for Shopping Center Property (continued)

(b) Tax and Insurance Allocation, Ratio, and Adjustment. In addition to the base rent above provided, and as additional rent, LESSEE shall pay its proportionate share of all taxes, general and special, assessed against every part of the entire real property of which the Leased Premises are a part, and also its proportionate share of the cost of all fire, windstorm and other hazard insurance carried upon the entire real property of which the Leased Premises are a part. LESSEE'S proportionate share of taxes and insurance costs shall be in the ratio that the floor area leased to LESSEE bears to the total floor area of the entire property of which the Leased Premises are a part, which ratio shall be applied to the total taxes assessed and insurance costs to determine LESSEE'S proportionate share. LESSOR shall estimate for the period from the effective date of this Lease to January 1st next following, the amount of LESSEE'S proportionate share of taxes and insurance costs, as provided above, based upon taxes and insurance premiums paid during the previous year. This proportionate share shall be the proportionate share of the LESSEE for the full year multiplied by the ratio that the number of months of this Lease prior to January 1st next following the execution of this lease, bears to twelve. LESSEE shall pay the amount so determined to LESSOR, in equal installments concurrent with payment of the base rental, commencing with the first day of the first full month of the term of this Lease, and ending with the rental payment due December 1st next following the effective date of this Lease. On or before January 1st next following the effective date of this Lease, and on or before each succeeding January 1st thereafter, LESSOR shall estimate LESSEE'S pro rata share of the taxes and insurance costs for the succeeding calendar year, as provided above, and shall notify LESSEE of the amount of said estimate. LESSEE shall pay to LESSOR monthly thereafter during the ensuing calendar year, concurrent with the payment of the base rental, 1/12th of the amounts so estimated.

LESSOR shall keep annual records of the amount of taxes assessed and insurance costs paid and shall compute LESSEE'S pro rata share thereof. Within a reasonable time after January 1st of each year following the effective date of this Lease, LESSOR shall notify LESSEE of said LESSEE'S proportionate share of the taxes and insurance costs. If the monthly payments previously made by LESSEE are not sufficient to pay said LESSEE'S proportionate share of the taxes and insurance, LESSEE shall pay to LESSOR, within thirty (30) days after receipt of notice of said deficiency, the amount by which the actual costs of said LESSEE'S proportionate share of taxes and insurance exceed the estimated amount paid by LESSEE. If the estimated amount paid by LESSEE exceeds the LESSEE'S share of the taxes assessed and the cost of insurance, LESSOR shall credit said excess to LESSEE and shall reduce the estimated amount to be paid by LESSEE for the ensuing year by that amount. LESSEE shall have the privilege of examining records and computations upon which charges are made under these provisions.

(c) Percentage Rent. In addition to the payment of the Base Rent and all other rents and payments required hereunder, LESSEE shall pay to LESSOR, annually, the amount, if any, by which ______________ percent (_____ %) of the gross sales of merchandise (as hereinafter defined) during each Lease Year exceeds the aggregate amount of base rent paid by LESSEE to LESSOR attributable to said lease year, the method of computation and manner and time of payment of said percentage rent being more fully set forth hereinafter.

(d) Statement of Revenue. LESSEE shall submit to LESSOR, at the close of each month or within 10 days thereafter, a statement, signed by LESSEE and the manager of the store, showing the "gross sales of merchandise" for each day of said month.

(e) Gross Sales of Merchandise Defined. The term "gross sales of merchandise," as used in this Lease, is hereby defined to mean and include all sales of merchandise of every kind and character, and to include all revenues from all departments and services and sources made from the Leased Premises, for both cash and credit, including all orders taken and merchandise sold from the Leased Premises and filled or delivered from or to any other store or place, excluding taxes and refunds.

Figure 12.2: Retail Premises Lease (continued)

Lease Agreement for Shopping Center Property (continued)

(f) Computation and Payment of Percentage Rent. Concurrently with the furnishing of the monthly statements of gross sales of merchandise as hereinafter provided, LESSEE shall pay to LESSOR, as an installment payment to apply on the percentage rent due hereunder, any amount by which the percentage listed in (c) above multiplied by the gross sales of merchandise as shown on the monthly statement exceeds one month's Base Rent at the then current rate. Said percentage rent shall be computed at the close of each month or within 10 days thereafter, and shall be payable monthly as aforesaid. However, such percentage rent shall be annualized and subject to adjustment at the end of each Lease year. Within 60 days after the close of each Lease Year hereunder, LESSEE shall submit to LESSOR its statement showing the gross sales of merchandise for such Lease Year. Concurrently therewith, LESSEE shall pay LESSOR the amount of the percentage listed in (c) above multiplied by the gross sales of merchandise as shown upon the statement for the Lease Year less the aggregate monthly installment payments of percentage rent as heretofore provided for which have been paid for the Lease Year. If the aggregate monthly installment payments on percentage rent exceed the annual percentage rent due the excess shall be applied on future annual percentage rents due hereunder and any unapplied balance shall be refunded at the end of the term of this lease.

(g) Lease Year Defined. For all purposes under this lease, the term "Lease Year" shall mean the period from the commencement date of the term of this lease to the anniversary date of the first day of the month in which the commencement date of the term of this lease occurs and each 12 months period thereafter.

(h) Books and Records. LESSEE shall keep, in the Leased Premises, a permanent and accurate record in accordance with generally accepted accounting principles, consistently applied, showing "gross sales of merchandise" for each day during the term hereof, which record shall include all supporting and allied records, including but not limited to cash register receipts and sales tax reports. All such records shall be open to LESSOR at all reasonable times for the purpose of determining and verifying the percentage rent due. LESSEE shall retain and preserve all sales slips, cash register receipts and all other records pertinent to "gross sales of merchandise" for at least one year following the close of each Lease Year.

(i) Audit. LESSOR may at any reasonable time audit the records of LESSEE. If LESSOR audits the records of LESSEE and such audit reveals a greater amount of "gross sales of merchandise" than LESSEE has reported to LESSOR, LESSEE shall immediately pay the full and true amount of percentage rental due and shall pay all costs of the audit after notice thereof. If "gross sales of merchandise," as shown by the audit, do not exceed those reported by LESSEE to LESSOR, the audit shall be at the expense of LESSOR.

3. CHANGE OF BASE RENT DUE TO COST OF LIVING (CPI). Base rent as provided herein shall be adjusted in the same proportion as the fluctuation in the U.S. Department of Labor's Consumer Price Index published by the Bureau of Labor Statistics. For the purposes of this paragraph, the base month will be the month next preceding the first full month of the term of this Lease and the monthly rental commencing with the 13th month of this Lease will fluctuate in the same proportion that said Consumer Price Index is higher or lower than such base month on a cumulative basis. Such proportion will be computed annually for the first month following the completion of each twelve (12) months of the Lease, and the new rent derived from such computation shall be in effect for the next twelve months. In no event however, will an adjustment be made which would reduce the Base Rental rate to an amount less than the rate set forth in this Lease. The necessary calculation for the adjustment required herein will be made as quickly as possible but in the event a rent paying date occurs before the adjustment can be calculated an amount equal to the then current unadjusted Base Rental rate will be paid by LESSEE to LESSOR on the rent payment date and as soon as the calculation of the adjustment has been made an additional payment will be immediately paid by LESSEE to LESSOR or a reduction on the next due Base Rental payments will be made, whichever is appropriate in order to cure any underpayment or overpayment of Base Rent.

Figure 12.2: Retail Premises Lease (continued)

Lease Agreement for Shopping Center Property (continued)

4. PARKING. LESSEE agrees to cause its employees to park only in such places as provided and designated by LESSOR for employee parking. Upon written request from LESSOR, LESSEE will within five days furnish the state automobile license numbers assigned the cars of all employees.

5. LIGHTING. LESSEE shall keep the display windows in the Leased Premises well lighted from dusk until 10:00 o'clock P.M. (local time) during each and every day of the term of this lease, and shall pay its portion of the cost of electric current and maintenance resulting from exterior lighting of the building and parking lot, based upon the ratio set out in 2(b) above.

6. MERCHANTS ASSOCIATION. Should there be an association of the merchants in the shopping center of which the Leased Premises are a part, LESSEE shall belong to such association and pay reasonable dues assessed by a majority of the members of the association. The obligation to pay such reasonable dues shall be an obligation under this Lease.

7. MAINTENANCE.

(a) Exterior. LESSOR shall be responsible for the maintenance of the exterior of the outside walls and Common Areas of the building, parking lot, roof, walkways, stairways, walks, drives, streets, alleys, yards, and other areas common to the premises of which the Leased Premises are a part. The pro rata cost of such maintenance shall, however, be paid monthly as billed, by the LESSEE to LESSOR in the ratio that the square footage of the Leased Premises bears to the square footage occupied by all tenants of the premises of which the Leased Premises are a part.

(b) Interior. LESSEE shall maintain and keep in good repair the interior of the Leased Premises and all electrical and plumbing fixtures and equipment in the interior, including but not limited to, exposed installations on floors, walls and ceilings, all installations of any kind made by LESSEE, all hardware, interior painting and decoration of every kind, and all doors, windows, and screens. LESSEE shall replace all broken or damaged glass on the Leased Premises at LESSEE'S sole cost. LESSEE will maintain and keep clear all floor drains and drain lines of all kinds in or upon the Leased Premises to their juncture with public sewer main.

(c) Heating and Air Conditioning. Heating and air-conditioning equipment, and hot water heaters, where present, shall be and remain the property of LESSOR. Where such equipment is installed by LESSEE, said equipment shall remain upon the Leased Premises at the termination of this Lease, and become property of LESSOR. LESSOR shall not be responsible for maintenance, repair, or replacement of any such equipment, or damage caused by or because of such equipment. LESSEE shall hold LESSOR harmless from any damage caused by or because of such equipment, and in the event damage to the Leased Premises or the premises of which the Leased Premises are a part occurs by or because of such equipment, LESSEE shall immediately, and at LESSEE'S sole cost, repair and restore the damaged premises to their original condition. In the event of LESSEE'S failure, for a period of five days, to begin such restoration, LESSOR may make the necessary repair and restoration and LESSEE shall reimburse LESSOR the cost thereof.

8. HOURS OF BUSINESS. LESSEE shall conduct its business in the Leased Premises during the regular and customary hours of such type of business and on all business days, and will conduct said business in a lawful manner and in good faith to the end that LESSOR may during the term of this lease receive the maximum amount of rental income reasonably to be anticipated from the conduct of said business.

9. AWNINGS AND WINDOW COVERINGS. LESSEE shall not install awnings or other fixtures on the exterior of the building without prior written consent of LESSOR. In the event the Leased Premises have any exposed windows not used for merchandise display, LESSEE will install, at LESSEE'S cost, venetian blinds or other window coverings specified by LESSOR. LESSEE shall keep and maintain all awnings, venetian blinds, and other window coverings in a state of repair satisfactory to LESSOR.

Figure 12.2: Retail Premises Lease (continued)

Lease Agreement for Shopping Center Property (continued)

10. SIGNS. LESSEE is privileged to provide a store identification sign of its choice subject to consent and approval of LESSOR as to the type, design, construction, material used, and method of mounting. Any sign shall be installed and maintained by LESSEE so as to prevent all exterior water from entering the Leased Premises. LESSEE is responsible for securing any necessary permits and the payment of any fees in connection with erection of said sign. Damage to persons or property as a direct or indirect result of LESSEE'S sign is an exclusive risk of the LESSEE.

11. TRADE FIXTURES. LESSEE may install such trade fixtures as are reasonable and proper in carrying out the business which LESSEE is authorized to conduct in the Leased Premises. If LESSEE is not in violation of any of the terms or conditions of this Lease at the termination thereof, or any extension thereof, LESSEE shall remove all trade fixtures, including signs, from the Leased Premises and restore said premises to their original condition, all at LESSEE'S expense, except for any alterations, additions, or improvements as provided for in Paragraph 14 of this lease. If LESSEE is in violation of any terms or conditions of this Lease, however, such trade fixtures shall remain on the Leased Premises and shall be subject to the terms of the Landlord's lien hereinafter contained.

12. ADDITIONAL BUILDING. LESSOR reserves the right at any time to build additional stories on the building occupied by LESSEE and to any building adjoining the same, and reserves the right to close any skylights and windows (except display windows) and to run necessary pipes, conduits, and ducts through the herein Leased Premises. LESSOR further reserves the right to use and lease such additional space in such manner as LESSOR, at its sole option, may choose.

13. NOT A PARTNERSHIP. Nothing contained herein shall be deemed or construed by the parties hereto, or by any third party, as creating the relation of principal and agent or of partnership or of joint venture between the parties hereto, it being understood and agreed that neither the method of computation of rent, nor any other provision contained herein, nor any acts of the parties hereto, shall create any relationship between the parties hereto other than the relationship of LESSOR and LESSEE.

Source: Floyd M. Baird

Source: Floyd M. Baird

Unit 12

When a tenant requires an option to renew a lease, it should be clear to the landlord that this entails giving up control of the property for both the lease period and the option period. In addition, an option may or may not be exercised when it becomes due. A tenant may ignore the option and move or decide to negotiate with the landlord for new terms, depending on market conditions at renewal time. Consequently, the terms of any renewal become a function of market conditions as they change from time to time.

Except for strip centers that have some unique quality of design or location, most rents are established on a regular payment basis over the term of the lease. Some special circumstances require the inclusion of a **percentage clause** (for example, a gas station lease might have a fixed rent plus a penny or two per gallon override). Some leases also contain a property tax clause, which requires that the tenant pay any future taxes exceeding the base amount in effect at the inception of the lease.

The owner of a strip center often finds that the success of the investment is very much a function of the success of the tenants as entrepreneurs. If tenants cannot show a profit in a particular location, no matter how low the rent is, they will probably be unable to pay it. On the other hand, if the tenants are doing well, rent is the least of their concerns.

Thus, as a general rule, a landlord's profits are very closely related to a tenant's success. In the case of a small store lease, the landlord-tenant relationship is one of interpersonal dependency, not just a legal binder. It is in the best interests of a landlord to help a tenant succeed, even to the point of decreasing rent during the start-up period to enable the tenant to become established. A **graduated lease** is extremely useful in this regard, starting with a low rent in the initial period and gradually increasing to accommodate a successful tenant's ability to meet a higher payment schedule. If the tenant fails, even at the lower rents, it is just as well because the sooner the unfortunate mismatch is recognized, the sooner the landlord can lease the building again.

Case Study 12.1 explores an example of strip center development.

CASE STUDY 12.1 Strip Center Development

This block-long property consists of 600 feet of frontage on a major thoroughfare and is 150 feet deep to a 20-foot alley. The investors rezoned the parcel to commercial—it had been apartment zoning—by inviting adjoining neighbors to participate in its design. They quickly eliminated any fast food, gas stations, or all-night markets to control noise and traffic. The architecture was to conform to the neighborhood and no unsightly signs or disturbing lights were erected. The alley was paved and a seven-foot wall was built on the house side of the alley to help buffer noise. All stores were set back from the main street a distance of 40 feet to allow for front parking.

The 43,200-square-foot building was designed to be built in nine stages of 60-by-80 feet each, starting from one corner. The building code required a 30-foot setback at each corner to allow for traffic visibility. The 60-foot modules were designed to be rented in multiples of 20 feet, with the tenants choosing the space they needed. Once the construction started, the buildings filled quickly and took nine months to rent. The final **tenant mix** is as follows:

Shoe store	100 feet
Ice cream parlor	40 feet
Bicycle shop	80 feet
Lamp shop	40 feet
Candy store	60 feet
Barber shop	40 feet
Carpet shop	60 feet
Beauty shop	40 feet
Real estate office	40 feet
Insurance office	40 feet

MANAGING COMMUNITY SHOPPING CENTERS

The management of a community shopping center usually involves the services of a professional who has had experience in dealing with national tenants as well as with more prominent local retailers. Besides the normal leasing duties of the manager, daily responsibilities include the supervision of maintenance personnel and security guards. These duties require an on-premises supervisor, although many community and neighborhood shopping centers are managed by companies with offices located away from the centers. The efficiency of these centralized activities expands a management company's ability to handle a number of shopping centers, plus other income properties, from a single main office.

Lease terms for major tenants usually range from 15 to 20 years, whereas local tenants' leases may range from only 5 to 10 years. Renewal options are often based on a right of first refusal. The leases of untried tenants invariably include a landlord's cancellation clause that can be exercised if the gross volume of business does not meet expectations.

The percentage lease is the tool employed to establish the landlord-tenant relationship in a community shopping center. Such a lease includes rent to be charged on the basis of a minimum rate against a percentage of the monthly gross business, but also includes an arrangement for an annual adjustment. This adjustment acts to balance the peak-season months against those when gross volume is low. The center's management must have access to each tenant's books to verify these figures, and provisions are made to hire outside auditors for periodic reviews to offset any possible disputes in rent computations.

To pay for the costs of maintaining the parking area and joint walkways, community shopping center tenants are usually charged a **common-area fee** in addition to their rent. These fees are also used to offset the charges incurred for advertising, flyers, bulk mailings, and parking area promotional activities. Common-area charges are usually based on the ratio of the tenant's floor area to the center's total floor area. Sometimes they are imposed as a flat charge.

Management often plays a more prominent role in the activities of community shopping centers than it does in those of neighborhood centers. Special promotions are continually designed to attract shoppers to the center. These activities may directly involve the tenants, as do sidewalk sales, or they might involve such outside attractions as carnivals or art fairs.

Community shopping center tenants often find it expedient to join together in an association whose elected leaders represent them in disputes with the management. The association often accepts responsibility for supervising activities designed to promote the center.

MANAGING REGIONAL SHOPPING CENTERS

Regional centers require at least one full-time manager to be on the premises and available during shopping hours. Management is responsible for securing new tenants, renewing existing leases, supervising daily operations, and dealing with shoppers' complaints. A full crew of maintenance engineers is available at all times, as is a corps of security guards charged with maintaining decorum and handling emergency situations. Because 60% of the shopping in this country occurs at night, lighting and security are important management responsibilities.

All regional centers include an active merchants' association to which, according to their leases, all tenants must belong. Together with the center's management, this association is responsible for the varied promotional activities essential to this form of shopping enterprise. Ranging from local artists' displays to seasonal programs of entertainment, regional promotional activities are a constant and demanding part of management responsibility. There are companies that specialize in promoting and bringing events to retail centers.

There are numerous shopping centers that combine many of the individual attributes of the three major types described. They are called hybrid shopping centers and fall somewhere in between the neighborhood, community, and regional classifications.

SUMMARY

More than any other type of real estate investment, apartments require the greatest amount of management participation in terms of physical maintenance and continuing tenant goodwill. The responsibilities increase with the number of apartments owned.

But all properties, including condominiums, cooperatives, strip centers, office parks, and industrial properties, also require management. In addition to handling leases, tenant issues, and maintenance, many properties are required by law to have an on-site manager to operate legally.

In a condominium, the association elects a board of directors to supervise the daily operations, most often through the services of a full-time resident manager.

Probably the most significant factor in the success of an office building investment is the establishment of a competitive but profitable rental schedule. Based on an annual rate per square foot of usable space, a required lease payment is a function of many variables, including competitive rents, the location and quality of the subject building, the services provided by management, and the floor in the building where the space is located.

Often, landlords will offer concessions when soliciting new office tenants. Unable, under many circumstances, to lower rents, a landlord may provide a free rental period to offset some of the tenants' move-in costs. Additional inducements offered to attract new tenants include the installation of interior partitions, floor covering, heating and cooling equipment, payment of utilities costs, and provision of janitorial services. Developers of new high-rise office projects sometimes offer to assume the liability for the balance of new tenants' old leases to induce them to move into their new building.

Invariably, an office lease includes special clauses designed to solve specific problems. Often, a tax clause is inserted that specifies the tenant's responsibility to pay any increase in taxes over the base year, in addition to the stipulated rent. Some leases include an escalation clause that allows the rent to be raised automatically to cover increased utility and maintenance expenses. An office building owner may include a subletting privilege in the lease but invariably reserves the right to approve the new tenant.

Although strip stores generally have a higher tenant turnover than do larger shopping centers, the tenancies of successful entrepreneurs may continue indefinitely. In addition, commercial tenants usually accept the responsibility for maintaining the structure, which, when coupled with long-term occupancy, appeals to a great many real estate investors.

Strip store rents are invariably based on a fixed amount for a set period, with the inclusion of escalation clauses for longer leases. Percentage clauses are usually included for those strip stores that occupy a unique or monopolistic site, such as a corner gas station. In most strip store leases, the tenant is able to secure an option to renew, which tends to place control in the tenant's hands.

In terms of management responsibilities and lease arrangements, the three types of shopping centers have much in common. Most tenants are required to pay a basic minimum rent plus or against a specified percentage of gross business. Thus, a landlord participates in the success of the tenants and capitalizes on the monopolistic quality of the center. In exchange, the management provides the maintenance and security required in such large projects.

Most centers require that their tenants join an association that assumes the responsibility for generating and supervising advertising and promotional activities designed to attract shoppers. In addition, the associations' directors usually represent the tenants in their negotiations with management regarding store hours, participation in promotions, and determination of assessments for CAM.

DISCUSSION TOPICS

1. Discuss the pros and cons of a lease versus a month-to-month tenancy from both the tenant's and the landlord's points of view.
2. Discover what concessions are being offered to prospective tenants from the manager of a high-rise office building in your area.

UNIT 12 EXAM

1. Our nation's trend toward service-oriented business activities is
   A. decreasing, but requiring more office space.
   B. increasing, but requiring less office space.
   C. decreasing and requiring less office space.
   D. increasing and requiring more office space.

2. Rental concessions usually include all of the following *EXCEPT*
   A. free rent for a specified time.
   B. carpets, drapes, and partitioning.
   C. lowering the rent.
   D. purchase of a prospective tenant's existing lease.

3. Which of the following definitions is *TRUE*?
   A. Tax clause: the landlord pays any increase in property taxes.
   B. Acceleration clause: the tenant pays an increase in rent to offset rising utility and maintenance charges.
   C. Escalation clause: the balance of rent is due in full before the lease expiration.
   D. Subleasing clause: the tenant has the right to rent the office space to someone else.

4. While studying the market for office space to establish the feasibility of a new project, the analyst should segment the market by all of the following attributes *EXCEPT*
   A. zoning.
   B. location.
   C. age.
   D. amenities.

5. In terms of requirements for a company's headquarters location, which of the following received top priority in a survey of nationwide organizations?
   A. Low cost
   B. Qualified labor supply
   C. Large functional space
   D. Social climate

6. The establishment of a rental schedule for an office building depends *LEAST* on which of the following?
   A. The economic stability of an area
   B. The owner's desired return on the investment
   C. The physical condition of the building
   D. The services provided

7. All of the following tenants generate traffic in a community shopping center *EXCEPT*
   A. a supermarket.
   B. a discount store.
   C. an auto parts shop.
   D. a furniture warehouse.

8. When a commercial tenant has the right to extend the lease at a price and terms established at the time of the lease inception, the lease provides for
   A. an option to renew.
   B. a right of first refusal.
   C. a right of subordination.
   D. a right of redemption.

9. When a tenant does $5,000, $6,000, and $7,000 gross business in each of three successive months, which of the following relationships is *FALSE*?
   A. Monthly rents of $500, $600, and $700 equals a $500 monthly minimum against 10% of the gross.
   B. Equal rentals of $500 per month for each of the three months equals $6,000 as fixed annual rental.
   C. Monthly rents of $500, $600, and $700 equals $6,000 per year as a graduated monthly rental.
   D. Monthly rents of $1,000, $1,100, and $1,200 equals a $500 monthly minimum plus 10% of the gross.

10. The type of shopping center that includes office towers and apartment buildings in its design is
    A. a regional center.
    B. a community center.
    C. a super-regional center.
    D. a strip store grouping.

UNIT 13

The Transaction: Contract to Closing

LEARNING OBJECTIVES

When you have completed this unit, you will be able to accomplish the following.

- Explain how an investment property transaction works from contract to closing.

KEY TERMS

1031 exchange	estimated settlement statement	net proceeds
addendum	estoppel letter	POC
assign	furniture, fixtures, and equipment (FF&E)	prorate
closing	financing contingency	risk of loss
consideration	indemnity	specific performance
contingency	letter of intent (LOI)	standby letter of credit
due diligence	liquidated damages	title commitment letter
earnest money		title insurance
		transaction facilitator

INTRODUCTION

Many deals have fallen apart over something other than sales price and time to close. When lawyers say, "The devil is in the details," they mean that more than price and terms are important to a real estate transaction. Contracts must include agreements regarding routine matters, such as time allowed for inspections and verification of data (**due diligence**), and also possible events that will hopefully never occur, such as default. All seller and buyer fears regarding potential problems must be examined, form the basis of some type of protective language, and then negotiated. The real estate contract both embodies the agreement of the parties regarding such matters and also provides a roadmap of instructions for the closing company. **Closing** is the process of exchanging documents and money to effectuate the purchase and sale. Things such as compensation of real estate agents may not be technically necessary to the contract itself, but are included to assist the closing company so it does not have to refer to multiple documents—a listing agreement and a sales contract—to determine allocation of funds at closing.

Residential owner-occupied real estate purchases are relatively straight forward. Usually, the buyer's real estate agent will have a generic purchase and sale contract prepared by the agent's office or a local association of REALTORS®. Buyers working without agents often have similar forms available to them, either from friends, the internet, or office supply stores. Contract negotiation begins when a buyer completes a form with the names of the parties, address, and legal description of the property, offer price, earnest money, escrow company, and perhaps some contingencies. A **contingency** is an event that determines whether the parties can cancel the contract or not without penalty. Common residential contingencies include the buyer's ability to obtain financing, the property passing certain inspections, and the seller's ability to transfer good title. Each contingency has a time limit so that if the contract is not canceled by agreed-upon deadlines, then the time-barred contingency is considered waived and no longer available.

After the residential buyer completes the contract, it is then transmitted to the seller, who will either sign or make a counter-offer by varying some of the terms. Depending on things like jurisdiction or property age, the seller might be required to attach various addenda to the contract. An **addendum** (plural: addenda) is an attachment to a contract. Common addenda are federally mandated lead-based paint disclosures and certain state-required seller property condition disclosures. When the parties reach an agreement and have a fully executed contract, it will then be forwarded to the closing company, sometimes also called an *escrow company* or a *settlement agent*. In some states, this is called *opening escrow*.

Virtually all real estate contracts include some type of negotiated **earnest money**. Earnest money is not consideration and is not necessary to make a binding contract. Instead, earnest money serves two other important functions. It is a strong indication of the buyer's financial strength and ability to close. A buyer who wants to buy a $1 million home with only $500 of earnest money might be engaging in wishful thinking or might be tying up a property while it looks for an ultimate buyer to whom it can flip the contract. Sellers require large earnest money deposits to weed out such buyers.

Earnest money is also generally specified as a sum of **liquidated damages** to be forfeited if the buyer does not complete the purchase (close) after removal of all contingencies. Liquidated damages are a preagreed sum of money that will compensate an innocent party for damages it might suffer if there is a default by the other party. It might be difficult to properly calculate the damage suffered by a seller if the buyer defaults. As a result, the parties will agree in advance that the damage will be $X. Typically, but not necessarily, that will be same amount as the earnest money.

In some states, the closing company holds the earnest money. In others, a licensed real estate agent will hold the money in a trust account and then deliver the funds to the closing company on the day of closing. In very large transactions, the earnest money might be a bank-issued **standby letter of credit**. The issuer agrees to pay a predetermined amount of money to another party—here, the seller—upon receipt of certain designated documents specifying the default. After default and bank payments to the seller, the bank must then pursue its customer—here, the buyer—for reimbursement. It is a substitute for earnest money but without the buyer needing to tie up cash for perhaps a lengthy time period.

Investment properties typically require a greater variety of negotiated terms and more complex contracts than owner-occupied residential properties. Investors will usually have a team of professionals available to assist them, including attorneys, engineers, accountants, facilities managers, and commercial lenders. Input from these various interest groups will lengthen the time between coming to an agreement regarding price, signing a contract, and closing on the transaction. The next section will discuss many of the contract terms.

REAL ESTATE CONTRACTS

Deal letter

The average residential property purchase begins with transmittal of a fairly standard contract form commonly used in that area, with blanks for things such as names of buyer and seller, price, and other terms. The average investment property purchase begins with a nonbinding **letter of intent (LOI)**, sometimes also called a *deal summary* and *letter of nonbinding agreement*. Purchasers initiate the process with a written offer that will contain some of the most important contract provisions, among those discussed next. What is important to one transaction might not be important to another one, so the letters are highly customized. At a minimum, the written offer will identify the property, propose a purchase price, outline a time period for due diligence items such as property inspections, and suggest a deadline for closing. The seller might counteroffer to vary some of the terms and also add some terms of his own. After the important elements are agreed upon, the parties will write and sign an LOI and then turn everything over to the attorneys for a final contract. This helps control legal fees so attorneys are not negotiating deal points. Negotiations between lawyers over subtle legal points can add weeks or months before there is a final agreement ready for signature.

Important contract provisions

Representations and warranties, definitions

Virtually all investment real estate contracts begin with representations and warranties, and then definitions. Representation and warranty clauses are called the *whereases* because they typically begin with "whereas," such as, "Whereas, the seller represents that the attached schedule of rents, security deposits, and lease expirations is true and accurate." They represent all of the underlying assumptions that propelled the parties into signing a contract. If one of the representations or warranties is inaccurate, the aggrieved party may be able to sue the other for fraud. The *Definitions* section provides the definition for important terms used in the contract, which might be different from the normally understood meaning for those terms. If so, then the contract definition is used. For example, a contract that includes all improvements on the land might define *improvements* as specific masonry buildings. If there were a very large metal building on the property, the seller could remove it before closing because it was not included in the definition of improvements. Parties often skim through these sections, dismissing them as mere boilerplate. They are, however, extremely important and should be carefully reviewed.

Parties

The correct legal names of the buyer and seller must be designated in the contract. A contract that incorrectly identifies an individual as the seller might not be enforceable if that person's corporation owns the property. If there are multiple owners, such as partners or spouses, then all parties with ownership interests should be named in the contract and execute it. Sometimes, the buyer will want the flexibility to **assign** the contract and sell its position to another buyer. In that case, the right of assignment will be specifically agreed upon. Buyers contemplating a tax-deferred like-kind exchange under Section 1031 of the Internal Revenue

Code will also reveal that in the contract and agree that an intermediary may hold title in the **1031 exchange**, if necessary.

Property

The parties will identify the property being sold by its full legal description. Use of only a street address is sometimes acceptable and enforceable, but never recommended. They will specify additional items in the transfer such as on-premises **furniture, fixtures, and equipment (FF&E)**; data such as tenant and property maintenance histories; and leases, websites, Facebook pages, and goodwill. Significant and unique items of personal property, such as important art work, will also be described in the contract. If there is goodwill built up in some component of the real estate, such as an operating self-storage facility or a signature building design, then those elements of the acquisition will be protected with noncompetition clauses. In most states, noncompetition clauses are enforceable only if they are limited in time and scope. The usual limit is three to five years and a defined area that represents the market place for the property.

Monetary terms

All contracts must describe the purchase price with some specificity. That is because all contracts require consideration to be enforceable. **Consideration**, in this context, is an exchange of promises—a promise to sell a particular property and a promise to pay a particular amount of money. It can be an exact dollar amount or an agreement regarding a method to calculate the ultimate dollar amount. For example, the purchase price of a newly constructed apartment complex might be a specific amount payable at closing and an additional percentage of gross collected rents on some future date after the property reaches stabilized occupancy. To be enforceable, the agreement regarding calculation must be so specific that a stranger to the contract could calculate it without any input from the principals. The amount of earnest money will also be agreed upon, as will the identity of the entity that will hold the earnest money until closing. If the seller will hold some or all of the financing, those terms must be spelled out in some detail, including amount financed, interest rate, monthly payments, maturity, and collateral. Complex transactions will also have clauses regarding the buyer's ability to extend the closing date for various reasons (usually related to due diligence) and a nonrefundable fee to be paid for each extension.

Interim activities

Buyers purchasing tenant-occupied properties specify restrictions on the seller's leasing activities between contract signing and closing. Otherwise, the seller could execute multiple leases at dramatically below-market prices in exchange for one-time up-front fees. There might be requirements related to routine maintenance and upkeep of the property and also specific repairs or capital improvements. The transaction itself might have to be kept confidential in order to not jeopardize other negotiations such as lease renewals. The parties will require proof that property insurance be kept in full force and effect until closing and spell out risk of loss. **Risk of loss** clauses detail who receives the money if there is an insurable loss and whether or not the buyer has to proceed to closing if the loss is over a certain size.

Allocation of purchase price

Sellers will have a certain tax basis in their properties. That is usually the seller's acquisition cost, plus capital improvements made afterward, minus depreciation deductions taken over the years. This is called the *adjusted basis*. The sales price will result in a return of the adjusted basis (not taxable), a recapture of prior depreciation deductions (currently taxed at a 25% rate), and profit, which is usually taxed at long-term capital gain rates. Some sellers will also have a goodwill component to the property. It is a matter of negotiation between the parties regarding how much of the purchase price will be allocated to land (which is not depreciable), depreciable improvements, personal property, and goodwill. The allocation agreed upon will have tax consequences for both parties and will have to be memorialized in the contract, and possibly also certain IRS disclosure forms.

Title

The parties will contractually agree regarding the type of deed to be executed by the seller and any related transfer documents. The type of deed will establish the seller's warranties regarding quality of title. Typically, the contract will set a deadline by which the seller must deliver a **title commitment** to the buyer. It is a written commitment by the title insurance company that it will insure title if certain itemized defects are removed by time of closing. The seller will have a deadline by which it must clear title defects, except those that will be satisfied at closing, such as a mortgage on the property. If the defects are not cleared by the deadline, the buyer will be able to cancel the contract and receive a refund of the earnest money. It is not uncommon for a buyer to agree to take the property subject to certain liens or title defects, but those should be spelled out in the contract or a subsequent amendment.

Due diligence

While a home buyer typically needs only a home inspection report, investors will generally require much more extensive inspections, reviews, and research, called *due diligence*. Outside professionals will be employed for assistance. Lawyers will review tenant leases and zoning issues. Accountants will comb through financial data for inconsistencies. Other accountants will prepare cost segregation analyses used for increasing income tax deductions in the early years of ownership. Engineers will report on things like structural integrity, code compliance, and water runoff control. Facilities managers will evaluate a building's ability to meet future needs for bandwidth, energy efficiency, and parking, and provide recommendations for repairs and improvements. Specialists might be needed to build complex financial models for three to five years into the future, based on information in current leases. Buyers will also need engineering reports regarding the possibility of environmental contamination, called a *Phase I*, and sometimes reports identifying types and amounts of actual contaminants, called a *Phase II*.

Accurate financial analysis of property is usually impossible before the parties enter into a contract. For example, a neighborhood shopping center buyer will need access to confidential tenant leases and retail sales to evaluate future revenues, especially if part of the rent is calculated as a percentage of sales. Investors contemplating changing a property's use may need an executed contract before they can even apply for subdivision approval or zoning variances. Consequently, some portion of due diligence will include the financial viability of the investment, not just matters related to the actual real estate.

Some contracts set specific time limits for each itemized area of due diligence such as document review, engineering, and governmental approvals, to name a few. Others set a time period within which to complete all due diligence that is generally 90 to 180 days after contract execution. Which approach is employed will depend on the type of property and the preferences of the parties involved.

Contingencies

Contingencies are events that may or may not occur that could result in the buyer being able to cancel the contract without penalty. A **financing contingency** is common in home purchase contracts, giving the buyer the right to cancel if it cannot secure financing within certain preagreed parameters such as interest rate and down payment. This is rare with investment properties. The market generally assumes that an investor will be able to secure the funds necessary to close. When there is a financing contingency, there is also a deadline by which the buyer must provide a lender commitment letter to the seller, or the seller will be allowed to cancel the contract. This prevents buyers from tying up properties while they engage in sometimes lengthy efforts to find a lender willing to take a chance on them.

Each party might have a corporate approval contingency that allows them to sign a contract immediately and begin due diligence, but obtain corporate approval before some specified later date. Income-producing properties will have contingencies related to review of the financial data for accuracy and consistency, with representations made before contract signing. Development land that is commonly sold on a price-per-square-foot basis will have contingencies related to surveys and verification of the size of the parcel. Utility contingencies require verification of power, size of gas lines, location of storm and sanitary sewer, and bandwidth availability. A frequent all-purpose contingency will state that if the buyer wishes to cancel for any reason by the end of the due diligence period, it may do so without penalty. Sellers, of course, usually want something worded more tightly, but that is a matter of negotiation.

Proration and security deposits

The parties will agree on a formula to **prorate** prepaid items and deferred payment itemsto split them according to the parties' period of ownership. Some rents for the month of closing will be paid before the closing date, and some afterwards. The parties must agree on a formula to decide how much belongs to the seller, how much to the buyer, and a date to settle the accounts. The seller will receive a credit for any prepaid maintenance contracts, equal to the prorated time period of buyer's ownership. The buyer will receive a credit for property taxes to be paid by her in the future, but which will often represent a period during which the seller owned the property. The buyer will agree to assume liability for security deposits. Amounts of money held as security deposits will have to be itemized by the seller and then verified by tenants, usually through a contractually required **estoppel letter**. This is a letter signed by each tenant agreeing on the amount of the security deposit, that no rent has been prepaid, that the landlord is not in default under any of his obligations, and that there are no verbal or side agreements regarding any matters at all, and all agreements are contained in the lease. In states that require separate escrow accounts for security deposits, the contract will specify transfer of the account. In other states, the better practice is for the seller to write a check at closing, transferring all security deposits to the buyer. Smaller transactions in nonescrow states will often simply give the buyer a credit against the purchase price for the security deposit liability assumed by the buyer.

Default

The well-worded contract will always have negotiated language related to default. If the buyer defaults, does it only forfeit the earnest money, or will it be liable for additional damages? If the seller defaults, will the buyer be allowed to sue for **specific performance** to enforce the terms of the sales contract, or will it be limited to damages only? Parties must agree as to the confidentiality of information disclosed to the buyer if the buyer then fails to go through with closing. Default provisions may require a seller to pay for the buyer's survey, tests, inspections, and loan commitment fees if the seller defaults, usually through inability to provide good title. There might be an agreement to engage in binding arbitration in case of a dispute, or agreements as to specific individuals to serve as mediators or private judges. There is often a jury-waiver provision in default clauses to avoid the risk of a runaway jury swayed by emotion rather than facts. Even in jurisdictions that automatically allow legal fees in the event of contract default, there will almost always be language about payment of attorneys' fees by the defaulting party.

Indemnity

Indemnity clauses make one party compensate the other for legal fees, expenses, and any settlement or judgment liability if the innocent party is sued as a result of actions or inactions of the other party. For example, federal hazardous waste laws make all owners of the property liable, even if an earlier party in the chain of title caused the toxic release. Regulators might require the buyer to engage in cleanup, also called *remediation*. In that case, the buyer will want an indemnity clause in the contract so it can recover those expenses from its seller. Other situations might include some tenant lawsuits, boundary line disputes, and escaped taxes. Escaped tax liability arises when the taxing authority realizes it has improperly assessed the property in the past, corrects that mistake, and then charges additional taxes to the current owner, but for a period going back several years. Such escaped tax liability is legitimately the seller's responsibility, but the buyer will have to pay them to avoid a tax lien sale. Indemnity clauses typically have a *basket*, or *deductible*, so that sums less than the stated amount will simply be borne by the innocent party and cannot be collected from the other. Such minimal, or de minimis, amounts are usually a negotiated small percentage of the contract value. A $3 million sale might have an indemnity clause deductible of $25,000, for example.

CLOSING

Closing is the name given to the exchange of money and documents. Smaller transactions are typically entrusted to disinterested third parties such as title companies, closing companies, or escrow agents. Larger ones usually take place in the offices of attorneys representing the buyer, seller, or lender. Home buyers and sellers are typically present at closing, accompanied by their real estate agents. It is not uncommon for commercial closings to take place without either party present. Instead, all documents will have been executed earlier and held in escrow, or they will be executed at closing by the attorneys under a power of attorney. Due to the prevalence of certified check fraud, the buyer's money is often sent via wire transfer to the offices of the closing agent. If personal, business, or certified checks are accepted, closing can be delayed until all funds are confirmed as collected and nonreversible.

The real estate contract will specify which party will bear the cost of various closing expenses or how they will share certain expenses. This is entirely a matter of negotiation between the parties. Expenses can include legal fees for documents such as the transfer deed, any correction deeds necessary to clear up title defects, and loan documents. There will usually be charges for the closing itself, wire transfers, and overnight delivery fees. Real estate commissions are paid at closing, according to the agreement of the parties. **Title insurance**, which insures the buyer's good title up to an agreed amount, has a certain base price that depends on the dollar value of the insurance. There will also be add-on charges for various additional coverages, called *riders*, such as ones for zoning, improvement location surveys, and presence of utilities. Another charge will add the buyer's lender as an additional insured. Buyers and sellers should be aware of the various title insurance requirements and costs in a transaction before blithely agreeing to pay or split title insurance expenses. Some expensive riders may be necessary only because of requirements by the buyer's lender. It would be imprudent for a seller to agree in advance to pay some or all of those items.

Several days before the date set for closing, parties should obtain an **estimated settlement statement** from the closing company and a final title commitment. Other documents might be needed for review, depending on the type of transaction. Usually, lender-related documents will have been the subject of separate negotiation and finalization between the buyer and her lender.

The seller's estimated statement will show the gross purchase price plus itemization of seller-paid expenses such as, typically, real estate commissions and title insurance. It will also list credits for prepaid items such as maintenance contracts. There might be deductions to satisfy the seller's mortgage, any other liens against the property, and other deductions for rents collected by the seller for the entire month but partially owed to the buyer under the prorate clause. Finally, the seller's estimated statement will show **net proceeds** to be paid to the seller at closing.

The buyer's estimated statement will start with the gross purchase price and then add expenses agreed to be paid by the buyer, such as loan document preparation. In commercial transactions, the buyer's agent might receive a share of the seller-paid real estate commission or may be paid separately by the buyer. If paid by the buyer, that expense will appear as a buyer expense. It is not uncommon for a buyer's agent to receive a share of the listing agent's commission, plus a buyer-paid bonus based on a percentage of the savings between the final negotiated sales price and original asking price. All items shown as debits or credits on the seller's side will also appear on the buyer's side as the opposite amount. A seller debit of $4,000 for collected rents will appear as a buyer credit for the same amount. If there is purchase money loan, the statement will list the sources and amounts of loan money. It will also show net cash the buyer must bring to closing.

Some items on the estimated statements may appear as **POC**, or *paid outside closing*. That is to alert the parties that a survey, for example, will not be paid from closing funds but will have to be paid separately by the responsible party. If the contract requires the seller to provide and pay for a survey, the buyer might want to know that expense will be POC. If the bill is not paid, the surveyor might be able to place a lien against the buyer's property. As a result, the buyer will want to follow up and make sure that POC item is actually paid by the seller.

It is critical for the parties to review all information on the estimated statement for accuracy, especially the areas that affect the cash buyer must bring to closing or the cash seller will receive at closing. For that reason, parties obtain estimated settlement statements as early as they can before closing.

The closing agent, even if an attorney, typically will not give legal explanations of any documents. At most, the closing agent might represent the company writing title insurance on the transaction. Other times, it is simply a **transaction facilitator**. It represents neither buyer nor seller unless specifically disclosed to all parties, who generally sign an acknowledgment of disclosure. Parties who desire legal advice should retain their own legal counsel to review documents and attend closing.

After closing, the settlement agent will deliver all deeds and mortgages or deeds of trust documents to the property-recording authorities for that jurisdiction. They rarely contact the tax assessor's office to assess the property in the new owner's name or claim any relevant exemptions, such as current-use exemptions. The buyer should make sure those steps are completed by his own personnel.

SUMMARY

Owner-occupied home sales generally have relatively short and unsophisticated contracts that involve very little negotiation. Closings for such transactions are fairly standardized, with all parties and the real estate agents in attendance. There is rarely any need for outside professionals. Investment properties, by contrast, usually generate contracts with a great number and variety of negotiated terms, depending on the size and type of property and details of the transaction and its financing. Investors contemplating a purchase would be well-advised to review a number of contracts for similar properties to educate themselves as to matters that should be negotiated and memorialized. Likewise, sellers should educate themselves as to common contract provisions for their type of property. Each should have already formed relationships with brokers, attorneys, accountants, surveyors, and engineers who might be needed as part of the sale or purchase team. With all of those elements in place, and a preclosing review of important closing documents, buyers and sellers can help ensure that their transactions will be as free of surprises as possible.

DISCUSSION TOPICS

1. Draft an LOI for the purchase of a 40-unit apartment complex that appears to have significant deferred maintenance (repairs that have not been made), a large number of tenant delinquencies, and possible Chinese drywall that will have to be remediated.
2. Ask a local closing company for a sample settlement statement for a home purchase, with names and property address redacted. Discuss the various line items, and then separately duplicate the math to see if you arrive at the same results for buyer funds due at closing and seller net proceeds payable at closing.

UNIT 13 EXAM

1. A common contingency in home purchase contracts is
   A. loan approval.
   B. purchase price.
   C. earnest money.
   D. real estate commission.

2. An amendment is a change to a real estate contract. Attachments to the original contract are called
   A. addenda.
   B. parapluie.
   C. amendments also.
   D. errata.

3. Earnest money
   A. indicates the buyer's ability to close.
   B. is necessary for an enforceable contract.
   C. must be at least 5% of the purchase price.
   D. all of the above.

4. Another phrase for a letter of intent is
   A. deal letter.
   B. LI.
   C. declaration of willingness to close.
   D. indemnity agreement.

5. Which contract price description would not be enforceable?
   A. Fair market value
   B. One hundred times gross collected rents for the month of closing
   C. Payoff amount for seller's first mortgage to ABC Bank, plus $25,000
   D. $22.19 per square foot according to survey to be ordered by seller

6. Allocation of purchase price includes
   A. parties' agreement regarding amount attributable to land.
   B. all charges on the final settlement statement.
   C. only the buyer's charges on the final settlement statement.
   D. refund of earnest money.

7. Estoppel letters help ensure
   A. no surprises in the landlord/tenant relationship.
   B. reimbursement to the buyer of expenses that belong to the seller.
   C. proper proration of taxes.
   D. the correct basis for IRS reporting.

8. Defaulting sellers who refuse to close
   A. can usually be sued for specific performance.
   B. can always be sued for specific performance.
   C. are limited to the earnest money for compensation.
   D. can always be sued for damages.

9. The clause that requires a party at fault to reimburse an innocent party who is sued by another is called
   A. indemnity.
   B. de minimis.
   C. res judicata.
   D. specific performance.

10. Which statement is *TRUE?*
    A. Closing companies represent neither buyer nor seller in a transaction.
    B. Sellers must pay for title insurance because sellers must deliver good title.
    C. Security deposits are prorated at closing.
    D. Estimated settlement statements cannot be requested earlier than 24 hours before closing.

GLOSSARY

1031 exchange An exception to paying a capital gains tax on a recent gain of a sale, a 1031 tax-deferred exchange allows a person to sell appreciated investment real estate and defer the payment of that capital gains tax by acquiring a like-kind replacement.

acceleration clause A contract provision that allows a lender to require a borrower to repay all of an outstanding loan if certain requirements are not met.

active income Income acquired in the pursuit of a taxpayer's main occupation.

active participation Owned at least 10% of a rental property and made management decisions or arranged for others to provide services (such as repairs) in a significant and bona fide sense.

ad valorem tax A tax levied according to value, generally used to refer to real estate tax. Also called the *general tax*.

addendum Any provision added to an existing contract without altering the content of the original. Must be signed by all parties.

adjustable-rate mortgage (ARM) A mortgage loan that has an interest rate that is changed (adjusted) periodically based upon an index agreed to between a borrower and a lender.

adjusted basis The adjusted basis of the property begins with the basis, which depends on the method of acquisition. Once the basis is determined, certain adjustments (additions to and subtractions from) are made over time to arrive at the adjusted basis. Capital gains profits are the difference between the realized selling price of the property and its adjusted basis.

air rights The right to use the open space above a property. Generally the surface is used for another purpose.

alternative minimum tax (AMT) Required if its application to the taxpayer's special preference items exceeds the regular tax amount.

Americans with Disabilities Act (ADA) Federal law that is designed to allow persons with disabilities reasonable access to public areas.

amortization The systematic repayment of a loan by periodic installments of principal and interest over the entire term of the loan agreement.

anchor tenant A major department store in a shopping center.

ancillary probate Process of settling an estate when property is located in a state other than the deceased's main residence.

annual percentage rate (APR) The effective or actual interest rate, which may be higher or lower than the nominal or contract interest rate because it includes loan closing costs.

Annual Property Operating Data (APOD) A form that lists a property's gross income, individual operating expenses, and net operating income.

annuity A series of regular payments or receipts over a period of years.

appropriation A taxing body authorizes the expenditure of funds and provides for the sources of the funding.

assemblage The process of combining two or more parcels of real estate into one.

assign The transfer in writing of interest in a bond, mortgage, lease, or other instrument.

assumable A loan that may be taken over (assumed) by a buyer when purchasing a parcel of real estate. Often requires the lender to approve the new buyer.

at-risk rule A rule disallowing investors from deducting more investment money from their taxable income than they have actually invested.

before-tax cash flow The money left after debt service has been subtracted from the net operating income and before income tax is paid.

betterments Improvements to property made by tenants.

big box Big box stores, so named because they are shaped like a large one-story box, typically buy their own land, sell it to a REIT or a subsidiary, and then lease it back. Examples of big box stores are Lowes, Walmart, and Costco.

blue-sky law Refers to the laws targeted to control "puffing" by land promoters.

boot Money or property given to make up any difference in value or equity between two properties in a 1031 exchange.

breakeven point That point at which gross income equals fixed costs plus variable costs.

breakeven ratio Analytical tool used by appraisers and investors that shows how well the gross operating income will cover cash requirements.

bridge loan A short-term loan used until a person or company secures permanent financing or removes an existing obligation.

build-out allowance Landlords often have a build out allowance for new tenants, quoted as a certain dollar amount per square foot of leased space. The build out allowance money can be used to customize the space for the tenant's needs and aesthetic demands.

build to suit A building to be constructed to serve the special needs of a specific tenant.

Building Owners and Managers Association (BOMA) An association of building owners and managers founded in 1921 to address issues in the building management industry.

bundle of rights Describes the owner's rights of control over property.

business park A preplanned conglomeration of buildings in one area designed to house activities of a business nature.

buyer's market When the supply of a commodity exceeds the demand.

c-store There are almost 150,000 c-stores, also called *convenience stores*, in the United States. They typically sell fuel, snacks and drinks, food staples such as breakfast foods and some canned goods, small sizes of pet foods, and hot food such as pizza and chicken wings.

capital gains income The taxable profit derived from the sale of a capital asset.

capitalization of income The *capitalization of income* model takes a snapshot of only one year of operating revenue and expenses. Subtracting expenses from the revenue yields a number called the *NOI*, which is expressed as an annual number.

capitalization rate The rate of return, based on purchase price, that would attract capital.

caps Limits to the increases in either the interest rate or payment amount under an adjustable-rate mortgage. Often includes an annual limit and a lifetime limit.

cash on cash The ratio of annual before-tax cash flow to the total amount of cash invested, expressed as a percentage.

ceiling An absolute maximum rate of interest that may be charged under an adjustable-rate loan.

central business district (CBD) An agglomeration of businesses and services in the center of a city; "downtown."

Chinese drywall Between 2001 and 2009, an estimated 100,000 U.S. homes were built with Chinese drywall, a defective product that emitted sulfurous gases and volatile chemicals.

closing An event where promises made in a sales contract are fulfilled and mortgage loan funds (if any) are distributed to the buyer.

collapsible corporation A corporation designed to exist only during the course of constructing a large project. After completion, it is dissolved.

collateral Property—real or personal—pledged as security to back up a promise to repay a debt.

come out of the ground A phrase that describes the construction of new properties.

commercial mortgage-backed securities (CMBS) A type of mortgage-backed security that is secured by mortgages on commercial *properties* instead of residential *real estate*.

common-area fee In condominiums, the charge for taxes, insurance, maintenance, and so forth, apportioned to each owner and, in shopping centers, to each tenant.

common-area maintenance (CAM) Among the expenses often included in a net lease are common-area maintenance (CAM) charges to cover maintenance costs on items shared by all the tenants, such as parking lots, atriums, public restrooms, hallways, and the like.

common areas Those areas in a condominium that are held as common elements.

community association Residential homeowners association in which membership is a condition of ownership of a unit in a planned-unit development, or of a lot for a home or a mobile home, or of a town house, villa, condominium, cooperative, or other residential unit which is part of a residential development scheme and which is authorized to impose a fee that may become a lien on the parcel.

community shopping center A type of center that is larger than a neighborhood center but smaller than a regional center.

Comprehensive Environmental Response, Compensation, and Liability Act (CERCLA) A federal law that defines liability for environmental cleanups.

compound interest Interest paid on interest earned.

conciliation An amicable, nonlitigious mediation that seeks to resolve complaints filed under the open-housing laws with the local commissioner, who investigates accordingly.

condominium The fee simple ownership of an apartment or a unit, generally in a multiunit building;, that includes an undivided interest in the common elements.

conduit Something through which other things travel, such as water or electricity. In tax law, a conduit is a mechanism that allows profits to travel through the vehicle that created the profits, without tax liability.

conduit loans Commercial mortgage-backed securities (CMBS), also called *conduit loans.* Such loans are originated through mortgage brokers. They are usually made for 10-year terms at fixed interest rates and are fully nonrecourse, meaning with no personal liability by the borrower.

congregate care center A form of housing in which tenants have access to a communal dining room, physical and social amenities, and, often, a health care center.

consideration (1) An exchange of promises. (2) Something of value that induces a person to enter into a contract.

construction loan An open-end mortgage loan, usually for a short term, obtained to finance the actual construction of buildings on a property.

contingency Provisions in a contract that require a certain act to be done or a certain event to occur before the contract becomes binding.

contract for deed A contract under which the purchase price is paid in installments over a period of time during which the purchaser has possession of the property but the seller retains title until the contract terms are completed; usually drawn between individuals. Also called a *land contract, installment contract,* or *agreement of sale.*

convenience store There are almost 150,000 convenience stores, also called *C-stores,* in the United States. They typically sell fuel, snacks and drinks, food staples such as breakfast foods and some canned goods, small sizes of pet foods, and hot food such as pizza and chicken wings.

conversion (1) To change to another use, as changing rental apartments to condominiums or lofts to apartments. (2) The appropriation of property that belongs to another.

cooperative A multiunit building whose title is held by a trust or corporation for the benefit of persons living in the building. The residents are beneficial owners of the trust or shareholders of the corporation, each possessing a proprietary lease.

corner of Main and Main The most important intersection in a community or in a downtown office area.

cosign Additional signatures in a real estate agreement providing extra guarantees.

cost recovery Depreciation from an accounting viewpoint is a theoretical loss of value for tax purposes and is more technically called *cost recovery.*

credit tenant A commercial tenant large enough, and financially strong enough, to be rated as investment grade. Some projects require national credit tenants, and others are satisfied with regional credit tenants.

curtesy rights The rights of a widower in the estate of his deceased wife.

cycle Events that repeat themselves on a regular basis; may be a business cycle, an economic cycle, or a real estate cycle.

dealer A person who purchases real estate and sells it to customers "in the ordinary course of her trade or business."

debt coverage ratio The number of times the annual net operating income will pay the annual debt service as required by the lender.

debt service The principal and interest payment on a loan.

deed of trust A financing instrument in which the borrower/trustor conveys title into the hands of a third-party trustee to be held for the beneficiary/lender. When the loan is repaid, title is reconveyed to the trustor. If default occurs, the trustee exercises the power of sale on behalf of the lender/beneficiary. Also called a *trust deed.*

deed restrictions Private restrictions on land use placed on property through provisions in a deed.

default Nonperformance of a duty; failure to meet an obligation when due.

defeasance The substitution of collateral.

defeasance option Allows the borrower to exchange another cash-flowing asset for the original collateral on the loan.

deferred exchange A time-delayed trading of like properties.

deficiency judgment The difference in the amount received at an auction of defaulted property between the amount owed and the amount received as an award to the lender.

demand The desire to acquire properties or services.

depreciation Appraisal: Loss of value due to physical deterioration, functional obsolescence, or economic obsolescence. Accounting: Allowable deduction for the recapture of the investment.

destination store Retail stores that combine several attributes to make it very attractive to the consumers.

discount A payment of less than the face amount of a security as a consequence of the contract interest rate being lower than the market rate.

discount rate The rate of interest charged by the Federal Reserve to its member banks to borrow money.

discounted cash flow The present worth of a series of receipts over time.

discretionary funds Money available for investment in excess of that needed for necessities.

discretionary trust A trust that may be changed at the will of its owners.

disintegration A period of decline when the property's economic usefulness is near an end and constant upkeep is necessary.

dower rights The rights of a wife in the estate of her deceased husband.

draws A system of payments made by a lender to a contractor as designated stages of a building's construction are completed.

due diligence An investigation to find all facts of material interest to an investor.

due-on-sale clause A clause in a mortgage or trust deed that stipulates that a borrower cannot sell or transfer the property without prior written consent of the lender. Also called an *alienation clause.*

earnest money Money deposited by a buyer under the terms of a contract, to be forfeited if the buyer defaults but to be applied to the purchase price if the sale is closed.

easy money When interest rates are low and funds for loans are plentiful.

effective gross income (EGI) The total income from the property.

effective rate The interest rate that is actually earned or paid on an investment, loan, or other financial product in a given time period, as a result of compounding interest.

Environmental Protection Agency (EPA) A federal agency that sets standards, determines how much pollution is tolerable, establishes timetables to bring polluters in line with its standards, and enforces environmental laws.

equilibrium a condition of stable value during the holding period.

escalation clause A clause in a loan instrument that provides for increases in payments or interest based on predetermined schedules or on a specified economic index, such as the cost-of-living index.

estimated settlement statement An itemized list estimating all charges that will be imposed upon the buyer and seller in a real estate transaction.

estoppel letter A document often used in due diligence in real estate, often completed or signed by a tenant.

eviction The legal dispossession of an errant borrower or tenant.

exchange To trade like properties, thus avoiding income tax liability under IRS 1031.

exculpatory clause (1) A clause sometimes inserted in a mortgage note in which the lender waives the right to a deficiency judgment. (2) As used in a lease, a clause that intends to relieve the landlord from liability for tenants' personal injuries and property damage.

factoring Receivables sold to generate cash flow.

Fair Housing Act A federal law that prohibits discrimination in the sale, rental, financing, or appraisal of most types of housing.

Fannie Mae A privately owned corporation, originally created as a federal agency, that provides a major secondary mortgage market.

feasibility analysis A market or financial analysis of a proposed investment with emphasis on the attainable income, probable expenses, and most advantageous use and design.

feasibility study A market or financial analysis of a proposed investment with emphasis on the attainable income, probable expenses, and most advantageous use and design.

fee simple ownership A title that is unqualified; the most complete form of ownership; conveys the highest bundle of rights. Also called *fee simple absolute title*.

FF&E Abbreviation for furniture, fixtures, and equipment, commonly used in commercial real estate contracts.

financing contingency Gives the buyer the right to cancel the contract if the buyer cannot secure financing within certain preagreed parameters.

first-generation space Space that has never been used and will be in need of lighting, wiring, partition walls, doors, and flooring, among other things.

fixed costs Those costs of operating a property that do not change with the occupancy level; for example, landscape maintenance.

fixed expenses Costs that are more or less permanent and vary little from year to year—such as real estate taxes and insurance for fire, theft, and hazards—and often stay the same no matter what the occupancy level of the property may be.

fixity Real estate that is permanently attached to the ground.

forbearance agreement An agreement to postpone, reduce, or suspend payment due on a loan for a limited and specific time period.

foreclosure Court action initiated by the mortgagee or a lienor for the purpose of having the debtor's real estate sold to pay the mortgage or other lien.

Foreign Investment in Real Property Tax Act (FIRPTA) A tax law that imposes U.S. income tax on foreign persons selling U.S. real estate.

forgoing The act of not doing something. Not accepting a benefit now, often in the hope of greater benefits later.

four major food groups Life companies look for loans in the four major food groups—multifamily, office, retail, and industrial.

franchise By private contractual agreement, a business that uses a designated trade name and operating procedures.

Freddie Mac An organization that operates much like Fannie Mae to provide a secondary market for mortgages issued by the members of the Federal Home Loan Bank system.

functional obsolescence Defects in a building or structure that detract from its value or marketability; usually the result of layout, design, or other features that are less desirable than features designed for the same functions in newer property.

general obligation bond System of financing in which the community is held responsible for making payments for capital improvements, usually included in property taxes.

general partnership A type of partnership wherein all the partners share in the operation, profit, and losses both jointly and severally.

general real estate tax A tax that is made up of the taxes levied on the real estate by government agencies and municipalities.

Ginnie Mae A federal agency created in 1968 to take over special assistance and liquidation functions of Fannie Mae. Ginnie Mae participates in the secondary market through its mortgage-backed securities pool.

going dark When the leases contain a clause specifying that the tenant has to remain open and continue its business on 100% of its premises, the landlord has the right to obtain specific performance of this provision. This covenant of continuous operation, also called a *going dark clause*, is designed to create the ambience of a successful center and ensure that the needs of the shoppers are met, regardless of retailer difficulties.

graduated lease A contract specifying rental increases in regular increments.

graduated payment loan A loan for which payments increase regularly over time.

gross rent multiplier (GRM) A capitalization method used for calculating the approximate value of an income-producing commercial property based on the property's gross rental income.

ground lease An agreement in which a tenant is permitted to develop a piece of property during the lease period, after which the land and all improvements are turned over to the property owner.

growth management Policies that control growth of a community.

highest and best use That possible use of property that will produce its greatest net income, and thereby develop its highest value.

hobby tax rules Rules that limit allowable deductions on enterprises that do not clearly show a profit motive.

homogeneous tenancy A business tenancy in which similar or complementary goods or services are offered.

horizontal regime Condominium ownership of a unit above ground.

hypothecation The act of pledging real estate as security without surrendering possession of the property.

income What is left after one subtracts expenses from revenue.

incremental taxes Additional taxes generated as a result of new industry moving into an area.

incubator industrial building A structure provided by the community to encourage growth of a new company.

indemnity A clause that makes one party compensate the other for legal fees, expenses, and any settlement or judgment liability if the innocent party is sued as a result of actions or inactions of the other party.

index A benchmark that is used to adjust the interest rate in an adjustable-rate loan; for example, the one-year Treasury bill.

industrial development bond Securities issued to pay for the development of a new industry, usually in the form of general obligation bonds.

industrial park A controlled development designed to accommodate specific types of industry.

infant industry Newly formed businesses.

inheritability Under our allodial system, the ability to leave property to heirs.

innocent landowner defense Applied to property purchased after 1986 and assumes that property owner "did not know and had no reason to know" of contamination at the time of purchase.

Institute of Real Estate Management (IREM) A professional association of real property managers that awards the Certified Property Manager designation.

International Council of Shopping Centers (ICSC) The global trade association of the shopping center industry, founded in 1957.

integration a condition of developing value when building new.

interest factor (IF) The proportion that determines the time value of money.

interim A use for property until it can be put to its highest and best use.

interim loan A short-term loan made during construction, to be replaced by a permanent loan upon completion.

internal rate of return (IRR) The rate at which the present worth of an annuity plus reversion exactly equals the investment price.

Interstate Land Sales Full Disclosure Act An act of Congress passed in 1968 to facilitate regulation of interstate land sales to protect consumers from fraud and abuse in the sale or lease of land.

investment trust A trust designed to act as an investment conduit for small investors that enables them to pool their resources.

irrevocable trust A permanent arrangement that cannot be changed until the goals of the trust have been met.

joint tenancy Ownership of real estate by two or more parties; includes rights of survivorship where the deceased's interest passes automatically to the surviving joint tenant(s).

joint venture The joining of two or more people in a specific business enterprise. A common joint venture is a type of equity participation arrangement in which a lender puts up funds, a developer contributes expertise, and the two become partners in the project.

junior loan Any loan that is not in first lien position.

labor-intensive A business depending more on labor than on machines.

land banking Purchasing and holding land for future development.

lease A written or oral contract between a landlord (the lessor) and a tenant (the lessee), transferring the right to exclusive possession and use of the landlord's real property to the lessee for a specified period and for a stated consideration (rent). Leases for more than one year must be in writing to be enforceable.

leasehold The tenant's legal interest in a property.

Letter of Intent (LOI) A nonbinding agreement stating two or more parties' desire to enter into a real estate transaction that provides an outline of the proposed transaction so the parties can negotiate before committing to a contract.

leverage Use of borrowed money to finance the purchase of an investment.

LIBOR A benchmark rate that some of the world's leading banks charge each other for short-term loans.

lien A legal claim that one party has against the property of another as security for a debt.

limited liability company (LLC) Enjoys a corporate form and the tax advantages of a partnership without the restrictions of an S corporation.

limited partnership A legal entity that includes a general partner who actively manages the investment, and limited partners, whose only personal liability is their investments. Income taxes vest at each individual partner level.

liquidated damages An amount predetermined by the parties to a contract as the total compensation to an injured party should the other party breach the contract.

liquidity Condition under which something can be sold promptly at market value.

living trust An arrangement whereby legal title to property is transferred by the owner (trustor) to a third person (trustee) to be held and managed by the trustee for the trustor's benefit and under the trustor's control for a certain period until specific goals have been attained. Also called an *inter vivos trust.* Established to facilitate the management of properties during the grantors' lives. Usually resolves into a testamentary trust on their deaths.

loan-to-value (LTV) A financial term used by lenders to express the ratio of a loan to the value of an asset purchased.

location Where the property is. An indispensable component for an evaluation analysis.

lock-out clause An absolute prohibition against an early prepayment.

loft building A large, warehouse-type building usually located in a central city area.

longevity The concept of real estate that recognizes the long-term nature of most real estate investments.

Low-Income Housing Tax Credits (LIHTC) Gave state and local LIHTC-allocating agencies the equivalent of $8.7 billion in annual budget authority in 2017 to issue tax credits for the acquisition, rehabilitation, or new construction of rental housing targeted at lower-income households.

mailbox money passive revenue.

mall The common walking areas of large shopping centers.

manufactured home Prefabricated homes built in a factory and transported to a lot for installation.

market analysis An analysis designed to uncover the conditions and trends of a marketplace.

market segmentation Due to the fractured aspect of the real estate business, the market tends to be local in nature and its conditions may vary greatly from location to location.

market study A study that analyzes market demand for a particular product or service.

market value The highest price for which a property would sell, assuming a reasonable time for the sale and a knowledgeable buyer and seller acting without duress.

minimum housing standards Minimum building and housing codes adopted by many communities to protect the health and safety of the public.

mineral rights Ownership rights to all minerals located on or under land and to the profits realized from the sale of these minerals.

minority ownership discount Reflects the notion that a partial ownership interest may be worth less than its pro-rata (proportional) share of the total business.

mortgage A document establishing real property as security for the repayment of a debt.

move clause Virtually all office leases have move clauses, which allow the landlord to move the tenant to comparable space in the building, as needed. The interpretation of what is comparable often gives rise to litigation between the parties.

municipal lien search While a title search should disclose any recorded liens or encumbrances on a property, there can be other unrecorded charges on a property that can later result in a lien. These charges may become the responsibility of the current property owner.

naming rights Branding rights for an office building. Wells Fargo Plaza in Houston, Texas, is not owned by Wells Fargo; it is owned by MetLife. Building branding can be a very important component of lease negotiations.

negative amortization Less than interest-only loan payments, which cause the balance of a loan to increase by the amount of the deficient interest.

neighborhood shopping center The smallest planned center.

net lease A lease requiring the tenant to pay the costs of operating the building, including maintenance, taxes, insurance, and repairs, in addition to the rent.

net operating income (NOI) The income left after all the operating expenses have been paid.

net present value (NPV) The present value of an investment's expected cash inflows minus the costs of acquiring the investment.

net proceeds Expenses—either prepaid or paid in arrears—that are divided or distributed between the buyer and the seller at the closing.

nominal interest rate The rate of interest defined in the contract.

nonrecourse A loan or other financial tool with no personal liability by the borrower.

note A signed instrument acknowledging a debt and promising repayment.

off-street parking Parking spaces on private land, as in shopping centers.

office park A preplanned conglomeration of buildings in one area designed to house activities of a business nature.

operating expenses Periodic and necessary expenses essential to the continuous operation and maintenance of an income property.

opportunity cost The amount of money that could be earned through alternative investments.

option An agreement to keep open an offer to sell or purchase property for a prescribed period.

overlay Micro-requirements in zoning codes that impose specific aesthetic or density requirements in some areas, but not others. For example, all properties zoned as low-density single-family residential might have no occupancy limits. If a particular area has a college/university overlay, it might limit occupancy to only three unrelated persons per house to avoid de facto dormitories housing 10 or more students in a four-bedroom house.

partially amortized loan A loan that has a series of payments—part principal and part interest—that is not sufficient to pay off the total loan at maturity. There is a remaining amount of principal (a balloon) that must be paid at the end of the loan term.

partnership An association of two or more individuals who operate a business as co-owners.

passive activity loss limitation All rental income is passive income. Passive losses can offset passive income, but not active income.

passive income Income from real estate rentals; owner does not take a role as manager.

percentage clause A clause in a contract that stipulates that a tenant pays a fixed percent of the gross income against a specified minimum rental.

permanence An attribute of real estate that recognizes that real estate investment is long term, complex, and often requires large sums of money.

personal property Movable property that does not fit the definition of realty.

Phase I Engineering reports regarding the possibility of environmental contamination.

Phase II Reports identifying types and amounts of actual contaminants.

Phase III The Phase III assessment details how an environmental cleanup is to be performed. It is the last phase before actual cleanup begins.

Phase IV The environmental remediation plan selected by an investor and engineers. It is the roadmap for remediation, just as engineering drawings are the roadmap for electrical and plumbing systems in a building.

Phase V An investor obtains Environmental Protection Agency approval for a Phase IV environmental cleanup plan.

Phase VI Gathers all necessary data to obtain regulatory approval that a cleanup site now meets all environmental standards after it has been remediated.

pierce the corporate veil A situation in which courts put aside limited liability and hold a corporation's shareholders or directors personally liable for the corporation's actions or debts.

plat An official map of an area that is recorded in the public record.

plottage The subsequent increase in value of a group of adjacent properties when they are acquired by the same owner and combined into one property.

POC The abbreviation for paid outside closing. These are items that are paid for separately by the responsible party.

portfolio income Income from interest, dividends, and royalties.

potentially responsible party (PRP) An entity that, under the Comprehensive Environmental Response, Compensation, and Liability Act (CERCLA), may be liable for the costs of an environmental cleanup.

present value The current value of a future sum of money or stream of cash flows given a specified rate of return.

present worth Discounting money to be received in the future to determine its value today.

pro forma NOI The standard form that shows calculations for income left after all the operating expenses have been paid.

pro forma profit and loss A standard profit and loss statement, also called a *P&L, income statement, earnings statement*, or *expense statement.* All record the revenue, costs, and expenses for a fiscal year or quarter, or other period of time.

profitability index The ratio of payoff to investment of a proposed project.

property Anything capable of being owned.

property tax lien A lien placed on real property until such time as the property tax bill is paid.

proprietary lease In a corporation cooperative, the lease issued to an individual shareholder occupant.

prorate Expenses—either prepaid or paid in arrears—that are divided or distributed between the buyer and the seller at the closing.

pyramiding A method of acquiring additional properties by refinancing equities.

railroad spur A branch line constructed to an industrial project for dockside loading and unloading.

real estate investment trust (REIT) An unincorporated trust set up to invest in real estate that must have at least 100 investors, with management, control, and title to the property in the hands of trustees.

real estate mortgage investment conduit (REMIC) A pool of mortgages in which investors may purchase proportionate interests.

real estate mortgage trust (REMT) A business trust similar to a REIT that invests in mortgage securities rather than in real estate.

real estate professional A licensee who legally conducts the business of real estate.

real estate A portion of the earth's surface, extending downward to the center of the earth and upward into space, including all things permanently attached thereto by nature or people, and all legal rights therein.

real property The rights of real estate ownership; often called the *bundle of legal rights*. See also *real estate.*

realized gain The amount by which the sale price of an asset exceeds its purchase price.

recaptured gain The gain received from the sale of depreciable capital property that must be reported as income.

recasting the financials The process of carefully inspecting, and perhaps changing, some of the seller's profit and loss numbers.

recognition clause A mortgage loan provision in which the vendor or mortgagee agrees in advance that if the promoter should default during the term of the agreement, the lender will respect the rights of subsequent lot owners and honor their contracts.

recognized gain Profit from the sale of an investment that is taxable in the current year.

recourse A legal agreement which gives the lender the right to pledged collateral in the event that the borrower is unable to satisfy the debt obligation.

regional center A large agglomeration of shops and stores in one location. Includes more than one department store.

regular corporation A corporation that is not an S corporation or LLC.

Regulation Z The truth-in-lending portion of the Consumer Credit Protection Act of 1968. It requires complete disclosure of the total costs involved in most credit activities.

relative scarcity A situation in which the consumer perceives a shortage and bids up the value of the commodity accordingly.

release clause A clause included in a blanket mortgage that provides that on payment of a specific sum of money, the lien on a particular parcel or portion of the collateral will be released.

remediation Corrective action to clean up an environmentally contaminated site to eliminate contamination or reduce the amount to an acceptable level.

rental concessions Perquisites offered to entice new tenants, such as free rent for a few months or build-outs in the form of partitions or paint.

repossession The act of placing property into the hands of the holder of the security after foreclosure.

request for proposal (RFP) A request to a professional for a rate chart or fee range for conducting due diligence on an investment property.

reserves A portion of earnings set aside to cover possible future losses.

retirement community A residential community designed to fit the needs and lifestyles of older persons.

return on investment (ROI) An annual percentage derived from dividing cash invested into net after-tax income.

revenue A measure of how much raw income a company is bringing in from sales of its products and services.

revenue bond Bonds to be repaid by the fees charged for the use of the funded project.

rezoning The process of changing from one land use to another, usually more intensive.

right of first refusal The right of a person to have the first opportunity to either purchase or lease a specific parcel of real property.

risk The possibility of loss.

risk of loss A clause that details who receives the money if there is an insurable loss and whether or not the buyer has to proceed to closing if the loss is over a certain size.

rooftops Households within an area, and the demographic data gathered from census studies and local chambers of commerce about the residents of those households.

royalty income Profits secured from mineral rights, oil wells, and publications. See also *portfolio income*.

S corporation A corporation with a maximum of 75 shareholders that is taxed like a partnership.

sale-leaseback-buyback A financing arrangement under which an investor purchases real estate owned and used by a business corporation, then leases the property back to the business; includes a buy-back option.

scheduled gross income (SGI) The amount of rental income the property could produce with 100% occupancy and with all tenants paying full rent.

secondary market A marketplace in which mortgages and trust deeds are traded. *See also Fannie Mae, Freddie Mac,* and *Ginnie Mae.*

Secured Overnight Financing Rate (SOFR) The SOFR index is based on the interest rates banks charge each other for overnight loans.

securities Something given, deposited, or pledged to make secure the fulfillment of an obligation, usually the repayment of a debt. Generically, mortgages, trust deeds, and other financing instruments backed by collateral pledges are termed securities for investment purposes.

self-directed IRA An Individual Retirement Account (IRA) provided by some financial institutions in the United States that allows alternative investments for retirement savings.

self-storage facility Neighborhood storage facilities usually designed as individual cubicles; accessible daily.

seller's market When demand exceeds supply.

senior loan Any loan that has priority over another.

setback requirement Local zoning and building code specifications stipulating the amount of open space to be preserved in the front, rear, and side yards.

severalty Ownership of property vested in one person alone.

sharing the market uplift A tenant may be able to sublease a unit for a rent higher than that stipulated in the original lease, and thus, make a profit on the landlord's investment. Often, leases require that these tenants provide the landlord with 50%–100% of any excess rent the tenant may collect from the subtenant. This is called *sharing the market uplift.*

sheltering Having income deemed as either nontaxable, as in the deduction of expenses, or as tax deferred, as in cost recovery (depreciation) deductions.

sinking fund A savings account designed to accumulate funds in anticipation of meeting a balloon payment.

site selection The process of determining the best location for a project.

sole and separate ownership Individual ownership by a married person.

special assessment A tax or levy customarily imposed against only those specific parcels of real estate that will benefit from a proposed public improvement like a street or sewer.

specific performance A legal action to compel a party to carry out the terms of a contract.

split-fee financing A financing arrangement wherein the lender purchases land and leases it to a developer, while at the same time, financing the construction of the improvements.

sponsor Because of the reliance on the borrower's management track record, it creates opportunities for investors with cash to partner with cash-poor, but management-experienced, persons on a project. This arrangement is so common that there is a name for the experienced person, who is called the *sponsor.*

spot zoning A single property with a permitted use not in conformity with the surrounding properties.

stabilized occupancy Concept is used to estimate future value of a property or project once it reaches its reasonable occupancy potential.

standby letter of credit A document from a bank that guarantees "payment of last resort" if a client does not fulfill a contractual commitment to a third party.

straight line The depreciation of real property in equal amounts over the allowed life of the property for tax purposes.

strip Part of a REMIC's assets; interest-only (IO) or principal-only (PO) portions of its inventory can be sold separately.

strip center These stores offer commodities and services of every nature and description and serve the neighborhood, as well as the entire city, with their wares. Like the smaller apartment and office buildings previously described, strip centers are also called *strip malls* and *convenience centers.*

strip store Store buildings found along a community's arterial roads.

subdivision restrictions Restrictions, often created by a city, that places minimum requirements in the development of any subdivision within the jurisdiction of that city.

subject to Becoming responsible, but not assuming personal liability, for an existing loan.

sublease The right of a primary tenant to rent a property to a subsequent tenant. Usually maintains the continued liability of the primary tenant.

subordination clause A clause in an agreement that states that the current claim on any debts will take priority over any other claims formed in other agreements made in the future.

super-regional center Regional shopping centers that include apartment and office buildings.

supply Products and services available for consumption.

surplus land Land that is not currently needed to support the existing improvement but cannot be separated from the property and sold off.

sweat equity The amount of equity created in a property by the work and improvements made by the direct labor of a person such as an owner.

syndicate A group of two or more people united for the purpose of owning an investment. A syndicate may operate as a corporation, general partnership, or limited partnership.

take-out commitment An agreement by a financial institution or another investor to make a long-term loan at a certain, stated date in the future.

tax clause In a lease, a clause requiring the tenant to pay any increase in property taxes over the base year's amount.

tax credit A credit applicable directly against taxes due; a 100% deduction.

tax levy The formal action taken to impose the tax, usually by a vote of the taxing district's governing body.

tax shelter A phrase often used to describe some of the tax advantages of real estate investment, such as deductions for depreciation, interest, taxes, and so forth.

taxable income The amount of income used to calculate how much tax an individual or a company owes to the government in a given tax year.

tenancy at sufferance A tenant who holds over after the end of the lease has a tenancy at sufferance. No notice is required to terminate the tenancy. A tenant who refuses to leave at the end of a lease may be charged double rent.

tenancy at will A tenancy at will may be terminated by either party that gives written notice as follows: year-to-year—3 months' notice before the end of any annual period; quarter to quarter—45 days' notice before the end of any quarter; month-to-month—15 days' notice before the end of any monthly period; and week to week—7 days' notice before the end of any weekly period.

tenancy by the entirety The joint ownership—recognized in most states—of property acquired by spouses during marriage. On the death of one spouse, the survivor automatically becomes the sole owner of the property.

tenancy in common A form of inheritable co-ownership under which each owner holds an undivided interest in real property.

tenant mix In a shopping center, the description of occupants by the types of businesses in which they are engaged.

term loan A loan to be paid in full at a specified time; not an amortizing loan.

testamentary trust A trust that commences on the demise of the trustor.

tight money When interest rates are high and funds for loans are scarce.

time-share A real estate ownership form that permits multiple purchasers to buy undivided interests in a resort condominium with the right to use the facility for a specified time period.

time value of money The present worth of future income.

title commitment A written commitment by the title insurance company that it will insure title if certain itemized defects are removed by time of closing.

title insurance A policy insuring a property owner or mortgagee against loss by reason of defects in the title to a parcel of real estate, other than encumbrances, defects, and matters specifically excluded by the policy.

topography The surface characteristics of land.

traffic counts Data tracks peak- and low-traffic volume by the number of vehicles that cross a certain point of a street location.

trailing 12 NOI calculated for the immediately preceding 12 full months.

tranche Parts of a REMIC's assets.

transaction facilitator One who represents neither buyer nor seller.

unauthorized practice of law Preparing documents such as non-Supreme Court-approved leases, deeds, notes, or mortgages is considered unauthorized practice of law—a third-degree felony. A licensee who advertises to prepare or review sales contracts for people not buying through the licensee is practicing law.

untenantable Unfit for tenants. A tenant may withhold rent if the landlord fails to maintain the property and it becomes untenantable.

value in use A specific use that defines a property's value.

variable costs Operating expenses of a property that will change with the occupancy level; for example, management fees based on rent collected.

variable expenses The expenses that vary according to the occupancy level such as supplies, water, and any management fees that are tied to the amount of rent collected.

variable interest rate An approach to financing in which the lender is permitted to alter the interest rate, with a certain period of advance notice, based on a specific base index. Monthly loan payments can then be increased or decreased or maturity can be extended, depending on how the base index fluctuates.

variance An allowance made in zoning codes that leaves the zoning in place, but allows a particular nonconforming use on the property. Usually, these are granted only if the property is not capable of supporting its zoned used.

warehouse building Buildings used for storage.

wraparound loan A new loan that encompasses any existing loan without disturbing the legal priority of an underlying loan.

ANSWER KEY

Unit 1

1. **A**
2. **D**
3. **D**
4. **C**
5. **D**
6. **A**

Unit 2

1. **C**
2. **C**
3. **B**

Unit 3

1. **B**

Unit 4

1. **C**
2. **D**
3. **C**
4. **B**
5. **A**
6. **C**
7. **C**
8. **D**
9. **B**
10. **C**

Unit 5

1. **C**
2. **D**
3. **B**
4. **C**
5. **D**
6. **D**
7. **B**
8. **A**
9. **C**
10. **D**

Unit 6

1. **C**
2. **D**
3. **B**
4. **B**
5. **D**
6. **B**
7. **C**
8. **C**
9. **D** 100,000 – 20,000 = 80,000 × 0.02564 = 2,051.2 × 10 = 20,512; 80,000 – 20,512 = 59,488 + 20,000 = 79,488
10. **B**

Unit 7

1. **B**

2. **B**

3. **A**

Unit 8

1. **B** 50,000 – 15,000 = 35,000 – 25,000 = 10,000 / 100,000 = 10%

2. **B** \$38,000 gross revenue – \$13,300 expenses = \$24,700 × 12 months = \$296,400 NOI; divide by 0.07 cap rate = \$4,234,286 indicated value

3. **C** \$38,950 gross revenue – \$13,547 expenses = \$25,403 × 12 months = \$304,836 NOI; divide by 0.07 cap rate = \$4,354,800 – \$4,234,286 = increased value of \$120,514. To check the math, capitalize only the net change in NOI (\$950 increased revenues – 247 increased expenses = \$703 × 12 months = \$8,436 / 0.07 = \$120,514

4. **A**

5. **B**

6. **B**

7. **D**

8. **A**

9. **B**

10. **D**

Unit 9

1. **A**

2. **D**

3. **B**

Unit 10

1. **A**

2. **A**

3. **A**

4. **A**

5. **A**

6. **C**

7. **C**

8. **D**

9. **B**

10. **C** 50,000 × 0.02 = 1,000 + (10,000 × 0.10 = 1,000) = 2,000 / 10,000 = 20%.

Unit 11

1. **A**

2. **D**

3. **C**

4. **D**

5. **C**

6. **C**

7. **A**

8. **C**

9. **C**

10. **C**

11. **D**

12. **C**

13. **B**

14. **C**

15. **D**

16. **C**

17. **D**

18. **C**

19. **C**

20. **C**

21. **B**

22. **B**

23. **B**

24. **B**

25. **C**

26. **B** 5,000 × 0.08 = 400 × 3.0373 = 1,214.92. 5,000 × 0.6355 = 3,177.50 + 1,214.92 = 4,392.42.

27. **C** 5,000 × 0.08 = 400 × 2.4018 = 960.72. 5,000 × 0.7118 = 3,559.00 + 960.72 = 4,519.72.

Unit 12

1. **D**
2. **C**
3. **D**
4. **A**
5. **C**
6. **B**
7. **D**
8. **A**
9. **C**
10. **C**

Unit 13

1. **A**
2. **A**
3. **A**
4. **A**
5. **A**
6. **A**
7. **A**
8. **A**
9. **A**
10. **A**

INDEX

S

T

U

V

W

Y

Z

Notes

Notes

Notes